AF737627

HIGHER EDUCATION AND THE LAW

HIGHER EDUCATION AND THE LAW

Editors

Sally Varnham
Patty Kamvounias
Joan Squelch

THE FEDERATION PRESS
2015

Published in Sydney by
The Federation Press
PO Box 45, Annandale, NSW, 2038.
71 John St, Leichhardt, NSW, 2040.
Ph (02) 9552 2200. Fax (02) 9552 1681.
E-mail: info@federationpress.com.au
Website: http://www.federationpress.com.au

National Library of Australia
Cataloguing-in-Publication entry

Higher education and the law / edited by Sally Varnham, Patty Kamvounias, Joan Squelch.

Includes index.
ISBN 978 176002 025 5 (pbk)

Education, Higher – Law and legislation – Australia.
Educational law and legislation – Australia.
Students – Legal status, laws, etc – Australia.

344.94074

© The Federation Press

This publication is copyright. Other than for the purposes of and subject to the conditions prescribed under the Copyright Act, no part of it may in any form or by any means (electronic, mechanical, microcopying, photocopying, recording or otherwise) be reproduced, stored in a retrieval system or transmitted without prior written permission. Enquiries should be addressed to the publisher.

Typeset by The Federation Press, Leichhardt, NSW.
Printed by OPUS Group in Australia.

Contents

Foreword

Universities and the Law – A View from the Legal Profession

Pamela Madafiglio and John Birrell

> Universities were once regarded as a societal opiate. Nowadays individual rights transgress the teaching machinery. The medieval university looked backwards; it claimed to be a library of old knowledge. The modern university looks forward, and is a factory of new knowledge. The relationships between students, staff and the university itself have grown to parallel those of the world of industry. Universities, however, have remained unique creatures with special problems not familiar to the rest of society or, for that matter, the courts.
>
> (Robert J Sadler, 1981)

As lawyers with a close association with Australian universities, in one case, for over three decades, we are pleased to be able to contribute a foreword to this very timely publication.

Australia's universities have evolved from learning institutions with a charitable (public) purpose to international commercial enterprises; their nature as unique entities within a changing landscape spawns many and diverse aspects of their relationship with the law in practice. We welcome this valuable resource as the first comprehensive exploration of the law and higher education in Australia.

Since the establishment of the first Australian universities in the 1850s, universities have grown significantly in number, diversity and complexity. The changing nature of universities is evident in their structure and functions, governance, funding, the relationships they have with staff, students and external stakeholders, and the ever increasing influence of external regulatory regimes.

Perhaps nothing symbolises the legal and social change universities have undergone more than the changed role of the University Visitor. With its origins in ecclesiastical law, its exclusive function was essentially to settle internal disputes according to the statutes, by-laws and rules of the particular university. During the 1980s, uncertainties, particularly as to jurisdiction and remedies, led to reforms to confine the role to ceremonial only (with the exception of Western Australia) and for universities to strengthen their grievance procedures generally. While once representative of complete autonomy in terms of a university's responsibilities and accountability towards its members, the diminution in the role made university operations subject to external scrutiny and so, can be seen to epitomise the changes that have occurred generally in the legal environment in which universities operate. However, as Sadler observed in 1981, while things were changing, the Visitor remains in many universities, clearly demonstrating that, as universities adapt to a modern environment and legal system, their links to tradition and the past remain.

Universities are now creatures of a body of legislation which is a mix of sector specific legislation (university or public) and non-specific legislation (enterprises generally). The chapters of this book are grouped into these two areas, referred to first as the Law **of** Higher Education, and secondly, the Law **and** Higher Education. They provide comprehensive coverage of many of the areas of operation upon which, from a practitioner's perspective, the law has substantial impact. Among these are: governance arrangements and the composition of governing bodies; commercial activities; methods of regulation and deregulation; the availability or otherwise of public law actions such as judicial review; and the many areas of both public and private law which govern relationships and responsibilities. These matters are of increasing importance as universities move further into a commercial, entrepreneurial scenario and are subject to the range of challenges created by global circumstances. Of the many recent examples are issues relating to the ownership of property created by a university's employees and students in the area of copyright, and in commercialisation of research as demonstrated by the well-known case of *UWA v Gray*. Legislation such as the *Defence Trade Controls Act 2012* (Cth) and its impact on the freedom of academics in relation to their research and dissemination of their findings is another example.

Underlying many of the legal issues facing universities today is the fundamental question as to the status of a university: is a university a public authority engaged in the provision of a public good, or is its nature now that of a private provider of educational services?

These days, it may be that a university can be a public authority for one purpose but not another, and there are increasing areas where the public (educational) versus private (commercial) capacity of the university comes to the fore. Surprisingly, this could be as seemingly trivial as how a university can control traffic and parking on its campus. This issue may have diminished in significance over the years, but it has posed considerable practical problems and raised the significant legal issue of whether the campus was a private or public place.

A modern university is involved in an often complex web of relationships, both internal and external. Many of the legal aspects relating to the relationships a modern university has with its students and student associations, and its academic and professional staff, are explored comprehensively here. Recent decades have seen a not insignificant amount of external complaint initiated by students against their universities, particularly in relation to equal opportunity and perceived discrimination. In terms of the relationship with collective student bodies, there was, in 2005 in New South Wales, a shift in approach with the introduction of voluntary student unionism. Universities had to provide more funding for student services which had greater legal and operational implications. While this involvement decreased again with the ability to charge student services and amenities fees under the amendments in the *Higher Education Legislation Amendment (Student Services and Amenities) Act 2011* (Cth) and the Guidelines made under that Act, its impact continues. It is evermore essential that both universities and students prioritise maintaining relationships built on respect and partnership, for however the relationship may be characterised, if it turns sour, it can have far-reaching consequences and affect the very fabric of a university.

Time has also seen a significant amount of litigation between universities and their staff, much of it involving former staff members bringing numerous legal actions against the relevant university. An extreme example is the litigious Dr Spautz, whose litigation against his university ranged from Local Court indictment proceedings for criminal defamation through to High Court habeas corpus and abuse of process proceedings. Dr Spautz was ultimately declared a vexatious litigant but he was, in the meantime, the catalyst for law reform in some areas.

In conclusion, this scholarly work provides both a theoretical and practical approach to the plethora of legislation and common law which increasingly governs the operation of universities, both internally and in their relationships with external stakeholders. While most areas of the law may be clear in their application, there are perennial issues which include:

- enabling statutes that have in some, but not all, respects evolved with the times;
- basic legal conundrums that remain unresolved in the university setting; and
- transcendent characteristics such as the public-private tension within a university and the special relationship between a university and its stakeholders.

Our conclusion is somewhat similar to Sadler's observations in 1981. Despite significant changes to the institutions themselves and to the legal and economic environment in which they operate, universities are still fundamentally creatures of statute. They have a public purpose and members and other stakeholders with diverse interests. As Sadler recognised, universities retain the marks of their medieval past while striding forward as factories of new knowledge. However, social, economic and political imperatives, combined with international variations and instabilities, mean that Australian universities operate in a constantly changing landscape. The legal challenge for universities today is balancing the tradition of learning with the modern realities they now face.

Pamela Madafiglio
Partner, Minter Ellison

John Birrell
Lawyer, Minter Ellison

Preface

Rob Behrens

Higher Education and the Law is an important, timely and granular study. It analyses rigorously the ways in which higher education law and general law have shaped Australian universities, their purpose, governance, operation and funding. A key strength of the book lies in its particularism in locating the provision and regulation of Australian higher education within a federal context, dealing with the emergence of universities from an historical perspective, and setting out how Australian demography influences the challenges to be addressed.

At the same time, the editors and authors never neglect how the forces of globalisation, marketisation, and the rise of student consumerism have altered horizons and changed behaviour in universities, and promoted their relevance to national economic and social renewal. All of this makes the subject area deeply relevant for comparative legal and public policy study.

The book was conceived, researched and written during a period of significant debate and change to the governance, regulation and funding of Australian universities. This period of change appears to be far from concluded. These facts give the text an immediacy and vibrancy. It is not only a reliable source for university administrators and managers, and scholars, but also an instrument of public policy for the choppy seas of university reform ahead.

Rob Behrens
Independent Adjudicator for Higher Education
England and Wales

About the Contributors

The Editors

Dr Sally Varnham is a Professor of Law at the University of Technology, Sydney. From 2011 to 2014, she was Chair of the University Academic Board and continues to be a member of the University of Technology, Sydney Council. Her main research interest is in law and policy relating to all sectors of education. She has a strong interest in the university-student relationship, particularly student engagement in decision-making and governance, and her current research is in this area. Sally is widely published in Australia and abroad and regularly presents at national and international conferences.

Patty Kamvounias is a Senior Lecturer in Business Law and Program Director for the Master of Commerce at the University of Sydney Business School. Her research interests include the application of public law and private law principles to higher education and the quality of teaching and learning. Patty has been involved in major research projects exploring student complaints and grievance handling in universities.

Dr Joan Squelch is an Associate Professor in the School of Law at the University of Notre Dame Australia (Fremantle). Joan holds qualifications in both education and law, and is admitted as a lawyer in the Supreme Court of New South Wales. She teaches constitutional law, administrative law and employee relations law. Her research interests include legal education, education and the law, education and human rights law, school governance and workplace bullying.

The Contributors

Rob Behrens has been Independent Adjudicator for Higher Education in England and Wales since 2008. Educated at Nottingham and Exeter universities as a UK civil servant, he worked on the South African transition from apartheid. He then became Secretary to the Committee on Standards Public Life, before appointment as Complaints Commissioner to the English and Welsh Bar in 2006.

Marcelle Burns is a Kamilaroi woman and Pre-doctoral Fellow in Law at the University of New England. Her research interests include Indigenous peoples and international law, native title, and Indigenous knowledges in legal education. Marcelle is a member of the National Indigenous Research and Knowledges Network, funded by the Australian Research Council.

Joy Cumming is a Professor of Education at the Australian Catholic University. She is recognised internationally for her work in educational assessment. In addition to educational qualifications, she holds a Juris Doctor degree and Graduate Diploma in Legal Practice and is admitted as a lawyer in the Supreme Court of Queensland. Her education law interests include examination of the impact of educational policy and legislation on schools and students, with major emphasis on legal and policy issues in assessment and accountability.

Dr Elizabeth Dickson is a Senior Lecturer in the Law School at the Queensland University of Technology. She teaches, publishes and presents in the area of discrimination law and consults for a variety of Queensland education institutions in respect of issues relevant to disability discrimination. Elizabeth co-edited the *International Journal of Law and Education* from 2004 until 2012.

Maxine Evers is a Senior Lecturer at the University of Technology, Sydney. Maxine served as Student Ombud at the University of Technology, Sydney from 2010 to 2012. In this position, she assisted students with grievances relating to the processes and policies relevant to their study. Maxine has a continuing research interest in the role of student ombudsmen.

Helen Fleming has worked for and within the Australian university sector for over 20 years, both in-house and in private practice. Helen's areas of practice and interest include governance and compliance, administrative law, intellectual property rights and charitable trusts. Helen is currently University Secretary and General Counsel at the University of Western Sydney.

Michael Fraser AM is Professor of Law, as well as Director of the Communications Law Centre, at the University of Technology, Sydney, Australia's independent, non-profit, public interest centre specialising in communications, media and online law and policy. Michael is Chairman of the Australian Copyright Council, Chairman of the Stolen Generations Testimonies Foundation, and a Director of the Dictionary of Sydney Trust.

Robert Horton is a Sydney solicitor and partner of Hicksons Lawyers who practises in the area of tort litigation with a special focus on the liabilities of both private and public educational institutions.

Katie Kossian is an employment lawyer working in the Sydney Employment and Safety team at Thomson Geer. Katie has worked both in-house and in private practice and holds a Master of Laws from the University of Sydney.

Dr Bruce Lindsay worked for many years as a senior student advocate and policy researcher in the tertiary education sector. He completed doctoral research on university decision-making at the Australian National University College of Law in 2010. He presently works in environmental law for Environmental Justice Australia, a specialist public interest community legal centre in Melbourne.

Ralph Mawdsley holds joint chairs as Professor of Law in the Cleveland-Marshall College of Law and the Roslyn Z Wolf Professor of Education, Cleveland State University, Cleveland, United States. He holds a PhD in Educational Administration and a Juris Doctor. He worked as a school principal and prosecutor before his academic career. He has an international reputation in school law. His education law specialties include School Law, Special Education Law, and Sports Law.

Bronwyn Olliffe is the Associate Dean (Teaching and Learning) in the Faculty of Law at the University of Technology, Sydney. From 2003 to 2006, Bronwyn served as the Student Ombud at the University of Technology, Sydney. An integral component of Bronwyn's administrative roles at the University of Technology, Sydney has been the enhancement of the student experience.

Dr Gaby Ramia is Associate Professor in public policy in the Graduate School of Government at the University of Sydney. His primary research interests include: international education and the welfare of international students; employment services and the welfare of the unemployed; and the relationship between social policy and industrial relations.

Dr Francine Rochford is a Senior Lecturer at La Trobe University. Her work on the law and policy of higher education includes her doctorate on the topic *Liability of the University in Negligence* (University of Melbourne), and a number of journal articles, conference papers and book chapters dealing with aspects of the law and policy of higher education.

Jacquie Seemann is a practising employment lawyer and heads the Sydney Employment and Safety team at Thomson Geer. Jacquie is a member of the New South Wales committees of both the Australian Labour Law Association and the ANZ Education Law Association, and will be teaching in the Master of Labour Law and Relations program at the University of Sydney in 2016.

Kerry Smith is currently Special Counsel with Hicksons Lawyers, Sydney, and practises in liability law. She has acted on behalf of educational institutions, defending a broad range of claims brought against them.

Myles Stilwell is legally qualified and before teaching at Massey University, New Zealand, he held a range of positions in the probation service. He teaches in dispute resolution, and is a mediator in student and staff disputes, as well as a Proctor investigating serious student misconduct.

Dr Nigel Stobbs has practised as a barrister of the Supreme Court of Queensland and of the High Court of Australia. He researches, lectures and consults in sentencing law and policy, in therapeutic jurisprudence and in Chinese legal systems, through the Queensland University of Technology Crime and Justice Research Centre.

Dr Anita Stuhmcke has researched and published widely with respect to regulation and social change. This interest extends to the investigation of ombudsmen, both as change agents and regulatory tools. Anita has served as an Assistant and Student Ombud at the University of Technology, Sydney and performs a variety of other grievance handling roles for both staff and students.

Abigail Tisbury is a Senior Associate at Hicksons Lawyers in Sydney and has conducted tort-based litigation for many years on behalf of a wide range of institutional clients, including education authorities.

Jade Tyrrell was the 2013 National President of the National Union of Students (NUS). Jade has served on a number of boards and committees during her time as a student representative including the 2013 SSAF review panel chaired by Arch Bevis and the University of Technology, Sydney Academic Board in 2012. Before taking up her role with NUS, Jade was the president of the Students' Association in 2012. She has also been an editor of the student magazine, Vertigo, and a first year law student mentor. Jade graduated from the University of Technology, Sydney in 2013 with a BA Laws/ Communications (Journalism).

Irene Watson belongs to the Tanganekald and Meintangk First Nations Peoples of the Coorong and south east of South Australia, and is currently an Australian Research Council Indigenous Discovery Awardee and Professor of Law at the University of South Australia, School of Law.

Mary Wyburn is a senior lecturer in Business Law at the University of Sydney Business School. Her current higher education research focuses on the ownership of intellectual property rights in commercialised research, the role of adverse findings of academic misconduct on admission to legal practice and authorship ethics.

Table of Cases

Table of Statutes

Queensland

South Australia

Introduction to Higher Education and the Law

Sally Varnham, Patty Kamvounias and Joan Squelch

Australia has a strong, vibrant and inclusive system of higher education. Over the past decades, while growing in size and stature, it has been subject to huge change, precipitated often by economic and political imperatives. Those who manage, govern, research and teach in universities have been required to be both proactive and reactive in the face of the shifting sands, all the while maintaining and growing a sector which has earned a considerable global reputation. It is impossible to overestimate the extent to which law and policy drive and govern these changes and their impact on the sector.

From the establishment in 1850 of Australia's first university, the University of Sydney, to the incorporation in 2013 of Australia's newest private university, the sector has owed its existence to legislation, both State and federal, which govern matters such as funding, management, governance and accountability. The statutory provision for the first universities in Australia was largely modelled on the UK system, in common with their policies, practices and in many cases, their physical environment.

The sector has grown exponentially, and while there are still vestiges of its UK legacy, it has developed a strong and unique character. Historically, the sector has been established, funded and regulated by a combination of State and federal legislation, recent decades however have seen increasing federal control. There are now 37 public universities and three private universities in Australia that dominate a higher education sector that includes a large number of private providers and a few overseas universities who operate campuses within Australia. All of these public and private providers are known as self-accrediting institutions and are registered and regulated according to law by the federal Tertiary Education Quality and Standards Agency or TEQSA. There are also a large number of non-self-accrediting providers (known as private providers) which may also be incorporated under the *Corporations Act 2001* (Cth). These are not only regulated but must be first be accredited by TEQSA in order to legally carry out operations.

The law plays a central role. It provides for many often complex external relationships, particularly between universities and governments and controls the operation, governance and management, funding and regulation of universities and their activities. It governs, to a large extent, the relationship between universities and its members – staff and students. A large and increasing body of general law impacts upon all a university's relationships and much of its operations.

This is the first Australian book dedicated entirely to the law relating to the provision of higher education. Its mission is to highlight and provide guidance on the law and current legal issues in areas which are considered to be most salient.

The book begins by outlining the framework of higher education provision. It then traverses a wide range of areas where the law impacts upon a university's external and internal relationships, from principles of fundamental rights such as anti-discrimination and equal opportunity, transparency and due process in decision-making, employment and student matters, to property rights such as copyright and ownership of intellectual property. Much of the law which affects all facets of life in Australia is analysed for its particular significance to the higher education sector.

As editors we have commissioned chapters from leading scholars and practitioners with knowledge and expertise in particular areas. Inevitably, there are crossovers and we have attempted wherever possible to cross reference to avoid repetition. Each chapter provides a unique resource for university managers, governors, administrators, academics, students, legal practitioners and all with an interest in the law as it relates to higher education. While it is intended to be useful as a practical and readable guide, it has academic rigour and encourages debate in its highlighting of the issues currently affecting each particular area. To further assist the reader, a list of References and Further Reading is available on The Federation Press website.

Within the confines of one book, it is impossible to cover every facet of the law relevant to the higher education sector. Universities of the 21st century are huge entrepreneurial enterprises, with responsibilities for international and national trading ventures and collaborations, large building projects, and controlling many millions of dollars annually. For these areas, we refer the reader to the general law relating to corporations, property and finance.

While the areas covered in the book have relevance to the many private non-self-accrediting institutions operating in Australia, we do not cover these providers specifically. This is the case also with the Vocational Education and Training (VET) sector, comprising institutes of technical and further education, known as TAFEs, adult and community education providers and agricultural colleges. Within this sector these are also a wide range of private providers, community organisations, industry skill centres and commercial and enterprise training providers.[1] VET may also be provided within schools and there are some dual sector universities which provide both higher education and vocational education and training. Apart from the general legal principles contained in statute and common law which have applicability to all education providers, this book does not specifically cover the VET sector.

We have not attempted to cover the multitude of ways in which the law traverses higher education, but to focus on those areas which have the most practical relevance. The well-researched and readable chapters by eminent scholars in their particular areas of expertise are at once interesting, informative and thought-provoking.

The world of higher education has a constantly changing landscape. The law both drives these changes and reacts to them. General law also does not stand still. This book endeavours to provide information, discussion and analysis, current as of 1 May 2015.

1 For further information on this sector, the reader is referred to the website of the Australia Skills Quality Authority (ASQA) which is the organisation of the Australian government responsible for the operation and regulation of the VET sector <www.asqa.gov.au>.

PART ONE

The Law of Higher Education

Chapter 1

The Legal Framework of Higher Education

Joan Squelch

I Introduction

The system of higher education in Australia is complex and diverse. It is also governed and regulated by a vast array of Commonwealth and State or Territory legislation and regulations. As an introductory chapter to the diverse legal themes and issues dealt with in this book, this chapter provides an overview of the composition of the higher education system in Australia, with the focus on universities, and the legal framework in which they operate. Consideration is given to the place of higher education in a federal system of government, the relationship between Commonwealth and State systems, the incorporation of universities, university governance, quality assurance and funding.

II Higher Education in a Federal System

In 1901, the Commonwealth of Australia was established as a federation under the *Commonwealth of Australia Constitution Act 1900* (the Constitution). Under the federal system, law-making powers are shared between the Commonwealth Parliament and the parliaments of the States. The Commonwealth can only make laws over matters that are granted by the Constitution. Concurrent powers over matters that both the Commonwealth and a State can make valid laws are listed in s 51 of the Constitution.[1] Education is not one of the listed powers and therefore education falls within the residual State matters. The Commonwealth does not have any power per se to make laws on higher education and universities. The Commonwealth 'possesses no specific power over such subjects as "education", "higher education" or "universities" in general'.[2] This was confirmed in *R v University of Sydney*, a case concerning Commonwealth control of university admission, in which it was held that 'the Commonwealth Parliament has no power to legislate with respect to the subject of education as such'.[3]

However, the provision and regulation of higher education has increasingly become a shared responsibility between the Commonwealth and States, with the Commonwealth gaining 'some significant Constitutional power over the area of

1 Sarah Joseph and Melissa Castan, *Federal Constitutional Law: A Contemporary View* (Lawbook Co, 2014).

2 Greg Craven, 'Commonwealth Power Over Higher Education: Implications and Realities' (2006) 1(1) *Public Policy* 3.

3 *R v University of Sydney* (1943) 67 CLR 95.

higher education'.[4] The power to influence, regulate and control universities is largely attributed to the Commonwealth government's control over funding and the power to grant funding subject to conditions. The Commonwealth government has also used the corporations power to pass laws relating to higher education.

The corporations power, s 51(xx) of the Constitution, empowers parliament to make laws with respect to 'foreign corporations, trading and financial corporations formed within the Commonwealth'. This provision applies to private and public universities. The courts have confirmed that universities are 'trading corporations', based on the test of whether or not a corporation conducts 'substantial' trading activities.[5] *Quickenden v O'Connor* (*Quickenden*),[6] in which an academic at the University of Western Australia challenged the validity of a certified agreement made under the *Workplace Relations Act 1996* (Cth), confirmed that universities may be characterised as trading corporations irrespective of the purpose of the corporation: a university may be a trading corporation 'if it engages in substantial or significant trading activities notwithstanding that trading is not its primary purpose'.[7] In *Quickenden*, the court noted that the 'activities cited are trading activities and are substantial' and although the university was not established for the purpose of trading 'at the time relevant to this case and at present, it does fall within that class'.[8] Trading activities of a university include the sale of publications, fees for services provided such as accommodation, fees from international students, parking fees, ticket sales from university events and the sale of computing equipment[9] (see Chapter 8 by Kamvounias).

This legislative power of the Commonwealth was further extended in *New South Wales v Commonwealth*,[10] which held that the corporation's power is not limited to trading aspects but allows regulation of matters such as employer-employee relations,[11] as was the situation in *Quickenden*. The Commonwealth therefore has the legislative power to exercise control in areas of teaching and research. This is illustrated by the Commonwealth government's implementation of the quality assurance framework under the *Tertiary Education Quality and Standards Agency Act 2011* (Cth) (*TEQSA Act*), which was passed under s 51(xx) (corporations), s 51(xxxix) (incidental power), and s 122 (power to make laws with respect to territories) of the Constitution.[12] Although the Commonwealth may regulate activities of universities, it does not have general powers of incorporation, as discussed below.[13]

4 Craven, above n 2, 1.

5 See also *R v Federal Court of Australia; Ex parte WA National Football League* (1979) 143 CLR 190, 208; *State Superannuation Board v Trade Practices Commission* (1982) 150 CLR 282, 304.

6 [2001] FCA 303. See also *E v Australian Red Cross Society* (1991) 27 FCR 310.

7 *Quickenden v O'Connor* [2001] FCA 303, [47].

8 Ibid [51].

9 Ibid [23].

10 *New South Wales v Commonwealth* (*Work Choices case*) (2006) 229 CLR 1.

11 Jim Jackson, 'Commonwealth Controls over Australian Schools, TAFEs and Universities via Tied Funding: Time for Constitutional Reform?' (2008) 13(2) *Australia & New Zealand Journal of Law and Education* 109.

12 *TEQSA Act* s 8.

13 In *New South Wales v Commonwealth* (1990) 169 CLR 482, referred to as the *Incorporation case*, in which certain provisions of the *Corporations Act 1989* (Cth) were challenged, it was held that the Commonwealth powers under s 51(xx) did not extend to regulating the formation of corporations.

III Higher Education Providers

The higher education system is made up of universities and various other higher education institutions that are either self-regulating or non-self-regulating providers.[14] There are currently 40 universities in Australia, of which 37 are public and three private.[15] In addition to the universities and other self-accrediting providers there are over 150 non-self-accrediting higher education providers that are listed on State and Territory registers.[16] These latter institutions are mostly private and provide a wide range of specialised education services.[17] The size of the higher educator sector is evident from student numbers. In 2013 there were a total of 1,313,776 domestic and international students enrolled at higher education institutions; an increase of 4.5 per cent from 2012, with 92.5 per cent of students enrolled in public universities.[18]

Vocational education and training (VET) providers, which mainly constitute non-self-accrediting providers (that is, providers whose courses are accredited by the Government Accreditation Authority), play a significant role in the economic development of the country by providing a wide range of highly professional and technical skills training for the workforce. The providers of VET comprise technical and further education institutes, adult and community education providers, agricultural colleges, industry skill centres, and commercial and enterprise training providers as well as community organisations that provide skills training. Some universities[19] and schools[20] also provide VET.[21] VET is 'provided through a network of eight state and territory governments and the Australian government, along with industry, public and private training providers that work together to provide nationally consistent training across Australia'.[22] VET is regulated by the Australian Skills Quality Authority (ASQA) pursuant to the *National Vocational Education and Training Regulator Act 2011* (Cth).

Self-accrediting[23] providers comprise public and private universities; for example, the Carnegie Mellon University, which is an Australian branch of an American

14 See *TEQSA Act* s 5 for a definition of 'higher education providers'.

15 The University of Notre Dame Australia situated in Fremantle and Sydney is a private not-for-profit university, Bond University situated in Queensland is a private not-for-profit university, and the newly established Torrens University is a private incorporated body. The Australian Catholic University (ACU) is not a private university but a public not-for-profit university funded by the Australian Government.

16 Australian Government, Department of Education, Employment and Workplace Relations <http://www.deewr.gov.au/highereducation/Pages/Overview.aspx>.

17 See, for example, MyUniversity <http://myuniversity.gov.au/OtherSelfAccreditingHigherEducationProviders>.

18 Australian Government. Department of Education. Higher Education Statistics. Student Data <https://www.education.gov.au/selected-higher-education-statistics-2013-student-data>.

19 See, for example, Victoria University <http://www.vu.edu.au/study-with-us/your-study-options/vet-in-schools>.

20 See, for example, Department of Education, Western Australia, <http://www.det.wa.edu.au/curriculumsupport/vetis/detcms/portal/>.

21 Australian Government, Australian Skills Qualification Authority, <http://www.asqa.gov.au/about-vet/australias-vet-sector.html>.

22 See Department of Education, Western Australia, above n 20.

23 *Higher Education Support Act 2003* (Cth) (*HESA*) sch 1.

research university;[24] the MCD University of Divinity; and other self-accrediting institutions and non-universities, including the Batchelor Institute of Indigenous Tertiary Education.[25]

All higher education providers are required to be registered with TEQSA and listed on a national register, which is intended to be the 'authoritative source of information on the status of registered higher education providers in Australia'.[26] To qualify as a higher education provider, an institution must meet the threshold standards[27] relating to provider standing, financial viability and sustainability, corporate and academic governance, academic quality and integrity, management and human resources, responsibilities to students, physical and electronic resources, and infrastructure, and offer at least one accredited course.[28]

For the remainder of this chapter, the discussion will focus on the university sector.

IV Incorporation of Universities and State Legislation

A Incorporation

Most universities are incorporated under their own legislation enacted by State parliaments. The Minister for Education is generally responsible for approving new universities, including the operation of universities external to Australia, as well as approving the operation of self-accrediting instructions and accrediting courses.[29]

The use of the name 'university' is also protected and regulated. 'University' is a restricted name that cannot be used without the consent of the Minister for Education. An education institution or an agent of an education institution is not permitted to use the word 'university' or represent an institution as a university unless it is an Australian university or a recognised overseas university.[30]

The University of Sydney[31] was the first university to be established in Australia in 1850 followed by the University of Melbourne in 1853,[32] the University of Adelaide in 1874[33] and the University of Tasmania in 1890.[34] The growth of university education in the first half of the 20th century saw the establishment of the following universities: the University of Queensland (1909);[35] the University of Western Australia (1912);[36] the

24 Carnegie Mellon University Australia <http://www.australia.cmu.edu/>.

25 *HESA* sub-div 16-B, ss 16.15 (Table A), 16.20 (Table B), 16.22 (Table C).

26 *TEQSA Act* (Cth) pt 3.

27 *Higher Education Standards Framework (Threshold Standards) 2011* made under s 58(1) of the *TEQSA Act*.

28 *TEQSA Act* s 25.

29 See, for example, *Higher Education Act 2004* (WA); *Higher Education Act 2001* (NSW); *Higher Education (General Provisions) Act 2008* (Qld); *Education and Training Reform Act 2006* (Vic) pt 4.3 div 5.

30 See, for example, *Higher Education Act 2004* (WA) s 6; see also *Business Names Registration (Availability of Names) Determination 2012* pt 2.

31 *University of Sydney Act 1989* (NSW).

32 *University of Melbourne Act 2009* (Vic).

33 *University of Adelaide Act 1971* (SA).

34 *University of Tasmania Act 1992* (Tas).

35 *University of Queensland Act 1998* (Qld).

36 *University of Western Australia Act 1911* (WA).

Australian National University (1946),[37] the only university established under federal law; and the University of New South Wales (1949).[38] The second half of the 20th century was characterised by a significant growth in university education with the addition of Monash University (1958)[39] and the emergence of more regional-based universities such as the University of New England (1953).[40]

Between 1964 and 1975 there was a dramatic increase with the establishment of nine new universities: Macquarie University (1964),[41] La Trobe University (1964),[42] the University of Newcastle (1965),[43] Flinders University (1966),[44] James Cook University (1970),[45] Griffith University (1971),[46] Deakin University (1974),[47] Murdoch University (1975)[48] and the University of Wollongong (1975).[49]

Since the 1980s, a number of universities have been incorporated, many of which have gained university status, following a long tradition of providing various forms of vocational-based training and the merging of different educational institutions, including: Curtin University of Technology (1987);[50] University of Technology, Sydney (1988);[51] Queensland University of Technology (1988);[52] University of Western Sydney (1988); Charles Sturt University (CSU) (1989);[53] Bond University (1989), incorporated under the *Companies (Queensland) Code*;[54] the University of Notre Dame Australia (1989);[55] University of Canberra (1989);[56] Victoria University of Technology (1990), renamed Victoria University in 2005;[57] University of South Australia (1990);[58] Australian Catholic University (1991), incorporated under the *Companies (Victoria) Code* and operating as a company limited by guarantee;[59] Edith Cowan University (1991);[60] Central Queensland University (1992);[61] University of Southern Queensland (1992);[62] RMIT University

37 *Australian National University Act 1991* (Cth).
38 *University of New South Wales Act 1989* (NSW).
39 *Monash University Act 2009* (Vic).
40 *University of New England Act 1993* (NSW).
41 *Macquarie University Act 1989* (NSW).
42 *La Trobe University Act 2009* (Vic).
43 *University of Newcastle Act 1989* (NSW).
44 *Flinders University of South Australia Act 1966* (SA).
45 *James Cook University Act 1997* (Qld).
46 *Griffith University Act 1998* (Qld).
47 *Deakin University Act 2009* (Vic).
48 *Murdoch University Act 1973* (WA).
49 *University of Wollongong Act 1989* (NSW).
50 *Curtin University of Technology Act 1966* (WA).
51 *University of Technology, Sydney, Act 1989* (NSW).
52 *Queensland University of Technology Act 1998* (Qld).
53 *Charles Sturt University Act 1989* (NSW). Charles Sturt University dates back to 1895, with the establishment of the Bathurst Experimental Farm <http://www.csu.edu.au/about/history>.
54 *Bond University Act 1987* (Qld) s 2.
55 *University of Notre Dame Australia Act 1989* (WA).
56 *University of Canberra Act 1989* (Cth).
57 *Victoria University Act 2010* (Vic).
58 *University of South Australia Act 1990* (SA).
59 *Australian Catholic University Act 1990* (NSW) s 3.
60 *Edith Cowan University Act 1984* (WA).
61 *Central Queensland University Act 1998* (Qld).
62 *University of Southern Queensland Act 1998* (Qld).

(1992);[63] Swinburne University of Technology (1992);[64] University of Ballarat (1993),[65] now named Federation University Australia;[66] Southern Cross University (1994);[67] University of Sunshine Coast (1999);[68] and Charles Darwin University (2004).[69] The ongoing establishment of universities has seen the new Torrens University Australia being established in 2013 as a private university.[70]

B *Functions of Universities*

Legislation incorporating universities do not define what a university is; however, universities may be defined by reference to their functions or objects.[71] Functions and objects of a university typically relate to the advancement and dissemination of knowledge, engagement in research, provision of tertiary qualifications, participation in national and international scholarship, research and consultancy, and engagement in discourse and public debate within the wider community. For example, the University of Technology, Sydney includes the following as main functions of the university:

> (a) the provision of facilities for education and research of university standard,
> (b) the encouragement of the dissemination, advancement, development and application of knowledge informed by free inquiry,
> (c) the provision of courses of study or instruction and the carrying out of research across a range of fields to meet the needs of the community,
> (d) the participation in public discourse,
> (e) the conferring of degrees, including those of Bachelor, Master and Doctor, and the awarding of diplomas, certificates and other awards,
> (f) the provision of teaching and learning that engage with advanced knowledge and inquiry,
> (g) the development of governance, procedural rules, admission policies, financial arrangements and quality assurance processes that are underpinned by the values and goals referred to in the functions set out in this subsection, and that are sufficient to ensure the integrity of the University's academic programs.[72]

V University Governance

The enabling legislation that establishes universities generally sets out the various governance structures and functions, which are supported by internal university

---

63 *Royal Melbourne Institute of Technology Act 2010* (Vic).
64 *Swinburne University of Technology Act 2010* (Vic).
65 *University of Ballarat Act 1993* (Vic). The University was one of the few Australian universities to take its name from an Aboriginal language word: 'Ballarat' meaning 'resting place'.
66 *Federation University Australia Act 2010* (Vic).
67 *Southern Cross University Act 1993* (NSW).
68 *University of the Sunshine Coast Act 1998* (Qld).
69 *Charles Darwin University Act 2003* (NT).
70 *Torrens University Australia Act 2013* (SA). Torrens University Australia Limited was incorporated as an Australian company on 3 January 2012. It is a member of the Laureate International Universities network. In October 2011, the South Australian government grant LEI Higher Education Holdings Pty Ltd authorisation to establish a university.
71 Jim Jackson and Sally Varnham, *Law for Educators: School and University Law in Australia* (LexisNexis Butterworths, 2007).
72 *University of Technology, Sydney Act 1989* (NSW) s 6.

statutes, regulations, policies and procedures. In general, statutory university governance structures include a council (or senate[73] or board of trustees[74]), the executive team consisting of the Vice Chancellor and executive managers, and an academic board (also referred to as academic senate). The establishment, powers and duties of university governance structures are derived from the respective university enabling legislation. See Chapter 2 by Varnham for further discussion on governance.

A University Council

The council (senate or board) of a university is the governing body (authority) of the university and is responsible for the overall strategic direction of the university. Chancellors are appointed to chair the council.[75] The powers and duties of councils are set out in the respective university enabling statute. A council is generally empowered to do anything necessary for the effective control and management of the university. Typically, council powers included conferring degrees, diplomas and certificates, appointing university staff, terminating staff appointments, managing and controlling the university affairs and property, acquiring and disposing of real property, making internal regulations and by-laws, and managing and controlling university finances.[76]

A university council has the power to make statutes, by-laws and regulations subject to the university's enabling legislation. The function of the statutes or by-laws is to regulate the internal organisation, management and administration of the university. Statutes may be made in relation to a number of matters, including the organisation, management and governance of the university; the academic board; employment of staff; discipline; academic dress and academic titles, ranks or positions; examinations; research; courses of study; intellectual property; student loans; endowments, traffic, property and amenities; and fees charged.[77]

A university statute or by-laws made by the council must be in writing, have the common seal of the university affixed, and generally be submitted to the Minister of Education for approval. University statutes and regulations must be made readily available to the public by whatever means a university council considers appropriate. Some university enabling legislation requires statutes or by-laws to be approved the Governor and then published in the Government Gazette.[78]

---

73 See, for example, the *Murdoch University Act 1973* (WA) s 17(1), which provides that the governing body of the university shall be the senate; the *University of Queensland Act 1998* (Qld) div 2.

74 *University of Western Sydney Act 1997* (NSW) ss 10, 22.

75 In March 2007 the Chancellors of the Australian universities formally incorporated as the University Chancellors' Council (UCC), which meets twice a year.

76 See, for example, *University of Western Australia Act 1911* (WA) div 3; *Murdoch University Act 1973* (WA) s 17.

77 See, for example, *University of Melbourne Act 2009* (Vic) s 29; *University of Sydney Act 1989* (NSW) s 36(1).

78 See, for example, *Murdoch University Act 1973* (WA) s 25; *Curtin University of Technology Act 1966* (WA) s 35(1); *Edith Cowan University Act 1984* (WA) s 27; *University of Sydney Act 1989* s 36(2); *University of Western Sydney Act 1997* (NSW) s 40; *University of Adelaide Act 1971* (SA) ss 22 and 23.

B University Executive

University enabling legislation makes provision for the office of the Vice Chancellor. The Vice Chancellor is the principal academic appointed by the university council as the chief executive officer of the university and, assisted by a team of executive managers, is responsible to council for the overall academic standards, management and administration of the university.[79]

C Academic Boards

University academic boards (also known as an academic council) have an important role in university governance as a policy-making body and advisory body to the university council. According to Universities Australia, 'the academic board or university senate has principal responsibility for providing academic leadership in the university's core activities of teaching and research training. The board oversees and has custodianship for academic standards'.[80]

VI Quality Assurance and Accreditation

Quality assurance and accreditation in higher education are now largely regulated by the Commonwealth's Tertiary Education Quality and Standards Agency (TEQSA) and the Australian Qualifications Framework.

A Tertiary Education Quality and Standards Agency

TEQSA was established in July 2011 by the *Tertiary Education Quality and Standards Agency Act 2011* (Cth) (*TEQSA Act*). The primary aim of TEQSA is to ensure that students receive a high quality education at any Australian higher education provider.[81] Key objects of the *TEQSA Act* are to regulate higher education using a standards-based quality framework and principles relating to regulatory necessity, risk and proportionality; to protect and enhance Australia's reputation for quality higher education and training services; and to increase its international competitiveness in the higher education sector.[82] To this end, TEQSA has extensive powers and functions as numerated in s 134 and includes the broad provision that TEQSA has the 'power to do all things that are necessary or convenient to be done for or in connection with the performance of its functions'. Importantly, TEQSA is empowered to carry out its functions within and outside of Australia, which is important given Australia's extensive international education market (see Chapter 5 by Ramia).

Higher education providers may apply to TEQSA for approval to be registered as a higher education provider in a particular category. The process is rigorous and

79 See, for example, *University of Tasmania Act 1992* (Tas) s 16; *University of Adelaide Act 1971* (SA) s 8. Similar provisions are found in the enabling statutes of other Australian universities.

80 Universities Australia, <http://www.universitiesaustralia.edu.au/page/about-us/committees---contacts/key-contacts/academic-boards/>.

81 Tertiary Education Quality and Standards Agency <http://www.teqsa.gov.au/>.

82 *TEQSA Act* s 3.

applicants are required to address comprehensive threshold standards, which were developed before the establishment of TEQSA, based on the existing National Protocols and National Guidelines for Higher Education Approval Processes.[83] The threshold standards comprise provider registration standards, provider category standards,[84] provider course accreditation standards, and the qualification standards. Provider registration standards include matters relating to financial liability and safeguards, corporate governance, academic quality and integrity, responsibility of students, human resources and infrastructure. The Higher Education Standards Panel, which is an expert advisory body established under the *TEQSA Act*,[85] is now responsible for reviewing and developing the threshold standards, and to provide independent advice to the Federal Ministers responsible for education and research.[86]

Another important function of TEQSA is the approval and accreditation of courses of study. The threshold standards for course accreditation are the qualification standards, which have been prepared based on the Australian Qualifications Framework (discussed below) endorsed by the Ministerial Council for Tertiary Education and Employment in April 2011 and implemented in July 2011.[87]

In order to ensure that registered higher education institutions comply with the quality assurance standards, TEQSA also has extensive compliance, investigative, monitoring and enforcement powers in relation to registered institutions over which it has control.[88] These include the power to enter the premises of institutions by consent or a properly executed warrant[89] and carry out searches and seizures.

B *Australian Qualifications Framework*

Australian universities are authorised by State and Territory legislation to accredit their own courses, but they must be in compliance with the Australian Qualifications Framework (AQF), which is Australia's national policy for regulated qualifications.[90] The AQF was first developed in 1995 as a council of the Ministerial Council for Tertiary Education and Employment and revised in 2011 and 2013.[91] The AQF covers higher education, vocational education and training, and school education. Government funding to universities, whether directly or indirectly, is inevitably linked to quality assurance and demonstrable compliance with quality standards. The AQF provides the qualification standards that underpin national regulatory and quality assurance

83 *Higher Education Standards Framework (Threshold Standards) 2011* (a legislative instrument under the *TEQSA Act*). Section 58(1) of the *TEQSA Act* provides that the Minister may, by legislative instrument, make standards. The Higher Education Standards have been under review and the final proposed Higher Education Standards Framework has been submitted to the Minister for Education <http://www.hestandards.gov.au/final-proposed-framework>.

84 Australian University, Australian University College, Australian University of Specialisation, Overseas University and Overseas University of Specialisation. The majority fall within the 'Australian University' category.

85 *TEQSA Act* pt 9.

86 Australian Government, Higher Education Standards <http://www.hestandards.gov.au/>.

87 Ibid.

88 *TEQSA Act* ss 70-73.

89 Ibid ss 90-91.

90 Australian Qualifications Framework <http://www.aqf.edu.au/>.

91 Ibid.

arrangements for education and training providers,[92] and ensures 'a national recognition and a consistent understanding of what defines each qualification type'. Under TEQSA legislation and in line with the AQF, higher education providers may offer higher education programs of learning leading to AQF qualifications at levels 5, 6, 7, 8, 9 and 10 of the AQF, which range from diplomas at level 5 to doctoral qualifications at level 10.[93] Each level reflects the depth and complexity of learning associated with each level, and provides a summary of the minimum knowledge, skills and application of knowledge and skills for each level. The AQF maintains a register of AQF qualifications and the organisations authorised to issue those qualifications.[94]

C International Students

International students make up a large cohort of students in Australian higher education (see Chapter 5 by Ramia). Higher education institutions that provide education and training services to overseas students studying in Australia on student visas must comply with the *Education Services for Overseas Students Act 2000* (Cth) (*ESOS Act*). The *ESOS Act* sets out the legal framework governing delivery of education to overseas students studying in Australia on a student visa. It aims to protect the interests of overseas students by setting minimum standards, and to enhance Australia's reputation for delivering quality education services.[95] Higher education providers are required to be registered for providing education services to overseas students (which essentially means all Australian universities). It is an offence under the *ESOS Act* to promote or provide courses to overseas students if the provider is not a registered provider.[96] The *ESOS Act* further provides for a legislative instrument, the *National Code of Practice for Registration Authorities and Providers of Education and Training to Overseas Students 2007*,[97] 'to provide nationally consistent standards for the registration and conduct of registered providers and the conduct of persons who deliver educational services on behalf of registered providers'.[98] Higher education providers that breach the *ESOS Act* may be subject to various penalties, which include conditions[99] being attached to their registration, and suspension or cancellation of registration.[100] The *ESOS Act* also provides for extensive powers to authorised employees[101] to monitor and search

92 Ibid.

93 For a detailed description of the standards and levels see the Australian Qualifications Framework July 2011 <http://www.aqf.edu.au/Portals/0/Documents/Handbook/AustQuals%20FrmwrkFirstEditionJuly2011_FINAL.pdf>.

94 Australian Qualifications Framework. AQF Register <http://www.aqf.edu.au/Portals/0/Documents/Register%20Policy%20-%20July%202011.pdf>.

95 *ESOS Act* s 4A.

96 *ESOS Act* s 8.

97 *National Code of Practice for Registration Authorities and Providers of Education and Training to Overseas Students 2007* <https://aei.gov.au/Regulatory-Information/Education-Services-for-Overseas-Students-ESOS-Legislative-Framework/National-Code/Documents/National_Code_2007_pdf.pdf>.

98 *ESOS Act* pt 4 s 34.

99 *ESOS Act* s 84.

100 *ESOS Act* pt 6.

101 *ESOS Act* s 5.

providers,[102] and for the production of notices to access information or documents that are relevant for monitoring purposes.[103]

VII Funding

Funding of higher education in Australia is complex. The Commonwealth government is primarily responsible for the public funding of higher education including public and private universities. However, universities increasingly have to rely on non-government sources of funding such as revenue from international students.

Currently, the *Higher Education Support Act 2003* (Cth) (*HESA*) is the primary piece of legislation through which universities receive funding. The *HESA* provides for the Commonwealth to give financial support for higher education and certain vocational education and training through grants and other payments made largely to higher education providers, and through financial assistance to students (usually in the form of loans).[104]

There are a range of grants for specific purposes including quality, learning and teaching, research and research training programs. The Commonwealth Grant Scheme is the main source of funding through which universities receive funding to subsidise the cost of student fees for domestic students enrolled in an undergraduate bachelor program across various disciplines.[105] Since 2012, public universities have been able to decide on the number of domestic students they enrol in bachelor programs (except for medicine) and therefore the funding received for the Commonwealth Supported Places (CSP). The funding is determined according to the formulae and principles set out in div 33 of the *HESA*.

The Higher Education and Research Reform Amendment Bill 2014 was introduced to the House of Representatives on 28 August 2014. The Bill sought to introduce far-reaching reforms to higher education. The main thrust of the reforms (ch 2 pt 2-2) was on deregulating fees, extending funding to education qualifications below the level of bachelors' degree and increasing funding to private universities and non-private higher education providers.[106] Key reform measures included: deregulation and the expansion of a demand driven system; a new Commonwealth Scholarship Scheme; the change of the HELP indexation rate from the Consumer Price Index to the Treasury 10-year bond rate; a new minimum level for repayment of HELP debts and increased funding to research under the Future Fellowship Scheme (schs 1-5).[107]

---

102 *ESOS Act* pt 7 div 3.

103 *ESOS Act* pt 7 divs 1, 2.

104 *HESA* ch 1 div 3 s 3.1. Financial assistance is provided in the form of HECS-HELP assistance for student contribution amounts; FEE-HELP assistance for tuition fees; OS-HELP assistance for overseas study; SA-HELP assistance for meeting student services and amenities fees imposed by higher education providers: s 3.10.

105 *HESA* ch 2 pt 2-2.

106 Higher Education and Research Reform Amendment Bill 2014 <http://www.aph.gov.au/Parliamentary_Business/Bills_Legislation/Bills_Search_Results/Result?bId=r5396>.

107 Australian Government, Department of Education and Training, Higher Education and Research Budget Information <https://www.education.gov.au/higher-education-and-research-budget-information>.

In September 2014, the Bill was referred to the Senate Education and Employment Legislation Committee to conduct an enquiry and submit a report on the Bill. The Senate Report of October 2014 made some key recommendations and recommended that the Bill be passed.[108] Nonetheless, in December 2014, the Bill was voted down by the Senate, leaving the university sector and other providers in limbo.[109] An amended Bill was subsequently tabled in parliament in March 2015 which followed the same fate as the previous Bill. The amended Bill was voted down by the Senate thereby halting, for the time being, proposed reforms to higher education funding including the contentious issue of deregulating university fees.

VIII Conclusion

Australian universities are generally established under State or Territory legislation and are self-regulating entities. University enabling statutes set out the structure, governance, powers and functions of universities, and provide universities with the autonomy and authority to make internal rules, regulations and policy according to which a university operates. To this extent, universities have been able to develop into distinctly different institutions. However, as the Commonwealth government has steadily extended its influence and control over higher education, largely through the broadening scope of the Constitutional corporations power, the governance and management of universities have become subject to an increasing amount of Commonwealth legislation and regulation, both specifically education legislation and general legislation covering all aspects of university life. The breadth of laws relating to various aspects of higher education are examined in the chapters that follow.

108 Standing Committees on Education and Employment <http://www.aph.gov.au/Parliamentary_Business/Committees/Senate/Education_and_Employment/Higher_Education/Report/b02>.

109 Eliza Borrello and Jonathon Gul, 'University Deregulation: Senate Rejects Education Minister Christopher Pyne's Push for Higher Education Reform', *ABC News*, 3 December 2014 <http://www.abc.net.au/news/2014-12-02/senate-rejects-governments-push-to-deregulate-universities/5935116>.

Chapter 2

University Governance: Responsibility and Accountability

Sally Varnham

> Governance is about the frameworks in which universities and colleges manage themselves and about the processes and structures used to achieve the intended outcomes – in other words about *how* higher education institutions operate.[1]

I Introduction

This chapter begins by setting the contextual background for higher education governance looking briefly at its historical development. Secondly, it outlines the legal framework and considers the various suggested models for governance through the lens of increasing managerialism and corporatisation of the sector. Finally, it discusses current trends and issues facing university governing bodies.

In 2006, a UK commentator wrote, with reference to the system of higher education there:

> A new emphasis on quality assurance and assessment has been established, in both teaching and research. More generally, globalisation and internationalisation have developed, together with the impact of new technology, especially in the fields of communications and information handling, as key drivers of change in higher education. Arguably, strongest of all the forces for change have been the growing influence of market forces and competition within higher education.[2]

He could well have been referring to higher education in Australia today. The sector is undergoing significant change, precipitated by a multitude of factors driven by international developments, economic factors and political imperatives.[3] This 'evolution' of higher education impacts considerably on institutional corporate and academic governance and the principles upon which it is founded. The sector is both driving and responding to phenomena variously referred to as 'massification', 'commodification' and 'corporatisation', accompanied and assisted by the rapidly accelerating impact of

---

1 P Maassen and B Stensaker, 'Interpretations of Self-Regulation. The Changing State – Higher Education Relationship in Europe' in R Begg (ed), *The Dialogue Between Higher Education Research and Practice* (Kluwer Academic Publishers, 2003).

2 J Taylor, '"Big is Beautiful". Organisational Change in Universities in the United Kingdom: New Models of Institutional Management and the Changing Role of Academic Staff' (2006) 31(3) *Higher Education in Europe* 251.

3 See Chapter 1 by Squelch.

technology. The market driven model with its principles of commercialisation and competition has led many universities to review the composition of their main governing bodies. They are responsible now for huge multi-faceted enterprises with increasing commercial and entrepreneurial imperatives and this leads inevitably to the need for accompanying expertise and focus of members.

In addition, governing bodies must consider how best to implement new teaching and learning methods and platforms afforded by technology to accommodate the new generation of students.[4] There is a strong emphasis on innovation and creativity and as well as having their primary focus on quality and standards, and the scholarship of teaching and learning and research, universities must pay increasing attention to the identification and amelioration of risk in the drive forward.[5] While enjoying a large measure of autonomy they are subject to considerable constraint and accountability under legislation and legislative instruments.[6]

II University Governance: An Historical Perspective to the Present Day

When Australian public universities were first established, there was no appropriate governance model from their UK counterparts. Public universities there, such as Oxford and Cambridge, comprised a collection of colleges and although they conferred university degrees, each college was managed and governed autonomously. The first model in Australian universities comprised a governing body over which the Chancellor both presided and had a strong influence. These bodies later took to seeking advice on academic matters, such as the establishment of new disciplines, from professorial boards comprising all the professors and heads of departments. By the middle of the 20th century, most Australian public universities had evolved to have a governing body presided over by a Chancellor; a Vice Chancellor as the Chief Executive Officer, usually but not always a senior academic at the head of the executive or management arm of the university's operations; and a professorial board entrusted with the maintenance of standards and quality, and later, for the formulation of academic policy. The Vice Chancellor had to look to the governing body for the allocation of resources in order to fulfil the university's functions and operations in terms of its strategic plan, and both he or she and this body in turn relied on the advice of the professorial board for oversight of academic matters and policy. This structure essentially remains, save for the replacement of the professorial board with a more representative academic governance body (see below).

The development of the Australian university sector and its governance in terms of accountability can be traced in three stages. First was its expansion assisted greatly

4 Within this context are exponential developments in course delivery, and the advent of MOOCs or Mass Online Open Courses.

5 The Tertiary Education Quality and Standards Agency (TEQSA) regulates according to principles relating to regulatory necessity, risk and proportionality and for this purpose it has developed a Regulatory Risk Framework. See Chapter 1 by Squelch for further discussion.

6 Jeanette Baird, 'International, Hierarchical and Market Influences on Australian University Governance' in Michael Shattock (ed), *International Trends in University Governance: Autonomy, Self-Government and the Distribution of Authority* (Routledge, 2014).

by Commonwealth support, from the Murray Report in 1957 to the 1975 demise of the Whitlam Government. This was followed by a period of little change until 1988 and the Dawkins era.[7] Since then, universities have faced much greater federal intervention through funding mechanisms, the push to corporatisation with greater accountability and less involvement of the States and 'government normative expectations of good university governance have been progressively refined through review and legislative change'.[8] It has been argued that the pressure to operate on corporate principles has led to a blurring between public and private good, created tensions between corporate and academic values, and posed threats to institutional autonomy.[9] Carnegie and Tuck put it in these terms: 'Indeed, the massification of higher education and on-going pressures from the state to attract and grow private sources of income, reduce expenditure, increase efficiency and encourage cross-sector competition, have brought into question the very idea of a university (Kennedy 2003) or the place of academic staff within them (Carney 2006)'.[10]

Academic governance, as the overseer of academic quality in a university,[11] and the corporate governing body which is ultimately accountable, are at the centre of this changing world.

III The Legislative Framework of University Governance

Legislation, outlined above in Chapter 1 by Squelch, confers generally wide ranging powers on university governing bodies for oversight of strategy and accountability. Specifically they are entrusted with ensuring effective management including responsible financial and risk management, and all academic matters pursuant to each university act, legislation and other instruments and codes. While ultimate accountability is with the corporate governing body, operational responsibility is delegated to management and to the academic governing body for academic matters.

A Federal Legislation

The primary federal legislation is the *Higher Education Support Act 2003* (Cth) (*HESA*). The purpose of *HESA* is essentially to provide for the funding of universities and a basis for accountability in return for that funding. The corporate governing body is ultimately responsible for ensuring that accountability. The requirements are set out in s 19.1 as:

---

7 See Chapter 1 by Squelch.

8 Jeanette Baird, 'Beyond Professionalism: Enhancing the Governance Culture for Australian University Governing Boards' (2006) 12 *Tertiary Education Management* 297, 301.

9 Margaret Thornton, *Privatising the Public University: The Case of Law* (Routledge, Taylor & Francis Group, 2012).

10 Gary Carnegie and Jacqueline Tuck, 'Understanding the ABC of University Governance' (2010) 69(4) *Australian Journal of Public Administration* 431, 433; KJ Kennedy, 'Higher Education Governance as a Key Policy Issue in the 21st Century' (2003) 2(1) *Educational Research for Policy and Practice* 55; S Carney, 'University Governance in Denmark: From Democracy to Accountability' (2006) 5(3-4) *European Educational Research Journal* 221.

11 Ibid.

- financial viability (sub-div 19-B);
- quality (sub-div 19-C);
- fairness – treating all students and prospective students fairly (sub-div 19-D);
- compliance – complying with all legislative instruments and provider compliance requirements (sub-div 19-E). Meeting the requirements of TEQSA registration: compliance with the Provider Standards (Higher Education Threshold Standards) and compliance with contribution and fee requirements (sub-div 19-F);
- compact and academic freedom requirements (sub-div 19-G) – all Table A and Table B providers[12] must enter into mission-based compacts with the federal Minister; and
- in accordance with s 19.115, each such provider must have a policy that upholds free intellectual inquiry in relation to learning, teaching and research.

Further standards for governance are set out in Commonwealth legislation and policy relating to overseas students: the *Education Services for Overseas Students Act 2000* (Cth) (*ESOS Act*) and the *National Code of Practice for Registration Authorities and Providers of Education and Training to Overseas Students 2007* (*National Code*).[13] A provider must fulfil the *ESOS Act* standards for governance in order to have CRICOS registration required to deliver courses to overseas students.

TEQSA may review or examine an entity's operations to assess whether it meets the standards prescribed by the *Higher Education Standards Framework (Threshold Standards) 2011* known as Threshold Standards.[14] Within these standards are Provider Standards which make provision for university governance (below).[15]

B State and Territory Legislation

The corporate governing body's powers and functions are set out in each individual university act passed by State and Territory legislatures, with some exceptions for example, the Australian National University (ANU) – governed by Commonwealth legislation, and the Australian Catholic University, which is incorporated under the *Corporations Act 2001* (Cth).

While using differing terminology, the university Acts generally confer wide ranging powers on the corporate governing body. These powers focus on budget, commercial activities, appointments and the responsibility to review and monitor the management of a university as a whole or the University's performance as a university. Examples are: *Australian National University Act 1991* (Cth): 'entire control and management of the University' and powers of Council which it cannot delegate. The *University of Melbourne Act 2009* (Vic) (and other Victorian university Acts such as the *Royal Melbourne Institute of Technology Act 2010* (Vic)) makes the governing body responsible for 'the general direction and superintendence of the University' and sets out its primary responsibilities as: mission, strategic direction, monitoring systems of

12 For a definition of these categories of providers, see Chapter 1 by Squelch.

13 Applications for inclusion on the Commonwealth Register of Institutions and Courses for Overseas Students (CRICOS) are now assessed by TEQSA. See Chapter 5 by Ramia.

14 *TEQSA Act* s 59.

15 These Threshold Standards are under review at the time of writing.

control and accountability, commercial activities, assessment and management of risk, overseeing and monitoring the academic activities of the university.[16]

The accountability requirements of university governance for federal public funding and adherence to national higher education priorities, are supplemented at State level by oversight through annual university audits and other such requirements. For example, in New South Wales this is through the *Public Finance and Audit Act 1983* (NSW) and each State has its equivalent. The corporate governing body of a university is ultimately responsible to ensure that universities use their resources effectively and efficiently and university policies are administered and implemented properly. An important facet of this responsibility is they must ensure that they have integrated, efficient and transparent approaches to risk management and compliance.[17]

IV Governance Bodies

There are variations in terminology used in legislation and practice for the governance bodies in Australian universities. The governing body with overall responsibility for the university is known as either the Council (University of Technology Sydney), Senate (University of Sydney) or Board of Trustees (University of Western Sydney) (all referred to here as 'the corporate governing body'). The body responsible for academic governance may be known as Academic Board (Southern Cross University), or Senate (Macquarie University) (all referred to here as 'the academic governing body'). The term 'Senior Executive' is used for university management, known as Vice Chancellor or Provost (this title may also be used for a Senior Deputy Vice Chancellor), and Deputy Vice Chancellors or Pro Vice Chancellors (these titles may vary), with the Faculty Deans or School Heads below them.

The unique nature of a university means that while the functions of these bodies are theoretically separate, the essential nature of their decision-making is necessarily intertwined.[18] The decisions of each one generally has impact upon the others, making a three-pronged approach essential. The integral nature of academic considerations to all university decision-making, particularly financial, is set out clearly by Shattock in his discussion of the 2012 crisis at London Metropolitan University:

> Even what may seem a purely financial decision may have a significant academic component: the closure of a course or a department, the decision to invest in a new building or the determination of tuition fees all involve academic as much as financial considerations. Good governance extends to academic decisions about course structures, appointments and the maintenance of academic infrastructures which, while they may have financial implications, are primarily about academic priorities which contribute to the academic reputation of the institution (itself an important component of financial viability).[19]

---

16 *University of Melbourne Act* (Vic) s 8(3) (and other Victorian university Acts have corresponding provisions).

17 Such audits are contained within the annual report to parliament by the Auditor-General of audits of key public sector bodies within the State.

18 See below for a discussion of Shared Governance.

19 Michael Shattock, 'University Governance' (2012) 16(2) *Perspectives: Policy and Practice in Higher Education* 56, 57.

Successive federal government reports have, since the Hoare Report in 1995,[20] raised issues relating to the size, composition, roles and responsibilities of governing bodies. Most recently university governance has received particular attention in the Provider Registration Standards of the Threshold Standards. These Threshold Standards are under review; consultation pursuant to the Consultation Draft April 2014 has been completed and the proposed new standards have been submitted for ministerial consultation and determination. Although the new standards will take a different form, the provisions for Corporate Governance (6.1) and Academic Governance (6.2) are substantially unchanged.

Importantly, both for accountability for government funds and retaining the support of both government and community, governance bodies must be seen to operate effectively. The governance structures of a university must ensure that all its facets, from property and finance to academic quality, equity and diversity, are managed efficiently and effectively, while maintaining university autonomy and academic independence.

In October 2014, TEQSA released Draft Guidance Notes on Corporate and Academic Governance, designed to reflect TEQSA's interpretation of the Threshold Standards as they relate to practice within the sector and provide guidance in relation to different cases.[21] They set out the core roles and responsibilities of the three components of institutional governance setting out the fundamental principle that while all three components are 'interdependent and overlapping … there needs to be a separation of, and clarity about, their principal roles and functions to ensure that governance is effective'.[22] So while it is a requirement in the Threshold Standards that there be a 'clear and discernible separation between corporate and academic governance' and 'a clear distinction between governance and management', shared responsibilities necessitate 'a balance between separation and cooperation'.[23]

Each component of governance is now considered separately.

A The Corporate Governing Body

Chaired by the University Chancellor, this is the primary governance body of Australian public universities. Its functions are set out in legislation and in the Provider Registration Standards (above). It has overall responsibility for the university's operations, its organisational resources and finances, and is accountable for the university's application of public funds. In the last few decades, these bodies have been increasingly 'professionalised' with smaller membership and less staff and student representation. In 2002, a National Conference on Governance highlighted the need for procedures for proper induction and review, better channels of communication between this body and the Executive, and professional development. A recognised need for improved university governance saw the implementation of the National Governance Protocols

20 The Higher Education Management Review <http://www.voced.edu.au/content/ngv8870>. See also <http://www.oecd.org/australia/33642632.PDF>.

21 Meaning the whole higher education sector which includes a large and diverse range of private providers in addition to universities.

22 Draft Guidance Note Corporate Governance, 1 October 2014, 2.

23 Ibid 3.

in 2004,[24] now replaced by the Voluntary Code of Best Practice for the Governance of Australian Universities (Voluntary Code) in 2011.[25] This provides that the corporate governing body should adopt a statement of primary responsibilities. While retaining ultimate responsibility it may delegate specific areas. Its functions are wide ranging and include the university's strategic direction and mission, oversight and management of the university and its performance, establishing policy and principles of procedure 'consistent with legal requirements and community expectations', approving and monitoring systems for control and accountability, overseeing and managing risk, overseeing and monitoring the university's academic activities, as spelt out in specific university legislation. There should be procedures in place of induction and professional development of members and biannual assessment of performance.

The Voluntary Code provides for membership not exceeding 22 and for the appointment of members with qualifications and experience commensurate with the requirements of the role, in terms of financial and commercial expertise with the ability to contribute to the effective operation of the body. Members must, at all times, act in the best interests of the university. While the Voluntary Code agrees on provisions for the appointment of external members and states that there should be 'a majority of independent members who are neither enrolled as a student nor employed by the university', it is otherwise silent on internal membership.

Provider Registration Standard 3.2 prescribes that this body must use a 'full range of expertise including higher education expertise and independent financial expertise' in order that the board's deliberations and decisions are sound and well-informed.

The Provider Registration Standards set out the specific responsibilities of the corporate governing body as: risk management (3.4); delegations in terms of decisions to be made by governance or management (3.5); strategic planning for the institution (3.6); academic governance including the maintenance of academic standards and quality assurance (3.7, 3.8). While the responsibility for the latter is delegated to the academic governing body, ultimate accountability for all the institution's operations rests with the corporate governing body (3.1).[26]

B *The Academic Governing Body*

This body's function is oversight of the core business of the university, teaching and learning and research, and it is the principal policy-making and advisory body on all academic matters and educational programs.[27] It is responsible to the corporate

---

24 The National Governance Protocols were implemented under the former government's reforms in higher education: The Hon Dr Brendan Nelson, *Our Universities: Backing Australia's Future* (Australian Department of Education, Science and Training, 2003).

25 Approved and endorsed by the Ministerial Council for Tertiary Education and Employment in July 2011.

26 Higher Education Standards Framework, which proposes to replace in part the *Higher Education Standards Framework (Threshold Standards) 2011.*

27 *The Purpose and Function of Academic Boards and Senates in Australian Universities*': a policy paper formulated that the National Conferences of Chairs and Academic Boards and Senates 2005 (Anthony Dooley), 2012 and 2013 (Paul Wormell and Peter McCallum). For varying perspectives, see also Julie Rowlands, 'The Symbolic Role of Academic Boards in University Academic Quality

governing body for assuring academic quality including academic freedom, academic integrity, assessment, admissions, and research conduct.

TEQSA gives a definition of academic governance in the glossary to its Regulatory Risk Framework (February 2012):

> Academic governance is a subset of the overall governance of an educational organisation, and deals with the framework that regulates academic decisions and academic quality assurance within the organisation. Academic governance includes the policies, processes, definitions of roles, relationships, systems, strategies and resources that ensure academic standards and continuous improvement in academic activities, and is concerned with the integrity and quality of the core higher education activities of teaching, research and scholarship.

This body has its origins in 'the community of scholars' and as such is generally collegial and representative of the university community – senior executive and management, academics and students. Under the newly proposed Higher Education Standards Framework, there is no requirement for an institution to have an academic governing body such as an academic board, with the provision for academic governance stating that:

> Process and structures are established and responsibilities are assigned to provide governance of academic policies, to maintain academic oversight of the quality of teaching, learning and research and research training [where research is undertaken by the higher education provider] and to provide academically-informed advice to the corporate governing body on academic matters.[28]

Universities, however, vest that function in a formally constituted academic governance body as described above. This body maintains all aspects of its operations through committees, such as teaching and learning, course accreditation, research and research training.

The TEQSA Draft Guidance Note 2014 sets out the activities of an academic governing body as: academic policy, processes and procedures, academic leadership, academic quality assurance, developing scholarship, staff professional development, maintenance of academic standards and protection of academic integrity. While oversight is with this body, the responsibility for implementation and management rests with the executive.[29]

C The Senior Executive or Management

This consists of the senior management of the university with the Vice Chancellor or Provost at the head of a group of Deputy Vice Chancellors or Pro Vice Chancellors with responsibility for the day to day organisation of all areas of university activities. Within the portfolio of each of these positions is a unit or department of staff such as managers, executive officers and secretaries. Senior management extends also to the Faculty Deans and Associate Deans with specific responsibilities. Each faculty has a Faculty Board made up of representatives from academic and professional staff, and students, and often (but not always) presided over by the Dean.

Assurance' (2013) 19(2) *Quality in Higher Education* 142; and Hilary Winchester, '*Academic Board and the Academy: Seizing the Moment*' (2007) <www.heqa.com.au>.

28 Higher Education Standards Framework Consultation Draft – April 2014, 6.2.1.

29 Ibid 6 and 7.

V Models of Governance: Shared Governance

While the roles, functions and principles of governing bodies are universal, differences between institutions in historical development, enabling legislation, institutional missions, sizes and cultures leads inevitably to differences in each governance body, and the balance between them. The values base of each institution and the manner in which it manages its relationships within and out in the external and political environment will dictate the approaches and dimensions of its governance operation. Whatever the particular flavour of institutional ethos, it is important that for the integrity of governance there must be, in relation to the university's central business, a balance of business-like approaches against the place of higher education as a public good and 'as an autonomous sphere for the development of a critical and productive democratic citizenry'.[30]

It is generally accepted that strong, collegial and representative university governance is best achieved through a 'shared governance' model, although inevitably there will be tensions between management and governance roles in practice. This is customarily seen as a triangular framework for the operation of governance functions,[31] and was proposed by Michael Shattock as an integrated governance framework best suited for avoidance of narrow commercial approaches and to enable universities to best 'fulfil their missions as social institutions'.[32] Although there have been variations proposed the holistic model,[33] an adaptation of the enterprise governance model of private entities, remains as:

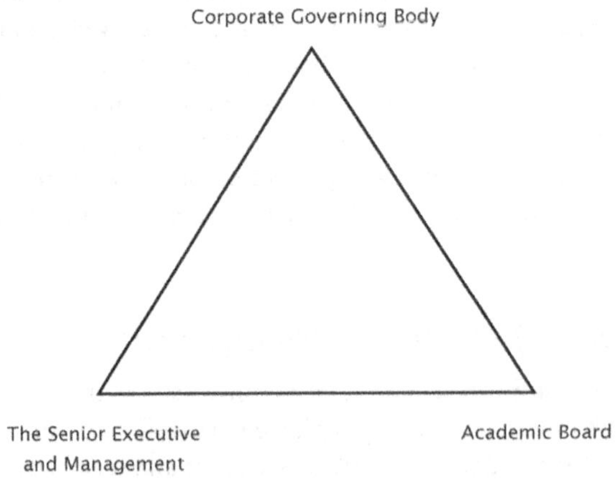

30 HA Giroux, 'The Corporate University and the Politics of Education' (2003) 2 *Revisita Praxis* 22, quoted in Jeanette Baird, 'Beyond Professionalism: Enhancing the Governance Culture for Australian University Governing Boards' (2006) 12 *Tertiary Education Management* 297, 299.

31 Sometimes referred to as the Clark triangle (1983).

32 Michael Shattock, 'Balancing Modern Concepts of University Governance' (2002) 56(3) *Higher Education Quarterly* 235 as discussed in Gary Carnegie and Jacqueline Tuck, 'Understanding the ABC of University Governance' (2010) 69(4) *Australian Journal of Public Administration* 431.

33 See, for example, a more radical 'corporate governance' model with an upper tier 'supervisory board' proposed by Roger Brown, 'What Do We Do About University Governance?' (2011) 15(3) *Perspectives: Policy and Practice in Higher Education* 87.

Carnegie and Tuck suggest an 'ABC' of university governance with academic governance placed first, so as to remind us of the imperative of the vital role of scholarship in universities.[34] Their thesis goes further to four separate, but overlapping, facets of scholarship: discovery, integration, application and teaching, all of which are integral to the governance function of a university. They then follow with business governance, being the financial performance of a university, and corporate governance, concerned with accountability and assurance as other key components of university governance. Acknowledging that this builds on the notion of shared governance, they refer to the ABC model as: 'a mission related integrated approach which focuses on the interdependence of scholarship, performance and conformance' which is designed to 'preserve the integrity of the organisational missions of public universities as social institutions'.[35] The appeal of this adaptation is that it strongly reinforces the true nature of universities and it is suggested that its validity is in principle within the framework of accountability provided by legislation.

VI Current Issues

A Composition of Governing Bodies

The balance in composition of membership of governing bodies is a key issue.[36] Importantly, members of a governing body must act in the interests of the university as a whole, and not be 'advocates of a particular group of constituents or a particular viewpoint'.[37] Edwards says that all sharing the same vision, and a trust in the constituents to effectively carry out the roles assigned to them, are vital elements of university governance. She argues for a collegial and participatory model with the essential component of transparency and accountability.

As national and global circumstances (particularly economic) and successive government policies push universities further towards the entrepreneurial commercial model, the nature and composition of corporate governing bodies is being called into question. Their central function renders them fundamentally different to corporations. Public universities are not concerned with shareholder profits and 'bottom lines' but rather with the key mission of teaching, learning and research, and thus developing the intellectual capital of the nation. While the demands of accountability and the magnitude and breadth of the 'business operations' of a university render it essential that the members of this body have sound business experience, expertise and acumen in terms of risk and assurance, it is equally important not to discount academics as a vital resource, and students as key constituents for the operations in which this body is engaged. It is inevitable in the current scenario that tensions arise between the different perspectives towards a university's operations.

34 Gary Carnegie and Jacqueline Tuck, 'Understanding the ABC of University Governance' (2010) 69(4) *Australian Journal of Public Administration* 431, 436.

35 Ibid 439.

36 Meredith Edwards, Deputy Vice Chancellor and Director, National Institute for Governance, University of Canberra, 'University Governance: A Mapping and Some Issues' (Paper delivered at the LifeLong Learning Network National Conference, Canberra, 2001).

37 Ibid 15.

Satisfying both primary interests of academic and financial viability makes the composition of the governing bodies crucial. Equally important is the framework setting the parameters of their functions and their mechanisms to achieve effective participation of all interests. This is put thus by Simon Marginson and Mark Considine:

> Governance is concerned with the determination of values inside universities, their systems of decision-making and resource allocation, their mission and purposes, the patterns of authority and hierarchy, and the relationship of universities as institutions to the different academic worlds within and the worlds of government, business and community without.[38]

Crucially, university governance embraces a number of relationships – both external and internal. Externally, it covers the relationship between the university, government and the community, each with often differing expectations and agendas (evidenced in Australia in recent years with changes of governments – both federal and State). In variance with private corporate governance, universities must also incorporate the requirements for accountability of both State and federal governments. Internally, university governance both covers, and is representative of management and the university community, academic and professional staff and students. All 'stakeholders' are of fundamental importance to the very nature of a public institution and the processes of governance bodies must be based on principles of participation, equity and collaboration.

This is an important challenge facing Australian universities today, with differing interventions by State governments. The Victorian Government in 2012 passed an amendment to the *Education and Training Reform Act 2004* (Vic) to remove the existing right of automatic election of staff and students to university main governing bodies and to provide that appointment will only occur by way of government or council election.[39] Appointments are based on holding the qualifications to perform the duties of the position of a director of a major institution. As a result, while staff and students may be elected to the corporate governing body as 'council-appointed' members, their election is not guaranteed and they will have to demonstrate adequate skills for the role. In New South Wales, the *Universities Governing Bodies Act 2011* (NSW)[40] provides that a university governing body may adopt or otherwise, standard governing body provisions to replace those for each university in their individual acts. The standard governing body provisions, set out in sch 1, provide for a participatory model with categories of members being official, elected, governing body-appointed members and ministerially-appointed members with no category at any time constituting a majority of the total members. The Constitution rules of each institution may prescribe the

38 Simon Marginson and Mark Considine, *The Enterprise University: Power, Governance and Reinvention in Australia* (Cambridge University Press, 2000), 7.

39 This measure continues to attract strong criticism from all sides, highlighted in Andrew Trounson, 'Melbourne University Slams New Victorian Laws on Councils' (26 October 2012) *The Australian*; and National Tertiary Education Union, 'Fight to Restore Representation on University Councils in Victoria' (1 February 2013) *ed Xpress* <www.nteu.org.au/women/blog/>. It has been reported that the Victorian Legislature is moving to overturn the legislative provision and require universities to restore elected staff and student representation on their Councils – see also Andrew Trounson, 'Staff, Students Return to Councils' (22 April 2015) *The Australian*.

40 *Universities Governing Bodies Act 2011* (NSW) s 4.

numbers of elected academic staff and non-academic staff members and elected student members, but at least one from each of these elected categories is mandatory. The total size of the governing body shall be no fewer than 11 or more than 22 members.[41]

B The Role of Students in University Governance[42]

Proposed deregulation of the sector and increased student fees point arguably to a need for a more systematised student voice in the standard, quality and delivery of the higher education in which they are investing significant time, energy and money. It has become fashionable to apply the supplier/consumer analogy to the university/student relationship.[43] Fundamental to this concept is the notion that 'passive' purchasers are acquiring a product or a service. This ignores the increasing focus on student-centred learning and importantly it ignores the importance of students' views into how the product will be developed, and into the maintenance and advancement of the quality and standards attached to their teaching and learning.[44]

As discussed in Chapter 3 by Tyrrell and Varnham, comparative jurisdictions are now emphasising 'student-driven' higher education, with calls for the student experience to be at the centre of strategy and innovation in universities.[45] In the United Kingdom, the Quality Assurance Agency (QAA, the UK equivalent of TEQSA), 'has been working at the forefront of engaging students in quality assurance and enhancement ...'.[46] In Europe, consideration of the role of students in university governance has been a key feature of the Bologna Project for European Higher Education.[47]

---

41 *Universities Governing Bodies Act 2011* (NSW) sch 1, div 1, s 3.

42 The student voice is discussed comprehensively in Chapter 3 by Tyrrell and Varnham.

43 See also Chapter 7 by Rochford, Chapter 10 by Stuhmcke, Olliffe and Evers, and Chapter 8 by Kamvounias. For a discussion of the appropriateness of this characterisation, see Patty Kamvounias and Sally Varnham, 'Getting What They Paid For: Consumer Rights of Students in Higher Education' (2008) *Griffith Law Review Special Issue* 306-332. Also, for a comprehensive discussion of the university/student relationship, see Patty Kamvounias and Sally Varnham, 'Legal Challenges to University Decisions Affecting Students in Australian Courts and Tribunals' (2010) 34 *Melbourne University Law Review* 140-180. The application of the 'consumer' model to students in the United Kingdom is discussed at length in Dennis Farringdon and David Palfreyman, *The Law of Higher Education* (2nd ed, Oxford University Press, 2012).

44 The governance role for students has formal recognition in cl 6.2.3 the *Proposed Higher Education Standards Framework Consultation Draft April 2014.*

45 Particularly in the White Paper *Higher Education: Students at the Heart of the System*, Department for Business, Innovation and Skills (BIS) June 2011.

46 Anthony McCiaran, Chief Executive QAA, Foreword to the University of Bath and QAA research publication: GM Van der Velden, AD Pool, JA Lowe, R Naidoo R and PC Pimentel Botas, *Student Engagement in Learning and Teaching Quality Management: A Study of UK Practices, Commissioned by the Quality Assurance Agency – Project Report* (UK Quality Assurance Agency and Bath University, 2013).

47 It is of interest to note that the role of students in university governance dates back historically to 13th century Europe when there was a strong dominance of students in universities such as Bologna. This feature however had largely faded by the mid-20th century with the exception of universities in some Latin American countries, for example the University of Cordoba in Argentina. In most comparative jurisdictions, student democratisation was replaced by the student/client/consumer concept. However, ME Menon discusses the significant involvement of students in the governance of Canadian Universities in 'Student Involvement in University Governance: A Need for Negotiated Educational Aims? (2003) No 9 *Tertiary Education and*

However the university/student relationship is to be framed, it is important to have effective mechanisms for embracing the views of the greatest constituents, in developing strategy and in framing quality and standards, and ultimately, in accountability.

VII Conclusion

Strong, innovative and strategic governance is essential to the success of a university and to the higher education sector as a whole. In the current climate, universities are 'defined by strong corporate executive control imposing economic performance targets in internal structures'[48] there is an ever increasing need to concentrate on the balance between the economic imperatives imposed on them and their fundamental mission of scholarship.

While the widely varying natures of Australian universities calls for differences in governance culture, it can generally be said that most have a shared governance model with the primary or corporate governance body being called the Council or Senate chaired by the University Chancellor,[49] and an Academic governance body which is responsible for the academic life of the university. The new 'professionalism' of the membership of governing bodies should come with a culture of engagement in university strategy and all operations but not at the expense of collegiality within the partnership model.[50] While this chapter looks primarily through a legislative lens, there is much commentary and debate relating to the nature of governance in the modern university, both internationally and within Australia.[51]

Never before in the history of Australia has the higher education sector been faced with so many challenges to its continued high national and global standing. In light of government policy driving deregulation of the sector and resultant higher fees for students, there has been a call for universities to refocus on their governance provisions and perhaps for the introduction of a new set of national guidelines following the UK lead.[52] Professor Paul Wellings, Vice Chancellor of the University of Wollongong says:

Management 233. See also ME Menon, 'Students Views Regarding their Participation in University Governance: Implications for Distributed Leadership in Higher Education' (2005) No 11 *Tertiary Education and Management* 167.

48 Simon Marginson and Tim Considine, *The Enterprise University: Power, Governance and Reinvention in Australia* (Cambridge University Press, 2000), quoted in Fabrice Henard and Alexander Mitterie, *Governance and Quality Guidelines in Higher Education: A Review of Governance Arrangements and Quality Assurance Guidelines* (Organisation for Economic Co-operation and Development (OECD) Directorate for Education, 2010), 30.

49 For composition of this body see, for example, the *Universities Governing Bodies Act 2011* (NSW).

50 In the discussion of 'overreach' of commercially-orientated governing bodies, it is of interest to note the empirical research conducted of university governing bodies before 2000, which revealed a feeling of 'disempowerment' or 'collective rubber-stamping': Jeanette Baird, *Repertoires of Governance of Members of Australian University Governing Boards* (PhD thesis, University of New England, Armidale, 2004).

51 See Michael Shattock (ed), *International Trends in University Governance: Autonomy, Self-Government and the Distribution of Authority* (Routledge, 2014), particularly Jeanette Baird, 'International, Hierarchical and Market Influences on Australian University Governance' in Michael Shattock (ed), *International Trends in University Governance: Autonomy, Self-Government and the Distribution of Authority* (Routledge, 2014).

52 'Time to Get Governance House in Order' (15 January 2015) *The Australian*, quoting Professor Wellings, Vice Chancellor of the University of Wollongong.

'Universities will need to be able to demonstrate that they are acting in the best interests of students and the communities they serve'.[53] Indeed, it is clearly becoming ever more important that universities have robust, nimble and representative processes to ensure their accountability, and to demonstrate that students get what they have paid for.

In this turbulent era, it is vital that universities maintain their focus strongly on teaching, learning and research as it is this scholarship which is the essence of their activities. It is essential, also, that universities not only maintain the expertise in their governance to ensure their effectiveness and integrity in their wide reaching entrepreneurial and commercial activities, but that they do not lose sight of the importance of input from all stakeholders. While it is probably accurate to predict that universities of the future will maintain their commercial orientation, governments and their policies will come and go. In the maelstrom, the best future will be assured universities by their maintenance of a staunch defence of a strong culture of partnership in their educational endeavour.

53 Ibid.

Chapter 3

The Student Voice in University Decision-making

Jade Tyrrell and Sally Varnham

I Introduction: What is 'The Student Voice'?

The term 'student voice' incorporates a rich diversity of perspectives. The concept has become prevalent within higher education discourse in the last decade, particularly in the United Kingdom and in Europe, and to a more limited extent in Australia where it is usually considered in the context of quality assurance and curricula.[1] The discussion considers how the student voice may be meaningfully incorporated in university decision-making and governance.[2] The increasing diversity of student bodies at Australian universities is well-recognised[3] and as this diversity increases the notion of 'the typical student' becomes problematic and divorced from reality. Many new types of students have entered the system including mature-aged, those who are first in their family to receive a university education, perhaps those from a low socio-economic background, international, Aboriginal and Torres Strait Islanders, postgraduates, those undertaking distance study, and others. Each has a different set of needs.[4] Higher education institutions are challenged to embrace successfully the views and interests of such a varied and complex group which must be considered alongside local undergraduate domestic students – still typically the overwhelming majority of the student population but no longer the sole voice for students.

This chapter suggests that the incorporation of the views of students requires the implementation of tailored and 'grassroots' strategies in conjunction with formal provisions. A holistic approach offers the greatest chance of incorporating the views of students and achieving fairness in ways that benefit the higher education community as

1 Catherine Bovill, 'Students and Staff Co-creating Curricula: An Example of Good Practice in Higher Education?' in Elizabeth Dunne (ed) *The Student Engagement Handbook: Practice in Higher Education* (Emerald Group Publishing, 2013), 461.

2 Fiona Campbell 'How to Hear and Heed the Student Voice' in Gerry Czerniawski and Warren Kidd (eds), *The Student Voice Handbook: Bridging the Academic/Practitioner Divide* (Emerald Group Publishing, 2011), 265, 266.

3 Hamish Coates, Daniel Edwards, Leo Goedegebuure, Marian Thakur, Eva van der Brugge and Fran van Vught, *Profiling Diversity of Australian Universities* (June 2013) <http://www.lhmartininstitute.edu.au/documents/publications/lhmi-acer-research-briefing-australian-institution-profilesupdated050613.pdf> .

4 Emmaline Bexley, Suzanne Daroesman, Sophie Arkoudis and Richard James, *University Student Finances in 2012. A Study of the Financial Circumstances of Domestic and International Students in Australia's Universities* (Universities Australia, July 2013), 6.

a whole. It is founded on an understanding that students, as key stakeholders in higher education, deserve a serious level of input and influence. A culture of student participation could flow from the course level to an institutional level. It could go beyond to decision-making processes of governments in formulation of higher education policy and educational quality assurance. Indications from overseas, particularly in Europe, and more recently in the United Kingdom, are that tailored, collaborative approaches to student engagement are beneficial to all.[5] Increased student satisfaction comes from the matching of expectations – more likely to be achieved through the engagement of the diverse student voice. While it is a challenge, to do it effectively would assist in achieving not only the best possible educational experience for students, it would also aid the development of the social capital of graduates armed with the skills of leadership, as valuable preparation for citizenships of a democratic society.

This chapter draws on the findings of Carey's research in the United Kingdom: that students interviewed felt that 'a partnership model should replace the paternalistic culture of higher education'.[6]

II Students as Partners for Collaboration

The development of partnerships with students is the key to universities being agents for change through the creation of internal democratic cultures.[7] In Europe, the student/university partnership is seen as an integral part of the Bologna Process of creating a European Higher Education Area. A meeting of European Ministers in charge of Higher Education in 2001 to discuss the report 'Furthering the Bologna Process', referred to: 'The involvement of ... students as competent, active and constructive partners'.[8] It marked the beginning of the official recognition of student involvement in higher education governance.[9] In Australia, this is a relatively new concept, which may not have been welcomed as wholeheartedly. Anecdotally, all too often decisions about students that have a direct impact on their educational outcomes or matters otherwise relevant to them are being made without a student 'in the room'.

A product of commercialisation of universities is to treat students as consumers of a product or a service. This characterisation implies market response which is obviously important. However, it places emphasis on the 'passive consumer',[10] ignores the value

5 GM Van der Velden, AD Pool, JA Lowe, R Naidoo and PC Pimentel Botas, *Student Engagement in Learning and Teaching Quality Management: A Good Practice Guide for Higher Education Providers and Student Unions* (UK Quality Assurance Agency and Bath University, 2013), 6 <http://www.bath.ac.uk/learningandteaching/pdf/student_engagement/Good_Practice_Guide_11.9.2013.pdf>. See also Elisabeth Dunne and Derfel Owen (eds), *The Student Engagement Handbook: Practice in Higher Education* (Emerald Group Publishing, 2013).

6 Philip Carey, 'Student Engagement: Stakeholder Perspectives on Course Representation in University governance' (2013) 38(9) *Studies in Higher Education* 1290-1303, 1295.

7 Sjur Bergan (ed), 'The University as Res Publica: Higher Education Governance, Student Participation and the University as a Site of Citizenship' (Council of Europe Publishing, 2004) <www.coe.int>.

8 Ibid 3 referring to *Towards the European Higher Education Area: Communique of the Meeting of European Ministers in Charge of Higher Education* (Prague, 19 May 2001).

9 Ibid 4.

10 Philip Carey, 'Student Engagement in University Decision-making: Policies, Processes and the Student Voice' (Doctoral Thesis, Lancaster University, United Kingdom, June 2013), 44,

of student input and lacks an understanding of the ability of students to take part in the academic community as partners.[11] It has been said that it detaches students from their experience[12] as learners, seeking educational and career success.

UK researcher Carey addressed the notion of the student as co-producer as an alternative or antidote to consumerism. He argued that consumerism is directly contrary to any movement towards student engagement, citing the argument 'that consumer status engenders passivity in students. They expect a degree of service that attends to their needs and requires a relatively modest personal investment'.[13]

In Europe, also, there is pushback against this categorisation. A statement of the European Students' Union known as the Budapest Declaration of 2011 said:

> Students are not consumers of higher education, but significant components within it. Consumers are not involved in the management of process, but students are co-responsible for higher education management, as higher education is developed for students. Students are the main beneficiaries of increasing the quality of [higher education]. Students should have more impact in decision-making and governance of higher education, which must be a community of students and professors who are equally responsible for its quality.[14]

We can keep a careful watch on the experiences in Europe and more recently the United Kingdom, where the student voice commands considerable attention today,[15] to illustrate the inherent benefits of student participation and the concept of partnership. In these jurisdictions, effective partnership and meaningful dialogue between universities and students is being recognised as best practice.[16] In 2012, the UK tertiary education regulator, the Quality Assurance Agency (QAA), commissioned research by the University of Bath to examine student engagement at all levels of higher education. Arguably, the performance indicators used in this study suggest that student involvement in organising freely, participating in agenda-setting and voting on issues which concern the academic community[17] are all ideal for the creation of collaboration through effective partnerships. The report included a finding that there are changing perceptions of the role of students held by institutions and by student unions, and the

---

citing A McCulloch, 'The Student as Co-producer: Learning from Public Administration About the Student-university Relationship' (2009) 34(2) *Studies in Higher Education* 171; Milica Popovic, General Rapporteur European Higher Education Area, *General Report: Student Participation in Higher Education Governance* (Aghveran, Armenia, 8-9 December 2011), 7.

11 Popovic, above n 10.

12 Julie Baldry Currens, 'How Might the Student Voice Affect Transformation in Higher Education?' in Gerry Czerniawski and Warren Kidd (eds) *The Student Voice Handbook: Bridging the Academic/Practitioner Divide* (Emerald Group Publishing, 2011), ch 15, 186.

13 Carey, above n 10. See Chapter 7 by Rochford.

14 Budapest Declaration: Governance and Student Participation. 21st European Student Convention, Prague, February 2011.

15 GM Van der Velden, AD Pool, JA Lowe, R Naidoo and PC Pimentel Botas, *Student Engagement in Learning and Teaching Quality Management: A Study of UK Practices, Commissioned by the Quality Assurance Agency – Project Report* (UK Quality Assurance Agency and Bath University, 2013). See also Student Engagement Partnership <http://www.hefce.ac.uk/about/howweoperate/si/studentengagement/>.

16 Ibid.

17 Ibid.

widespread perception is increasingly that of the student as 'stakeholder', while 'partner' is an ideal to strive for in programs and disciplines generally.[18]

III Effective Student Representation as a Tool for the 'Student Voice'

The diversity of higher education providers necessarily means that no one model of student representation can apply to achieve the same degree of success in every environment. As the UK QAA Best Practice Model suggests, diversity demands the creation of a tailored representation model, with student representation at all levels that is catered not only to the institution, but different groups of students.[19]

The spread of representation should begin at a faculty level and filter up to the highest of governance within an institution to successfully develop a culture.[20] Strategies to incorporate students' perspectives and to encourage student involvement using a top-down approach will inevitably not result in enough grassroots support for engagement and active participation in the long-term, and in every institution there needs to be two to three tiers of student representation with active channels of communication for maximum cooperation and overall gain.

Below is a critique of student representation as currently provided, and ideas for working towards a culture, rather than the current scattered approach.

A Higher Level – the Corporate Governing Body: University Senates and Councils[21]

This level includes sub-committees, working groups and initiatives of the relevant governing body.

In Australia, the most instructive source of law on this issue is the *Higher Education Support Act 2003* (Cth) (*HESA*) and individual enabling Acts of Parliament which set out the formation and governing body of each university. Where relevant, university legislation provides for student membership, the roles or duties are not described in any detail and there are no quotas for student representatives beyond basic requirements for a certain number of under-graduate and postgraduate student to have elected positions.

The trend over the last decade for university councils to downsize is worrying unless accompanied by provision for the student voice to remain and be strengthened. A clear indication that the view behind the trend is not universally held was provided by Victoria when, in 2012, it moved to be the only State in Australia where student and staff representation on university councils was not guaranteed. Carol Nicoll, the then Commissioner of TEQSA, was quick to write to universities reminding them of their

18 GM Van der Velden, AD Pool, JA Lowe, R Naidoo and PC Pimentel Botas, *Student Engagement in Learning and Teaching Quality Management: A Good Practice Guide for Higher Education Providers and Student Unions* (UK Quality Assurance Agency and Bath University, 2013), 28.

19 Ibid 6.

20 See Philip Carey, *Student Engagement in University Decision-making: Policies, Processes and the Student Voice* (Doctoral Thesis, Lancaster University, United Kingdom, June 2013).

21 See Chapter 2 by Varnham.

obligations as a condition of registration, pursuant to the *Higher Education Standards Framework (Threshold Standards) 2011* (Threshold Standards). Clause 6.8 provides that they must have 'student representation within its deliberative and decision-making processes' and to encourage 'students to participate in these processes'.[22] The Victorian provision removing the automatic right of election of students to governing bodies, amending the *Education and Training Reform Act 2006* (Vic), is in direct contradiction to an ethos of student representation.

B Faculty Level

This includes sub-committees of faculties, teaching and learning and course committees. This level of student representation and involvement is governed largely by individual faculties and their policies. There is inevitably inconsistency across disciplines and it has proved to be the most difficult level at which to keep students actively engaged. Models suggest targeted strategies for recruitment and retention of student representatives that are based on an understanding of the mechanisms to achieve change and how decision-making at a faculty level operates in the broader institutional context.[23]

C Course/Class/Subject level

This could involve 'subject liaisons' or representatives of a particular cohort nominated as a designated point of contact. There is obvious advantage for students to have representation at this level that is one of their number (in the sense that they are accessible and approachable) and with their best interests at heart (in the sense that they have the ability to raise concerns at a higher level and affect change in real terms).[24]

D Informal Liaison Structures

The QAA/Bath Good Practice Guide[25] points to the benefit of informal processes at every level enabling easy reporting and communication through a representative network. These processes provide access for representatives and a focus for their voices to be heard in a variety of forums including inductions, mentoring, training and support through recognition. Regular informal discussions between student representatives

---

22 It must be noted that the Threshold Standards are currently undergoing a review process and the Consultation Draft of April 2014 provides in cl 6.1.3 that: 'The governing body takes steps to create an organisational culture where … informed decision making by students is supported and students have opportunities to participate in the deliberative and decision making processes of the higher education provider' – although there is a footnote which states that this neither requires nor precludes student membership of a governing body or other governance structures of the provider. Clause 6.2.3 however states that: 'Students have the opportunity to participate in academic governance'. See Chapter 1 by Squelch and Chapter 2 by Varnham.

23 GM Van der Velden, AD Pool, JA Lowe, R Naidoo and PC Pimentel Botas, *Student Engagement in Learning and Teaching Quality Management: A Good Practice Guide for Higher Education Providers and Student Unions*' (UK Quality Assurance Agency and Bath University, 2013), 19.

24 For a discussion of student course representation, see P Carey, 'Student Engagement: Stakeholder perspectives on course representation in university governance' (2013) Vol 38(9) *Studies in Higher Education* 1290.

25 Van der Velden et al, above n 23, 6.

and decision-makers can be most effective and this helps to provide a mechanism for feedback and genuine consultation.[26]

E Other Provision for Student Participation

1 Students' Rights Charters

Students' rights charters provide another mechanism through which the importance of the student voice may be recognised. An example of such a charter is the Budapest Declaration, adopted in February 2011 at the European Student Convention. There are different examples of student charters at various Australian universities. One example is the Student Charter of Rights and Responsibilities at the University of Western Australia. In Clause 5 Student Representation there is implied an important direction to the university:

> 5.1 Every student has the right:
> (a) to have their opinion represented through the Student Guild on all matters affecting students;
> (b) to representation on major decision-making bodies of the University either through direct election or by nomination through a recognised student body; and
> (c) to have the right, notwithstanding the existence of formal representation, to convey personal or collective opinion to the Vice-Chancellor.[27]

Most of such Charters, however, are regarded simply as statements of principle which are not necessary incorporated in real terms into university processes.

2 Student Surveys

In Australia, there is a heavy reliance placed on survey results from student feedback and as an indicator of what students want.[28] However, there are suggestions from abroad that a more successful determinant is collaboration and active student participation. While surveys can be representative of the student experience to some extent, they are self-selecting mechanisms and the experiences of all student groups may not be captured in quality measurement instruments. Students may be cynical as to the extent to which results of instruments such as the University Experience Survey[29] are implemented or largely ignored.[30]

---

26 See Van der Velden et al, above n 23 – the place of informal measures such as these is discussed in the Good Practice Guide <http://www.bath.ac.uk/learningandteaching/pdf/student_engagement/Good_Practice_Guide_11.9.2013.pdf>.

27 <http://www.student.uwa.edu.au/life/charter>.

28 All universities have their own Student Feedback Survey instruments. There is now also the Australia-wide University Experience Survey (UES) which is stated to 'help universities in Australia and government to improve your experience as a university student'. See also C Lawson, *Student Voices: Enhancing the experience of international students in Australia*', Australian Education International, June 2012.

29 M Klemenic, 'The Public Role of Higher Education and Student Participation in Higher Education Governance' in J Brennan and T Shah (eds), *Higher Education and Society in Changing Times: Looking Back and Looking Forward* (Centre for Higher Education, Research and Information, 2011), 4.

30 Ibid.

All universities in Australia have student associations, and there are also national student bodies, such as the National Union of Students (NUS).

IV The Role of Independent Student Organisations

A strong and well-funded independent student organisation within a university is best-placed to represent and facilitate the student voice and to draw on the student body for feedback. A student organisation can be an invaluable source of information to inform and influence strategy, policy and development.[31] This was an important finding in the Bath Report, where it was considered 'striking' that student unions in the United Kingdom, as opposed to higher education institutions themselves, took a clear lead in the of improvement of representation for underrepresented groups, and in the development of performance indicators for student engagement.[32] At its best, a student union can act as a conduit or a lynchpin for collaboration between students and the institution.

However, there is a very real sense in some institutions that in practical terms the contributions of students are often taken for granted or not taken seriously, and the acknowledgment of student contribution is not yet common.[33] There are also many barriers to participation in these student associations which may result in a growing disconnect between current students and institutional governance.[34] The low level of interest may be due to a number of factors including the nature of student life with its pressures on the availability of students and competing priorities for their attention, the perception by students and institutions about the role of students in the higher education community and a cynicism towards the existing frameworks for student participation in higher education governance.

It follows that while student representative organisations have the ability to play a vital role in the realisation of the student voice in higher education, there needs to be greater recognition, collaboration and support for their efforts. Student organisations have the most potential to bridge any real or perceived divide between an institution and its students.

V The Student Voice in Student Services – Beyond the Classroom

In 2005, the introduction of Voluntary Student Unionism (VSU)[35] and the absence of student union fees brought about the need for greater university funding of services beyond the classroom. In 2011, while still keeping VSU in place, a Student Amenities

31 Van der Velden et al, above n 23, 8.

32 GM Van der Velden, AD Pool, JA Lowe, R Naidoo and PC Pimentel Botas, *Student Engagement in Learning and Teaching Quality Management: A Study of UK Practices, Commissioned by the Quality Assurance Agency – Project Report* (UK Quality Assurance Agency and Bath University, 2013), 27 <http://www.bath.ac.uk/learningandteaching/pdf/student_engagement/Project_Report_11.9.2013.pdf>.

33 Ibid 26.

34 Sjur Bergan (ed), *The University as Res Publica: Higher Education Governance, Student Participation and the University as a Site of Citizenship* (Council of Europe Publishing, 2004), 16.

35 *Higher Education (Abolition of Compulsory Up-front Student Union Fees) Act 2005* (Cth).

Fee was able to be levied from students, pursuant to the *Higher Education Legislation Amendment (Student Services and Amenities) Act 2011* (Cth). This change has been accompanied by strong moves to facilitate student participation and to encourage incorporation of the student voice beyond quality assurance and standards in educational matters, to facilitate a positive experience outside the classroom. In Australia, protocols for student participation made in respect of the Student Services and Amenities Fee (SSAF) exist. The *Student Services, Amenities, Representation and Advocacy Guidelines* (*SSARA Guidelines*), were created under *HESA* pursuant to the 2011 amendment Act. Chapter 3 of the Guidelines contains the National Student Representation Protocols (NSR Protocols), which set benchmarks for representation and access to services. They were amended in 2013 by the Panel on the Review into the Guidelines Associated with the Student Services and Amenities Fee, in order to strengthen and clarify the provisions for student representation and the provision of student services.[36] The SSARA Guidelines are arguably the most instructive instrument on student representation in Australia. They recognise the importance of student engagement and representation in higher education. In particular, the essence is captured here:

> 3.1.2. Student engagement underpins quality teaching and learning. HEPs should support student engagement and representation through the provision of clear consultative arrangements, including with student representatives and major student organisations recognised by the HEP where appropriate.[37]

The 2012 academic year was the first year of operation of the SSAF and the associated Representation Guidelines. The frameworks deal largely with representation at an institutional level, not a faculty, department or a national level.[38] Furthermore, the Representation Guidelines were not a condition of grant for higher education providers nor could penalties be imposed for breaches.[39] One could argue that enforcement mechanisms for student representation are a 'toothless tiger' compared to those for other requirements such as quality assurance.

The Representation Guidelines as a whole also largely deal with consultation generally and the distribution of the Student Services and Amenities Fee (SSAF) but are silent on more specific issues such as obligations to guarantee student influence in decision-making and on policy through institutional representation, which is where students' concerns lie more generally.

While these Protocols must be considered in their context, they could be said to indicate an ethos of student participation and engagement which goes well beyond the inclusion of the student voice in the provision of student services. They do give validity to and reinforce the argument for extension into university and academic matters including educational quality standards, institution-wide information provision, research and development and curriculum design.

36 Representation Guidelines Review Panel, *Review of the Student Services, Amenities, Representation and Advocacy Guidelines Made Under the Higher Education Support Act 2003* (2013).

37 *Student Services, Amenities, Representation and Advocacy Guidelines 2013*, 3.1.2.

38 Ibid (see 3.2 generally).

39 Note: Section 19.67 of the *HESA* now provides that a Higher Education Provider (HEP) that receives a grant in a particular year must comply with the Requirements of the Representation Guidelines as those guidelines were in force on the 30 June just before the year.

VI Next Steps – Where to From Here?

A *The Need for a Culture of Participation*

The student voice is that of an increasingly diverse student body. The challenge is for higher education institutions to listen and respond to its changing needs. To keep up with the wants and needs of students, they need to have students at the core of everything that they do, making the incorporation of the student voice a continuous process.[40] Future challenges for Australia, recognised also in the United Kingdom,[41] include incorporating the student voice into curriculum design; understanding the make-up of the student body and the implications of this; recognising the need for increased student engagement and participation; and devising mechanisms for collaboration. While the autonomy of higher education providers is important, it cannot come at the expense of student representation and the university's engagement with its community, both within and outside, and with modern society.[42]

Currently lacking any real culture of student participation, universities face significant challenges in making any engagement effective. Perhaps the greatest is the low level of interest students have towards the governance of their higher education institution.[43] This is evidenced by the fact that voter turnout in student elections is typically low. To combat this lack of engagement, long-term strategies that incorporate principles of best practice will provide assistance in recognising the 'student voice' more effectively. This is a culture that needs to be developed from the commencement of a student's time in higher education.

For the 'student voice' and student representation to have a real and valuable role, processes need to be:

- Flexible: Although mechanisms for engagement should be tailored and reflective of student diversity, they should also be responsive to change.
- Embedded and layered: Across all levels of any given institution in a higher education institution, student representatives should be valued and guaranteed inductions, ongoing training and development to assist them in their roles. Perhaps students with particular roles should receive a small stipend or payment to acknowledge the time and effort required of this role. This could create an expectation that the role should be taken seriously, that it carries obligations and requires the student to be responsible for attending and participating.
- Accessible and genuine: Provision for student representatives is an important step, but formal and informal provisions for student representation must be distinguished from what occurs in practice. Formal provision for representation, for example on governance bodies is only a small part of the picture. For

---

40 Popovic, above n 10, 4.

41 Fiona Campbell 'How to Hear and Heed the Student Voice' in Gerry Czerniawski and Warren Kidd (eds), *The Student Voice Handbook: Bridging the Academic/Practitioner Divide* (Emerald Group Publishing, 2011), 265, 266.

42 Ibid.

43 Derfel Owen, *Student Representation in the United Kingdom* (Quality Assurance Agency for Higher Education (QAA) presentation, 14 October 2011) <http://www.aqu.cat/doc/doc_23771451_1.pdf>.

the reasons discussed above in this chapter it should not be considered to be the end story of engagement or participation.

- Formally recognised in leadership terms: The student's participation in the higher education community needs to be formally recognised as a role that involves the acquisition of skills and competencies relevant to future employment. In addition to this, they require the provision of resources to carry out their duties successfully.
- Meaningful: Roles in frameworks should not exist without effective implementation, simply to pay 'lip service' to government or institutional requirements or structures. Engagement breeds legitimacy and the performance of elected representatives once in office is important. A balance must be struck between placing too much emphasis on formal positions and introducing holistic strategies to encourage meaningful participation and influence through effective representation.
- Recognised as valuable by the higher education community: This is not simply as 'clients' or 'economic units', but as partners. Students should be able to identify with the institution, and actively engage in the groups or communities within it. The function of the university experience as a whole for students is not only to educate, but it is to generate skills, create leaders and to encourage active participation in our democracy. Provisions must therefore be made for incorporating aspects of student representation into the core fabric of any functioning university community in addition to teaching, learning and research priorities – participation in civics, citizenship and democracy is arguably just as important as objectives to pursue.

VII Conclusion

Effective student representation is the means by which students are engaged in a learning environment which in turn derives great benefits from their input. It also encompasses their ability to influence decisions in a real sense. Students should not merely be provided with a voice in a formal or legal sense, but they need to be heard. Providing students with the ability to raise issues from a subject level to the institution-wide level can provide inherent benefits to the institution as a whole,[44] and foster a culture of engagement, democracy and leadership. Such mechanisms offer the opportunity for improvements to be made in an institution through partnership, which fosters active participation of students[45] in the scholarly community.

Despite this, however, it is a fact that it remains increasingly difficult to engage students in the area of higher education governance and representation in general.[46] There can be general confusion or uncertainty on the part of students and institutions regarding the form student representation will and should take and how to engage

44 Van der Velden et al, above n 23, 19 <http://www.qaa.ac.uk/Publications/Podcasts/Transcripts/Pages/student-engagement-research-projects.asp>.

45 Gerry Czerniawski and Warren Kidd (eds), *The Student Voice Handbook: Bridging the Academic/Practitioner Divide* (Emerald Group Publishing, 2011).

46 Sjur Bergan (ed), *The University as Res Publica: Higher Education Governance, Student Participation and the University as a Site of Citizenship* (Council of Europe Publishing, 2004), 8.

most effectively, which can often include limited access for students as well as limited strategies that may be in place to integrate student participation in institutions' democratic processes. This is not necessarily borne from any ill will.

Development of a culture of representation from the bottom up is essential and the student organisation plays a valuable part in this. It is well-placed to collaborate with institutions to facilitate student engagement due to its unique position in being run by, or at least primarily driven by students themselves. To this end, they understand the pressures faced by students, their diversity of needs and their increasingly demanding work hours.

Chapter 4

Indigenous Knowledges: A Strategy for First Nations Peoples Engagement in Higher Education

*Irene Watson and Marcelle Burns**

I Introduction

This chapter will consider the position of First Peoples' engagement with higher education from the perspective of the embracing of Indigenous knowledge. This necessarily involves the taking of a wider view, to look through the lens of the administration of justice, and in so doing to attempt to develop more sophisticated and effective practices of inclusion. The authors argue for improving the methodological approach of including Indigenous knowledge so as to more effectively resolve matters that come before the law, as well as addressing historic and ongoing colonial injustice.

They will explore methodologies for social inclusion within the legal order, framed within the context of inclusion in higher education. Critiques have led to programs for inclusion of Indigenous knowledges and experience. Similarly, commitments to social justice have led to acceptance of the need for reform to formal law, administration and education. However, beyond inclusion of First Peoples[1] in governance projects, there has been no attention to developing appropriate methodology. This oversight has meant Indigenous knowledges are misrepresented or co-opted even while being included. Judith Butler asks: 'How do we understand those sets of conditions and dispositions that account for the "state we are in" (which could, after all, be a state of mind) from the "state" we are in when and if we hold rights of citizenship or when the state functions as the provisional domicile for our work?'[2] For First Peoples, these questions have a particular theoretical resonance and practical implication. How do First Peoples express and retain an Indigenous identity within the state? Many First Peoples assert that we

* This chapter has developed from the Australian Research Council 2013 Discovery Indigenous Award project *Indigenous Knowledges: Law, Society and the State* by Chief Investigator Irene Watson, and acknowledges the support and comments made by Kathy Bowrey. This chapter is a collaboration with Marcelle Burns, a member of the Australian Research Council funded National Indigenous Research and Knowledges Network, whose recent research focuses on Indigenous knowledges and cultural competency in legal education and academic standards.

1 Throughout this chapter we use Indigenous Peoples, Aboriginal Peoples, and First Peoples interchangeably.

2 Judith Butler, Gayatri Chakravorty Spivak, *Who Sings the Nation-state*? (Seagull Books, 2007).

are subjects in international law, while the state asserts we are their Indigenous Peoples and exist within the domestic paradigm of the state.

The 1967 Constitutional Referendum is attributed as being a key turning point in the recognition of Aboriginal Peoples within the Australian nation-state. The referendum is credited with creating the conditions for 'equality' for Aboriginal Peoples by empowering the Commonwealth to legislate to improve the socio-economic conditions of the First Peoples. However, the precise nature of these Commonwealth powers are somewhat open-ended – as was shown in *Kartinyeri v Commonwealth*.[3] Access to and participation in education has long been regarded as a key element of improving the socio-economic status of Aboriginal Peoples. Yet some 40 years later, the promise of equality the referendum proffered has not been realised. The participation of Aboriginal Peoples within higher education is yet to reach parity with other Australians.[4] Aboriginal Peoples comprise 2.2 per cent of the Australian population and 1.4 per cent of university enrolments, and First Peoples remain the most disadvantaged group in Australian society. Recent reviews of Australia's higher education system, such as the *Bradley Review*[5] and the *Behrendt Review*,[6] have recognised the need to improve Aboriginal Peoples' access and outcomes in higher education through a number of strategies, including the incorporation of Indigenous knowledges within university curricula. These strategies form part of a broader government agenda which purports to improve the socio-economic standing of First Peoples, seeking to 'close the gap' in the life chances and opportunities available to Aboriginal Peoples when compared to the majority of the Australian population. These reviews also coincide with the introduction of the Tertiary Education Quality and Standards Agency (TEQSA)[7] and the *Higher Education Standards Framework (Threshold Standards) 2011* which seek to ensure that higher education meets Australia's social and economic needs by creating minimum standards and threshold learning outcomes to promote and provide consistency across higher education programs respectively.[8]

The chapter will critique the current strategies for the inclusion of Indigenous knowledges in higher education, and in so doing it will examine whether these standards are truly 'inclusive' or whether they merely serve to further assimilate Aboriginal Peoples into the mainstream. It starts from the position that the difficulties of including

3 In part, *Kartinyeri v Commonwealth* (1998) 195 CLR 337 was a Constitutional law case involving the 'race power' of the Australian Constitution. The plaintiffs, sought a declaration from the High Court that an Act of the Commonwealth parliament, the *Hindmarsh Island Bridge Act 1997* (Cth), was unconstitutional under s 51(xxvi), arguing that to exclude specified places from the scope of the *Aboriginal and Torres Strait Islander Heritage Protection Act 1984* (Cth) would effectively discriminate against Ngarrindjeri people. The High Court decided there was no implied Constitutional power to prohibit the making of laws that have the effect of being racially discriminatory.

4 Australian Government, *Review of Higher Education Access and Outcomes for Aboriginal and Torres Strait Islander People Final Report* (*Behrendt Review*) (2012), 6-7.

5 Australian Government, *Review of Australian Higher Education: Final Report* (*Bradley Review*) (2008).

6 *Behrendt Review*, above n 4.

7 Pursuant to the *Tertiary Education Quality and Standards Agency Act 2011* (Cth).

8 It must be noted that these standards are under review with the proposed Higher Education Standards Framework yet to be introduced <http://www.hestandards.gov.au/higher-education-standards-framework>. See Chapter 1 by Squelch and Chapter 2 by Varnham.

Indigenous knowledge should not be underestimated. Ongoing racism, exclusion and the (at best) mixed progress to date on meaningful inclusion suggests there is a strong need for significant research and meaningful consideration of the 'how to' part of the problem. Critical thinking requires us to examine current practices and experiences of inclusion as a marker of a political and intellectual landscape that is in need of rethinking in order to articulate political possibilities beyond those offered by the existing discursive framing of the problem.

The critique will examine two key areas of higher education policy to demonstrate how current approaches to inclusion promote assimilation of Aboriginal Peoples' knowledges and laws within existing power structures rather than providing recognition on terms that are meaningful to Aboriginal Peoples. This chapter will use as its focus the Australian Learning and Teaching Council's *Bachelor of Laws: Learning and Teaching Academic Standards Statement*,[9] as they provide a clear example of how Indigenous knowledges are excluded in the current regulatory framework of higher education. The academic standards for law are also examined because the exclusion of Indigenous knowledges within legal education has a significant impact in terms of more meaningful recognition of Indigenous Peoples. It will be argued that these frameworks are deficient to achieve inclusion beyond current assimilationist models and therefore are limited. The chapter will also outline other policy developments in higher education such as the Universities Australia *Best Practice Framework*,[10] and *Guiding Principles for Indigenous Cultural Competency*.[11]

II The Higher Education Policy Landscape

The *Bradley Review* identified the need for tertiary institutions to include Indigenous knowledge in the curriculum in order to improve access to higher education and educational outcomes for Indigenous Peoples.[12] It recognised that '[a]s the academy has contact with and addresses the forms of Indigenous knowledge, underlying assumptions in some disciplinary areas may themselves be challenged'.[13] The following discussion will review the extent to which these recommendations have been implemented, particularly in the regulation of legal curriculum.

The *Behrendt Review* stressed that tertiary institutions should adopt a 'whole-of-university' approach to improving Indigenous student access and outcomes – with Indigenous education units taking responsibility for student support, and faculties taking responsibility for promoting academic success.[14] Some key recommendations that promoted these objectives included developing Aboriginal and Torres Strait Islander (ATSI) teaching and learning strategies across the curriculum and increasing ATSI representation across senior management and university governance structures.[15]

---

9 Australian Learning and Teaching Council, *Bachelor of Laws: Learning and Teaching Academic Standards Statement* (2010).

10 Universities Australia, *Guiding Principles for Developing Indigenous Cultural Competency* (2011a).

11 Universities Australia, *National Best Practice Framework for Indigenous Cultural Competency* (2011b).

12 *Bradley Review*, above n 5, xxiii.

13 Ibid 32-33.

14 *Behrendt Review*, above n 4, xii.

15 Ibid xxii-xxiv.

In a background paper to the review, Rigney found that there was an uneven commitment to the inclusion of Indigenous knowledges in curriculum, with current approaches falling into three categories: (1) Indigenous knowledge is invisible; (2) Indigenous knowledge is taught in a single unit of Indigenous studies; (3) Indigenous perspectives are embedded across all programs and courses.[16] Rigney argued that universities were in an 'Indigenous perspectives in the curriculum' 'historic moment' which provides an opportunity for Indigenous knowledges to be 'built in not bolted on' to curriculum.[17] However, the review also raised concerns that the teaching of Indigenous knowledges in universities is uneven, is poorly resourced and is not adequately supported by university policies.[18] It also noted that while there is no Indigenous specific standard within the *Higher Education Standards Framework (Threshold Standards) 2011* the 'teaching and learning standards provide TEQSA with sufficient power to evaluate and monitor the quality of Indigenous-specific curriculums and teaching'.[19] As the discussion below demonstrates, however, teaching and learning standards in law do not adequately specify or address Indigenous content in curricula.

Significantly, the review urged universities to develop and implement strategies to 'improve the cultural understanding and awareness of staff, students and researchers including the provision of cultural competency training' as one aspect of building the capacity of universities to support Indigenous student success.[20] The *Behrendt Review* also endorsed the Universities Australia cultural competency project (discussed below) as part of developing 'quality teaching' of Indigenous perspectives and to support an Indigenous graduate attribute.[21] Although there has been no formal government response to the *Behrendt Review*, the university sector is starting to embrace its recommendations and is moving towards incorporating Indigenous knowledges and cultural competency in all degree programs. However, using legal education as an indicative example, it would appear that the incorporation of Indigenous knowledges are constrained within existing frameworks which do not recognise Aboriginal Peoples' knowledges and law on terms that are meaningful to First Peoples.

III Legal Academic Standards: A Virtual Terra Nullius?

The introduction of the Australian Qualifications Framework (AQF) for all tertiary education programs has prompted the development of Australian Learning and Teaching Council's (ALTC) *Bachelor of Laws: Learning and Teaching Academic Standards Statement*.[22]

The ALTC Standards are now the industry benchmark by which all degrees will be accredited under the new AQF framework and they constitute the minimum standards for university courses. While the standards in law are broadly framed they may be regarded as indicative of the content that must be included in LLB programs. The ALTC

16 Ibid 95.
17 Ibid 96.
18 Ibid 98.
19 Ibid 98.
20 Ibid xxiv.
21 Ibid 96-97.
22 ALTC, above n 9.

Standards establish 'Threshold Learning Outcomes' (TLOs) for law degrees organised around the themes of knowledge; ethics and professional responsibility; thinking skills; research skills; communication and collaboration; self-management.[23]

The ALTC standards were developed during 2010 through an 'iterative consultation process' which included members of the judiciary, admission authorities, the legal profession, regulators, academics, students and recent graduates.[24] Notably, the consultation process did not outline any specific methodology for engaging with Aboriginal Peoples, and as Rodgers-Falk has observed, there was minimal input from organisations with an Indigenous focus.[25]

The TLO relating to knowledge requires that law students acquire an understanding of the 'fundamental areas of legal knowledge', the Australian legal system, and its underlying principles and concepts, including international and comparative contexts.[26] Students are also required to learn about the 'values of justice and ethical practice, and the broader contexts within which legal issues arise.'[27] However, the knowledge necessary to gain a law degree is limited to the 'Priestley 11',[28] and does not include any specific reference to Aboriginal Peoples' knowledges and law. While the ALTC Standards include a statement on the nature and extent of legal education which acknowledges that law is shaped by many perspectives – *including Indigenous perspectives*,[29] these are regarded as part of the broader context of law, which, it is envisaged, may be 'extended' to include Indigenous 'perspectives'.[30] Given that by definition 'perspectives' are limited to 'a mental view'[31] – as opposed to 'knowledge' which is 'the fact or state of knowing; [a] perception of fact or truth'[32] – it would appear that the ALTC standards preserve the dominance of the mainstream legal system in the way they conceptualise 'law'. As such, the ALTC standards are assimilationist in their focus, and offer little by way of challenging the current status quo – the partial and incomplete recognition of Indigenous law 'within' existing legal frameworks. The ALTC standards perpetuate a virtual *terra nullius* whereby Aboriginal Peoples' law is not given full or equal recognition within the state. If legal education is to contribute to creating a more inclusive social order it needs to, at the very least, critique the existing conditions that maintain such dominance and recognise that Aboriginal Peoples' have 'knowledge' of law, grounded in their own epistemologies, that are valid perceptions of 'fact or truth'.

---

23 Ibid 10.

24 Ibid 1.

25 Ibid 26-28, Appendix 2: List of submissions received; Phillip Rodgers-Falk, *Growing the Number of Aboriginal and Torres Strait Islander Law Graduates: Barriers to the Profession* (Background paper to the *Review of Higher Education Access and Outcomes for Aboriginal and Torres Strait Islander People Final Report* (*Behrendt Review*)) (Australian Government, 2012), 17.

26 Ibid 10.

27 Ibid.

28 Ibid 13; the current eleven 'prescribed areas of knowledge' are: Criminal Law and Procedure; Torts; Contracts; Property; Equity; Company Law; Administrative Law; Federal and State Constitutional Law; Civil Procedure; Evidence; and Ethics and Professional Responsibility.

29 Ibid 8, emphasis added.

30 Ibid.

31 *Macquarie Concise Dictionary* (6th ed, Pan Macmillan, 2013), definitions of perspectives includes 'a mental view or prospect', 880.

32 Ibid 652.

IV Moving Beyond 'Perspectives': Indigenous Knowledges and Curricula

Despite the failure of legal academic standards to adequately address Aboriginal Peoples' knowledges within legal education, there have been some developments within the broader university sector to include Indigenous knowledges in all university curricula. These developments have been driven by a broader social justice agenda to address Indigenous 'disadvantage' and 'close the gap' in the life chances and opportunities available to Aboriginal Peoples, when compared to other Australians.

In 2007 *Ngarpartji Ngarpartji – Yerra: Stronger Futures,* the report of the former Indigenous Higher Education Advisory Council (IHEAC),[33] outlined a number of strategies for improving the participation of First Peoples in higher education, including making Indigenous cultural competency a graduate attribute for all students.[34] In addition, IHEAC's *Principles and Practices of Cultural Competency: A Review of the Literature 2008* outlines some general principles relating to the introduction of Indigenous cultural competency in university programs.[35] Significantly, the review identified only two law and justice programs which incorporated elements of Indigenous inclusive curriculum, and noted that one of these programs was not sustained in the long term.[36] Both the *Bradley Review*[37] and the *Behrendt Review*[38] endorsed IHEAC's call to include Indigenous cultural competency in university curricula.

Universities Australia has developed *Guiding Principles for Developing Indigenous Cultural Competency* (*Guiding Principles*),[39] and a *National Best Practice Framework for Indigenous Cultural Competency* (*Best Practice Framework*).[40] The *Guiding Principles* and *Best Practice Framework* outline a holistic approach to promoting Indigenous cultural competency within universities through addressing five key areas: university governance; teaching and learning; Indigenous research capacity; human resource management; and external engagement. Broadly, these documents recognise the need to promote social inclusion by building relationships with First Peoples communities and increasing their involvement in university governance; incorporating Indigenous knowledges and cultural competency in curriculum; building the capacity of universities to engage in research that is beneficial to First Peoples; increasing the numbers of Indigenous staff at all levels of university operations; and through more meaningful engagement with First Peoples and working in partnership with local communities.[41]

---

33 Now renamed the Aboriginal and Torres Strait Higher Education Advisory Council. See generally <www.education.gov.au/aboriginal-and-torres-strait-islander-higher-education-advisory-council>.

34 Indigenous Higher Education Advisory Council, *Ngarpartji Ngarpartji – Yerra: Stronger Futures* (2007), 4-5.

35 Indigenous Higher Education Advisory Council, *Principles and Practices of Competency: A Review of the Literature* (2008), 5.

36 Ibid 34-36. These programs were the Bachelor of Laws at Griffith University, and the Bachelor of Justice at Queensland University of Technology.

37 *Bradley Review,* above n 5.

38 *Behrendt Review,* above n 4.

39 Universities Australia, above n 10.

40 Universities Australia, above n 11.

41 Universities Australia, above n 10, 175-190.

The *Guiding Principles* recommend that teaching and learning in universities should include Indigenous cultural competency as a formal graduate attribute or quality; Indigenous knowledges and perspectives should be embedded in all university curricula to provide students with the knowledge, skills and understandings which form the foundations of Indigenous cultural competency; and Indigenous knowledges and perspectives of the First Peoples of Australia should be incorporated into programs according to a culturally competent pedagogical framework.[42] Significantly, Universities Australia's definition of cultural competency recognises that Indigenous cultural competency goes beyond learning *about* Indigenous Peoples, and also 'includes the ability to critically reflect on one's own culture and professional paradigms in order to understand its cultural limitations and effect positive change.'[43] Therefore, the current move towards Indigenous cultural competency in university curriculum may have the potential to shift existing paradigms that currently limit the inclusion of Indigenous Peoples in existing social frameworks.

Moving towards curriculum that is inclusive of First Peoples and their knowledges is not, however, without significant methodological challenges. It is critical that such moves do not perpetuate the conditions and dispositions that have led to the current piecemeal and fragmented recognition of First Peoples' law within existing legal frameworks whereby the dominant culture can prescribe the criteria and scope of 'inclusion'. It is also important that forms of inclusion are not dictated by the dominant culture, because to do so risks the further assimilation of Aboriginal Peoples within the mainstream, and threatens the ongoing existence of Aboriginality itself. Therefore, there is a critical need to ensure that methodologies for inclusion promote and enhance Indigenous wellbeing on terms that are viewed as progressive and inclusive by First Peoples. To accept less would only serve to further entrench colonial power over First Peoples.

Clearly, higher education policy has identified the incorporation of Indigenous knowledges within university courses as a means of promoting more inclusive curricula for First Peoples and to also build the capacity of other Australians to work more effectively with First Peoples. Arguably, these initiatives have the potential to create the space for a more inclusive social order and more meaningful engagement with First Peoples at a community level. They also highlight the need to critically reflect upon and challenge existing forms of knowledge that may constitute barriers to a more inclusive social order. Such critical reflection requires a willingness to engage with Indigenous knowledges in ways that are meaningful to Aboriginal Peoples. There are, however, significant questions about whether the current approaches to 'inclusion' can achieve these goals.

V Inclusion on Whose Terms?

In the 1980s and 1990s feminist and critical legal scholars began to question the liberal premise of universality and neutrality of the law.[44] The limitations of a largely legal

42 Ibid 9.

43 Ibid 3.

44 Margaret Thornton, *The Liberal Promise: Anti-discrimination Legislation in Australia* (Oxford University Press, 1990); Margaret Davies, 'The Ethos of Pluralism' (2005) 27 *Sydney Law Review* 87.

positivist framework and the further problems around accounting for the impact of colonialism on Indigenous knowledges compound the difficulties for recognition and what that 'recognition' might look like. The notion of redressing systemic disadvantage by revisiting presumptions of Indigenous inclusion has met with steadfast resistance. This may be seen in relation to Native Title, Aboriginal Heritage Protection, and interpretation of the 'Best Interests of the Child' test in family law and also in the Northern Territory Intervention.[45] Programs for inclusion have included the gradual emergence of Indigenous academics within the academy and some research funding that target Indigenous 'issues'.[46] Within law, current approaches construct Indigenous persons as a special subject and we can see this in relation to a number of areas including international and human rights law; criminal; and property law. Each of these areas corresponds to discrete areas of bureaucratic responsibility for development of appropriate law and policy, but there has been no attention to developing appropriate methodologies of inclusion of Indigenous knowledges. There has been little headway in progressing dialogue that centres Indigenous knowledge within the policy purview of the state.

VI What About Recognition?

The dispersed capacity of Aboriginal Peoples to participate in determining the content of Aboriginality has led to the misrepresentation of Indigenous knowledges in international and domestic law and social policy development.[47] Notwithstanding the United Nations' completion of the *Declaration on the Rights of Indigenous Peoples* and the Australian government's belated acceptance of that Declaration in 2009, Aboriginal Peoples continue to be amongst the world's most disadvantaged.[48]

While there is a substantial body of research on the belated and conditional recognition of Aboriginal Peoples in the 20th century, views constructed in the 16th, 17th and 18th centuries continue to prevail. They deny that First Peoples' laws and relationships to their territories are legitimate forms of political organisation and ownership.[49] There has been no major Australian or international research aimed at evaluating how the exclusion of an Aboriginal knowledge-centred approach from international and domestic law has contributed to miscarriages of justice. Instead, models which aim for the assimilation of Aboriginality continue to be developed to accommodate claims

45 Irene Watson, 'In the Northern Territory Intervention, What is Saved or Rescued and at What Cost?' (2009) 15 *Cultural Studies Review* 45.

46 *Bradley Review*, above n 5 <http://www.deewr.gov.au/highereducation/review/pages/reviewofaustralianhighereducationreport.aspx>.

47 Sharon Venne, *Our Elders Understand Our Rights: Evolving International Law Regarding Indigenous Rights* (Theytus Books, 1998); Isabelle Schulte-Tenckhoff, 'Re-assessing the Paradigm of Domestication: The Problematic of Indigenous Treaties' (1998) 4 *Review of Constitutional Studies* 239.

48 Irene Watson and Sharon Venne, 'Talking up Indigenous Peoples Original Intent, in a Space Dominated by State Interventions' in Elvira Pulitano (ed), *Indigenous Rights in the Age of the UN Declaration* (Cambridge University Press, 2012), 87-109; SJ Anaya, *Indigenous Peoples in International Law* (Oxford University Press, 2004).

49 Sharon Venne, above n 47; Peter Fitzpatrick, *Modernism and the Grounds of Law* (Cambridge University Press, 2001).

for the equality of Aboriginal rights.[50] The need for an analysis of the exclusion of Aboriginal-centred approaches in research and cross-disciplinary engagement is acute, because Australian and international law and social policy developments have largely ignored the question and the validity of Aboriginal knowledge as an essential approach to questions of participatory inclusion, justice and coexistence.

The question of Aboriginality and its interpretation has not been explored by Australian judicial systems beyond the incorporation of Aboriginal content which sits within existing legal frameworks. Examples can be found in the Aboriginal Courts, also known as the Nunga or Koori Courts.[51] Rather than reflect upon the problem of inclusion from an Australian perspective, many turn to overseas experience for leadership. Canadian courts are often referred to as being more advanced in their recognition of Aboriginal ways of interpreting rights as in, *Delgamuukw v British Columbia*.[52] However, this approach is disputed by a growing body of Aboriginal academics[53] and is evidenced in decisions such as *Ermineskin Indian Band and Nation v Canada*.[54]

From the 1970s, we saw the Australian government enact Aboriginal land rights legislation, creating statutory land councils and local government councils, and in the 1990s it enacted the common law recognition of Aboriginal title. In general, these initiatives are viewed as providing effective Aboriginal rights to land and governance, but the vulnerability of Indigenous relationships to land and the failings of these laws has become apparent.[55]

In 1986, the Australian Law Reform Commission *Report into Aboriginal Customary Law*[56] inquired into the extent to which First Peoples had power to apply their laws and practices. It recommended wider recognition within the framework of the Australian legal system in the areas of criminal, family, property and intellectual property laws. Almost 20 years later the Northern Territory, Western Australian and New South

50 Irene Watson, 'Sovereign Spaces, Caring for Country and the Homeless Position of Aboriginal Peoples' (2009) 108 *South Atlantic Quarterly* 27.

51 So-called Aboriginal courts such as the Nunga Court in South Australia, Koori Courts in Victoria, Circle Sentencing in NSW, and the former Murri Courts in Queensland. See generally Heather McRae, Garth Nettheim, Thalia Anthony, Laura Beacroft, Sean Brennan, Megan Davis, Terri Janke, *Indigenous Legal Issues Commentary and Materials* (Law Book Company, 2009), 573-578. Typically these courts operate under established sentencing laws with the involvement of First Peoples Elders and community members in the sentencing process.

52 [1997] 3 SCR 1010. An Indigenous knowledges approach to Indigenous law and land was not considered by the court.

53 John Borrows, *Recovering Canada: The Resurgence of Indigenous Law* (University of Toronto Press, 2002); Sharon Venne *Our Elders Understand Our Rights: Evolving International Law Regarding Indigenous Rights* (Theytus Books, 1998).

54 [2009] SCC 9. The Supreme Court of Canada dismissed the appeals of the Ermineskin Nation and Samson Nation, two Cree bands from Alberta, against the Crown regarding the breach of fiduciary obligations in the management of oil and gas royalties. Crown interpretations of treaty arrangements were privileged over that of the Cree Peoples version of the agreement.

55 Watson, above n 50; Watson, above n 45; Ann Curthoys, Ann Genovese, Alexander Reilly (eds), *Rights and Redemption: History, Law and Indigenous People* (University of New South Wales Press, 2008).

56 Australian Law Reform Commission, *The Recognition of Aboriginal Customary Laws, Report No 31* (Australian Government Printing Service, 1986).

Wales governments held similar inquiries.[57] The Western Australian report proposed a number of substantive, procedural and policy reform measures in an attempt to recognise Aboriginal laws, and the Northern Territory Law Reform Committee recommended that 'traditional' law could be, where relevant, recognised by judges and government decision-makers, as long as it did not conflict with Australian law and did not fail the repugnancy test. The New South Wales Law Reform Commission recommended consideration of 'customary laws' where relevant in the sentencing of Aboriginal persons. The above have all been fragmentary attempts at the inclusion of Aboriginal law and culture.[58] In addition, they have been accompanied by requiring Indigenous Peoples to meet qualifying criteria and positivistic evidentiary burdens of proof regarding identity, community, geographical continuity, cultural conformity and so on.[59] In particular, native title processes have been criticised due to the 'crushing' burden of proof and the demands on parties which have been described as 'unprecedented in adversarial litigation.'[60] Beyond the particular subject demands on Aboriginal actors, this process places an additional burden on claimants to identify with democratic, liberal, inclusive, and universal jurisprudence. First Peoples who do not adhere to this model are excluded, and these kinds of exclusions impact upon the inclusion or otherwise of Indigenous knowledges within the higher education sector. It is widely recognised that Aboriginal knowledge of law and culture largely remain excluded from existing legal and political frameworks of recognition. Where Australian courts have translated Aboriginal Peoples into their law narrative, there has been little shift in their thinking about Aboriginal Peoples' colonised and racialised identities.[61]

Intra-community violence has dominated contemporary debate about the legal relevance of Aboriginal law and culture. This occurred in the context of the Northern Territory Intervention, when the idea of backward Aboriginal Peoples inhabiting violent communities developed to support the intervention.[62] The popular resonance of this politic was also demonstrated in January 2007 after the death in custody of Palm Islander Doomadgee. Following the announcement that there was sufficient evidence to prosecute police Sergeant Hurley for the death of Doomadgee, the president of the

---

57 Chris Cuneen and Melanie Schwartz, *Customary Law, Human Rights and International Law: Some Conceptual Issues* (Background Paper No 11, Law Reform Commission of Western Australia, 2005), 429-450; Greg McIntyre, *Aboriginal Customary Law: Can It Be Recognised?* (Background Paper No 9, Law Reform Commission of Western Australia, 2005), 4-5; New South Wales Law Reform Commission, *Sentencing Aboriginal Offenders* (Report No 96, 2000), xi.

58 Larissa Behrendt and Lorretta Kelly, *Resolving Indigenous Disputes: Land Conflict and Beyond* (Federation Press, 2008); Mick Dodson, 'Opinion: From "Lore" to Law' (1995) 3 *Aboriginal Law Bulletin* 2.

59 Isabelle Schulte-Tenckoff, 'Misrepresenting the Potlatch' in C Gerschlager (ed), *Expanding the Economic Concept of Exchange: Deception, Self-Deception and Illusions* (Kluwer Academic Publisher, 2001).

60 Tom Calma, *Native Title Report 2007* (Australian Human Rights Commission, 2007), 6.

61 Irene Watson, *The Recognition of Cultural Background in Indigenous Sentencing* (Sentencing Conference, National Judicial College of Australia, ANU College of Law, 2008) <http://njca.anu.edu.au/Professional%20Development/programs%20by%20year/2008/Sentencing%20Conference%202008/papers/watson.pdf>.

62 Patricia Karvelas, 'One Law for All: Howard' (29 May 2006) *The Australian* <http://www.theaustralian.news.com.au/printpage/0,5942,19288622,00.html>; Irene Watson, 'Aboriginal Women's Laws and Lives: How Might We Keep Growing the Law?' in Martin Hinton, Daryl Rigney, Elliott Johnston (eds), *Indigenous Australians and the Law* (Cavendish, 2008).

Police Union declared that if the Queensland government was going to prosecute one of its members, then the Queensland Police would withdraw from remote communities, and allow 'tribal law' to police them.[63] The ensuing debate illustrated the power of the popular culture to construct Aboriginality and perceptions of Aboriginal law and culture. It would be naïve to assume that these developments do not have judicial ramifications as well as ramifications as to how Indigenous knowledges might be included within the higher education sector.

VII Conclusion: The Need for Legal Theory

Legal scholarship and reform-oriented legal research has sought to find more effective ways of incorporating Indigenous knowledges. The inclusion of Indigenous content within the western academy now also provides opportunities for a greater interaction and inclusion of Aboriginal knowledges.[64] However, beyond the more obvious and welcome recruitment of Indigenous researchers to work on governance programs affecting Indigenous people, there has been little development of methodologies or strategies of inclusion. The primary mechanism for Indigenous inclusion is by a methodology of co-option. Indigenous resources are called upon to participate in programs as cultural informants, commenting upon a proposal or plan of action as stakeholders in the consultation or as 'partners' with the state or other institutions. Often one or a small number of Indigenous persons carry the institutional expectation of 'speaking for' the many diverse and distinct First Peoples that have been historically excluded.[65]

Beyond critique, Judith Butler suggests that one solution to the exclusion of Indigenous knowledge may come from developing a process of cultural translation.[66] For Butler the universality concept compels an understanding of culture and the need for cultural translation for the universal to emerge. Inclusion of Indigenous knowledge is currently hampered by paltry scholarship that risks essentialising and speaking for those it cannot.[67] It is this factor that will impact upon the possibility for a broader understanding and inclusion across the higher education sector.

The ultimate goal is to reassess practices for inclusion and develop practical possibilities for the centering of Indigenous knowledges that will assist the legal profession in developing their knowledge of First Peoples. Such a process would go beyond the translation of Aboriginal laws and culture that has in most instances been effected by western expertise and interpreters and would enable the inclusion of Indigenous

63 T Koch and M McKenna, 'Top Cop Steps in Over Police Union Strike Action' (2007) *The Daily Telegraph* <http://www.news.com.au/dailytelegraph/story/0,22049,21134071-5005941,00.html>.

64 Laurelyn Whitt, *Science, Colonialism, and Indigenous Peoples, the Cultural Politics of Law and Knowledge* (Cambridge University Press, 2009).

65 Irene Watson, 'Aboriginal Sovereignties: Past, Present and Future (Im)Possibilities' in Suvendrini Perera (ed), *Our Patch, Enacting Australian Sovereignty Post-2001* (Network Books Symposia Series, Australia Research Unit, Curtin University of Technology, 2007).

66 Judith Butler, 'Restaging the Universal: Hegemony and the Limits of Formalism' in Judith Butler, Ernesto Laclau, Slavoj Žižek (eds) *Contingency, Hegemony, Universality: Contemporary Dialogues on the Left* (Verso Publishing, 2000).

67 Watson, above n 65, 23.

knowledges of law from a First Peoples standpoint. The work of Davies[68] outlines the need for a pluralistic attitude in the contemporary Australian context, arguing that diversity should not be reduced to or explained by a singular attitude, and that while legal plurality exists it is poorly understood and rarely theorised.[69] Australia's failure to engage with the practical and theoretical understandings of legal pluralism has left it lagging 'behind other Western liberal democracies'.[70] This is due mainly to a lack of a rich analytical approach to the different modes of law. A critique of those positions from an Indigenous knowledges perspective has not yet made a significant contribution and existing works on this topic are limited in their analysis of the problem. There is work to be done in developing a critical Aboriginal theoretical response that will identify and evaluate the impact of the exclusion of Indigenous knowledges on Aboriginal Peoples' lives and its significance to the development of the legal profession of the future. This is work that will be invaluable to the advancement of Indigenous Peoples' lives as it will also be to the future engagement with higher education.

68 Davies, above n 44; Drucilla Cornell, 'uBuntu, Pluralism and the Responsibility of Legal Academics to the New South Africa' (2009) 20 *Law and Critique* 43, a discussion on the value of including uBuntu in the laws of South Africa.

69 Luke McNamara, 'Equality Before the Law' (2004) 11 *Polyethinic Societies: The Construction of Normative Criminal Law Standards*, E-Law <http://www.murdoch.edu.au/elaw/issues/v11n2/mcnamara112.html>.

70 Davies, above n 44, 105.

Chapter 5

The Regulation of International Higher Education

Gaby Ramia

I Introduction

International education in Australia is covered by a significant body of formal regulation, with extensive legislation dealing directly with international *higher* education and accompanying regulations to guide not only universities, both public and private, but also tertiary and technical colleges in their dealings with students. In this chapter, the focus is on how international education is regulated in, and in relation to, Australia's public universities, unless otherwise stated. Public universities constitute the vast majority of the university sector, with only three private universities and a few overseas-based private universities with Australian branches.[1] Outside of national laws, Australia is a signatory to the World Trade Organization's (WTO) *General Agreement on Trade in Services* (GATS), though as discussed below, in practice, this has had little effect on the higher education sector to date. Indeed, despite its increasingly important global drivers, international education is regulated mainly by and within the nation-state.

Like most developed countries, Australia has rules on eligibility for migration through the channel of completed educational qualifications. These rules have evolved over recent years in response to demand and supply conditions, in particular professions and trades, and to the concerns of governments over education quality, and thus the quality of graduates who apply to stay in Australia long-term or permanently after graduation.[2] There are also rules on the provision of 'transnational higher education' (TNHE), which refers generally to education through offshore branch campuses and distance programs as well as cross-border franchising, twinning degrees, program articulation, virtual and distance-based teaching and learning, and programs delivered within transnational institutional partners.[3]

Australia also provides external forums for the investigation and resolution of international student grievances. For international students in private post-secondary institutions, the federal government has established the office of the Overseas Students

1 StudyinAustralia (2014) <http://www.studyinaustralia.gov.au/global/australian-education/universities-and-higher-education>.

2 Gaby Ramia, Simon Marginson and Erlenawati Sawir, 'The Regulation of International Student Welfare in Australia' (2013) 71 *Journal of Australian Political Economy* 106.

3 Vik Naidoo, 'Transnational Higher Education: A Stocktake of Current Activity' (2009) 13(3) *Journal of Studies in International Education* 310.

Ombudsman, which is available only if complaints are not resolved to the student's satisfaction at the level of the institution. All students at public colleges and universities have access to the relevant State or Territory ombudsman if grievances are not resolved by the institution, though these procedures are relatively remote avenues of redress (see also Chapter 11 by Kamvounias). Finally, there is Australian legislation and accompanying regulations applying to universities but also other forms of tertiary and technical education, which incorporate student fee protections and limited pastoral care rights but also guidance to providers on their compliance; namely, the *Education Services for Overseas Students Act 2000* (Cth) (*ESOS Act*) and the *National Code of Practice for Registration Authorities and Providers of Education and Training to Overseas Students 2007* (Cth) (*National Code*). The *ESOS Act* and the *National Code* combined are commonly referred to as the 'ESOS Framework'.

This chapter analyses the Australian international education regulation regime, reflecting generally on its central legal and policy provisions, including those dealing with: trade, transnational education, student migration, quality assurance, provider compliance, and student rights. In order to provide an understanding of the international context within which Australian regulation operates, the first section of the chapter briefly reviews the implications of globalisation for national higher education systems. The second section reviews the relevant trade, transnational education, student migration and quality assurance provisions in the Australian system. The third section analyses the ESOS Framework in particular, which is the most directly applicable legal instrument, while the fourth and final section discusses the implications of the analysis for the debate on international education law and policy in Australia.

II Globalisation and the Regulation of Higher Education

Universities have increasingly opened up to the wider world and global developments influence their status, strategies and everyday operations.[4] Some countries have been significantly enriched economically by developing and expanding the export of their education services. Australia is among them, currently ranking fifth in the world on total absolute numbers of international students and ranking first on the basis of international enrolments as a proportion of total enrolments.[5] On this measure, Australia is the world's most internationalised higher education system.

International education both responds to, and reflects, globalisation. Held and McGrew's authoritative definition refers to globalisation in terms of 'the expanding scale, growing magnitude, speeding up and deepening impact of interregional flows and patterns of social interaction'.[6] Providers of international education and their students

4 Philip G Altbach, *Tradition and Transition: The International Imperative in Higher Education* (Sense Publishers, 2007); Michael Apple et al (eds), *Globalizing Education: Policies, Pedagogies, and Politics* (Peter Lang, 2005); Shelleyan Scott and Kathryn C Dixon (eds), *The Globalised University: Trends and Challenges in Teaching and Learning* (Black Swan Press, 2008).

5 OECD, *Education at a Glance 2013* (OECD, 2013), 307.

6 David Held and Anthony McGrew, 'The Great Globalisation Debate: An Introduction' in David Held and Anthony McGrew (eds), *The Global Transformations Reader* (Polity Press, 2000), 1, 4.

are agents and subjects of each of the dimensions of globalisation, and both student and provider are touched simultaneously by rules and customs in local, national and global spaces.[7] Marginson and Rhoades combine these three dimensions, arguing for a 'glonacal' heuristic, which implies systematic consideration of 'three intersecting planes of existence, emphasizing the simultaneous significance of global, national, and local dimensions and forces'.[8]

In the context of globalisation, the insights offered by comparative analysis of international education in different countries is important, allowing not just consideration of similarity in national responses to universal pressures, but also differences. Comparative research acknowledges that nations, and education providers, face global regulation from unequal and non-equivalent positions.[9] At the most basic level, some nations are net exporters, and some are net importers, of education. Whichever is the case, most nations, driven by varying national policy agendas, can and do pursue the internationalisation of education. For example, in contrast to some comparative researchers who stress intra-regional country similarities,[10] in their comparison of Hong Kong, Malaysia and Australia, McBurnie and Ziguras[11] argue that national higher education policies vary according to the central rationale of the national regime. While Hong Kong is mostly motivated by student consumer protection, Malaysian authorities mainly see international education as a means to advance nationalist goals including the building of local education infrastructure and the preservation of Islamic values and identity. Australian policy is geared toward projecting the perception of a quality education system. Whatever the central motivation, international education policy serves purposes beyond the cross-border accessibility of education services.

III International and Domestic Law and Policy

The most significant global initiative relating to the regulation of international education has been the involvement of the World Trade Organization (WTO) through its *General Agreement on Trade in Services* (GATS). This is a multilateral agreement among the entire 159 country membership of the WTO to liberalise the provision of services across borders in ways similar to the liberalisation of trade in products.[12] GATS allows for four 'modes of supply'. In relation to international education these are: Mode of Supply 1, 'cross-border delivery' of education services, whereby services are delivered by distance, in tele-education, education testing services and via the internet; Mode of Supply 2, 'consumption abroad', which involves the physical movement of students from one country to another to undertake their studies; Mode of Supply 3, 'commercial

7 Gaby Ramia, Simon Marginson and Erlenawati Sawir, *Regulating International Students' Wellbeing* (Policy Press, 2013).

8 Simon Marginson and Gary Rhoades, 'Beyond National States, Markets, and Systems of Higher Education: A Glonacal Agency Heuristic' (2002) 43(3) *Higher Education* 281.

9 Simon Marginson and Marcela Mollis, 'Comparing National Education Systems in the Global Era' (2000) 42(2) *Australian Universities Review* 53.

10 Ka Ho Mok, *Education Reform and Education Policy* (Routledge, 2006).

11 Grant McBurnie and Christopher Ziguras, 'The Regulation of Transnational Higher Education in Southeast Asia: Case Studies of Hong Kong, Malaysia and Australia' (2001) 42(1) *Higher Education* 85.

12 WTO, *Services Trade* (2014) <http://www.wto.org/english/thewto_e/whatis_e/tif_e/org6_e.htm>.

presence', which includes course offerings abroad through branch campuses or subsidiaries of institutions, franchising, and twinning or other articulated arrangements; and Mode of Supply 4, 'presence of natural persons', which covers the temporary movement of teachers, lecturers and other education personnel across borders.[13]

By virtue of their membership, all WTO member nations are signatories to GATS, but the majority of them have so far made no commitments on education in respect of whatever level including higher education.[14] Given that international education has been undergoing continual growth on a global basis[15] and in Australia,[16] regardless of the strength of commitments to GATS, it is generally agreed in the literature that it would be difficult to imagine GATS having a major impact on the strategies of individual nations in the foreseeable future.[17]

The migration dimension of international education, whereby international students seek to stay in the host country on a permanent or long-term basis beyond the time taken for studies, has a stronger and more direct relationship with international education regulation than does multilateral trade. Governments see international education partly as a means, through international student graduates, to contribute to innovation, technical and trade skills enhancement and labour-force development.[18] Australia is no exception, with approximately 20 per cent of its incoming economic migrants since 2000 being international students.[19] Migration is not only an outcome of international education in Australia; it is also a key motivation on the part of students. One 2007 study found that 65 per cent of (then) currently enrolled international students in Australia intended to apply for permanent residency.[20]

In the context of the internationalisation of education, new and emerging regimes of quality regulation are required.[21] Van Damme[22] suggests four such regimes, each of which is at least partially aspirational. The first would see efforts to increase international cooperation on quality, encouraging some convergence on the standards and issues seen as most important. The second would involve the upgrading of international networking and exchange in arrangements such as cross-border quality assessment projects. A third would develop validation and meta-accreditation of quality assurance

13 OECD, *Internationalisation and Trade in Higher Education: Opportunities and Challenges* (OECD, 2004), 33-37.

14 Jandhalaya Tilak, *Trade in Higher Education: The Role of the General Agreement on Trade in Services (GATS)* (UNESCO, 2011).

15 OECD (2013), above n 5.

16 Ramia et al, above n 7, 59-71.

17 Jane Knight, 'Crossborder Education in a Trade Environment: Complexities and Policy Implications', Paper delivered to *Workshop on Implications of WTO/GATS or Higher Education in Africa*, African Association of Universities, Accra Ghana, April (2004), 27-29; NV Varghese, 'GATS and Higher Education: The Need for Regulatory Policies', *Research Papers IIEP* (IIEP/UNESCO, 2007).

18 Allan Findlay, 'An Assessment of Supply and Demand-Side Theorizations of International Student Mobility' (2010) 49(2) *International Migration* 162.

19 Shanthi Robertson and Anjena Runganaikaloo, 'Lives in Limbo: Migration Experiences in Australia's Education-Migration Nexus' (2014) 14(2) *Ethnicities* 208.

20 Ibid 210.

21 Dirk van Damme, 'Trends and Models in International Quality Assurance in Higher Education in Relation to Trade in Education' (2002) 14(3) *Higher Education Management and Policy* 93.

22 Ibid.

systems and agencies. Finally, a fourth model would involve the creation of a fully-fledged global agency overseeing quality assurance.

In the Australian context, quality is dealt with in the National Protocols for Higher Education Approval Processes[23] administered by the Tertiary Education Quality and Standards Agency (TEQSA).[24] TEQSA is owned and funded by the State and federal governments but formally stands independent of government, having responsibility for quality audits of higher education institutions (see also Chapter 1 by Squelch). TEQSA audits cover 'both public and private universities, Australian branches of overseas universities, and other higher education providers with and without self-accrediting authority'.[25] University foundation and ELICOS programs are also included.

As well as reporting on providers' performance in relation to quality, TEQSA applies the qualification standards specified in the Australian Qualifications Framework (AQF).[26] More generally, TEQSA provides advice to government, providers and other stakeholders on quality enhancement and assurance, and liaises with similar quality assurance bodies in other countries, including those of the United Kingdom, Singapore, Hong Kong, Malaysia and the European Union.[27] It also recognises and cooperates with regional fora such as the Asia-Pacific Quality Network and works within the UNESCO/OECD *Guidelines on Quality Provision in Cross-border Higher Education*.[28] TEQSA's main responsibility in relation to transnational higher education is to ensure that the overseas teaching operations of Australian institutions adhere to the quality standards of both Australia and the host country.[29]

IV The ESOS Framework

The ESOS Framework, comprised of the *ESOS Act* and the *National Code* together, is the instrument which bears most directly and specifically upon Australian providers of international education and their international students. The ESOS Framework covers not only higher education institutions but also all other post-compulsory education providers, and schools. It excludes Australian transnational education ventures

23 MCEETYA, *National Protocols for Higher Education Approval Processes* (2007) <http://www.scseec.edu.au/site/DefaultSite/filesystem/documents/Reports%20and%20publications/Archive%20Publications/Higher%20Ed/Revised-Nat%20Protocols%20HE%20Approval%20Process.pdf>.

24 TEQSA, *About TEQSA* (2014) <http://www.teqsa.gov.au/about>.

25 Ibid.

26 AQF, *Australian Qualifications Framework* (2013) <http://www.aqf.edu.au/wp-content/uploads/2013/05/AQF-2nd-Edition-January-2013.pdf>.

27 TEQSA, *International Engagement* (2014) <http://www.teqsa.gov.au/about/international-engagement>.

28 TEQSA, *TEQSA International Strategy* (2013) <http://www.teqsa.gov.au/sites/default/files/TEQSAInternationalStrategy.pdf>.

29 TEQSA, Information Paper: TEQSA's Approach to Regulating the Offshore Provision of Regulated HE Awards (2013) <http://www.teqsa.gov.au/sites/default/files/RegulatingOffshoreProvisionOfRegulatedHEAwardsInfoSheet.pdf>; TEQSA, International Higher Education Providers Seeking to Offer Higher Education in Australia (2014) <http://www.teqsa.gov.au/sites/default/files/FAQs_InternationalProvidersinAustralia.pdf>.

physically operating offshore,[30] which are dealt with in the rules and conventions of the jurisdiction in which they operate, though – depending on the commitments made by the country in question – they may also be subject to the regional and global fora discussed above.[31]

The *ESOS Act* is designed to provide 'tuition assurance, and refunds for overseas [ie, international] students for courses for which they have paid', in cases where the course has not run; 'to protect and enhance Australia's reputation for quality education and training'; and 'to complement Australia's migration laws by ensuring providers collect and report information relevant to the administration of the law relating to student visas'.[32] The *National Code*, established under pt 4 of the *ESOS Act*, specifies nationally consistent standards which providers must meet in order to be registered as education providers for international students. The *National Code* also 'identifies the roles and responsibilities of the Australian Government and State and Territory governments in discharging their regulatory functions'.[33]

The *ESOS Act* recognises student rights, though mainly with relation to the assurance of funds expended by students in the form of tuition fees. Specifically, the *ESOS Act* mandates that providers not engage in 'misleading or deceptive conduct' in connection with recruitment or provision of courses.[34] The *ESOS Act* also requires providers to refund course fees if the provider defaults and fails to provide a course at the location or on the agreed starting day.[35] Provision is also made for student default on payment of course money.[36] These protections are backed by the Overseas Students Tuition Fund (OSTF), to which providers must contribute each year. The OSTF exists to provide refunds to students and to reimburse providers who provide students with alternative courses when a provider has failed to discharge its obligations.[37] The *ESOS Act* also prescribes a variety of rights and responsibilities for providers, particularly in relation to OSTF contributions,[38] general enforcement of the Act's terms and conditions, and monitoring of providers and sanctions in case of non-compliance.[39]

National reputation and quality, though not quality assurance, are addressed within the *National Code* through the imposition of nationally consistent standards on providers. The standards relate to: 'pre-enrolment engagement of students', including marketing information and practices, formalisation of enrolment, and the use of education agents;[40] 'care for and services to students', including provision relating to students

30 David Woodhouse and Antony Stella, 'Regulation and Quality Assurance of Higher Education Institutions in Australia' (Paper presented at International Workshop on Institutional and Programme Accreditation (IWIPA), Bangalore, India, 2011) <http://ieeexplore.ieee.org/xpl/articleDetails.jsp?arnumber=6221146&tag=1>.

31 Stéphan Vincent-Lancrin and Sebastian Pfotenhauer, *Guidelines for Quality Provision in Cross-Border Higher Education: Where Do We Stand?* (OECD Directorate for Education, 2012).

32 *ESOS Act* s 4B.

33 *National Code* s 1.2.

34 *ESOS Act* s 15.

35 *ESOS Act* ss 46A-46F, Provider defaults.

36 *ESOS Act* ss 47A-47H, Student defaults.

37 *ESOS Act* pt 5.

38 *ESOS Act* ss 53A-53D.

39 *ESOS Act* pts 6-7, Provider defaults.

40 *National Code* Standards 1-4.

under 18 years of age, and student support services in general;[41] 'students as consumers', including students transferring between registered providers, and student complaints and appeals;[42] the student visa program, including student completion within expected study duration, the monitoring of student attendance and course progress, course credit, and course deferral, and enrolment suspension or cancellation;[43] and finally 'staff, educational resources and premises', and changes to the ownership and management of registered providers.[44]

On the protection of student rights the *National Code* provides for 'student welfare and support services'[45] and 'nationally consistent standards for dealing with student complaints and appeals'.[46] Where international students are under 18 years of age, the Australian government must be satisfied that appropriate arrangements are in place for student accommodation, support and general welfare arrangements during the whole of the period that they are under the age of 18 and studying onshore in Australia.[47] Yet accommodation and living arrangements are the only specified requirements, with 'support and general welfare arrangements'[48] being mentioned, but left largely undefined. Where students are over the age of 18, the responsibilities of providers are prescribed with less detail again. Students must have access to support services and orientation programs to provider staff who assess and administer these services and programs. In addition, providers must have 'critical incident policies' in place for all students; a critical incident being defined as 'a traumatic event, or the threat of such (within or outside Australia), which causes extreme stress, fear or injury'.[49] Finally, under Standard 8 of the *National Code* providers are required to offer students 'internal' processes for handling complaints and appeals, implying processes within the provider institution, and where independent mechanisms are requested by students, the student and the provider are bound by the decision.[50]

V Issues and Controversies

Australia is one of the world's most attractive destinations for international students.[51] As Wilkins, Balakrishnan and Huisman find in their review of research on factors influencing student country destination choice for higher education, one consideration continuously

41 *National Code* Standards 5-6.
42 *National Code* Standards 7-8.
43 *National Code* Standards 9-13.
44 *National Code* Standards 14-15.
45 *National Code* Standard 6.
46 *National Code* Standard 8
47 *National Code* Standard 5.
48 *National Code* Standard 5.1a.
49 *National Code* Standard 6. Though each provider must have a critical incident policy on hand and in writing, notably '[t]he details of your [the provider's] Critical Incident Policy do not need to be shared with students at orientation'. See Australian Education International, *National Code* pt D, Standard 6 (2014) <https://www.aei.gov.au/Regulatory-Information/Education-Services-for-Overseas-Students-ESOS-Legislative-Framework/National-Code/nationalcodepartd/Pages/ExplanatoryguideD6.aspx>.
50 *National Code* Standard 8.5.
51 OECD 2013, above n 5.

cited by students as being important is the cost of living.[52] Though Australia was once a more affordable location than most of its major competitor nations, the increase in the value of the Australian dollar over the last five years has resulted in significantly higher living costs for international students.[53] Indeed, a 2013 report by Chinese Bank HSBC revealed that Australia is the highest-cost study destination in the world, being more expensive to live and study in than the United States, the United Kingdom and Europe.[54]

One trade-off for a relatively expensive education, for students who can afford it, is satisfaction with living conditions and the study experience. In the latest available research by Australian Education International (AEI), the federal government's international education agency, high levels of satisfaction are found among international students studying and living in Australia.[55] Eighty-eight per cent of higher education students, 89 per cent of vocational college students and 89 per cent of English language students reported overall 'satisfaction with living' in Australia. Rates of overall 'satisfaction with studying' were similar, being 85 per cent for higher education students, 87 per cent for vocational college students and 91 per cent for English language students.[56]

Another trade-off for an expensive education is the perceived quality of the education, which as discussed above, is given great importance by the Australian government in policy and law. A key indicator of quality is seen in perceptions of Australian education among prospective international students; that is, students who are yet to choose their destination country but are looking to choose. In one study, which was conducted for the US-based Institute of International Education (IIE) and applied to higher education only,[57] prospective students from countries across Africa, Asia, Europe and Latin America were asked about their perceptions of higher education in Australia, Canada, Japan, China, Germany, France, the United Kingdom and the United States. Survey respondents placed Australia in the position of third lowest of the eight countries in terms of quality, with only 19.2 per cent of them agreeing with the statement that Australia is a 'high quality higher education system'. The figures in relation to the other seven countries in descending order were: 75.6 per cent for the United States, 49.9 per cent for the United Kingdom, 33.2 per cent for Canada, 30.7 per cent for Germany, 23.2 per cent for France, 18.6 per cent for Japan and 3.5 per cent for China.[58] The take-home message is that, at least among prospective students, Australia ranks lower than most of its major rival countries in terms of perceived quality.

---

52 Stephen Wilkins, Melodena Stephens Blakrishnan and Jeroen Huisman, 'Student Choice in Higher Education: Motivations for Choosing to Study at an International Branch Campus' (2012) 16(5) *Journal of Studies in International Education* 413.

53 International Education Advisory Council, *Australia – Educating Globally: Advice from the International Education Advisory Council* (Commonwealth of Australia, 2013), 28.

54 HSBC, *Study Costs Most in Australia* (2013) <http://www.hsbc.com/news-and-insight/2013/study-costs-most-in-australia>.

55 AEI, *International Student Survey 2012: Overview Report* (2013) <https://aei.gov.au/research/Publications/Documents/2012%20ISS%20Overview%20Report_PDF_Web%20version_FINAL.pdf>.

56 Ibid.

57 Patricia Chow, *What International Student Think About US Higher Education: Attitudes and Perceptions of Prospective Students in Africa, Asia, Europe and Latin America* (2011) <file:///C:/Users/gramia/Downloads/IIE_Student_Attitudinal_Survey_Report.pdf>.

58 Ibid 6.

An expensive education might also be traded off against general student wellbeing in the destination country. In the IIE research cited above, Australia ranked fourth on 'student support services' and fifth on student safety.[59] The *ESOS Act* and the *National Code* were not designed to regulate student safety. However, the *National Code* does refer to the requirement for providers to provide 'an age and culturally appropriate orientation program that includes information about' a range of support services.[60] These services include legal services, emergency and health services, complaints and appeals, and 'any student visa condition relating to course progress and/or attendance as appropriate'.[61] The important point is that the specification is for *information* about the services, and not the provision of these services. There are no substantive minimum standards. Providers must 'provide the opportunity for students to access welfare-related support services', but these are 'to assist with issues that may arise during their study, including course progress and attendance requirements and accommodation issues'.[62] Importantly, 'assistance with issues relating to' services is not the same as mandating the provision of those services, whether on campus or elsewhere. Thus there is no requirement, for example, that international students be guaranteed or offered housing, adequate and affordable or otherwise. In short, the 'welfare-related' aspect of services are not well defined in the body of the *National Code*, though Appendix A specifies that welfare and support services 'may include thorough direct provision *or referral*, information/advice about' a wide range of issues.[63]

This raises questions for government and providers and in recent years there has been significant public and scholarly attention devoted to the question of international student wellbeing.[64] There is ample evidence of concern over issues such as student safety from crime,[65] housing quality and quantity,[66] personal finances,[67] and discrimination and exploitation in part-time and casual employment.[68] The *Review of the ESOS Act*,[69] conducted by The Honourable Bruce Baird, recognised these issues, alongside others which were recognised by the government in the 2010 amendments to the Act as discussed in the previous section of this chapter. On 'student support' and the 'educational experience', Baird made clear that while the *ESOS Act* could not alone be the vehicle for reform, and that '[g]overnments, providers, students, agents and the broader Australian community all have a role to play', the government should

59 Ibid.

60 *National Code* Standard 6.

61 Ibid 6.1f.

62 Ibid 6.3.

63 The italics represents the author's emphasis.

64 This debate is reviewed comprehensively in two sources: Ramia et al, above n 2, 113-117; Ramia et al above n 7, 84-90.

65 Chris Nyland, Helen Forbes-Mewett and Simon Marginson, 'The International Student Safety Debate: Moving Beyond Denial' (2010) 29(1) *Higher Education Research and Development* 89.

66 Franlin Obeng-Odoom, 'Far Away From Home: The Housing Question and International Students in Australia' (2012) 34(2) *Journal of Higher Education Policy and Management* 201.

67 Helen Forbes-Mewett et al, 'Australian University International Student Finances' (2009) 22(2) *Higher Education Policy* 141.

68 Chris Nyland et al, 'International Student-Workers in Australia: A New Vulnerable Workforce' (2009) 22(1) *Journal of Education and Work* 1.

69 ESOS Review, *Stronger, Simpler, Smarter ESOS: Supporting International Students* (Commonwealth of Australia, 2010).

address them in policy and law 'outside of ESOS'.[70] In particular, Baird highlighted problems relating to 'student safety, accommodation, employment, transport and health matters'.[71] Importantly, international students in Australia have access to health services equivalent to those under Medicare but these are purchased on a commercial and non-subsidised basis.[72] International students are provided with public transport concession cards on the same terms as are local students in all States except New South Wales, which now has partial concessions which do not match those enjoyed by local students, and Victoria, which has announced similarly limited concessions, though slightly more generous than those in New South Wales.[73]

The Victorian government's *Overseas Student Education Experience Taskforce*[74] and the New South Wales government's *International Education and Research Industry Taskforce*[75] identified similar problems in relation to student support services and wellbeing and made similar recommendations, as did the Council of Australian Governments' (COAG) *International Students Strategy*[76] and the Commonwealth Senate's Education, Employment and Workplace Relations References Committee inquiry into the *Welfare of International Students*.[77] Finally, in recognition of the importance of the human rights of international students, the Australian Human Rights Commission has developed its *Principles to Promote and Protect the Human Rights of International Students*.[78]

Scholars have been more systematically critical on these questions than government-sponsored inquiries. Marginson and his colleagues provide the best example of comprehensive work highlighting the need for more effective government policy on student welfare.[79] They conducted in-depth interviews with 200 international students studying in Australia, finding that a broader range of life domains are potentially important focal points, including all of those listed above, plus health, transport, English language proficiency, social and family networks, and dealings with the immigration office. They acknowledge that the vast majority of international students in Australia have a positive overall life and study experience, but the existence of the minority who do not is for them evidence that student wellbeing is in need of regulatory reform.[80]

---

70 Ibid iv.

71 Ibid.

72 Simon Marginson et al, *International Student Security* (Cambridge University Press, 2010), 18-19.

73 John Ross, 'Overseas Students to be Stung on Discount Travel' (12 March 2014) *The Australian* <http://www.theaustralian.com.au/higher-education/overseas-students-to-be-stung-on-discount-travel/story-e6frgcjx-1226851774160>.

74 Victorian Government, *Overseas Student Education Experience Taskforce (Victoria)* (Victorian Government, 2008).

75 New South Wales Government, *Industry Action Plan: NSW International Education and Research* (NSW Government, 2012).

76 Council of Australian Governments, *International Students Strategy for Australia* (COAG, 2010).

77 Commonwealth Senate Education, Employment and Workplace Relations References Committee, *Welfare of International Students* (Commonwealth of Australia, 2009).

78 Australian Human Rights Commission, *Principles to Promote and Protect the Human Rights of International Students* (AHRC, 2010).

79 Marginson et al, above n 72.

80 Ibid 3-9.

Finally, a particularly important area for reform has been the connection between international education and migration, as recognised by scholars[81] and the Australian government, expressed mainly through its *Review of the ESOS Act*[82] and the *Strategic Review of the Student Visa Program* (*Strategic Review*).[83] Arguing that existing provisions in migration legislation were too rigid, the ESOS Review recommended that the *ESOS Act* 'be amended to enable a more flexible approach to current visa cancellation requirements for students who are reported for failing to maintain satisfactory course progress or attendance'.[84] Also, responding to what many saw as the ability of vocational colleges to engage unscrupulous offshore agents, the ESOS Review recommended 'introducing financial penalties for providers whose offshore agents act unethically',[85] and 'requiring all provider payments to agents to be contingent upon disclosure of the recruiting agent and their commission structure to both students and regulators'.[86] In the context of a high Australian dollar and falling enrolments in 2010-2012,[87] the migration program was perceived by the *Strategic Review* to be too tight,[88] thus disadvantaging Australia's ability to maximise its market share in the international education market and hampering its ability to allow university-educated migrants to stay permanently.

The thinking behind this is important. As discussed in Section III above, more than half, approximately 65 per cent,[89] of international students in Australia have the intention, while still enrolled, to become permanent residents post-graduation. If they cannot become permanent residents they may not study in Australia and may instead study in another, competitor, country. Recognising this, the *Strategic Review* recommended that international students graduating from Bachelors and Masters by coursework programs receive two years' subsequent work rights.[90] All higher degrees by research graduates, meaning PhDs and Masters by research, should receive unlimited work rights.[91]

These measures were introduced almost as recommended by the *Strategic Review*, the difference between recommendation and policy enacted being that research degree graduates are allowed four years, rather than unlimited, work rights.[92] The result in any case is a more migration-friendly international education regime.

---

81 Reviewed in Shanthi Robertson, *Transnational Student-Migrants and the State: The Education-Migration Nexus* (Palgrave Macmillan, 2013).
82 ESOS Review, above n 69.
83 Australian Government, *Strategic Review of the Student Visa Program 2011* (Australian Government, 2011).
84 ESOS Review, Recommendation 9.
85 ESOS Review, Recommendation 12a.
86 ESOS Review, Recommendation 12c.
87 Julie Hare, 'Fall in Overseas Students Costs $1bn' (3 August 2012) *The Australian* <http://www.theaustralian.com.au/higher-education/drop-in-overseas-students-costs-1bn/story-e6frgcjx-1226441801202>.
88 *Strategic Review*, above n 83.
89 Robertson and Runganaikaloo, above n 19, 210.
90 *Strategic Review*, above n 83, Recommendation 4.1, 4.2.
91 Ibid Recommendation 7.
92 VisAustralia, *Work Rights for Students* (2014) <http://www.visaustralia.com/en/latest-news/50-work-rights-for-international-students.html>.

Chapter 6

'The Next Two Decades are Going to Be Transparency':* Regulatory Challenges for Universities

Helen Fleming

I Introduction

Universities have been described as one of history's most robust institutions:[1] constantly reinventing themselves: most recently, from a model of a self-governing 'community of scholars', focused on academics and their research, into a 'multiversity' business model, focused on the needs and aspirations of students and the economic future of Australia.[2] Much of this transformation has been driven by Commonwealth government policy over the last 30 years, but at the same time has led to increased regulatory control and scrutiny. While some commentators, like Justice Michael Kirby, argue that the concepts of public accountability and transparency for publicly funded corporations have been accepted since colonial times,[3] these are only recent (and not uncontroversial) additions to the general university lexicon.

II A Brief Overview of the Australian University Regulatory Framework

A *University Legislative Framework*

All Australian public universities are established as statutory corporations under Commonwealth, State or Territory legislation[4] with stated primary objects and functions

* Altered from original quote, 'The next two decades are going to be privacy' from 'The Short List', *The West Wing*, Episode 9, 1999, Warner Bros Television.

1 Andrew Gilbert, 'Enterprise and Change in Australian Universities: Change, Continuity and the Idea of the University' in Pamela Kinnear (ed), *The Idea of a University: Enterprise or Academy?* (Conference papers, Manning Clark House and the Australia Institute, 26 July 2001).

2 See Denise Bradley, Peter Noonan, Helen Nugent and Bill Scales, *Review of Australian Higher Education: Final Report* (Department of Education, Employment and Workplace Relations, 2008).

3 Michael Kirby, *Public Funds and Public Power Beget Public Accountability* (University of Canberra, Corporate Governance ARC Research Project, Corporate Governance in the Public Sector, 9 March 2006), 14.

4 See, for example, *Australian National University Act 1991* (Cth), *University of Canberra Act 1989* (ACT), *University of Sydney Act 1989* (NSW), *Charles Darwin University Act 2003* (NT),

of teaching and research (see also Chapter 1 by Squelch).[5] These statutes emphasise their very public status. For example, the preamble to the original statute that established Australia's first university, the University of Sydney, contains the following statement:

> Whereas it is deemed expedient for the better advancement of religion and morality and the promotion of useful knowledge, to hold forth to all classes and denominations of Her Majesty's subjects resident in the Colony of New South Wales, without any distinction whatsoever, and encouragement for pursuing a regular and liberal course of education … [6]

The Commonwealth assumed full responsibility for funding universities in 1974[7] and thus achieved a dominant position over higher education policy because of its ability to attach conditions to university grants.[8] That dominance was consolidated with the introduction in the 1980s of the Higher Education Contribution Scheme (HECS)[9] and Unified National System.[10] The result is that, in many respects, public universities are now very highly regulated. The university sector has, at times, reacted negatively to what it perceives as unnecessary interference with institutional autonomy.[11]

B Universities as 'Public Authorities' or 'Government Agencies'

Australian public universities are regulated by a combination of Commonwealth, State and Territory regulatory regimes as 'public authorities' or 'government agencies' as defined in the particular legislation: either because they are established by legislation for a public purpose,[12] are prescribed as such by regulation,[13] or are named directly.[14]

This chapter focuses on three regulatory regimes: freedom of information, whistleblower protection and privacy of personal (including health) information. The theme of this chapter is that, in these three areas at least, there is still some tension between university ideas about transparency and accountability and expectations of the broader community.

University of Queensland Act 1998 (Qld), *University of Adelaide Act 1971* (SA), *University of Tasmania Act 1992* (Tas), *University of Melbourne Act 2009* (Vic), *University of Western Australia Act 1911* (WA).

5 See, for example, *University of Western Sydney Act 1997* (NSW) s 8.

6 *University of Sydney Act 1850* (NSW) 14 Vic No 31.

7 Department of Education, Science and Training, *The National Report on Higher Education in Australia* (Canberra, 2001).

8 Higher education was the responsibility of State and Territory governments until 1974 when the Commonwealth, with the agreement of the States and Territories, assumed direct funding of universities.

9 John S Dawkins, *The Challenge for Higher Education in Australia* (Australian Government Publishing Service, 1987).

10 The Honourable John S Dawkins, MP, *Higher Education: A Policy Discussion Paper* (Green paper, Australian Government Publishing Service, 1987).

11 See, for example, David Dixon, *TEQSA, the AQF and the Regulatory Threat to Australian Legal Education* (undated) <http://www.clmr.unsw.edu.au/article/compliance/regulatory-threat-australian-legal-education>.

12 See, for example, *Government Information (Public Access) Act 2009* (NSW) sch 4, cl 2(1)(b); *Freedom of Information Act 1991* (SA), s 4(1) (definition of 'agency').

13 See, for example, *Freedom of Information Regulations 2009* (Vic) sch 3.

14 See, for example, *Right to Information Act 2009* (Tas) s 5 (definition of 'public authority'), para (ab).

III Freedom of Information

It has been said that the traditions of secrecy that were a hallmark of successive British governments were imported into and dominated Australian public affairs until only recently.[15] Previously, a 'mere curiosity and desire to see and inspect documents' was not considered a sufficient reason to allow members of the public the right to inspect public records.[16] Like governments, universities have been accused of being opaque about their internal affairs, although this may have more to do with protection of institutional autonomy and academic freedom than protection of official secrets.

The enactment of freedom of information (FOI) laws throughout Australia provided legally enforceable rights of access to government documents as part of a greater ideal to promote government accountability and transparency.[17] Like the governments that introduced those laws, universities implemented policies and procedures that, on the face of it, indicated a commitment to openness and transparency. However, and like those governments, universities have sometimes gone to extraordinary lengths to use exemptions to deny access to information.

A recent study in the United Kingdom[18] made findings that may also be true of Australian universities: that awareness of FOI responsibilities was generally good among general staff but 'significantly poorer' among academic staff and that attitudes among senior management varied between institutions, ranging from supportive to 'begrudging compliance' and to resistant.[19] The study attributed some of this to general lack of training and awareness. Nonetheless, it also found that the biggest improvements in universities, following introduction of FOI legislation, were greater transparency, improved information and records management and professionalism among staff.[20]

The most contentious FOI cases for Australian universities have tended to involve access to or disclosure of (and not necessarily in this order) student marks and examination papers, referees' reports and vice chancellors' salary packages. Each category is discussed below. A common theme is that access or disclosure threatens institutional autonomy and academic integrity.

15 Paul D Finn, *Official Information, Integrity in Government Project, Interim Report 1* (Australian National University, 1991).

16 *R v Southwold Corp; Ex parte Wrightson* (1907) 97 LT 431.

17 Victoria was the first State to introduce freedom of information laws in Australia, see *Freedom of Information Act 1982* (Vic), followed by the *Freedom of Information Act 1982* (Cth), *Freedom of Information Act 1989* (ACT), *Freedom of Information Act 1989* (NSW) (superseded by the *Government Information (Public Access) Act 2009* (NSW)), *Freedom of Information Act 1991* (SA), *Freedom of Information Act 1991* (Tas) (superseded by *Right to Information Act 2009* (Tas)), *Freedom of Information Act 1992* (WA), *Freedom of Information Act 1992* (Qld) (superseded by *Right to Information Act 2009* (Qld)) and *Information Act 2002* (NT).

18 Daniel Swallow and Gabrielle Rourke, *The Freedom of Information Act and Higher Education: The Experience of FOI officers in the UK* (Department of Political Science, University College London, June 2012).

19 Ibid 6.

20 Ibid 9.

A Access to Student Assessments

In one of the earliest FOI cases involving a university,[21] several graduates of the Australian National University (ANU) sought access to their university assessment reports, including assessment of their honours theses. At the time, feedback to students about their performance was uncommon, and access to examiners' reports almost unheard of. ANU resisted disclosure, relying principally on two exemptions:[22] first, that disclosure would prejudice or limit the exchange of opinions between examiners and prevent free and frank assessment: and second, that the interests of the students in obtaining this information was essentially limited to private interests, rather than public or community interests. The Administrative Appeals Tribunal (AAT) rejected the first argument.

> I accept that some examiners may feel threatened by such disclosures and that there is a possibility that their approach to assessment of student work may be consequentially affected. On the other hand, there is, I think, much to be said for the view ... that an academic in assessing the work of a student must be prepared to make judgments honestly and impartially, and be prepared to stand by those judgments. Indeed, those are the characteristics of a good academic.[23]

However, in a case where a student sought access to examinations papers of other students (with names redacted),[24] the AAT denied access on the grounds that the public interest test was satisfied and "disclosure could reasonably be expected to prejudice the effectiveness of procedures for the conduct of examinations."[25]

This issue still remains contentious, even though universities now routinely provide feedback to students about their performance. More recently, in *University of Melbourne v McKean*[26] the university claimed an exemption for access to marking guides and an examination paper for a different reason: that 'the use or uses for which the document was prepared have not been completed'.[27] However, that argument failed because the uses for which those documents had been created were completed once academic results were published following assessment. A media statement issued by McKean shortly after the court's decision is instructive: not only did he want to find out why he received the marks that he did, perhaps with a view to challenging them; it leaves no doubt about his (arguably misplaced) sense of entitlement around what he termed as his 'investment' in higher education:

> I wanted value for money. Not only that, but I wanted good marks, and if I didn't get them, I wanted a good reason why.[28]

---

21 *Re James v Australian National University* (1984) 6 ALD 687.

22 See *Freedom of Information Act 1982* (Cth) s 36 (internal working documents and deliberative processes) and s 40 (prejudice to effectiveness of procedures for conduct of examinations).

23 *Re James v Australian National University* (1984) 6 ALD 687, 703, Deputy President Hall.

24 *Re Redfern v University of Canberra* (1995) 38 ALD 457.

25 *Freedom of Information Act 1982* (ACT) s 40(1) and (2).

26 [2008] VSC 325.

27 *Freedom of Information Act 1982* (Vic) s 34(4)(c).

28 Bernard Lane, 'Ex-student Wins Legal Fight with Uni Over Exams' (1 September 2008) *The Australian*.

More than 30 years after the decision in *Re James v Australian National University*, some universities still resist disclosure of examiners' identities. This is despite a more recent finding by the Victorian Civil and Administrative Tribunal that the vast majority of examiners are not concerned about remaining anonymous, and that community expectations require higher levels of accountability and transparency around examination of students' theses.[29]

B Access to Referees' Reports

Appointment and promotion of academic staff in universities is, for the most part, a formal and complex process, that has at times been criticised for lack of transparency, particularly with respect to the promotion of female academics.[30] Part of the process involves obtaining referees' reports. While it is common for candidates to nominate referees they consider favourable to them, universities often claim a convention of treating referees' reports as confidential on the grounds that this encourages candour. In some cases, referees may be asked to sign a confidentiality agreement.

In *Re Kamminga v Australian National University* (*Kamminga*),[31] an academic applied for access to a referee's report, following two unsuccessful applications for appointment. ANU denied under a number of exemptions, including those relating to deliberative processes[32] and materials obtained in confidence.[33] ANU also claimed a convention of confidentiality for referees' reports, even if these were not explicitly marked as confidential.

The tribunal accepted that the convention existed, and exempted the referees' reports as materials obtained in confidence.[34] In doing so, it applied the decision of Gummow J in *Corrs Pavey Whiting and Byrne v Collector of Customs of Victoria and Alphaharm Pty Ltd*,[35] which held that in order to rely on that exemption, the following elements had to be established: first, that the person who provided the information must be able to identify the information, with specificity, and not simply in global terms; second, that the information has the necessary quality of confidentiality (and is not common or public knowledge), third, that the information was received in circumstances that imported an obligation of confidence and fourth, that there is actual or threatened misuse of the information and that unauthorised use would be of detriment to the person who provides it.[36]

However, the tribunal disallowed the 'deliberative processes' exemption.[37] It did not accept ANU's argument that the threat of disclosure could lead to less candid reports,

---

29 *Darwish v Deakin University* [2002] VCAT 87, [23]-[25], [31].

30 See, for example, Hilary Winchester, Colleen Chesterman, Shard Lorenzo and Lyn Browning, *The Great Barrier Myth: An Investigation of Promotion Policy and Practice in Australian Universities* (National Colloquium of Senior Women Executives in Australian Higher Education, Australian Vice Chancellors' Committee, 2005).

31 (1992) 26 ALD 585.

32 *Freedom of Information Act 1982* (Cth) s 36(1).

33 *Freedom of Information Act 1982* (Cth) s 45(1).

34 *Freedom of Information Act 1982* (Cth) s 45(1).

35 [1987] FCA 266.

36 Ibid [14] (Gummow J).

37 *Freedom of Information Act 1982* (Cth) s 36(1).

and compromise the selection of high quality staff. The tribunal was particularly concerned that:

> there may be cases where adverse comment is made on an applicant which is unfounded or out of context. The goal of selecting the best staff in such cases would be facilitated by allowing applicants access to the reports.[38]

A similar argument was pressed in *Re Rindos and University of Western Australia.*[39] UWA drew a comparison with the practice in universities in the United States where the confidentiality convention does not exist, and claimed that little value was placed on referee reports obtained from that country.[40] However, the assertion was rejected due to lack of evidence to support it.[41]

However, more recently in *Van der Wall v University of Sydney* (*Van der Wall*)[42] the tribunal accepted that the equivalent 'in confidence' exemption under the New South Wales FOI legislation[43] applied. The tribunal, adopting a broader construction, held that disclosure would be contrary to the public interest.[44] It accepted the university's argument that there was a convention of confidentiality, and that its recruitment and selection processes would be compromised if confidentiality was not assured.[45] However, *Van der Wall* can probably be distinguished on its facts because the applicant was another academic who disapproved of the appointment.[46]

One issue not addressed in *Kamminga* was whether the exemption for breach of confidence applied to contractual, as well as equitable, breach.[47] Following that case, a number of universities adopted the practice of including a 'no guarantee of confidentiality' paragraph in their standard letters of request for referees' reports. Croucher criticises this practice because, in her view:

> universities left themselves exposed to having to argue under a provision like cl 13(b) of the FOI Act (NSW) when, in a somewhat overcautious or uncertain response to FOI legislation, some routinely included in their letters to referees seeking reports the disclaimer that, because of FOI legislation, strict confidentiality could not be guaranteed. Such a statement seems to undermine the assertion that the information was indeed invested with the necessary quality of confidence to attract a breach of confidence action.[48]

Moreover, she argues that referees' reports can and should be written in a considered and fair manner, and may even be negative or critical, as long as this is explained.[49]

---

38 *Kamminga*, [15].
39 [1995] WAICmr 20. See also *Freedom of Information Act 1992* (WA).
40 [1995] WAICmr 20, [34].
41 Ibid [66]. See s 102(1) of the *Freedom of Information Act 1992* (WA).
42 [2008] NSWADT 213. The relevant Act was the *Freedom of Information Act 1989* (NSW).
43 *Freedom of Information Act 1989* (NSW) sch 1 cl 13(b).
44 *Van der Wall*, [24], following *Howell v Macquarie University* [2008] NSWCA 26.
45 *Van der Wall*, [44] and [45].
46 Ibid [29].
47 *Kamminga*, [23].
48 Rosalind F Croucher, 'Confidentiality, Shadow Boxing, and Proper Processes – the FOI Challenge in Recruitment and Promotion Processes in Australian Universities' (2007) 38(2) *University of Toledo Law Review* 599, 605.
49 Ibid 615.

C Vice Chancellors' Salary Packages

In recent years, there have been many attempts by journalists and the National Tertiary and Education Union to find how out much Australian university vice chancellors earn. They argue that while universities (and especially their vice chancellors) complain about cuts to funding by governments, resulting in cuts to staffing levels, vice chancellors' salary packages continue to rise.[50]

In New South Wales, most universities were initially prepared to release part or all of these details, but some resisted, often relying on confidentiality clauses in the employment contracts of those vice chancellors. In *Fomiatti v University of Western Sydney (No 2)*[51] the tribunal found that the confidentiality exemption[52] applied to both the original employment contract and to two subsequent variations of it.[53] The New South Wales Ombudsman subsequently attacked this decision as essentially enabling universities to 'contract out' of the New South Wales *Freedom of Information Act* by pre-determining that exemption.[54]

More recently, universities have largely abandoned resistance to disclosure, and details of vice chancellors' salaries are now published routinely in annual reports and in newspapers. However, these are now often accompanied by unflattering headlines.[55] One has to wonder whether this is media revenge for an initial lack of transparency.

IV Whistleblower Protection

Universities occasionally experience what could be described as 'spectacular failures' in corporate governance. The University of Queensland is a recent example: that university's Vice Chancellor and Deputy Vice Chancellor resigned following allegations of nepotism in enrolment processes, which resulted in adverse findings by the Queensland Crime and Corruption Commission.[56] The Independent Commission Against Corruption (ICAC) also found that the Head and Deputy Head of the University of Newcastle Graduate School had engaged in corrupt conduct in failing to apply the University of Newcastle's plagiarism policy in relation to overseas students and to properly investigate plagiarism allegations.[57] Both of these cases came to light because whistleblowers were willing to come forward and press their concerns. Professor Ted Steele, a well-known whistleblower in the university sector, was dismissed from the University of Wollongong

50 See, for example, Anthony Gough, 'While Universities Cry Poor Over Funding Cuts, Some Vice-Chancellors are Well on their Way to Million-dollar Salaries' (20 April 2013) *The Courier Mail*. A similar debate rages in the United Kingdom. See, for example, David Lyttleton, 'Higher Education Pay Survey, 2013' (28 March 2013) *The Times Higher Education*.

51 [2006] NSWADT 210.

52 *Freedom of Information Act 1989* (NSW) sch 1, cl 13(a).

53 *Fomiatti v University of Western Sydney (No 2)* [2006] NSWADT 210, [16].

54 New South Wales Ombudsman, *Annual Report 2007-2008* (22 October 2008), 148.

55 See, for example, Amy McNeilage, 'Uni Bosses Earn 10 Times More than Staff' (25 August 2013) *Sydney Morning Herald*; Bernard Lane, 'Big Pay for the Poor Performers' (6 June 2012) *The Australian Higher Education*.

56 Ken Levy, *An Examination of Suspected Official Misconduct at the University of Queensland* (Crime and Misconduct Commission Queensland, 13 September 2013).

57 Independent Commission Against Corruption, *Report on Investigation into the University of Newcastle's Handling of Plagiarism Allegations* (30 June 2005).

(but subsequently reinstated) after he accused it of 'soft-marking' and lowering academic standards for full fee paying, and especially overseas, students.[58]

The Commonwealth and all Australian States and Territories have now enacted stand-alone whistleblowing laws,[59] as well as protective provisions into other legislation.[60]

Whistleblowing has also occurred in research environments, most famously at the University of New South Wales (UNSW) when members of his own research team made more than 450 separate allegations against Professor Bruce Hall (Hall affair). These included scientific fraud, financial fraud, workplace bullying and incorrect attribution of journal articles. UNSW commissioned a number of inquiries,[61] including one by former High Court judge and University of Technology Sydney Chancellor, Sir Gerard Brennan (Brennan inquiry). This triggered a number of legal actions by Professor Hall, including an attempt to restrain UNSW from publishing the Brennan inquiry's report[62] and to seek judicial review in relation to it;[63] and a defamation action against the Australian Broadcasting Commission.[64] Moreover, the Vice Chancellor and Dean of Medicine, Professors Rory Hume and Bruce Dowton, resigned. As one headline described it, it was '[a]n academic train crash that need not have happened'.[65]

Despite perceptions that Australians perceive whistleblowers in a negative light, a *Newspoll* survey carried out in 2012 for Griffith University and the University of Melbourne revealed 81 per cent support; although of that number only 53 per cent felt there was a general acceptance within Australian society.[66] A not dissimilar result occurred in a similar survey by the University of Greenwich conducted in the United Kingdom in the same year.[67]

Under common law employment rules (see also Chapter 14 by Seemann), employees owe their employer a duty of good faith that also includes a duty to bring to their employer's attention any issues of misconduct or corruption. However, they can find themselves exposed to adverse action, ranging from isolation to dismissal. As Commissioner Fitzgerald put it:

---

58 *NTEIU v University of Wollongong* [2001] FCA 1069.

59 See *Public Interest Disclosure Act 2013* (Cth); *Public Interest Disclosures Act 1994* (ACT); *Public Interest Disclosures Act 1994* (NSW); *Public Interest Disclosures Act 2008* (NT); *Whistleblowers Protection Act 1994* (Qld); *Whistleblowers Protection Act 1993* (SA); *Public Interest Disclosures Act 1992* (Tas); *Whistleblowers Protection Act 2001* (Vic); *Public Interest Disclosures Act 2003* (WA).

60 See, for example, *Government Sector Employment Act 2013* (NSW) s 69(1)(b) (public sector employees); *Fair Work (Registered Organisations) Act 2009* (Cth) ss 337A-337D (whistleblowers who report corruption of trade union or employer organisations or their officials).

61 For a chronology of the 'Hall affair', see Martin B Van Der Weyden, 'Managing Allegations of Scientific Misconduct and Fraud: Lessons from the "Hall affair"' (2004) 180 *Medical Journal of Australia* 150.

62 *Hall v University of New South Wales* (unreported, NSWSC, 25 February 2003, Levine J).

63 *Hall v University of New South Wales* [2003] NSWSC 542; *Hall v University of New South Wales* [2003] NSWSC 539; *Hall v University of New South Wales* [2003] NSWSC 669.

64 *Hall v Swan* [2009] NSWCA 371.

65 Linda Doherty, 'An Academic Train Crash That Need Not Have Happened' (27 April 2005) *Sydney Morning Herald.*

66 Griffith University, *Australia Not an 'Anti-dobbing' Culture: First Whistleblowing Survey Results* (Media Release, 6 June 2012).

67 Wim Vandekerchove, *UK Public Attitudes to Whistleblowing* (University of Greenwich, 15 November 2012) <http://ssrn.com/abstract=2176193>.

> If either senior officers and/or politicians are involved in misconduct or corruption, the task of exposure becomes impossible for all but the exceptionally courageous or reckless, particularly after indications that such disclosures are not only unwelcome but attract retribution.[68]

Despite statutory protections from reprisals,[69] whistleblowers are often not in a position of power relative to the person against whom the whistle is blown. Moreover, the allegations are often very serious. All of these factors combine to create disincentives for whistleblowing. Despite some modernisation of university governance structures following the introduction of the *National Governance Protocols* in 2003 (see also Chapter 2 by Varnham), senior university academics and administrators still wield significant power.[70] Moreover, universities are not always well equipped to investigate these types of matters internally. The jurisdiction to investigate, make findings and take appropriate action is found in the employment (usually through a staff enterprise agreement) or student relationship. Despite potential serious consequences, including dismissal or expulsion, these investigative processes are administrative in nature, and thus have nowhere near the sting of compulsion and consequences for failure to appear or to tell the truth as, for example, the royal commission powers of a regulatory body such as ICAC. Moreover, depending on the complexity of the case, it can also be difficult to investigate allegations with the necessary degree of confidentiality. This is particularly so for allegations involving adverse behaviours, such as workplace bullying, that often rely on witness evidence rather than a paper trail. Another complicating factor is that, by the time the whistle is blown, the workplace or classroom may already be dysfunctional.

Problems can also occur with the investigation process. For example, the Brennan investigation panel in the Hall affair was criticised for failure to include a scientist with relevant expertise.[71]

With such a volatile mix, it is no surprise that university whistleblowing systems can sometimes fail, with serious legal and reputational consequences.

From his insights into the Hall affair, Van Der Weyden articulates five key lessons for investigating scientific fraud or misconduct.[72] It is submitted that these lessons can and should be adopted and applied by universities more broadly as part of a comprehensive whistleblowing regime as follows:

Lesson 1: Allegations of a serious nature, and *always* when they involve senior staff, should be investigated by one or more investigators with appropriate qualifications and expertise, who are independent, and preferably external to the university. It may also be appropriate to ask an external regulator (such as ICAC) to investigate, or to at least have some input into any terms of reference or investigatory expertise. In cases involving

68 Gerald E Fitzgerald, *Report of a Commission of Inquiry Pursuant to Orders in Council* (Fitzgerald Report, 3 July 1989), 134.

69 For example, the *Public Interest Disclosures Act 1994* (NSW) s 9A.

70 Craig McInnis, 'Renewing the Place of Academic Expertise and Authority in the Reform of University Governance' in William G Tierney (ed), *Governance and the Public Good* (State University of New York Press, 2006), 119.

71 See, for example, Margaret Rice, 'A Call for Integrity in the Goldfish Bowl' (22 December 2006) *Sydney Morning Herald*,.

72 Van Der Weyden, above n 61, 149-151.

academic or scientific fraud, an investigation panel should include at least one person with expertise in the same discipline as the person under investigation.

Lesson 2: Investigators should be given clear terms of reference. In some cases, further allegations can come to light during the course of an investigation, which can add to its complexity and length. If so, universities should seek legal advice as to how those further issues should be investigated: either by widening existing terms of reference of the existing investigator or referring it to another investigator if different skills or expertise are required. It is absolutely critical that investigations are as thorough as possible, out of fairness to the person under investigation and to ensure procedural integrity.

Lesson 3: Universities should proactively manage confidentiality to minimise any risk of reprisal towards a whistleblower, and also manage the whistleblower's own expectations about confidentiality. This can be very challenging because whistleblowing laws include a requirement to keep the very fact of the disclosure and the identity of the whistleblower confidential. Whistleblowers do not always appreciate that their identity and evidence may, for reasons of procedural fairness, have to be disclosed, particularly where the only available evidence is their own testimony. Moreover, in a small workplace, the identity of the whistleblower may be immediately obvious. For these reasons, whistleblowers should never be given an unequivocal guarantee of confidentiality.

Lesson 4: Workplaces sometimes fall into a state of conflict and instability either before or during an investigation. Universities need to proactively manage these risks as early as possible: otherwise, a dysfunctional workplace, with consequent legal and reputational risks can result. This needs to be done in a way that does not result in any reprisals against the whistleblower (such as moving that person to another part of the university against his or her wishes), and expose the university to breach of applicable whistleblowing laws.[73]

Lesson 5: Decisions or outcomes flowing from an investigation should have high levels of transparency, although this does not necessarily mean these should be made public. Van Der Weyden criticises the process used in the Hall affair, where the Vice Chancellor, before making his decision, considered the Brennan inquiry report and Professor Hall's written response to it (which itself included reports from six experts in immunology).[74]

Van der Weyden's commentary is understandably concerned with integrity in investigations of scientific fraud. He and others have repeatedly called for the establishment of an independent office of integrity in scientific research.[75] However, and in fairness to Professors Hume and Dowton, the processes used in the Hall affair were overlaid with complex and unwieldy misconduct processes prescribed by UNSW's then current academic staff enterprise agreement.[76] Unfortunately, some of those processes still persist in a number of university staff agreements, despite attempts at reform.[77] The

73 See, for example, *Public Interest Disclosures Act 1994* (NSW) s 20; *Public Interest Disclosure Act 2013* (Cth) pt 2.

74 Van Der Weyden, above n 61, 151.

75 See, for example, Mark Solomons, 'Senator Defends Performance of Scientific Misconduct Inquiries after QUT case' (21 August 2013) *Courier Mail*.

76 *University of New South Wales (Academic Staff) Enterprise Agreement 2000*.

77 See, for example, cll 43 and 45 of the *University of Western Sydney Academic Staff Agreement* (2009-2012).

key lesson here is that any decision must always be, and be seen to be, justifiable and proportionate to the finding of fact made.

Managing the expectations of both the whistleblower and the subject of the complaint about the progress and outcomes of an investigation is also critical.[78] Whistleblowers can often feel aggrieved or suffer reprisals if the allegations ultimately prove to be untrue or unsubstantiated by the evidence, no matter how honestly they are made. They also need to understand that, in some cases, the evidence may simply not be sufficient to sustain the allegation, no matter how thorough the investigation.

Much has been said and written in scholarly articles and the media[79] about the moral courage it takes for people to blow the whistle: arguably, it takes even more moral courage for organisations to investigate thoroughly and fairly, and to decide outcomes proportionate to the findings made.

V Management of Personal and Health Information: Privacy vs Transparency Challenges

As with most other organisations, the information technology revolution has transformed records management in universities. Minimum standards of record keeping are mandated under State and Territory laws for Australian public universities.[80] While this has led to improved student services and business systems, universities have had to balance efficiency in record keeping with privacy considerations. In a networked 'cloud', and often also decentralised environment, the Registrar's Office is no longer the sole repository of student information; and the Human Resources Office is no longer the sole repository of staff information. Personal or health information may be collected, stored and used throughout a university for a myriad of purposes.

A *Privacy of Personal and Health Information in New South Wales*

In New South Wales, universities are required to manage personal and health records in accordance with, respectively, the *Privacy and Personal Information Protection Act 1998* (NSW) (*PPIP Act*) and the *Health Records Information Privacy Act 2002* (NSW) (*HRIP Act*).[81]

78 See New South Wales Ombudsman, *Managing Information Arising out of an Investigation: Balancing Openness and Confidentiality* (May 2009), 7-8.

79 See, for example, Robert W Kolodinsky, 'Moral Courage in Organisations: Doing the Right Thing at Work' (12 April 2012) 107 *Journal of Business Ethics* 547.

80 *Archives Act 1983* (Cth); *Territory Records Act 2002* (ACT); *State Records Act 1998* (NSW); *Public Records Act 2002* (Qld); *State Records Act 1997* (SA); *Archives Act 1983* (Tas); *Public Records Act 1973* (Vic); *State Records Act 2000* (WA).

81 See also *Privacy Act 1988* (Cth); *Health Records (Privacy and Access) Act 1997* (ACT); *Information Act 2002* (NT); *Information Privacy Act 2009* (Qld); *Personal Information Protection Act 2004* (Tas); *Information Privacy Act 2000* (Vic); *Health Records Act 2001* (Vic). South Australia and Western Australia do not have specific data privacy laws enacted but South Australia has a privacy committee and a privacy instruction requiring the South Australian government agencies to comply with a set of Information Privacy Principles. The *Freedom of Information Act 1992* (WA) includes some privacy principles applicable to Western Australian government agencies, for example s 32. The Australian Capital Territory has adopted a modified version of the *Privacy*

Students and staff are just as concerned as the broader community about how their personal and health information is managed, and are quite prepared to press a complaint for any perceived breach.[82] Privacy claims are also sometimes used by students as a means of seeking redress for grievances, principally around dissatisfaction with grades.[83] However, this is probably a reflection of the challenges that students face in trying to fit their particular grievance into a cause of action quite unsuited to deal with it.[84]

B Challenges for Universities – Students with Mental Health Issues

It has been acknowledged widely, both in Australia and overseas, that the number of university students with mental health issues is generally on the increase. This is particularly so for overseas students who, in many cases, are the first in their family to study at university and often carry the heavy burden of high expectations.[85] Moreover, the percentage of university students with mental health issues appears to be higher than for the general population.[86]

In this context, an increasing challenge for Australian universities relates to the use and disclosure of students' personal or health information to third parties (such as police, ambulance services or hospitals) where their behaviour poses a health and safety risk.

The most well-known example of a failure to properly manage privacy issues is the Virginia Tech University massacre in the United States in 2007, in which a student killed 32 students and staff and injured another 17 before taking his own life. An independent review convened by the then Governor of Virginia concluded that one of the main contributing factors was the failure within the various departments of the university (including the faculty, the student counselling service and campus security) to share information.[87] The student had a long history of mental health issues and student disciplinary action, and was known to various departments of the university. However, the resulting dots were never joined to identify the student as a risk and take remedial action. The investigation revealed that confusion about US federal privacy

---

Act 1988 (Cth), see *Australian Capital Territory Government Service (Consequential Provisions) Act 1994* (Cth).

82 See, for example, *AKL v University of Western Sydney* [2013] NSWADT 147.

83 See, for example, *DO v University of New South Wales* [2003] NSWADTAP 9 and *Vice Chancellor, Macquarie University v FM* [2005] NSWCA 192 and the commentary about that case in Patty Kamvounias and Sally Varnham, 'Legal Challenges to University Decisions Affecting Students in Australian Courts and Tribunals' (2010) 34 *Melbourne University Law Review* 140, 143.

84 Jim Jackson, Helen Fleming, Patty Kamvounias and Sally Varnham, *Student Grievances and Discipline Matters Project: Final Report* (Australian Learning and Teaching Council, 2009), 14.

85 See, for example, Helen M Stallman and Ian M Shocet, 'Prevalence of Mental Health Problems in Australian University Health Services' (June 2009) 44(2) *Australian Psychologist* 122; Sarah Wang, Susan Lee and Zahra T Wahid, *University Student Mental Health: The Australian Context* (Australian Medical Students' Association, 11 September 2013).

86 Stallman and Shocet, above n 85, 122.

87 Virginia Tech Review Panel, *Mass Shootings at Virginia Tech: Report of the Review Panel Presented to Governor Kaine, Commonwealth of Virginia* (Virginia Tech Report, August 2007).

laws[88] contributed to the tragedy despite the existence of an 'emergency exception' allowing for limited disclosure to protect health and safety.[89]

The panel's review revealed widespread lack of understanding, conflicting practice, and laws that were poorly designed to accomplish their goals.

> The widespread perception is that information privacy laws make it difficult to respond effectively to troubled students. This is only partially correct ... A narrow interpretation of the law is the least risky course, notwithstanding the harm that may be done to others if the information is not shared.[90]

In Australia, universities have to manage mental health issues for both staff and students in compliance with a large array of laws: privacy laws,[91] record keeping laws,[92] workplace health and safety laws,[93] disability discrimination laws[94] and, in the case of staff, industrial laws (particularly as these relate to adverse actions).[95] Navigating these can be a challenge for mental health professionals in university counselling and other health services.

However, in New South Wales at least, courts and tribunals have applied a broad approach to the term 'use' in the context of disclosure within an organisation. In *AW v Vice-Chancellor, University of Newcastle*[96] the tribunal held that disclosure of a student's health information by that university's complaints officer to a person in the university's counselling service did not amount to a breach of Health Privacy Principle 10[97] which prescribes limits on the use of health information. This was because the disclosure had occurred for the primary purpose of investigation of the student's complaint. However, how broadly 'use' will be interpreted depends on the primary purpose for which the health or personal information is collected in the first place. Any secondary purposes will depend on how closely these are related to the primary purpose.

The *PPIP Act*, like the equivalent Commonwealth legislation,[98] has a regime for privacy protection in the form of 'Information Protection Principles' that sets out requirements for dealing with personal information. Relevantly, the *PPIP Act* contains exemptions in some limited circumstances: where the agency believes, on reasonable grounds, that disclosure is necessary to prevent or lessen a serious and imminent threat

---

88 See *Americans with Disabilities Act 1990*, the *Family Education and Privacy Act 1974* (*FERPA*) and the *Health Insurance and Portability and Accountability Act 1996*.

89 20 USC § 1232G(B)(1)(I) (2006)

90 Virginia Tech Report, above n 87, 63.

91 See above n 81.

92 See above n 80.

93 See *Work Health and Safety Act 2011* (Cth); *Work Health and Safety Act 2011* (ACT); *Work Health and Safety Act 2011* (NSW); *Work Health and Safety (National Uniform Legislation) Act 2011* (NT); *Work Health and Safety Act 2011* (Qld); *Work Health and Safety Act 2012* (SA); *Work Health and Safety Act 2012* (Tas); *Occupational Health and Safety Act 2004* (Vic); *Occupational Safety and Health Act 1984* (WA).

94 See *Disability Discrimination Act 1992* (Cth); *Discrimination Act 1991* (ACT); *Anti-Discrimination Act 1977* (NSW); *Anti-Discrimination Act 1992* (NT); *Anti-Discrimination Act 1991* (Qld); *Equal Opportunity Act 1984* (SA); *Anti-Discrimination Act 1998* (Tas); *Equal Opportunity Act 2010* (Vic); *Equal Opportunity Act 1984* (WA).

95 *Fair Work Act 2009* (Cth) pt 3-1 (adverse action provisions).

96 [2008] NSWADT 86, [27]-[29].

97 *Health Records Information Privacy Act 2002* (NSW) sch 1, cl 10.

98 *Privacy Act 1988* (Cth).

to the life or health of the individual concerned or another person;[99] disclosure to a law enforcement agency for the purpose of ascertaining the whereabouts of an individual who has been reported to the police as a missing person;[100] and in circumstances where it is reasonably necessary to investigate an offence, where there are reasonable grounds to believe that an offence has been committed.[101]

Likewise, the *HRIP Act* contains similar exemptions.[102] However, disclosure under any of these exemptions is not necessarily straightforward: each potential disclosure must be considered and based on the particular merits of the case. A particularly difficult challenge is deciding when a threat is sufficiently 'serious and imminent' to warrant disclosure.

In order to rely on this exemption, the following elements must be satisfied: first, that there are reasonable grounds for the belief or view held, and secondly that the threat is *both* serious and imminent. In *McMahon v RMIT University*[103] the Tribunal held that a reasonable belief need not be a wholly subjective belief or even factually correct. However, there must be circumstances where it is reasonable to form that belief at the time a decision to disclose is made. In order to be 'serious', the threat must be important or grave.[104] In order to be 'imminent' the threat must be pending or likely to occur at any moment, applying its ordinary dictionary meaning.[105] The Tribunal held that the provision is to be construed narrowly and cannot, for example, be relied upon as a means to resolve any liability or insurance coverage concerns.[106] The Australian Law Reform Commission has criticised the requirement of imminence as too restrictive: it argues that this could lead agencies to take an overly conservative view and refrain from taking preventative action until it is too late.[107] Moreover, it also fails to take account of cases where a person's mental health deteriorates over a period of time. For international students, the consequences can be particularly severe: in many cases, they do not have the support of nearby family or friends.

Conversely, there is the question of a university's duty of care towards a student with mental health issues. The extent of such a duty has been considered in the United States in the context of prevention of student suicide where two lower courts were prepared to impose a duty of care in claims for wrongful death.[108] In *Shin v Massachusetts Institute of Technology*, the court found that there was a 'special relationship' that existed between the university and student, because that university was aware of previous suicide attempts by that student and the student had indicated an intention to try and commit

99 *Privacy and Personal Information Protection Act 1998* (NSW) s 18(1)(c).

100 *Privacy and Personal Information Protection Act 1998* (NSW) s 23(5)(b).

101 *Privacy and Personal Information Protection Act 1998* (NSW) s 23(5)(d)(ii).

102 *Health Records and Information Privacy Act* 2002 (NSW) sch 1: Health Information Privacy Principles 10(1)(c), 11(1)(c), 11(1)(h) and 11(1)(j).

103 [2012] VCAT 1423, [82], [84].

104 Ibid [84].

105 Ibid [84]. See also *FM v Vice-Chancellor, Macquarie University* [2003] NSWADT 78, [55].

106 See, for example, *MT v Director General, New South Wales Department of Education and Training* [2004] NSWADT 194, [194]-[197]; *Director General, New South Wales Department of Education and Training v MT (GD)* [2005] NSWADTAP 77, [75].

107 Australian Law Reform Commission, *For Your Information: Australian Privacy Law and Practice* (ALRC Report 108, 12 August 2008), paras 25.82-25.87.

108 *Schieszler v Ferrum College* 236 F Supp 2d 602 (WD Va 2002); *Shin v Massachusetts Institute of Technology* No 020402, 2005 WL 1869101 (Mass Super Ct, 27 June 2005).

suicide again.[109] As one commentator argues, universities can find themselves stuck 'between a rock and a hard place', despite exemptions in emergencies.[110] In Australia, it is at least conceivable that failure to disclose could give rise to a prosecution for breach of work health and safety laws: alternatively, disclosure where the threat is 'serious' but not sufficiently 'imminent' risks exposure to a claim for breach of privacy.

Gray argues that, because of these restrictions, US universities are reluctant to notify parents or others about a student's suicide attempts or inclinations. Some have adopted the 'Joffe Model', where students who attempt, or intend to commit, suicide are required to attend four mandatory counselling sessions, or else face expulsion.[111] However, others have not done so for fear of claims of unlawful disability discrimination. A variation on this model has been adopted in Australia, where students can be required to take involuntary leave of absence on medical grounds, thus minimising the need to deal with any unacceptable behaviour as student misconduct.[112]

However, the difficulty with these methods is that they involve an element of compulsion, and thus expose institutions to claims for unlawful disability discrimination. Gray argues:

> Instead of the duty to prevent suicide, the duty to notify parents or others about a student's suicidal intent is more likely to become a universal change in higher education law. Amending FERPA to allow universities to feel less exposed to liability when disclosing information regarding a student's suicidal ideation will help universities discharge the duty, if any, to notify and may correspondingly encourage courts to impose this duty.[113]

In the end, there is and can never be a single or ideal strategy for managing student mental health issues. One criticism is that most university models focus more on risk rather than support and intervention strategies. It is submitted that the *PPIP Act* only serves to entrench such attitudes with the requirement for a threat to be imminent as well as serious, and in a climate where students are already often reluctant to disclose a mental illness (if diagnosed) or obtain help, for fear of stigma or unfair treatment. Instead, removal of the imminence requirement, as recommended by the Australian Law Reform Commission, will go a considerable way to encourage a more positive focus on the health of the individual affected, as well as risk. Or, if you like: a more transparent, and less defensive, approach.

VI Conclusion

In an increasingly regulated environment, universities are under increasing pressure to embrace and incorporate transparency into all aspects of their operations: how

109 *Shin v Massachusetts Institute of Technology* No 020402, 2005 WL 1869101 (Mass Super Ct, 27 June 2005).

110 Carrie E Gray, 'The University-Student Relationship Amidst Increasing Rates of Suicide' (Annual 2007) 31 *Law and Psychology Review* 137.

111 Ibid 150. The Joffe model is a reference to Paul Joffe, 'An Empirically Supported Program to Prevent Suicide in a College Student Population' (2008) 38 *Suicide and Life Threatening Behaviors* 87.

112 See, for example, Australian National University, *Medical Leave Statute* (2007) and *Medical Leave Rules* (2013).

113 Gray, above n 110, 152.

they teach and assess students; how they recruit and promote employees; and how they investigate complaints, to name a few. Arguments about attacks on institutional autonomy or academic freedom no longer appear to hold sway. As discussed in this chapter, secrecy only allows problems to escalate and fester. Transparency instead fosters a culture of questioning and innovation: the very principles and values that universities are supposed to champion.

PART TWO

The Law and Higher Education

Chapter 7

The Contract Between the University and the Student

Francine Rochford

I Introduction

It is commonly understood that the relationship between universities and their students is governed, at least partially, by contract.[1] This seems to be conceded even in jurisdictions in which the matter has not been the subject of authoritative pronouncement, as in the case of Australian jurisdictions. However, this was not the historical position. Case law established that historically the relationship was primarily one of status – a continuing, institutional conferral of position as an incident of a relationship rather than as a consequence of agreement. This chapter reconciles these two positions, as least as far as can be attempted with the current state of the law in Australia. University structures and practices[2] have changed in line with the contractual understanding to such an extent that contractual intention is likely to be established, however this is not inconsistent with the existence of internal rules and procedures aligned with a status relationship, failure to follow which may trigger administrative remedies.

This analysis will briefly articulate the 'status' interpretation of the relationship between the student and the university, and recount the transition from status to contract. The analysis will then consider cases which provide authority to ground a contractual interpretation of the modern relationship, and provide an analysis of the formation of such a contract. However, the relationship between the university and the student is rarely litigated on the basis of contract, potentially because of imbalances of power, the availability of more expeditious statute-based or administrative remedies, or because of the lack of attraction of contractual remedies. This suggests that the contractual designation is at the least unhelpful, and perhaps simply a rhetorical explication of the relationship.

---

1 See David Palfreyman, 'Phelps … Clark … and Now Rycotewood? Disappointment Damages for Breach of the Contract to Educate' (2003) 15 *Education and the Law* 237. In the United States, see *Ross v Creighton University*, 957 F 2d 410 (7th Cir 1992); Alec Samuels, 'The Student and the Law' (1972-1973) 12 *Journal of the Society of Public Teachers of Law* 252 posits a hybrid relationship.

2 See Jane Kelsey, 'Privatizing the Universities' (1998) 25 *Journal of Law and Society* 51.

II From Status to Contract – the Reinterpretation of the University-Student Relationship

Historically, the university was described as a 'little municipality' and the relationship was one of 'status'; a condition conferred by law and not created by the acts of the parties in which the 'creation, continuance or relinquishment and the incidents are a matter of sufficient social or public concern.'[3] There have been a number of cases in which courts have rejected the contractual analysis as, 'although perhaps in one sense ... not quite absolutely and metaphysically a misnomer, but in a legal point of view it is a misnomer – it is not a legal contract.'[4]

Under a 'status' analysis, students stand in relation to the university as corporators stand in relation to other forms of corporation. The relationship is governed by the by-laws of the university corporation (see also Chapter 1 by Squelch). Typically, Australian students – both undergraduate and postgraduate – become members of the university pursuant to the statute creating the university.[5] As members, students submit to the incidents of that relationship. Like members of a corporation, students 'enjo[y] their membership of the foundation as a result of having been admitted to office therein.'[6] Membership designates status. This does not discount the operation of contract in non-domestic matters, but where a matter is internal or 'domestic' the court declines jurisdiction. The visitor has exclusive jurisdiction[7] which is an element of the 'status' relationship.[8]

3 See Geoffrey MacCormack, 'Status: Problems of Definition and Use' (1984) 43 *Cambridge Law Journal* 361; Francine Rochford, 'The Relationship Between the Student and the University' (1998) 3 *Australia & New Zealand Journal of Law and Education* 28.

4 *Thomson v University of London* (1864) 33 LJCh 625, 638.

5 For example, in New South Wales the *University of Sydney Act 1989* (NSW) s 4 establishes the university, and it is incorporated by s 5. In the case of this university, students and graduates form part of the university (s 4). Similar provisions exist in the *University of New South Wales Act 1989* (NSW) ss 4-5, *University of Newcastle Act 1989* (NSW) ss 4-5, *University of Technology, Sydney Act 1989* (NSW) ss 4-5, *University of Wollongong Act 1989* (NSW) ss 4-5, *University of New England Act 1993* (NSW) ss 4-5 and the *University of Western Sydney Act 1997* (NSW) ss 5-6. In the Northern Territory the *Charles Darwin University Act* s 4 continued the corporate form of the previous *Northern Territory University Act*, and s 7 includes graduate and undergraduate students in the composition of the university. In South Australia, the *University of Adelaide Act 1971* (SA) s 4 continues the university as a body corporate (s 4(3)) composed, *inter alia*, of students graduate and undergraduate (s 4(2)). Section 4 of the *University of Tasmania Act 1992* (Tas) continues the existence and corporate form of the University of Tasmania, and the university includes undergraduate students (s 5). Interestingly, s 5(2) allows any person within the statutory constitution of the university to 'make a statutory declaration that he or she has a conscientious objection to being a member of the University', and give it to the Vice Chancellor, upon which he or she will cease to be a member of the university. Victorian university statutes were re-enacted in a more modern form in 2009-2010 and bear significant commonality. The *University of Melbourne Act 2009* (Vic) continues the university as a body corporate (s 4) including students as members (s 4). Other Victorian legislation follows this model: see the *Monash University Act 2009* (Vic), *University of Ballarat Act 2010* (Vic), *La Trobe University Act 2009* (Vic), *Royal Melbourne Institute of Technology Act 2010* (Vic).

6 Peter M Smith, 'The Exclusive Jurisdiction of the University Visitor' (1981) 97 *Law Quarterly Review* 610, 639.

7 *Thomson v University of London* (1864) 33 LJCh 625, 634.

8 *R v University of Hull Visitor; Ex parte Page* [1993] AC 682; *R v University of Nottingham; Ex parte K* [1998] ELR 184.

The existence of the exclusive visitorial jurisdiction provides one explanation for the relative rarity of cases litigated in relation to the university-student relationship, because 'internal matters' have traditionally not been reported in authorised law reports. The presumption that university disputes are not suitable for judicial pronouncement is now widely challenged[9] and the jurisdiction of the visitor has been severely attenuated by statute, or removed altogether.[10] Even where it has been held to apply, Australian courts have, on occasion, found the visitorial jurisdiction compatible with the contractual analysis.[11] In *Bayley-Jones v University of Newcastle*,[12] Allen J concluded that there was no difficulty in construing a contract which incorporated the terms arising from the rules of the university, but which was within the exclusive jurisdiction of the visitor.

In the absence of a visitor with exclusive jurisdiction over matters of internal discipline, internal university disciplinary processes (see also Chapter 9 by Lindsay) and the university ombudsman (see also Chapter 10 by Stuhmcke, Olliffe and Evers) still exist. However, these may be consistent with the analysis of the relationship as contractual – in the same manner as a contractual arbitration clause. Nevertheless the contractual analysis is given priority in modern analyses of the relationship. Since the 1960s, commentators have favoured a contractual interpretation of the university-student relationship.[13] It is argued that a 'rigorously followed contract theory could provide a means for creating and preserving student rights.'[14] These analyses often posit that the remedies available to students seeking a contractual remedy are more protective than the 'internal' rules of a university and, where it existed, the exclusive jurisdiction of the visitor.[15]

III The Student Contract

Universities vary in their statutory form,[16] relationship with students and enrolment procedures. A typical analysis of the contract between the student and the university identifies enrolment or registration as the point at which contractual terms must be

9 David M Price and Peregrine WF Whalley, 'The University Visitor and University Governance' (1996) 18 *Journal of Higher Education Policy and Management* 45, 48; Peter M Smith, 'The Exclusive Jurisdiction of the University Visitor' (1981) 97 *Law Quarterly Review* 610; William Ricquier, 'The University Visitor' (1978) 4 *Dalhousie Law Journal* 647.

10 See generally Bruce Lindsay, 'Complexity and Ambiguity in University Law: Negotiating the Legal Terrain of Student Challenges to University Decisions' (2007) 12 *Australia and New Zealand Journal of Law and Education* 7 (see also Chapter 9 by Lindsay).

11 *Murdoch University v Bloom and Kyle* [1980] WAR 193, 198. See also *Thomas v University of Bradford* [1987] AC 795, 823-824.

12 (1990) 22 NSWLR 424.

13 HWR Wade, 'Judicial Control of Universities' (1969) 85 *Law Quarterly Review* 468, 471. See also DC Holland, 'The Student and the Law' (1969) 22 *Current Legal Problems* 70, quoted in JW Bridge 'Keeping Peace in the Universities: the Role of the Visitor' (1970) 86 *Law Quarterly Review* 531, 548.

14 Note, 'Developments in the Law – Academic Freedom' (1968) 81 *Harvard Law Review* 1045, 1146.

15 See, for example, *R v Committee of the Lords of the Judicial Committee of the Privy Council acting for the Visitor of University of London; Ex parte Vijatunga* [1988] 1 QB 322.

16 Modern universities are typically statutory corporations, although some charter corporations still exist. Other forms, such as trusts, are not typical in universities following the English tradition.

available to the student who accepts those terms either impliedly or expressly.[17] However, the parameters of that contract, and whether it contains an explicit promise to educate, are not clear. Judicial authority is scarce in the Australian jurisdictions.[18] Authorities in the United States typically involve private institutions.[19] In the United Kingdom, which bears closer resemblance to Australia's publicly funded higher education environment, cases seem to have resolved that there is a contract to educate.[20] In New Zealand, there is judicial authority[21] that the relationship between the student and the university is contractual and some universities have embarked on a process designed to make the contract explicit.[22] Often, however, a contract is conceded, and the parties' assumption that the enrolment agreement contains the contractual terms has meant that the claim has often not been fully interrogated. Australian courts have not had the opportunity to make a strong precedent in relation to the contractual point, largely because most cases have been brought in relation to consumer protection legislation,[23] discrimination,[24] freedom of information[25] or in application for administrative remedies.[26] Moreover, the cases that have run to trial have tended to involve self-represented litigants, and so will often be unsatisfactory in their analysis or argument for the purposes of useful precedent.[27] The court can only make rulings based on the arguments presented by the

17 Sally M Furay, 'Legal Relationship Between the Student and the Private College or University' (1970) 7 *San Diego Law Review* 244, 263.

18 See cases referred to below n 27.

19 *Anthony v Syracuse University* 130 Misc 249, 223 NY Supp 796 (Sup Ct 1927), rev'd 224, App Div 487, 231 NY Supp 435 (1928).

20 *Clark v University of Lincolnshire and Humberside* [2000] 1 WLR 1988; [2000] 3 All ER 752; *Moran v University College Salford* [1994] ELR 187; *D'Mello v Loughborough College of Technology* [1970] CLY 2888; (17 June 1970) *The Times*; *Sammy v Birkbeck College* (3 November 1964) *The Times*; *Lyall v Service* (1863) 2 M 115; *Jex-Blake v Senatus Academicus of University of Edinburgh* (1873) 11 M 784; *Cadells v Balfour* (1890) 17 R 1138 and *Green v Peterhouse* (10 February 1896) *The Times*. See Dennis J Farrington and David Palfreyman, *The Law of Higher Education* (2nd ed, Oxford University Press, 2012).

21 *Grant v Victoria University of Wellington* [2003] NZAR 185. For analysis, see Julia Pedley and Virginia Goldblatt, 'The Development of a Student Contract and Improvement in Student Disciplinary Procedures at Massey University' (2007) 12 *Australia and New Zealand Journal of Law and Education* 73.

22 Pedley and Goldblatt, above n 21.

23 See *Yee Tak On v Dr Linda Hort (ANU College)* [2012] FMCA 391 and *Ejueyitsi v Bond University* [2012] FCA 1514. See generally Francine Rochford, 'Traders of the Lost Ark – lectures and liability' (2001) 13 *Education and the Law* 127; Sally Varnham, 'Straight Talking, Straight Teaching: Are New Zealand Tertiary Institutes Potentially Liable to Their Students Under Consumer Protection Legislation?' (2001) 13 *Education and the Law* 303; Patty Kamvounias and Sally Varnham, 'Getting What They Paid For: Consumer Rights of Students in Higher Education' (2006) 15 *Griffith Law Review* 306; PH Clarke, 'University Marketing and the Law: Applying the Trade Practices Act to Universities' Marketing and Promotional Activities' (2003) 8 *Deakin Law Review* 304.

24 See *Hinchliffe v University of Sydney* [2004] FMCA 85; *University of Wollongong v Metwally* (1984) 158 CLR 447; *W v Flinders University of South Australia* [1998] HREOCA 19; *Sluggett v Flinders University of South Australia* [2000] HREOCA 26; *Elmaraazy v University of New South Wales, Professor Dennis, Professor Heseltine and Professor Richards* [1996] HREOCA 17.

25 See *Luck v University of Southern Queensland* [2009] FCAFC 73.

26 See *Griffith University v Tang* (2005) 221 CLR 99; *Ex parte King; Re University of Sydney* (1943) 44 SR (NSW) 19 and *Ex parte Forster; Re University of Sydney* [1963] SR (NSW) 723.

27 See *Edwards v Commonwealth (No 2)* [2012] FMCA 702, [6] and *Dudzinski v Kellow* [1999] FCA 390.

parties, and self-represented litigants will often not present coherent legal arguments based on precedent.

The other factor diminishing the amount or value of precedential authority is the existence of internal dispute resolution processes. 'Most if not all Australian universities ... possess hybrid tribunals' – the universities originally exercised purely consensual jurisdiction, and retain domestic features, but they now have statutory support.'[28] Whereas this was previously represented by the jurisdiction of the visitor, 'domestic' dispute resolution procedures now appear to be at least partially grounded in contract. Typically, the university's internal procedures will have to have been exhausted before a court will exercise jurisdiction, although if the procedure is grounded in contract (rather than an application for an administrative law remedy), this is probably not mandatory.[29]

IV The Contract to Enrol

A university-student contract will typically be analysed in two contexts: the contractual force of rules, policies and procedures incorporated on enrolment and a more generalised contract to educate. This will often be analysed as a 'contract to enrol' followed by a 'contract to educate'. Traditional contract law principles will determine whether terms are incorporated and promissory using an offer-acceptance analysis.[30] By this analysis, the terms must be in existence and available at the point of enrolment to avoid any post-enrolment terms failing for want of consideration.[31] However, this matter is not often analysed in great detail: '[t]he bench generally assumes that the provisions of the university-student contract are to be found in all of the statements contained in the admissions application, the registration form, the school's rules and regulations and the catalogue'.[32] It is possible to analyse the publication of a prospectus (or handbook) as an invitation to treat, an offer of a place to a student as a contractual 'offer', and the student's completion of enrolment procedures as the 'acceptance'. Consideration could be in the form of the student narrowing their opportunity to accept another university offer[33] or possibly as compliance with the university rules. Alternatively, it could be argued that the student's application through the relevant admissions bodies was an 'offer', and a university's provision of a place was a contractual 'acceptance', but that would be less likely, given that students typically elect several courses.

There are potential inconsistencies in the argument that there is a 'contract to enrol' in this form: the capacity to accept a second round offer, the process of confirmation of enrolment, and the typical failure of universities to make any effort to enforce the 'contract' against students who withdraw before confirmation, but these inconsistencies are not irreconcilable with the contractual analysis, particularly contracts affected by legislation. Legislative 'cooling off' periods provide similar examples. The process of

28 JRS Forbes, *Disciplinary Tribunals* (2nd ed, Federation Press, 1996), 12-13.
29 *Clark v University of Lincolnshire and Humberside* [2000] 3 All ER 752.
30 See N Seddon, R Bigwood and M Ellinghaus, *Cheshire & Fifoot Law of Contract* (LexisNexis Butterworths, 2012), ch 3.
31 'Payment' for the promise by providing a benefit or suffering a detriment.
32 Alvin L Goldman, 'The University and the Liberty of Its Students – A Fiduciary Theory' (1966) 54 *Kentucky Law Journal* 643, 652.
33 Farrington and Palfreyman, above n 20, 338.

annual re-enrolment is also not an overwhelming obstacle to the contractual analysis, given the existence of rolling contracts and other variants. In any event, 'formal offer and acceptance is only one way of manifesting assent. There is no reason in principle why contracts cannot be formed in stages, provided the circumstances or prior practice makes this clear or adequate notice is provided. This insight is neither revolutionary nor reactionary'.[34] The enrolment process, carried out with no opportunity for negotiation of terms, and purportedly incorporating great volume of material by reference, is not dissimilar to a range of standard form commercial transactions.

Few Australian cases expressly consider the matter, and even very recent cases have been ambivalent about the contractual aspect. In *Edwards v Commonwealth (No 2)*[35] the court analysed the contract of employment between a medical student, the Department of Health and Ageing, and the University of Sydney in the provision of a scholarship for a medical place with conditions attached. The court rejected Edwards' argument that the university's cancellation of his enrolment was a breach of contract (amongst other things), noting:

> Assuming that Mr Edwards' relationship with the University should be analysed as one of contract, then he has failed to persuade me that any of its actions were in breach of his rights under a contract. … If his enrolments were a matter of contract, then the rules of the Medical School, including their relevant amendments from time to time, formed part of the terms of the contract under which he hoped to be provided with a medical education.[36]

Even if there is a contract, it is unlikely that the entirety of the relationship is contractual. The existence of legislation and associated statutory instruments will attract the administrative law jurisdiction, and enforceability of university rules is not dependent on contract. The relationship between the terms of the proposed contract and the rules of the university was considered in *Gramotnev v Queensland University of Technology*[37] in connection with employees of the university. Gramotnev argued that incorporation of the relevant policies, procedures and statutes was effected by reference in the letter of appointment, which stated that '[t]he terms and conditions of your appointment are prescribed by …'.[38] The university argued that there was a distinction between contractual terms and conditions and non-contractual documents that are 'not contractually binding or in many instances even capable of being contractually binding'.[39] There is significant authority to support this distinction.[40] Whether terms have been incorporated into a contract by reference depends on whether 'a reasonable person in the position of a promisee would conclude that a promisor intended to be contractually bound by a particular statement'.[41] In *Soliman v University of Technology*

---

34 Randy E Barnett, 'Consenting to Form Contracts' (2002) 71 *Fordham Law Review* 627, 644.
35 [2012] FMCA 702.
36 Ibid [139].
37 [2013] QSC 158. See also *Victoria University of Technology v Wilson* [2004] VSC 33 and *University of Western Australia v Gray (No 20)* [2008] FCA 498.
38 Ibid [13].
39 Ibid [15].
40 Including, in relation to university rules, *Soliman v University of Technology, Sydney* [2008] FCA 1512 and subsequent proceedings.
41 *Soliman v University of Technology, Sydney* [2008] FCA 1512, [65].

Sydney, the preamble of the contract indicated that the contract was 'subject to' the relevant provisions of the documents referred to – including the University Act and by-laws. The court noted that '[t]hese are legislative instruments capable of alteration from time to time without any involvement of the applicant. This indicates … [that the reference] identifies relevant information capable of affecting the parties' contractual relations rather than documents intended to be binding and enforceable as part of their contractual relations'.[42]

Similar arguments apply to the relationship between a student contract and university statutes, rules and by-laws. These are the context within which the contract is to be read, and will potentially constrain the contract, rather than being documents incorporated into the contract by reference.[43] Questions of timing and sufficiency of notice become irrelevant, since no notice is required to support the enforceability of legislation or legislative instruments as would be the case in incorporation of a contractual promise. Using this argument, university by-laws and other statutory instruments made by properly constituted authority and within power are not contractual and decisions made under those instruments are more appropriately challenged through administrative law. Student disciplinary procedures, including academic progress and misconduct, will typically fall within this category and will also be subject to the conventions of natural justice (see also Chapter 9 by Lindsay).

There remains a large and variable 'grey' area consisting of course documentation, subject descriptions and searchable database and handbook entries that may be found to be promissory and incorporated into the university-student contract. Most course documentation will be subject to express disclaimer (for example, the institution may expressly state that they may not offer a particular subject or a particular course or may withdraw or vary a subject or course at any time), in which case, consumer protection legislation may be a less costly and more expeditious avenue of redress for a student (see also Chapter 8 by Kamvounias).

V The Contract to Educate

A 'contract to educate' follows on from the 'contract to enrol', and potentially contains promises to provide learning and teaching facilities. A 'failure to teach' case may be appropriately founded in contract only where a university has withdrawn a course, or where a subject necessary to complete a course is unavailable – so that the university has not complied with the terms of its own prospectus.[44] Again, these claims would be affected by legislation and the university's own rules, the university's capacity under those rules and its compliance with the appropriate procedures. Alternative grounds – that the university failed to comply with an implied term that services or facilities were available, would more commonly be asserted under consumer protection legislation.

42 Ibid [67].

43 A similar argument was asserted in *New South Wales Lotteries Corporation Pty Ltd v Kuzmanovski* [2011] FCAFC 106.

44 *University of Texas Health Science Center at Houston v Babb* 646 SW 2d 502 (1982) (Texas Court of Appeal) – subject to the reservation that the institution may modify it within reason: *Foley v Benedict* 55 SW 2d 805 (1932); Farrington, above n 20, 338.

There is a longstanding reluctance on the part of the courts to adjudicate on matters involving academic or pastoral judgment.[45] Courts are not, in general, willing to overrule the decision of an examiner. In relation to a general 'standard' to which an institution is required to teach, there are few relevant authorities. In *Ross v Creighton University*[46] the US court recognised that, although the relationship between the university and the student was, at least in part, contractual, a claim for breach of contract could not be sustained for a failure to educate to a certain level. The policy reasons for such reluctance included the reluctance of the court to revisit expert academic decisions and to place themselves in the position of examiners. In *Yee Tak On v Dr Linda Hort (ANU College)*[47] although the proceedings were primarily concerned with the application for summary dismissal, Neville FM did take the opportunity to say:

> It is not uncommon that courses in educational institutions ... are not delivered to the absolute, highest quality. ... However, it is one thing for educational courses, to be, among other things, of varying quality: it is quite another for the delivery of a course to provide a base, in law, for a dissatisfied student to claim the relief sought.[48]

VI Contractual Remedies

Even if a contract exists between the student and the university, this does not mean that a contractual remedy will best serve a student's interests. The contract is not freely negotiated, and more closely resembles a *contrat d'adhésion*[49] – particularly if the contract does incorporate the rules of the institution. A student will rarely be seeking to terminate the contract, given the multiple opportunities available to withdraw from the course without penalty. A student may be seeking relief to prevent suspension of a course, or to prevent a university from withdrawing a course, in which case equity might provide injunctive relief in the event that there is no more suitable common law remedy.[50] However, the university's capacity to make such a decision, and the procedures by which it is implemented, are typically clearly delineated in university legislation in which case administrative remedies are more appropriate.

It is arguable that a contractual claim may provide a more attractive option if damages are sought. Contractual damages are based on the principle that the award should place the plaintiff in the position they would occupy if the defendant had performed,[51] including expectation loss or loss of benefits or wasted expenditure or

45 *Griffith University v Tang* (2005) 221 CLR 99, 156 (Kirby J); Farrington and Palfreyman, above n 20, 333. See Sally Varnham, 'Decisions of Academic Judgement and Discipline in New Zealand Tertiary Institutions: Do Cheats Prosper?' (2001) 13 *Education and the Law* 390; see the decision in *Re Humzy-Hancock* [2007] QSC 34, analysed in J Joy Cumming, 'Where Courts and Academe Converge: Findings of Fact or Academic Judgment' (2007) 12 *Australia and New Zealand Journal of Education and the Law* 97.

46 957 F 2d 410 (1992).

47 [2012] FMCA 391.

48 Ibid.

49 'Take it or leave it': Farrington, above n 20, 338.

50 DH Clark, 'Rethinking the Role of Specific Relief in the Contractual Setting' in J Berryman, *Remedies: Issues and Perspectives* (Carswell, 1991), 141.

51 *Robinson v Harman* (1848) 1 Ex 850; 154 ER 363.

reliance damages,[52] and loss of opportunity.[53] A student may typically be seeking to recover lost expenditure as a result of enrolment – moving expenses, loss of income, residential and living expenses that would not otherwise be outlaid. Reliance losses are likely to feature in an award of damages in this area, since it is difficult to quantify the benefit that was to have been received under the contract.[54] *Buckingham v Rycotewood College*[55] provides relatively marginal authority from the United Kingdom for the payment of damages for the delivery of a poorly delivered course and enables the Australian authority of *Baltic Shipping v Dillon*[56] to be applied. This case is an exception to the ordinary rule that damages are not available for distress where the contract involved an express or implied promise to provide pleasure, entertainment, relaxation or the prevention of molestation or vexation.

However, the student would bear the onus of proving the extent of damage, must prove that the damage was caused by the breach, damages recoverable are limited by the remoteness principle and the student is required to mitigate loss.[57] All of these factors weigh heavily against a student in a generalised 'failure to teach' action.

VII Conclusion

Despite the ubiquity of the contractual analysis, some commentators are unconvinced of the welfare-enhancing capacity of the contractual regime, claiming that contract theory 'unduly favours the institution and has been of limited effectiveness in conferring rights upon students'.[58] The university is in the position to make the terms of the contract, without negotiation. The student would have to establish breach and damage and causation are difficult to prove. There are few relevant cases to provide strong precedent for an intending plaintiff, and those cases that exist are contradictory or insufficient. This is due in part to the existence of multiple and more expedient mechanisms for resolution of disputes between students and universities, and also to the predominance of unrepresented litigants in this area. Arguments presented in litigation are frequently poorly defined, and courts and tribunals are frequently not provided with sufficient information to enable a useful judicial statement – nor have the claims enabled them to do so. Accordingly, the contractual analysis remains a theoretical possibility amongst a range of arguably more appropriate mechanisms for resolving disputes between universities and students. Where this is the case many universities have sought to clarify the relationship by defining the limits of the potential contract, thus potentially reifying the relationship.

It is likely, given the very strong consumer protection environment, that generalised 'failure to teach' cases will be determined on the basis of consumer protection law,

52 *Commonwealth v Amann Aviation Pty Ltd* (1991) 174 CLR 64.
53 *Sellars v Adelaide Petroleum NL* (1994) 179 CLR 64, 102.
54 *McRae v Commonwealth Disposal Commission* (1951) 84 CLR 377.
55 Re liability, *Buckingham v Rycotewood College* (unreported, 26 March 2002, Oxford County Court); and re the calculation of damages, *Rycotewood* (unreported, 28 February 2003, Warwick Crown Court).
56 (1993) 176 CLR 344.
57 See Seddon, Bigwood and Ellinghaus, above n 30, ch 23.
58 See above n 14.

which is not reliant on contract, (see also Chapter 8 by Kamvounias) and challenges to decisions of the university will be determined on the basis of administrative law (see also Chapter 9 by Lindsay).

Given the poor performance on contract in legal challenges by students against universities, it is surprising that contract continues to feature so prominently. The euphemistic inclusion of 'student contracts' to assert expectations on students suggests that the contractual analysis is a shift towards transparency in the relationship, rather than a legal interpretation of the relationship.

Chapter 8

Students and the Australian Consumer Law

Patty Kamvounias

I Introduction

Changes to government policies and approaches to higher education have resulted in a rapid expansion of the sector and a 'marketisation' of the academy.[1] Students are increasingly being characterised as 'customers' of the services provided by higher education institutions whether in the public or in the private sector.[2]

Australia has had a single national consumer law since 1 January 2011. The Australian Consumer Law (ACL)[3] introduced provisions dealing with unfair terms in consumer contracts,[4] replaced provisions on implied terms in consumer contracts with new consumer guarantees in relation to goods and services,[5] and retained the general

1 Gabriel Baldwin and Richard James, 'The Market in Australian Higher Education and the Concept of Student as Informed Consumer' (2000) 22(2) *Journal of Higher Education Policy and Management* 139; Kathryn McMahon, 'Universities and Market Discourse' (2001) 27(1) *Monash University Law Review* 105; Francine Rochford, 'The Contested Product of a University Education' (2008) 30(1) *Journal of Higher Education Policy and Management* 41; Mike Molesworth, Richard Scullion and Elizabeth Nixon (eds), *The Marketisation of Higher Education and the Student as Consumer* (Routledge, London, 2011).

2 See, for example, Damien Considine, 'The Loose Cannon Syndrome: University as Business and Students as Consumers' (1994) 37 *Australian Universities' Review* 36; Patty Kamvounias, 'Students as Customers and Higher Education as Industry: A Review of the Literature and the Legal Implications' (1999) 3(1) *Academy of Educational Leadership Journal* 30; Patty Kamvounias and Sally Varnham, 'Getting What They Paid For: Consumer Rights for Students in Higher Education' (2006) 15 *Griffith Law Review* 306; Eddie Mark, 'Student Satisfaction and the Customer Focus in Higher Education' (2013) 35(1) *Journal of Higher Education Policy and Management* 2; David Palfreyman, 'Quality & Consumerism in Higher Education' (2013) 17(3) *Perspectives: Policy and Practice in Higher Education* 107.

3 The Australian Consumer Law (ACL) appears in sch 2 to the *Competition and Consumer Act 2010* (Cth) (*CCA*). The ACL applies as a law of the Commonwealth to the conduct of corporations: *CCA* s 131(1). State and Territory application legislation applies the ACL provisions to the conduct of persons generally: *Australian Consumer Law (Tasmania) Act 2010* (Tas) ss 5-6; *Consumer Affairs and Fair Trading Act 1990* (NT) ss 26-27; *Fair Trading Act 1992* (ACT) ss 6-7; *Fair Trading Act 1987* (NSW) ss 27-28; *Fair Trading Act 1989* (Qld) ss 15-16; *Fair Trading Act 1987* (SA) ss 13-14; *Fair Trading Act 1999* (Vic) ss 8-9; and *Fair Trading Act 2010* (WA) ss 18-19.

4 ACL ch 2 pt 2-3.

5 ACL ch 3 pt 3-2 div 1.

prohibition on misleading or deceptive conduct[6] and the prohibition of specific false or misleading representations.[7]

This chapter examines the application of these key provisions in the ACL to students and higher education providers. The chapter begins with a discussion of the legal relationship between students and education providers which is key to the application of the unfair contract terms provisions. This is followed by an analysis and examples in the context of higher education of the consumer guarantees and misleading or deceptive conduct. The chapter concludes with observations about issues in this area of the law.

II Unfair Terms in Consumer Contracts

A *Students and Educational Institutions – Is the Relationship Contractual?*

The relationship between a student and a private school or college is based on the contract entered into by the parties[8] so that any dispute that may arise, for example, about the payment of fees, will be determined pursuant to ordinary contract law principles.[9] The relevant court or tribunal will look to the terms of the contract to decide whether or not fees claimed are payable in the circumstances. In *Commonwealth v Ling*[10] the court implied a term into each of the agreements between students and a private college that fees paid would be refunded in full if the students were unable to obtain the necessary visa to enable them to study in Australia.

In relation to public universities, there is case authority in other jurisdictions[11] that the relationship between a student and a university is partly based on contract.[12] There is no clear judicial authority on this point in Australia, although in relation to private universities, there is authority that the source of student rights 'is primarily contractual'.[13] There have been cases where the Australian courts have been prepared to assume that the relationship between a student and a public university should be analysed as one of contract[14] and the omission to plead a breach of contract in conjunc-

6 ACL ch 2 pt 2-1 s 18.

7 ACL ch 3 pt 3-1.

8 In the case of private schools, the contract would be between the school and the student's parents or guardians.

9 In relation to private schools, see *Bosnich v Christ Church Grammar School* [2011] VCAT 1738; *Mears v Sydney Anglican Schools* [2013] NSWSC 535. In relation to private colleges, see: *LeFroy v Australasian College Broadway* [2011] NSWCTTT 287.

10 (1993) 44 FCR 397. This was confirmed on appeal: *Ling v Commonwealth* (1994) 51 FCR 88.

11 See *Clark v University of Lincolnshire and Humberside* [2000] 1 WLR 1989; [2000] 3 All ER 752; *Grant, Woolley, Staines and Grant v Victoria University of Wellington* (unreported, NZHC, Wellington Registry, CP 312/96, Ellis J, 13 November 1997).

12 See also Francine Rochford, 'The Relationship Between the Student and the University' (1998) 3(1) *Australia and New Zealand Journal of Law and Education* 28; Martin Davis, 'Students, Academic Institutions and Contracts – a Ticking Time Bomb?' (2001) 13(1) *Education and the Law* 9; Ruth Deech, 'The Student Contract' (2009) 43(1) *The Law Teacher* 3.

13 *Orr v Bond University* (unreported, QSC, No 2337/96, Dowsett J, 3 April 1996), 6.

14 See *Brackenreg v Northern Territory University* [2004] NTMC 43; *Edwards v Commonwealth (No 2)* [2012] FMCA 702, [139].

tion with an application for judicial review has been questioned.[15] Nonetheless, in a recent challenge to a decision to suspend a student for misconduct, Beech-Jones J was not so certain that the relationship was governed by a contract between the university and the student.[16] See also Chapter 7 by Rochford where the nature of the legal relationship between students and universities is discussed in more detail.

B ACL Provisions on Unfair Contract Terms

The relationship between a student and an educational institution must be a contractual relationship for the unfair terms provisions in the ACL to apply.

An unfair term in a standard form 'consumer contract' will be void and unenforceable.[17] For the purposes of the ACL, a 'consumer contract' is a contract for the supply of goods or services to an individual who acquires the goods or services wholly or predominantly for personal, domestic or household use or consumption.[18] All contracts will be presumed to be 'standard form', that is, contracts that have not been negotiated, unless proved otherwise.[19] To determine whether a contract is not standard form, the court must consider a number of relevant matters, including: the bargaining power of the parties, whether the contract was prepared by one party before any discussion occurred between the parties, whether others were also required to accept or reject the terms of the contract in the form they were presented, whether others were given an effective opportunity to negotiate the terms, and whether the terms take into account the specific characteristics of the parties or the particular transaction.[20]

A term of a consumer contract will be unfair if it causes significant imbalance in the rights and obligations of the parties, is not reasonably necessary to protect the legitimate interests of the supplier, and causes detriment to the acquirer (whether financial or otherwise).[21] To determine whether a term is 'unfair', the court must consider the contract as a whole[22] and must also determine whether the term is 'transparent', that is, whether or not it is expressed in reasonably plain language, legible, presented clearly and readily available to any party affected by the term.[23]

'Unfair' terms may include terms that permit one party (but not the other) to, for example, avoid or limit performance of the contract, terminate the contract, vary the terms of the contract, renew or not renew the contract, unilaterally vary the characteristics of the services supplied under the contract or unilaterally determine whether the contract has been breached or to interpret its meaning.[24]

---

15 *Griffith University v Tang* [2004] HCATrans 227 (Kirby J).
16 *X v University of Western Sydney (No 3)* [2013] NSWSC 1329, [43]-[44].
17 ACL s 23(1).
18 ACL s 23(3).
19 ACL s 27(1).
20 ACL s 27(2).
21 ACL s 24(1).
22 ACL s 24(2).
23 ACL s 24(3).
24 ACL s 25(1). For a discussion of these provisions in the ACL see SG Corones, *The Australian Consumer Law* (2nd ed, Lawbook Co, 2013), 221-254; Justin Malbon and Luke Nottage (eds), *Consumer Law and Policy in Australia and New Zealand* (Federation Press, 2013), 129-153.

If there is a contract between a student and an educational institution, it would not be difficult for that contract to be characterised as a standard form 'consumer contract'[25] to supply educational services to an individual for personal use and so within the scope of the ACL. All educational institutions should be reviewing their policies and the terms in any contracts they have with their students to ensure compliance with the ACL; the risk of non-compliance is that a term that is found to be 'unfair' will be not be enforceable against a student.

C Examples of Unfair Contract Terms in Education Contracts

There is little case law on the new unfair contracts regime and no case authority yet involving students. However, there are some cases where the terms of an education contract have been examined to determine whether or not they are 'unfair' pursuant to other remedial legislation.[26] These are discussed here as examples of terms that may also be 'unfair' and unenforceable under the ACL.

A school's refund policy was not an 'unfair' term in circumstances where the parents were given the opportunity to read the policy in Chinese before signing the contract.[27] A requirement of one term's fees in lieu of notice of withdrawal from a school was also not 'unfair'.[28]

However, the following terms have been found to be 'unfair': a term that allowed a cooling off period of only five days if a student wanted to cancel their enrolment[29] and a term that allowed students to be dismissed if they failed to maintain a certain number of points under the college's 'professional conduct system'.[30] A term requiring payment of all course fees if a student was prevented from completing a course because of a serious medical condition or an accident through no fault of their own would also be considered 'unfair'.[31]

Unfair terms in consumer contracts are also regulated in the United Kingdom where investigations of universities' contracts with students have found that, depending on the circumstances, it may be 'unfair' for universities to have terms allowing unilateral changes to courses and regulations[32] and terms allowing the imposition of academic sanctions when students owe small amounts or the debt is disputed.[33]

---

25 See *Zhang v Kilmore International School Ltd* [2007] VCAT 1977.

26 For example, *Consumer Claims Act 1998* (NSW); *Fair Trading Act 1999* (Vic).

27 *Zhang v Kilmore International School Ltd* [2007] VCAT 1977, [34]-[36].

28 *Bosnich v Christ Church Grammar School* [2011] VCAT 1738.

29 *Ncube v Open Colleges Pty Ltd* [2012] NSWCTTT 79, [6].

30 *Lan v International College of Management Sydney Pty Ltd* [2007] NSWCTTT 299. This term was unenforceable because the system was purely arbitrary and there were no guidelines for the number of points that could be deducted for any infringement.

31 See *Ncube v Open Colleges Pty Ltd* [2012] NSWCTTT 79, [6].

32 Office of Fair Trading, *Unfair Contract Terms Guidance Annexes – Guidance for the Unfair Terms in Consumer Contracts Regulations 1999* (September 2008).

33 Office of Fair Trading, *Universities Terms and Conditions: An OFT Report* (February 2014).

III Consumer Guarantees

A The ACL Consumer Guarantees

The ACL includes consumer guarantees based on the implied warranties and conditions that applied under previous consumer protection legislation but providing a separate statutory cause of action.[34] The consumer guarantees are automatically granted by the ACL to every supply of goods or services in trade or commerce to a consumer and cannot be waived or excluded.[35] Liability for failure to comply with consumer guarantees cannot therefore be avoided by inserting statements to that effect in course materials or handbooks.

Remedies in relation to the consumer guarantees exist independently of the law of contract and depend on whether the failure to comply with the guarantee is a 'major' failure and whether the failure can be remedied.[36] If the failure to comply is a major failure or cannot be remedied, the ACL allows the consumer to decide which remedy is preferred, including compensation for any reduction in the value of the services or termination of the contract for the supply of the services and compensation for money paid.[37] Consumers also have rights to compensation for any reasonably foreseeable loss or damage incurred.[38]

For educational institutions, the relevant guarantees are those that apply to persons supplying services to consumers. The ACL imposes guarantees that the services will: be rendered with due care and skill;[39] be fit for a particular purpose made known to the supplier;[40] achieve a result made known to the supplier or person by whom any prior negotiations in relation to the acquisition of the services was conducted[41] and be supplied in a reasonable time (unless a term in the contract deals with this).[42]

'Services' are defined to include a contract for or in relation to the provision of, or the use or enjoyment of facilities for amusement, entertainment, recreation or instruction.[43] Services such as teaching, research supervision, consultancy, accommodation, recreation, parking etc would therefore fall within the statutory definition.

Services must be provided to a 'consumer' for the consumer guarantees to apply. For the purposes of the consumer guarantees, if the amount payable for the services is less than $40,000, the person who has acquired services of any kind is a 'consumer'; or if the amount payable exceeds $40,000, the person is a 'consumer' only if the services were

---

34 Under *Trade Practices Act 1974* (Cth) s 74 terms were implied into contracts for the supply of services to a consumer. If suppliers did not supply their services with due care and skill, consumers could bring legal action for breach of contract. The ACL now provides both the consumer guarantees and the remedies for failure to comply with the guarantees. See Malbon and Nottage, above n 24, 97-127; Jeannie Marie Paterson, 'The New Consumer Guarantee Law and the Reasons for Replacing the Regime of Statutory Implied Terms in Consumer Transactions' (2011) 35(1) *Melbourne University Law Review* 252.

35 ACL s 64.

36 ACL pt 5-4 div 1.

37 ACL pt 5-4 div 1.

38 ACL pt 5-4 div 2.

39 ACL s 60(1).

40 ACL s 61(1).

41 ACL s 61(2).

42 ACL s 62.

43 ACL s 2(1)(b)(ii).

'of a kind ordinarily acquired for personal, domestic or household use or consumption'.[44] Only if the amount payable for educational services exceeds $40,000 will a court have to consider the nature of the services but it would be unlikely for a court to characterise education as anything other than a service acquired for personal use. Students would therefore fall within the definition of 'consumer' for the purposes of the ACL.

B ACL Guarantee that Services will be Rendered with Due Care and Skill

'Due care and skill' is not defined in the ACL but it is not a guarantee that services be provided at a standard of excellence.[45] The Explanatory Memorandum to the Bill that introduced the ACL states that the service provider must have 'an acceptable level of skill' in the particular area of service supplied and must exercise 'due care' in supplying the service.[46] Applicants would need to adduce evidence of acceptable standards (that would depend on matters such as the type of services, any applicable industry standards and any representations as to the skill or experience of the service provider) and evidence of failure to comply with those standards. The need to prove failure to exercise care and skill means an action for breach of the consumer guarantees will overlap with a common law action in negligence (see also Chapter 15 by Horton, Smith and Tisbury).

The cases indicate the difficulties facing students who allege lack of due care and skill in the provision of educational services. The courts will consider evidence *inter alia* of the qualifications and experience of teaching staff, teaching and examination practices and reports of external course reviewers[47] to determine whether the learning environment provided was 'appropriate'.[48] Courts have also noted that 'the attainment of an education requires input from … the learner'[49] and that it is reasonable to allow adult students to take responsibility for their own learning 'in the face of clear guidance set out in the course documents and reiterated by [teaching staff]'.[50] In dismissing claims by disgruntled failed students, the courts have also commented on the absence of applications from other students in a similar position[51] and noted that '[t]he success of the overwhelming majority of students … is itself testimony of the quality of the teaching'.[52]

Nonetheless, curriculum design, admission standards and research supervision have been identified as potential problem areas for higher educational institutions

44 ACL s 3(3).

45 In *Mears v Sydney Anglican Schools* [2013] NSWSC 535, [5] the court was satisfied that the services were provided at a reasonable standard of care. Commentators disagree as to whether 'due care and skill' is the same as the common law standard of 'reasonable care' in negligence. See Stephen Corones, 'Consumer Guarantees and the Supply of Educational Services by Higher Education Providers' (2012) 35(1) *University of New South Wales Law Journal* 1, 10; Russell V Miller, *Miller's Australian Competition and Consumer Law Annotated* (36th ed, Lawbook Co, 2014), 1662.

46 Explanatory Memorandum, Trade Practices Amendment (Australian Consumer Law) Bill (No 2) 2010 (Cth) [7.59].

47 *Abramova v Oxford Institute of Legal Practice* [2011] EWHC 613 (QB), [69].

48 *Qayam v Shillington College* [2007] NSWCTTT 620.

49 Ibid.

50 *Abramova v Oxford Institute of Legal Practice* [2011] EWHC 613 (QB), [68].

51 *Yee Tak On v Dr Linda Hort (ANU College)* [2012] FMCA 391, [23].

52 *Abramova v Oxford Institute of Legal Practice* [2011] EWHC 613 (QB), [69].

and the guarantee of 'due care and skill'.[53] Due care needs to be taken to ensure that courses meet minimum threshold standards set out in the Australian Qualifications Framework (see also Chapter 1 by Squelch) and satisfy any relevant professional body requirements, to ensure admission of students with appropriate academic skills, and to ensure supervisors have appropriate qualifications and experience.

C ACL Guarantees that Services Will Be Fit for a Particular Purpose or Achieve a Result Made Known to the Supplier

The 'purpose' and/or 'result' made known to a secondary school/supplier of educational services, for example, might include entry to university.[54] The 'purpose' and/or 'result' of a university legal education, for example, will include but might be much broader than entry into the legal profession.[55]

Corones has identified the following conduct that may constitute a breach of the consumer guarantees as to fitness for purpose: offering courses that are not accredited but require accreditation by the relevant professional bodies; allowing international students into courses without ensuring they have appropriate level of English language proficiency; failing to provide English language support services to international students after enrolment; failing to provide appropriate library and computing services to all students; and failing to provide a learning environment that complies with health and safety legislation.[56]

Another possible breach of the guarantee that an educational service be fit for a disclosed purpose may occur where students advise a university of their special needs before enrolment and a university accepts the enrolment but fails to provide the support the students require (see also Chapter 13 by Dickson).

IV Misleading or Deceptive Conduct and False or Misleading Representations

A Overview

Section 18 of the ACL prohibits persons in trade or commerce from engaging in conduct that is misleading or deceptive or likely to mislead or deceive.[57] In addition to this general prohibition, the ACL also prohibits specific false or misleading representations about goods or services, the most relevant prohibitions in connection with the

53 Corones, above n 45, 11-19.

54 See *Weir v Geelong Grammar School* [2012] VCAT 1736, [160].

55 See Lynden Griggs, 'Knowing the Destination Before the Journey Starts – Legal Education and Fitness for Purpose' (2007) 14 *eLaw Journal* 315.

56 Corones, above n 45, 20.

57 This section replaced *Trade Practices Act 1974* (Cth) s 52 which prohibited a 'corporation' in trade or commerce engaging in misleading or deceptive conduct. See Francine Rorke, 'The Application of the Consumer Protection Provisions of the *Trade Practices Act 1974* (Cth) to Universities' (1996) 12 *Queensland University of Technology Law Journal* 176; Jim Jackson, 'The Marketing of University Courses Under Sections 52 and 53 of the *Trade Practices Act 1974* (Cth)' (2002) 6 *Southern Cross Law Review* 106; Philip H Clarke, 'University Marketing and the Law: Applying the Trade Practices Act to Universities' Marketing and Promotional Activities' (2003) 8 *Deakin Law Review* 304.

supply of educational services being: false or misleading representations that services have sponsorship, approval, performance characteristics, accessories, uses or benefits;[58] and false or misleading representations that the person making the representation has a sponsorship, approval or affiliation.[59]

A contravention of the general prohibition in s 18 is often also a contravention of one of the specific prohibitions in s 29.[60] The main difference is that a breach of the general prohibition on misleading conduct may result in a claim for damages but does not constitute an offence under the ACL, while breach of a specific prohibition can incur a penalty or a fine.[61]

The litigation advantage of s 18 is that there is no need for a student applicant to prove a 'contract' with an educational institution and there is no need to satisfy a court that a student is a 'consumer' for the student to bring an action for misleading or deceptive conduct.

B Are Education Providers Trading Corporations?

ACL prohibitions are directed at the conduct of 'persons' including 'corporations'.[62] A 'corporation' is defined to mean a body corporate that: is a foreign corporation, is a trading corporation formed within the limits of Australia, or is incorporated in a Territory.[63]

Incorporated private education providers that charge fees for courses are clearly 'trading' corporations subject to the ACL. The position of public providers is less clear. All Australian public universities are statutory corporations but does this mean they are also 'trading corporations'? (see Chapter 1 by Squelch).

In a case involving a staff challenge to the validity of a certified agreement between the University of Western Australia and the National Tertiary Education Industry Union, the full court of the Federal Court held that the university was a 'trading corporation' because its trading activities (for example, buying, selling and renting property, investing, sale of publications, parking and student accommodation) were 'a substantial, in the sense of non-trivial, element albeit not the predominant element of what the university does'.[64] The court did not have to decide whether the provision of educational services within the statutory framework of the *Higher Education Funding Act 1988* (Cth) was 'trading' and different views were expressed on this question.[65] Subsequent statutory changes, allowing universities to set their own fees and encouraging competition between universities and non-university providers, mean it is highly likely that the education services provided by universities will be considered to be

58 ACL s 29(1)(g).
59 ACL s 29(1)(h).
60 See, for example, *Oldroyd v Sea School International Pty Ltd* [2013] NSWCTTT 361.
61 Penalty or fine of up to $1,100,000 for corporations and up to $200,000 for individuals: see ACL ch 4 pt 4-1, Offences relating to unfair practices; ACL ch 5 pt 5-2 div 1, Pecuniary penalties.
62 *CCA* s 131(1).
63 *CCA* s 4(1). 'Corporation' is defined in accordance with s 51(xx) of the Commonwealth Constitution because the Act relies on its validity on *inter alia* the 'corporations' power in s 51(xx).
64 *Quickenden v O'Connor* (2001) 184 ALR 260, [51].
65 *Quickenden v O'Connor* (2001) 184 ALR 260, [51] (Black CJ, French J); [106] (Carr J).

provided by 'trading corporations'. Indeed, in *Mathews v University of Queensland*, Spender J simply accepted that the university was 'a corporation' for the purposes of the student's claim for misleading or deceptive conduct.[66]

C Conduct of Education Providers 'In Trade or Commerce'?

The phrase 'trade or commerce' is defined in the ACL as meaning 'trade or commerce within Australia or between Australia and places outside Australia and specifically includes any business or professional activity whether or not carried on for profit.[67]

Section 18 of the ACL is only concerned with conduct '*in* trade or commerce' which the High Court has said involves activities which of their nature bear a trading or commercial character.[68] Generally, internal communications between employees will not occur 'in trade or commerce' but external communications by businesses to promote their commercial interests will be conduct 'in trade or commerce'.[69]

Conduct 'in trade or commerce' would therefore include representations to prospective students about the merits of a course[70] whether made in websites or course guides[71] or in any written contracts or oral statements made by the education provider. Publication of marketing brochures and material,[72] a fee schedule,[73] and an advertisement of a full fee paying postgraduate course[74] have all been held to be conduct 'in trade or commerce'.

A distinction must also be made between representations in promotional materials and representations or communications with students after they have enrolled. If a lecturer provides information in a lecture that is misleading, the application of the ACL may be precluded because the conduct is not 'in trade or commerce'. For example, representations that lecturers would provide statements of goals and nature of assessments and be available for discussion with students are not conduct 'in trade or commerce'.[75]

D Conduct that is Misleading or Deceptive or Likely to Mislead or Deceive

The onus is on the student to prove a contravention of the statutory prohibitions. An allegation of misleading conduct or a false representation will not be sustained if, for example, the education provider submits evidence to support the statements in

66 *Mathews v University of Queensland* [2002] FCA 414, [10].

67 ACL s 2. See *Shahid v Australasian College of Dermatologists* [2008] FCAFC 72, [30]; *Monroe Topple & Associates Pty Ltd v Institute of Chartered Accountants in Australia* [2001] FCA 1056, [147] [150]; [2002] FCAFC 197, [78].

68 *Concrete Constructions (NSW) Pty Ltd v Nelson* (1990) 169 CLR 594, 602.

69 Corones, above n 24, 88.

70 *Venianakis v International College of Australia* [2000] VCAT 1456.

71 *Shahid v Australasian College of Dermatologists* [2008] FCAFC 72.

72 *Weir v Geelong Grammar School* [2012] VCAT 1736.

73 *Rowe v Emmanuel College* [2013] FCA 939, [46].

74 *Fennell v Australian National University* [1999] FCA 989.

75 *Mathews v University of Queensland* [2002] FCA 414. See also *Plimer v Roberts* (1997) 150 ALR 235, 258; *Chapman v Luminis Pty Ltd (No 5)* [2001] FCA 1106, [178]; and Francine Rochford, 'Traders of the Lost Ark – Lectures and Liability' (2001) 13(2) *Education and the Law* 127, 132-139.

prospectuses and elsewhere about affiliations with relevant professional bodies;[76] or to indicate that the material in the handbook, the advertising for the course and other material is consistent with what was made available to the student.[77] If there is no evidence that the applicant was misled about the qualifications required for a course or the nature of the teaching in the course;[78] or no evidence in the pre-contractual documents and statements that conveys a misrepresentation as alleged by the student,[79] the action will fail.

However, if there is evidence of a false representation or misleading conduct, then the ACL will be contravened. Examples include: representations about online degrees when the college was not authorised to grant degrees or enrol students;[80] misrepresentations about the accreditation of childcare courses;[81] misrepresentations about paid employment opportunities when what was being offered was a training course;[82] misrepresentations that students could obtain a licence to work on completion of a course;[83] and failing to inform students that the course in which they had enrolled did not have the required approval.[84] It would also be misleading to promote courses that had been superseded and to guarantee successful completion of a qualification and subsequent employment.[85]

Steve Jones was reportedly the first student to commence legal proceedings against a university because of misleading advertising.[86] Jones' concerns about a master's degree at Deakin University were about outdated study materials and the fact he was attending classes with undergraduate students using the same materials and having the same assessments.[87] Soon after, in *Fennell v Australian National University*, Sackville J commented that such cases 'might be said to be a by-product of a relatively new phenomenon in Australian tertiary education, namely competition among Universities for full fee paying graduate students'.[88] His Honour was considering a claim by a postgraduate student that he was induced by a false representation to enrol in an MBA program. The court found that a newspaper advertisement about the degree was ambiguous and reflected carelessness on the part of those who drafted or approved it because it gave the impression that the university would be responsible for organising a work placement for every applicant in the program when the course handbook made it clear that prime responsibility for finding a placement was with

---

76 *St Clair v College of Complimentary Medicine Pty Ltd* [2008] NSWCTTT 1309.

77 See *Qayam v Shillington College* [2007] NSWCTTT 620; and *Weir v Geelong Grammar School* [2012] VCAT 1736.

78 *Cui v Australian Tesol Training Centre* [2003] NSWCTTT 329.

79 *Edwards v Commonwealth (No 2)* [2012] FMCA 702.

80 *ACCC v Australasian Institute Pty Ltd* (unreported, ACCC media release 251/99, 22 December 1999).

81 *ACCC v Black on White Pty Ltd* [2001] FCA 372.

82 *ACCC v Zanok Technologies Pty Ltd* [2009] FCA 1124.

83 *Venianakis v International College of Australia* [2000] VCAT 1456.

84 *Oldroyd v Sea School International Pty Ltd* [2013] NSWCTTT 361.

85 See Australian Skills Quality Authority Report, *Marketing and Advertising Practices of Australia's Registered Training Organisations* (Australian Government, 16 December 2013).

86 Geoffrey Maslen, 'His Master's Angry Voice' (12 July 1994) *The Bulletin* 27.

87 Ibid. The matter was settled so a court never considered the merits of the claim which nonetheless generated adverse publicity for the university at the time.

88 [1999] FCA 989, [1].

the individual student.[89] However, the court dismissed the proceedings because it was satisfied on the evidence, that Fennell had been informed at interviews before he enrolled that while the university would assist, he was primarily responsible for the work placement arrangements.[90]

The prohibition in s 18 of the ACL is often used by businesses against competitors who engage in conduct that is misleading or likely to mislead. Rival education providers have brought legal actions for misleading conduct in relation to, for example, the use of deceptively similar business names[91] and misrepresentations in the course of comparative advertising.[92]

E Appropriateness of Available Remedies

Should a student succeed in establishing that an educational institution has engaged in misleading conduct, the court or tribunal must then determine the appropriate remedy. The remedies available under the ACL include declarations, injunctions and corrective advertising orders but in most cases students will be seeking damages.[93]

Where there is evidence of loss, students have been compensated. In some cases, damages have been assessed as the full cost of course fees that had been wasted on courses that had been misrepresented to the students.[94] Claims for lost earnings and costs for textbooks and sundries such as internet, photocopying, and paper have also been considered.[95] Claims for compensation for distress and inconvenience are often found not justified on the evidence[96] although this is not always the case.[97]

But damages claims will not be successful if no loss or damage has been pleaded or there is no evidence of loss or damage.[98] In *Fennell v Australian National University*, Sackville J noted that after he completed the MBA, the student secured employment at a much higher salary and commented that it was unclear why damages should be awarded 'without taking into account the economic benefits flowing from completion of the program'.[99]

---

89 Ibid [34].

90 *Fennell v Australian National University* [1999] FCA 989, [44].

91 *College of Law Limited v Australian National University* [2013] FCA 492 deals only with pre-trial issues in relation to the discovery of certain documents. See Hannah Low, 'College of Law Name Dispute Settled' (23 May 2014) *Australian Financial Review* 32.

92 *Re Typing Centre of NSW Pty Ltd v Northern Business College Limited* [1989] FCA 115.

93 Damages for breach of ACL provisions are available pursuant to ACL s 236.

94 See *Venianakis v International College of Australia* [2000] VCAT 1456; *Oldroyd v Sea School International Pty Ltd* [2013] NSWCTTT 361. Even though the applicants got some benefit in terms of learning, completion of the courses did not lead to the employment qualifications that had been promised.

95 *Brackenreg v Northern Territory University* [2004] NTMC 43, [199].

96 See *Fennell v Australian National University* [1999] FCA 989; *Venianakis v International College of Australia* [2000] VCAT 1456.

97 *Shahid v Australasian College of Dermatologists* [2008] FCAFC 72, [255]. See also David Palfreyman, 'Phelps … Clark … and now Rycotewood? Disappointment Damages for Breach of the Contract to Educate' (2003) 15(4) *Education and the Law* 237.

98 *Mathews v University of Queensland* [2002] FCA 414, [23]; *Kwan v University of Sydney Foundation Program Pty Ltd* [2002] NSWCTTT 83.

99 [1999] FCA 989, [10].

V Conclusion

The ACL sets standards of conduct for all those acting in trade or commerce. Education providers, both public and private, should have measures in place to ensure the fairness of their rules and policies, the quality of their programs and the accuracy of their promotional material. Higher fees may mean higher student expectations of their educational experience. In a more competitive and costly higher education environment, ACL training should be mandatory so that all education providers and their staff understand their responsibilities under the ACL.

The ACL cannot provide redress for all student complaints. If students are dissatisfied with their results or with decisions about their academic progress or conduct, the ACL cannot assist because nothing in the ACL allows for the review of adverse decisions. For this, students need to rely on administrative law principles so that the fairness of decision-making processes can be reviewed through internal dispute resolution processes (see also Chapter 9 by Lindsay and Chapter 10 by Stuhmcke, Olliffe and Evers) or externally (see also Chapter 11 by Kamvounias).

Chapter 9

Student Conduct and University Discipline

Bruce Lindsay

I Introduction

Higher education in Australia remains dominated by public universities and the general approach to governance is to conceive of the university in the historic sense of a self-regulating educational body of higher learning and research (see also Chapter 1 by Squelch and Chapter 2 by Varnham).

The institutional and purposive context of the university is significant for an understanding of the legal situation of the student, of concepts and norms of student conduct, correlative norms of transgression and misconduct, and institutional handling of such transgression. This chapter is concerned with the fair and rational treatment of students in the public university system – in short, the application of administrative justice to the university's dealings with its students in disciplinary cases.[1] Universities possess broad, enabling powers to give effect to schemes for the regulation of conduct and discipline. The enabling Act will include powers to enact subordinate legislation, rules and/or policy, including for discipline (see also Chapter 1 by Squelch).

It is within this framework that universities enact disciplinary rules, which are commonly expressed as a proscriptive *misconduct* code. The misconduct or disciplinary code falls within the overarching discretion of the university to maintain order and good governance. 'Misconduct' will not necessarily be limited strictly to what is in the written code,[2] but there will nevertheless be some form of constraint on the scope of 'misconduct': '[Q]uestions of misconduct, moreover, inevitably carry overtones of moral and social evaluation and judgments about what sort of behaviour is acceptable'.[3] There needs to be at least something discreditable[4] in the impugned conduct.

---

1 Similar standards of treatment are likely apply to students attending private higher education providers, in particular as implied terms of the student's contract with the provider, although questions of the student contract and its terms are not settled in Australia. See *Bayley-Jones v University of Newcastle* (1990) 22 NSWLR 424, 436; *Herring v Templeman* [1973] 3 All ER 569.

2 *Soliman v University of Technology, Sydney* [2012] FCAFC 146, [28]-[34].

3 DJ Galligan, *Due Process and Fair Procedures: A Study of Administrative Procedures* (Clarendon Press, 1996), 372. Misconduct in an academic context need not necessarily be a matter of moral turpitude: *Re La Trobe University; Ex parte Wild* [1987] VR 447.

4 *Re La Trobe University; Ex parte Wild* [1987] VR 447, 456-457, citing *Mercer v Pharmacy Board of Victoria* [1968] VR 72, 85.

There is a structural distinction between matters of 'academic' misconduct and 'general' or non-academic breaches of misconduct codes. Academic misconduct bears directly on the academic processes of the university. The objective of such prohibitions is to secure the university against conduct that would or may threaten educational or intellectual operations of the institution, or processes ancillary to them.[5] Most disciplinary action taken by universities against students is likely to fall into the categories of academic misconduct.[6] 'Non-academic' misconduct can be a residual category of other breaches, especially affecting property or persons or otherwise adverse to the 'good government' and order of the institution. This conduct may appear 'quasi-criminal' in character.[7]

II Acting Fairly

Through the exercise of disciplinary powers, universities have the capacity to affect the status of persons enrolled as students and who, all things being equal, will progress through a course of study and graduate with the award of an academic qualification. The exercise of these powers clearly affects students' legal rights[8] and interests.[9] In particular, the university has the power to dissolve its relationship with the student, regardless of the wishes of the student. Whether as a matter of private law or public law,[10] the university is obliged to proceed fairly and rationally, that is to say, in a quasi-judicial manner.[11] Procedural fairness comprises two basic principles, or 'limbs': the right to a fair hearing (the *audi alteram* principle) and the right to be heard by an impartial decision-maker (the rule against bias, or the *nemo judex* principle). This section deals primarily with the fair hearing rule.

Axiomatically, the requirements of procedural fairness depend on the particular circumstances at issue and what is required for a university decision-maker to proceed fairly may vary. For example, requirements in a disciplinary matter will differ from those in a dispute about unsatisfactory academic progress or academic assessment.[12]

Extended judicial consideration of university discipline cases in Australia has been limited. In other jurisdictions, the approach to the question of what is required for procedural fairness in university misconduct cases has varied from a quite strict analogy to court-like proceedings and a quasi-criminal characterisation[13] to a less rigorous

5 See, for example, Debbie Papy-Carder 'Plagiarism in Legal Scholarship' (1984) 15 *University of Toledo Law Review* 233, 241.

6 Bruce Lindsay, 'Rates of Student Disciplinary Action in Australian Universities' (2010) 52(2) *Australian Universities Review* 27.

7 See *Bray v University of Melbourne* [2001] VSC 391.

8 See *R v Senate of the University of Aston* [1969] 2 All ER 964, 973H (Donaldson J); also *Bray v University of Melbourne* [2001] VSC 391, [9]-[11]; also, more recently, *Durney v Victoria University* [2014] VSC 161, [34].

9 *X v University of Western Sydney (No 3)* [2013] NSWSC 1329, [3].

10 See Francine Rochford, 'The Relationship Between the Student and the University' (1998) 3 *Australian and New Zealand Journal of Law and Education* 28; also *Clark v University of Lincolnshire and Humberside* [2000] 1 WLR 1988; *Bayley-Jones v University of Newcastle* (1990) 22 NSWLR 424, 436; *X v University of Western Sydney (No 3)* [2013] NSWSC 1329, [43]-[44].

11 *University of Ceylon v Fernando* [1960] 1 All ER 631; *Glynn v Keele University* [1971] 1 WLR 487.

12 *R v Cambridge University; Ex parte Persaud* [2000] EWHC 374 (Admin), [20]-[21]; see also Kirby J's reference to this authority in *Griffith University v Tang* (2005) 221 CLR 99, [166].

13 *Flanagan v University College Dublin* [1988] IR 724.

approach.[14] In earlier English cases,[15] obligations on universities to act in a fair manner were accompanied by relatively minimal direction as to content, such as requirements to give notice, afford an oral hearing and approach the matter with an open mind.

It has been said that university discipline should not be 'over-judicialised', because these forums are 'essentially domestic',[16] and the dealings between students and universities are primarily 'consensual' or contractual, albeit with statutory underpinnings (see also Chapter 7 by Rochford). Forbes[17] has described the university setting as 'hybrid', combining domestic and statutory characteristics. The main reason for retaining a 'domestic' characterisation of university tribunals[18] is that they contain no coercive powers to compel witnesses or the production of documents, nor the power to take evidence on oath. Further, university disciplinary proceedings are ordinarily conducted in private and there is no absolute privilege against defamation action.[19]

The 'domestic' qualities of university tribunals ought to be qualified. The status of 'hybridity' is not static. Applying robust standards of procedural fairness to university decision-makers, in a manner analogous to statutory tribunals, is appropriate. Since the early flush of judicial decisions and application of natural justice to universities in the 1960s and 1970s, higher education has transformed radically and continues to do so. Universities are now mass institutions, within an industrialised higher education sector. Wielding considerable social and economic power, universities are subject to extensive public regulation, including under higher education funding and regulatory legislation and migration law.[20]

Judicial approaches in Canada to questions of procedural fairness are instructive. Caution expressed by the Canadian Supreme Court[21] on over-judicialising university hearings has been qualified by more recent approaches of provincial superior courts which have held 'a university student ... is entitled to a high standard of justice', analogous to sanctions under professional employment.[22] The Canadian courts have increasingly insisted on high standards of procedural fairness and scope for adversarial methods, such as rights to cross-examination where issues of credibility arise.[23]

---

14 *Kane v Board of Governors of the University of British Columbia* (1980) 110 DLR (3d) 311, 321.

15 *University of Ceylon v Fernando* [1960] 1 All ER 631; *Glynn v Keele University* [1971] 1 WLR 487.

16 *Tadros v Charles Sturt University* [2008] NSWSC 1140, [150]; *Bell v Victoria University of Wellington* [2010] NZHC 2200, [78], [158]; JR Forbes, 'University Discipline: A New Province for Natural Justice?' (1970-1971) 7 *University Of Queensland Law Journal* 85. See also *Kane v Board of Governors of the University of British Columbia* (1980) 110 DLR (3d) 311.

17 JRS Forbes, *Justice in Tribunals* (4th ed, Federation Press, 2014), [2.18]-[2.20].

18 See Forbes, above n 16.

19 See Forbes, above n 16, 87-88. Absent malice, statements made may be protected by qualified privilege: eg *Defamation Act 2005* (Vic) s 30. It is questionable that a claim of susceptibility to an action in defamation would be sufficient to avoid the obligation of the decision-maker to make the case (and material on which it is based) known to an accused: see *Re Macquarie University; Ex parte Ong* (1989) 17 NSWLR 113, 137.

20 *Higher Education Support Act 2003* (Cth); *Tertiary Education Quality and Standards Agency Act 2011* (Cth); *Education Services for Overseas Students Act 2000* (Cth); *Migration Act 1958* (Cth).

21 *Kane v Board of Governors of the University of British Columbia* (1980) 110 DLR (3d) 311.

22 *Khan v University of Ottawa* [1997] CanLII 941, per Laskin JA (Brooke JA concurring). The approach of the New Zealand High Court has been somewhat to the contrary: *Bell v Victoria University of Wellington* [2010] NZHC 2200, [78].

23 *Healey v Memorial University of Newfoundland* (1992) 106 Nfld & PEIR 305; *Deng v University of Toronto* [2011] ONSC 835.

The continuing 'domestic' qualities of university tribunals, such as evidenced in a lack of coercive powers and hearings in private, do remain relevant. This may necessitate a cautious approach to fact-finding by university decision-makers.[24]

Characterisation of university tribunals and the application of procedural fairness might also have regard to broad-based human rights legislation, including the right to a fair hearing, in relevant jurisdictions. This includes Victoria[25] and the Australian Capital Territory.[26] 'Domestic' qualities notwithstanding, the application of human rights legislation to university hearings may further diminish rigid characterisation of those hearings as 'private' or 'voluntary.' Application of human rights legislation to university actions has not yet come before tribunals or courts. In Victoria, judicial consideration of the scope of the fair hearing right suggests university disciplinary actions would likely fall within the ambit of 'civil proceeding' for the purposes of fair hearing requirements under human rights law.[27]

A Standards and Models of Fairness in the Hearing Rule

There is a lack of overarching principle guiding the content of fair hearing procedure in Australian law.[28] An 'intuitive'[29] approach is preferred, founded on the broad and open standard that 'practical injustice'[30] must be avoided and that a 'reasonable and fair procedure' adopted.[31] Factors guiding the content of fairness include the statutory context of decisions, the consequences of decisions, the balance of justice with expediency ('cost/efficiency'), the question of urgency, the nature of the decision-maker, and what legitimate expectations may be in play.[32] This all occurs with regard to the underpinning model of 'judicial fairness,' or 'adversarial adjudication as a backdrop,'[33] overlaid with the diverse and complex procedural arrangements resulting from the nature of administrative decision-making in a particular case.[34]

'Fairness' in university 'circumstances' is complicated by:

- the 'hybrid' and evolving nature of public universities and relationships within them;
- the development of Australian administrative law and its incremental application to universities; and
- the various types of decisions within the category of university disciplinary action.

24 *Hall v University of New South Wales* [2003] NSWSC 669, [168].
25 For example, *Charter of Human Rights and Responsibilities Act 2006* (Vic) s 24(1).
26 *Human Rights Act 2004* (ACT) s 21(1).
27 See *Kracke v Mental Health Review Board* [2009] VCAT 646, [406]-[419].
28 Mark Aronson and Matthew Groves, *Judicial Review of Administrative Action* (5th ed, Thomson Reuters, 2013), [8.10], [8.90].
29 Ibid 491 [8.10].
30 *R v Minister for Immigration and Multicultural Affairs; Ex parte Lam* (2003) 214 CLR 1, 12-14 (Gleeson CJ).
31 *Kioa v West* (1985) 159 CLR 550, 627 (Brennan J).
32 Compare Aronson and Groves, above n 28, [8.50]-[8.80]; see also Galligan, above n 3, 247-252.
33 Aronson and Groves, above n 28, [8.100]; also Galligan, above n 3, 241-247.
34 See the extended discussion of procedural factors in Aronson and Groves, above n 28, [8.250]-[8.410].

1 Statutory Context

Statutory context is a key consideration.[35] For universities, this context is unique. Universities are corporate entities operating with wide autonomy, especially over academic matters. They have statutory basis and form, legislative powers, extensive systems of delegation and prolific decision-making requirements (see also Chapter 1 by Squelch).

As a matter of public policy, considerable judicial immunity is granted to universities in carrying out academic functions and applying academic judgment to decision-making,[36] including disciplinary decisions. 'Academic independence'[37] remains weighty.[38] For decisions to be immune from judicial intervention[39] they must be 'academic' in nature, an exercise of judgment, and lawful.[40] 'Lawful' here may include exercising the decision-making power in good faith, not acting unreasonably, or with bias.[41] 'Academic' qualities in university decisions do operate with constraints. In English law at least, the boundaries of academic immunity are becoming more tightly policed,[42] not only for *bona fides*, rationality and impartiality but arguably also for the validity and standard of expertise underpinning academic opinions.[43]

2 Nature of the Dispute

Not all misconduct matters are the same. Some hearings may involve numerous sources of oral evidence, some turn mainly on documentary evidence, some involve factual disputes as distinct from disputes over policy, rules, law and/or their application. Some turn more than others on issues of academic judgment.

Allegations of misconduct referring to subjective or intentional elements will need to be separately brought to the student's attention,[44] and findings about a student's conduct in relation to such elements must be reasonably open on the evidence available.[45]

---

35 *Re Minister for Immigration and Multicultural Affairs; Ex parte Miah* (2001) 206 CLR 57, 94, [130] (McHugh J).

36 See generally the commentary in Dennis Farrington and David Palfreyman, *The Law of Higher Education* (2nd ed, Oxford University Press, 2012), [12.40]-[12.45].

37 *Griffith University v Tang* (2005) 221 CLR 99, 156-159 [165]-[171] (Kirby J).

38 *Clark v University of Lincolnshire and Humberside* [2000] 1 WLR 1988; *R (on application of Mustafa) v Office of the Independent Adjudicator for Higher Education* [2013] EWHC 1379 (Admin); *Bell v Victoria University of Wellington* [2010] NZHC 2200.

39 *Clark v University of Lincolnshire and Humberside* (2000) 1 WLR 1988, [12] (Sedley LJ).

40 *R (on application of Mustafa) v Office of the Independent Adjudicator for Higher Education* [2013] EWHC 1379 (Admin), [44].

41 In *R (on application of Mustafa) v Office of the Independent Adjudicator for Higher Education* [2013] EWHC 1379 (Admin), citing *Moroney v Anglo-European College of Chiropractic* [2008] EWHC 2633 (QB), judicial intervention into decisions of academic judgment is considered on grounds of *bona fides* and whether an academic judgment is 'perverse'.

42 See *R (on application of Mustafa) v Office of the Independent Adjudicator for Higher Education* [2013] EWHC 1379 (Admin); also *R v Universities Funding Council; Ex parte Institute of Dental Surgery* [1993] EWHC 5 (Admin); *R (on the application of Persaud) v Cambridge University* [2001] EWCA Civ 534.

43 *R (on the application of Persaud) v Cambridge University* [2001] EWCA Civ 534, [39]-[41].

44 *Bell v Victoria University of Wellington* [2010] NZHC 2200, [159]-[170].

45 Ibid [173].

The nature of the proceedings will also depend on issues of urgency in circumstances where an expedited or truncated procedure is required and appropriate, usually for reasons of necessity, such as where there is an immediate threat of harm to a person.

There may be a balance to be struck between adversarial and inquisitorial methods. Adversarial approaches will provide for greater control and direction of the hearing by the parties involved, including the student, such as in the calling and questioning of witnesses, determining lines of inquiry, and marshalling evidence. Inquisitorial methods presume a central role for the decision-maker in the conduct, organisation and direction of the hearing. Disciplinary proceedings are typically accusatorial in nature, and adversarial practices, such as cross-examination, have evolved as particular techniques to elicit truth and test evidence. Once cross-examination enters into the procedural matrix, issues of examination-in-chief, representation, and tendencies to trial-like characteristics also become more compelling.[46]

The inquisitorial approach is open to university decision-makers,[47] however this is not a licence to inflexibly or unreasonably avoid adversarial practices where these are appropriate.[48].

3 Nature of the Decision-Maker

When considering the approach to be taken by university disciplinary bodies, it is also important to consider the nature of the decision-maker. Depending on the type of matter being dealt with, it may be heard by either an academic panel or an administrator.

University decision-makers in misconduct cases will typically be 'lay' decision-makers, that is, not lawyers. They may, especially in academic misconduct cases, be in the position of experts entitled and required to bring their knowledge and expertise to bear on the facts to be found and judgments to be made in the case.[49]

4 Consequences for the Student

The consequences of disciplinary action for students may be grave, if, for instance, there is the possibility that disciplinary action will lead to exclusion. For international students, for whom enrolment and participation attaches to their right to reside in Australia, the consequences of disciplinary action and penalties affecting course attendance and progress will be particularly serious. For law students, adverse disciplinary findings can also throw into question a future career. For other professions, there may be flow-on reputational issues, even where disciplinary proceedings are held in private and not the subject of public or official record.

46 See Forbes, above n 17, [12.76]-[12.96].

47 *Simjanoski v La Trobe University* [2004] VSC 180, [22].

48 In *Simjanoski*, the court described the discipline hearing as 'inquisitorial or partially inquisitorial': *Simjanoski v La Trobe University* [2004] VSC 180, [22], a point emphasised on appeal: *Simjanoski v La Trobe University* [2004] VSCA 125, [6] (Calloway JA).

49 *Simjanoski v La Trobe University* [2004] VSC 180, [25]-[30]; compare *Bell v Victoria University of Wellington* [2010] NZHC 2200, [78].

B Model Content of Procedural Fairness in Student Discipline Hearings

As 'the circumstances' at issue in disciplinary actions against students vary significantly, a schema of procedural models is suggested.[50]

First, there are circumstances in which it is desirable or appropriate for prominence to be given to adversarial techniques such as cross-examination or representation by a lawyer or professional advocate. A preference for this approach is indicated where:

- the facts or the credibility, knowledge or perceptions of witnesses are in dispute;
- the allegations are particularly grave;
- the consequences for the student are especially serious;
- the student is vulnerable or likely to face substantial difficulties presenting their own case. For example, students with mental health problems, students with a disability, or students for whom language or cultural difficulties would place them at a real disadvantage in making their case or defending their own interests; and/or
- the dispute turns on questions of fact, as much or more than issues of academic judgment, or the dispute involves complex issues of law, policy or practice.

The broad spectrum of procedural mechanisms should be canvassed or applied. There is learned opinion against adoption of methods such as cross-examination into administrative hearings, particularly where no coercive powers operate.[51] Yet there is also opinion the other way: 'Whenever disputed facts are in issue, cross-examination remains one of the best means by which adverse testimony can be tested for reliability'.[52] Variations and modifications to these techniques are possible and appropriate,[53] and, in the absence of such methods for testing evidence within adjudicative processes, greater obligation will fall back onto the (inquisitorial) decision-maker. In absence of the trial analogy, there are circumstances where fact-finding needs to be approached with 'caution',[54] if not ingenuity.[55] Consideration also needs to be given as to whether or in what ways students may need to be represented in order to organise and present their case, as well as to best assist the decision-maker. Representation in university hearings commonly involves non-legal advocacy.

The second model of procedural fairness involves those cases where facts may be in dispute or there is a dispute over the interpretation or application of rules but it is more appropriate for inquisitorial methods to apply to the adjudicative process. These may be cases where there are no witnesses other than the student, or no real dispute over the credibility, perceptions or knowledge of witnesses, other than the student. Much evidence may be in documentary form, such as in plagiarism cases, but the case may still be complex

50 Farrington and Palfreyman indicate the role to be played by proportionality in the organisation of procedural standards and rigour: Farrington and Palfreyman, above n 36, [12.49].

51 Forbes, above n 16, 98-100.

52 Geoffrey Flick, *Natural Justice: Principles and Practical Application* (2nd ed, Butterworths, 1984), 77-94; see also *University of Ceylon v Fernando* [1960] 1 All ER 631.

53 Flick, above n 52, 85-86.

54 *Hall v University of New South Wales* [2003] NSWSC 669, [168].

55 See the approach taken by the Inquiry in *Hall v University of New South Wales* [2003] NSWSC 669, [164]-[166].

or contentious. There may be a significant role for academic judgments in the decision-making process, and the disciplinary body is likely to take an active and central role in the inquiry. An 'accuser', such as the academic staff member referring the complaint or an investigating officer preparing the case, is not necessarily present. Fairness will be served by notice, the oral hearing and capacity to make oral and written submissions, a right to representation (although not necessarily legal representation), written reasons that deal with key substantive issues, and broad rights of appeal or internal review.[56]

In light of recent superior court cases in Victoria[57] and New South Wales,[58] university authorities would be well-advised also to ensure that full and adequate disclosure is made to students of the case against them and of the materials and evidence to which they may need to respond. The quasi-judicial character of university disciplinary proceedings, notably those in which a student is at risk of exclusion, is reinforced in these decisions.[59]

There is a third model of procedure in which the requirements of fairness recede, as it has been said, toward 'nothingness'.[60] Situations of 'emergency', or interim, action are held to be those where there is little or no requirement to provide for the right to be heard so long as the status quo ante is maintained until a fuller hearing can be convened.[61] In light of the decision in *X v University of Western Sydney (No 3)*,[62] caution should be taken, however, as to what is genuinely 'emergency' action and what is less than critical or imperative, even if serious.[63] In that case, a student was suspended by the university, pending a hearing of substantive allegations against him (charges of sexual assault), and given no clear notice of the allegations at the time of the suspension or an opportunity to respond to the action or the charges. The New South Wales Supreme Court found against the university on the ground of fairness.

Even in urgent situations, clear notice of what is being alleged, even if in a manner proportionate to the circumstances, should be provided.[64] Prejudice to course progress should be minimised.

The third model of procedure is also relevant for preliminary investigations or inquiries into disciplinary complaints before disciplinary hearings proper. Preliminary inquiries in the university, where otherwise properly conducted (for example, in good faith), are unlikely to attract duties of procedural fairness.[65] A student's interests and rights may be affected if a complaint or charge proceeds, but fairness in the decision-making process needs to be looked at as whole, including preliminary investigation and principal hearing.[66] Moreover, initial inquiries regarding student conduct are likely to be distinguishable by virtue of occurring in private, not in the public domain.[67]

---

56 Compare Bruce Lindsay, 'University Hearings: Student Discipline and Fair Procedures' (2008) 15(3) *Australian Journal of Administrative Law* 146.

57 *Durney v Victoria University* [2014] VSC 161.

58 *X v University of Western Sydney* [2014] NSWSC 82.

59 See, for example, *Durney v Victoria University* [2014] VSC 161, [34] (Garde J).

60 *Kioa v West* (1985) 159 CLR 550, 616 (Brennan J).

61 See Forbes, above n 17, [9.1]-[9.2].

62 [2013] NSWSC 1329.

63 *X v University of Western Sydney (No 3)* [2013] NSWSC 1329, [60]-[76].

64 Ibid [63]-[65].

65 *Wilde v University of Sydney* [2002] NSWSC 954.

66 Compare *South Australia v O'Shea* (1987) 163 CLR 378, cited in *Wilde v University of Sydney* [2002] NSWSC 954, [34].

67 *Wilde v University of Sydney* [2002] NSWSC 954, [37]-[38].

III Other Aspects of Decision-Making: Acting Impartially and Rationally

The 'second limb' of the procedural fairness doctrine requires a decision-maker to act impartially, that is, absent of bias and with a mind open to persuasion. University bodies operate to the standard applicable to statutory decision-makers, as distinct from private associations or 'clubs', in that conduct amounting to apprehended[68] as well as actual bias[69] must be avoided. The test for apprehended bias is that a fair-minded, informed observer *might* conclude that the decision-making *might* not be impartial.[70] This standard may be modified where proceedings are held in private,[71] although the objective risk of perceived bias remains the substantive test. Where inquisitorial approaches are the norm, this can be, on occasion, a delicate balancing act.[72]

As well as acting fairly and impartially, it is required that disciplinary decision-makers make decisions that are rational or reasoned, based upon evidence and not arbitrary. It has been said that procedural fairness and rational decision-making are linked.[73] As with administrative tribunals generally, decisions of university disciplinary bodies will be reviewable for legal error on grounds of relevance and reasonableness, on grounds of bad faith or improper exercise of power in decision-making. Each element of legality has received at least some consideration in university cases before the courts.[74]

In applying principles of legal rationality, decision-makers would do well also to be mindful of procedures of proof, such as requirements that decisions have some basis in evidence of probative value and that, while obligations to discharge an onus of proof generally do not apply in administrative hearings, an accuser may bear the burden of proof in disciplinary cases in circumstances of uncertainty.[75] An obligation to persuade the disciplinary body of a fact ought not to fall upon a student in disciplinary hearings.

Rationality of decision-making is associated with the requirement to consider relevant considerations and dismiss irrelevant considerations, on the one hand, and not to make decisions that are 'manifestly unreasonable',[76] on the other hand. This is a distinction made in law, where the latter standard presents a high bar of legal error,

---

68 *Simjanoski v La Trobe University* [2004] VSC 180, [31]-[39].

69 See *Re Macquarie University; Ex parte Ong* (1989) 17 NSWLR 113 for an instance of actual bias (in a staff dismissal case).

70 *Webb v R* (1994) 181 CLR 41; *Ebner v Official Trustee in Bankruptcy* (2000) 205 CLR 337.

71 *Re Refugee Review Tribunal; Ex parte H* (2001) 179 ALR 425, [28] (Gleeson CJ, Gaudron and Gummow JJ, the standard considered but not decided); *Hot Holdings Pty Ltd v Creasy* (2002) 210 CLR 438, [68] (McHugh J).

72 *Re Refugee Review Tribunal; Ex parte H* (2001) 179 ALR 425, [31].

73 *Australian Broadcasting Tribunal v Bond* (1990) 170 CLR 321, 367 (Deane J).

74 As to the application of good faith to academic decisions, see *R v Universities Funding Council; Ex parte Institute of Dental Surgery* [1993] EWHC 5 (Admin); *R (on application of Mustafa) v Office of the Independent Adjudicator for Higher Education* [2013] EWHC 1379 (Admin), [52]. As to judicial consideration of improper purposes, see *Ivins v Griffith University* [2001] QSC 86.

75 *McDonald v Director-General of Social Security* (1984) 1 FCR 354; *Minister for Health v Thomson* (1985) 60 ALR 701, 712; *Secretary, Department of Social Security v Willee* (1990) 96 ALR 211.

76 *Minister of Aboriginal Affairs v Peko-Wallsend Ltd* (1986) 162 CLR 24, 41 (Mason J), in reference to the classic statement of unreasonableness in *Associated Provincial Picture Houses Ltd v Wednesbury Corporation* [1948] 1 KB 223.

for decisions that exhibit serious irrationality or illogicality[77] or verge on arbitrary or capricious, although the distinction is not necessarily clear.[78]

In *Bell v Victoria University of Wellington*,[79] the New Zealand High Court expressed reservations about the reasoning approach taken by a university appeals committee to findings of plagiarism by a student who had in one part of her assessment for the particular subject, included references to certain materials but had not additionally shown how these materials were used in the main assessable text. Accommodating latitude to university decision-makers, the court held the decision was not so 'plainly irrational as to be wrong in law'.[80] Hence, the original decision was not unreasonable in the sense of serious irrationality. However, the court found the university appeal body had fallen into reviewable error in not accounting for instances of citation in the student's work in its analysis of plagiarism.[81] The university acted irrationally in not taking into account relevant considerations. The failure of the particular analytic approach of the disciplinary committee, rather than absurdity of approach or outcome, was at issue. University decision-makers may wish to note the forensic method of the court in this case.

IV Conclusion

University discipline and student conduct are persistent concerns in the institutional life of Australia's public universities. Particular preoccupations with student conduct may have changed over time, and will continue to do so as the nature of higher education and its delivery evolves. Universities regulate conduct by reference to inclusive codes and adopt quasi-judicial procedures such that internal decision-makers parallel the approach of statutory tribunals. Much of this chapter has dealt with the challenges of fair and rational decision-making in university discipline cases. As discussed, the application of these broad principles to this setting remains an unfolding process, as administrative law standards are incrementally applied to these circumstances and as the university sector continues to expand and evolve. Notwithstanding this dynamic process, essential tenets of administrative justice, including fair and rational treatment, will remain fundamental to how the public university does and should treat its single largest constituency, the students.

77 *Re Minister for Immigration and Multicultural Affairs; Ex parte Applicant S20/2002* (2003) 198 ALR 59; see Aronson and Groves, above n 28, [5.200], [6.390]-[6.500].

78 See *Minister for Immigration and Citizenship v Li* (2013) 249 CLR 332, [30] (French CJ).

79 *Bell v Victoria University of Wellington* [2010] NZHC 2200.

80 Ibid [140].

81 Ibid [81]-[113].

Chapter 10

Resolution of Student Grievances within Universities

Anita Stuhmke, Bronwyn Olliffe and Maxine Evers

I Introduction

Effective complaint[1] resolution is an ongoing challenge for universities. Grievances will arise within universities and with persons and organisations external to the institutions across any one of the vast array of activities a university undertakes. Similarly to many large institutions, each Australian university prescribes its own complaint resolution procedures and policies and provides complaint handling units and bodies staffed by its own academics and administrative staff.

This chapter examines the internal resolution of student grievances by Australian public universities. Private universities, while covered by similar principles to those discussed here,[2] are not analysed. The chapter begins with an overview of the legislative necessity for public universities to provide for internal grievance handling. It then outlines the specialist bodies created, funded and operated by universities to resolve student disputes and discusses the mechanisms of internal and external dispute resolution pathways available to students in the event that internal complaint resolution by the university fails to offer adequate redress.

II Legislation

Universities in Australia are largely responsible for maintaining their own quality and standards. The *Higher Education Support Act 2003* (Cth) (*HESA*) imposes an obligation on higher education providers[3] to operate at a level of quality which meets the Threshold Standards within the meaning of the *Tertiary Education Quality and Standards Agency Act 2011* (Cth) (*TEQSA Act*), and that meets the requirements which are imposed on the provider under the *TEQSA Act*[4] (see also Chapter 1 by Squelch). *HESA* also requires that all students and all applicants for admission must be treated fairly by the higher

1 The terms 'complaints', 'grievances' and 'disputes' are used interchangeably in this chapter.

2 See discussion in Patty Kamvounias and Sally Varnham, 'Legal Challenges to University Decisions Affecting Students' (2010) 34(1) *Melbourne University Law Review* 140.

3 Higher education providers include universities, self-accrediting and non-self-accrediting entities: see *HESA* s 3.5.

4 *HESA* s 19.15.

education provider[5] which must have grievance and review procedures for dealing with student complaints.[6]

The former Australian Universities Quality Agency (now the Tertiary Education Quality and Standards Agency (TEQSA)) in its audit reports made several recommendations concerning student grievances and appeal processes, most of which refer to greater transparency.[7] As a result, the *Higher Education Standards Framework (Threshold Standards) 2011*[8] specifically set out the higher education provider's responsibilities to students. These require the higher education provider to define and meet its responsibilities to students, including the provision of information, support and equitable treatment. Of special note is the section addressing student grievances:

> 6.4 Students have ready access to effective grievance processes, which enable them to make complaints about any aspect of the higher education provider's higher education operations, including operations provided by other entities on behalf of the higher education provider, without fear of reprisal, and which provide for review by an appropriate independent third party if internal processes fail to resolve a grievance.

The Threshold Standards also require that students be provided with information and have access to advocacy support in relation to the higher education provider's academic and procedural rules.[9] The higher education provider has the further responsibility to have 'student representation within its deliberative and decision-making processes and encourages students to participate in these processes'.[10]

TEQSA encourages students who have a complaint about a higher education provider to first contact the provider. Students who have a complaint concerning compliance with the Threshold Standards may lodge a complaint with TEQSA.[11]

Universities Australia, the peak body representing all Australian universities, developed the *Voluntary Code of Best Practice for the Governance of Australian Universities* (*Voluntary Code*). This *Voluntary Code* was approved in 2011 and includes the provision that:

> A university should codify its internal grievance procedures and publish them with information about the procedure for submitting complaints to the relevant ombudsman or the equivalent relevant agency.[12]

The Minister for Education has the power to revoke the approval of a higher education provider if the Minister is satisfied that the higher education provider has breached a

---

5 *HESA* s 19.30.

6 *HESA* s 19.45.

7 Jim Jackson, Helen Fleming, Patty Kamvounias and Sally Varnham, *Student Grievances and Discipline Matters Project* (ALTC, 2009).

8 The *Higher Education Standards Framework (Threshold Standards) 2011* is made under s 58(1) of the *TEQSA Act*.

9 *Higher Education Standards Framework (Threshold Standards) 2011* s 6.6.

10 *Higher Education Standards Framework (Threshold Standards) 2011* s 6.8.

11 <http://www.teqsa.gov.au/complaints>.

12 Universities Australia, *Voluntary Code of Best Practice for the Governance of Australian Universities* s 9, <https://www.universitiesaustralia.edu.au/efficiency-and-governance/legislation-and-governance/University-Governance/University-Governance#.U6PohZh--Uk>.

quality and accountability requirement or breached a condition imposed on the body's approval.[13]

Even without any legislative requirement for effective grievance handling, it is incumbent on universities to have an effective process for managing the disputes which inevitably arise in every community. The more effective the internal processes for resolving grievances, the less likely that those grievances will be taken to external bodies for resolution resulting in savings of time, money and stress for both the university and the complainant and possibly of the reputation for the university.[14]

III Models for Internal University Grievance Handling

The structures, policies and processes a university maintains to ensure that its grievance handling systems are appropriate and transparent within the legislative framework is a matter for each university.[15] The parties' rights to privacy must, of course, be rigorously observed (see also Chapter 6 by Fleming) as must fundamental legal principles such as procedural fairness (see also Chapter 9 by Lindsay).

Whatever model is employed, it is vital that students are able to navigate their university's processes easily and effectively. One model of a clear and concise hierarchy of steps for students to follow[16] sets out the different types of problems students may encounter and ensures that FAQs and contact information are clearly set out on the university's website.

Where a university has policies and procedures specifically relevant to a complaint then generally those policies and procedures must be followed to access the institution's grievance handling process.[17] There is a common emphasis on university websites that the institution's preference is, where possible, for grievances to be raised informally with the university officer who is directly responsible for resolving the matter.[18] Where the informal process does not resolve the matter then a complaint is often referred to the staff member who is responsible for managing grievances within a faculty or administrative unit such as an Associate Dean or Director.[19] If this initial stage of the formal process is not successful then the formal grievance handling process is accessed.[20]

---

13 *HESA* s 22.15.

14 Hilary Astor, 'Improving Dispute Resolution in Australian Universities: Options for the Future' (2005) 27(1) *Journal of Higher Education Policy and Management* 49.

15 Guidance is available to universities reviewing their grievance handling procedures in publications such as Jim Jackson, Helen Fleming, Patty Kamvounias and Sally Varnham, *Student Grievances and Discipline Matters Project Good Practice Guide for Handling Complaints and Appeals in Australian Universities*, May 2009 or in New South Wales Ombudsman, *Complaint Handling at Universities: Best Practice Guidelines*, December 2006.

16 Jackson et al, above n 7, 13.

17 Anita Stuhmcke, 'Grievance Handling in Australian Universities: The Case of the University Ombudsman and the Dean of Students' (2001) 23(2) *Journal of Higher Education Policy Management* 181.

18 Bruce Lindsay, 'University Discipline and the "Higher Education Crisis": Student Advocates' Experiences and Perceptions of Quasi-judicial Decision Making in the University Sector' (2009) 31(4) *Journal of Higher Education Policy and Management* 327, 339.

19 Sally Varnham and Maxine Evers, 'The Challenges and Opportunities of the Role of Student Ombudsmen in an Australian University' (2011) 22(4) *Australasian Dispute Resolution Journal* 228.

20 Lindsay, above n 18.

While the university 'visitor' as an internal adjudicator was until relatively recently a feature of some Australian universities, the visitor now mainly performs ceremonial functions and has no dispute resolution jurisdiction.[21]

As might be expected when there is such diversity across the university sector in Australia, the requirement to have an effective grievance process has been interpreted in different ways by different universities. However four common models can be identified:

- the university ombudsman – variously referred to as Ombuds, Student Ombud, Student Ombudsman, University Student Ombudsman and University Ombudsman;
- Dean of Students;
- Complaints Manager/Grievance Officer; and
- Academic Manager.

A University Ombudsman

In Australia, there are few legislative guidelines on the use of the term 'ombudsman'.[22] Instead, a 'light touch' accreditation scheme has emerged through the membership criteria administered by ANZOA (the Australian New Zealand Ombudsman Association) which is rigorous in determining which organisations may become full members.[23] Internal ombudsmen, such as the university ombudsman, are generally ineligible to be part of this organisation – ANZOA currently describes the use of 'internal ombudsman' as a 'contradiction in terms'.[24] Nevertheless, similarly to public sector ombudsman and private industry ombudsman, the university ombudsman is widely viewed within the sector as 'an independent officer of the university who receives and investigates complaints from students about administrative injustices or maladministration'.[25]

There has been a slow growth in the adoption of an ombudsman within Australian universities since the first ombudsman office was established in 1977 at the University of New England. In addition to the 12 universities[26] with an ombudsman office currently, at least two other universities have established an office which was subsequently

21 For a discussion of the university visitor in Australian universities, see Kamvounias and Varnham, above n 2, 147-150. The Australian Catholic University does, however, retain a 'visitor' who can review a student appeal or complaint in relation to a matter which has not been resolved to the student's satisfaction and where there is no external body with jurisdiction in relation to the matter, see <http://www.acu.edu.au/policy/student_policies/university_visitor_policy_-_students>.

22 By contrast, see the New Zealand *Ombudsmen Act 1975* s 28A. One exception is the requirement in the South Australian *Ombudsman Act 1972* (inserted in 2002) to prohibit government agencies from using the term 'ombudsman' to describe a process or procedure by which the agency investigates and resolves complaints against itself.

23 John McMillan, 'What's in a Name? Use of the Term "Ombudsman"' (Presentation to the Australian and New Zealand Ombudsman Association, Melbourne, 22 April 2008) <http://www.ombudsman.gov.au/files/22_April_2008_Whats_in_a_name_use_of_the_term_Ombudsman.pdf>.

24 ANZOA website <http://www.anzoa.com.au/ANZOA%20Policy%20Statement_Ombudsman_Essential%20Criteria.pdf>.

25 Stuhmcke, above n 17, 182.

26 The twelve universities with an ombudsman office are: Central Queensland University, Charles Sturt University (also has a Dean of Students), La Trobe University, Macquarie University, Monash University, Queensland University of Technology, RMIT University, Southern Cross

disbanded.[27] The majority of the universities with an ombudsman office have been accredited since 1988.

Although there are many similarities between university ombudsman offices there is no one single model. The 'terms of reference' of a university ombudsman's office govern the way in which the office operates, covering such matters as appointment, authority to enquire, the conduct of complaint, report of investigation and annual reports.[28] Informal dispute resolution processes are most commonly followed and one of the challenges for these offices is 'to achieve procedural and substantive fairness in the informal processes they administer'.[29]

In common with the public administration model, the university ombudsman office is generally an 'office of last resort'.[30] Before a complainant can lodge a request for assistance, all reasonable steps must have been taken to resolve the grievance within the relevant faculty, school or other unit in the university. Generally, the university ombudsman investigates whether the policies and procedures of the university were followed and applied and makes a decision to resolve the particular dispute. Depending on the terms of reference, the university ombudsman may also be able to make recommendations for systemic improvements across the university. This is an important component of continual quality improvement of administrative procedures. In the majority of institutions, the university ombudsman deals with student grievances only.[31]

B Dean of Students

The Dean of Students' role at the five universities[32] with such an office has been interpreted by each institution in very different ways. At the Australian National University, students are invited to make the Dean of Students aware of issues which they have confronted so that 'the Dean can ensure that student concerns are communicated to important deliberative and decision making University committees'.[33] The Dean of Students at the University of Newcastle appears to take an advisory or supporting role for students and also resolves informal complaints. Another function of the Dean of Students at Newcastle is to receive formal complaints which are then forwarded to the University Complaints Manager.[34] At the University of Wollongong, 'The Dean of

University, University of New England, University of South Australia, University of Technology Sydney, University of the Sunshine Coast.

27 Stuhmcke, above n 17, 184.

28 See, for example, the University of Technology, Sydney Student Ombuds Office Terms of Reference, <http://www.ombuds.uts.edu.au/terms.html>.

29 Rachael Field and Michael Barnes, 'University Ombuds: Issues for Fair and Equitable Complaints Resolution' (2003) 14(3) *Australasian Dispute Resolution Journal* 198, 204.

30 See, for example, the process for making a complaint to the Student Ombud at the University of South Australia at <http://w3.unisa.edu.au/ombud/Process/>.

31 Two exceptions to this are the University Ombudsman at Charles Sturt University and the University Ombudsman at the University of New England. Staff grievances are managed usually through other internal processes and the grievance handler is determined by the type of grievance and the applicable university policy.

32 Australian National University, Charles Sturt University (also has a University Ombudsman), Newcastle University, University of Canberra and University of Wollongong.

33 Australian National University website <www.anu.edu.au/dos/>.

34 <http://www.newcastle.edu.au/current-students/support/solving-issues/dean-of-students>.

Students is the Students' Ombudsman and investigates unresolved academic grievances which have been submitted previously to the Faculty or unit and other serious grievances unresolved by the Faculty or Professional Units'.[35] This Dean of Students would appear to have much in common with a university ombudsman office.

As Stuhmcke[36] has noted, whether the grievance handler is called an ombuds, ombudsman or Dean of Students, these offices have similar functions in handling grievances. The different models identified are not mutually exclusive and more than one may apply.

C University Complaints Manager/Grievance Officer

Where a Complaints Manager/Grievance Officer has been appointed, the power and authority of that Officer will be found in the University's Complaints Resolution Policy and Procedures (or similarly named documents[37]). Usually this type of Office manages both student and staff formal complaints and while it may not handle informal complaints, it is often this Office which will provide advice to a complainant about who to approach in the first instance. Informal complaints are usually dealt with by other staff members within a faculty, school or unit and on the basis that an informal process is better able to quickly resolve many smaller matters.

University Complaints Resolution Procedures generally provide a limited right of appeal.[38] For example, an appeal may be restricted to matters where the complaint has not been resolved within a reasonable time or where there has been a procedural irregularity in the handling of the matter or where new evidence is available.[39] The appeal may be lodged with the Vice Chancellor, the Registrar or with a specified unit.[40] In some cases, the right to appeal is limited to one ground only,[41] and if this is not applicable, a complainant who wishes to appeal is directed to refer the matter to the relevant external ombudsman or agency.

D University Academic Managers

In some universities, there is no separate grievance handling unit or specified complaints manager. Rather, an academic management position, such as a Head of School, is named as the appropriate authority with whom to lodge a grievance when the

35 University of Wollongong website <www.uow.edu.au/student/services/dos/index.html>.

36 Stuhmcke, above n 17.

37 See, for example, the University of Western Sydney Complaint Handling and Resolution Policy available at <http://policies.uws.edu.au/view.current.php?id=00098>.

38 New South Wales Ombudsman, *Complaint Handling at Universities: Best Practice Guidelines* (2006) recommend that good complaint handling practice provides at least one level of appeal from initial decisions determining complaints, at B-24.

39 See, for example, the University of Western Sydney DDS-Complaint Handling and Resolution Policy s 67 available at <http://policies.uws.edu.au/view.current.php?id=00098>.

40 See, for example, the University of Newcastle Complaints Resolution Procedure available at <www.newcastle.edu.au/policy/000898>.

41 See, for example, the University of New South Wales where an appeal is limited to procedural matters only at <https://student.unsw.edu.au/complaints>.

informal process has not resolved the issue.[42] The appropriate position is determined by the type of grievance which broadly can be divided into three categories: grievances about academic decisions and matters, grievances about administrative processes and grievances about an individual. If a complainant is dissatisfied with the initial decision, an appeal is usually available to the next level of management such as the Registrar[43] or the relevant Deputy Vice Chancellor or in some cases there is an Appeal Committee of Academic Board.[44]

IV Internal Regulation and Reporting

Each university will determine its own internal auditing and evaluation processes for its student complaints handling units. The most common approach to reporting is through the Annual Reports of the complaints handling units[45] or as part of the university's Annual Reports.[46] These reports may refer to the unit's terms of reference and may set out details about students' complaints, including the nature of the complaint, the source of the complaint, that is, the faculty in which the student was enrolled, and the trend in the number of complaints. Visibility and communication of these reports is ensured by publication on university websites. For example, the authors of this chapter have served as Student Ombuds at the University of Technology Sydney, where the office produces its own Annual Report, including data on the nature of complaints.

The nature of complaints of UTS students has remained constant during the period between 2009-2010 and 2013-2014 and includes concerns relating to assessment, special consideration and exemption from subjects and courses. The complaints relating to assessment are relevant to academic decisions and are similar to the findings of a study of students who litigated against universities between 1985 and 2006 that a substantial number of litigated cases related to academic decisions.[47] Astor also identified that half of the cases during the period alleged discrimination, although the majority of those cases were found not to have a cause of action in discrimination law.[48] Statutory breaches, including anti-discrimination laws, were also identified as a basis for student complaints in the final report of the *Student Grievances and Discipline Matters Project*.[49]

Given that public universities are under the jurisdiction of the relevant State, Territory or Commonwealth ombudsman's office (see also Chapter 11 by Kamvounias), to ensure transparency of internal processes and procedures and to enable compliance

42 See, for example, the University of Western Australia University Policy on Student Complaint Resolution available at <http://www.student.uwa.edu.au/life/complaints/policies/policy>.

43 See, for example, the University of Melbourne Student Complaints and Grievances Procedure <http://msl.unimelb.edu.au/feedback/grievance>.

44 See, for example, Flinders University, Student Appeals and Complaints <http://www.flinders.edu.au/ppmanual/student/appeals-and-complaints.cfm>.

45 See, for example, University of Technology, Sydney <http://www.ombuds.uts.edu.au/annual.html>.

46 See, for example, University of Melbourne <http://www.unimelb.edu.au/publications/archives.html#Annualreports>.

47 Hilary Astor, 'Why Do Students Sue Australian Universities' (2010) 21 *Australian Dispute Resolution Journal* 20, 30.

48 Ibid.

49 Jackson et al, above n 7, 114.

with any request for information from the relevant ombudsman, it is essential for the internal units that deal with complainants to have relevant data and records. This is a partially regulated area with State and Territory legislation providing for the keeping of records and documents by public institutions. In New South Wales, for example, the *State Records Act 1998* requires public offices to make and keep full and accurate records of the office's activities.[50] Although the Act also provides for the implementation of standards and codes for best practice for records management,[51] there is no statutory requirement for a centralised management system of complaints' records. A lack of centralised records is an area of concern as this information is:

> critical to identifying and rectifying systemic failures and other issues, such as behaviour patterns or types of complaints by reference to student demographic or faculty or school demographic.[52]

Ensuring proper processes and appropriate reporting is important for a wide range of reasons from commercial risk-management obligations to the provision of a positive student experience. It is also important for the reputation of universities.

Further mechanisms for internal monitoring and evaluation of complaint handling processes and procedures include feedback from students, students' associations and other relevant internal stakeholders, such as university legal services, counselling services and equity and diversity units.[53]

A significant concern with internal reporting is the absence of consistency across universities and the potential for unsatisfactory delivery of a fair and transparent system for handling student grievances. This is an area where the relevant State, Territory or Commonwealth ombudsman's office may be able to use its statutory authority to implement best practice standards to assist universities in internally centralising their records and externally ensuring uniformity.

V External Review of University Grievance Handling

The role of the student ombudsman or grievance handling unit as decision-maker of administrative processes is open to challenge if there is a lack of procedural fairness adhered to by the unit. Such issues may only be identified when an aggrieved student takes their concern outside the university.

Astor's study found that after discrimination-based cases, the most prevalent student claims related to unfair decision-making.[54] Astor's analysis of the case law evidenced that students were having to 'shoe-horn' their complaints in order to have a cause of action.[55] She concludes that, instead of costly litigation, some cases should have been resolved within the university.[56]

50 *State Records Act 1998* (NSW) s 12.
51 *State Records Act 1998* (NSW) s 13.
52 Jackson et al, above n 7, 83.
53 Jackson et al, above n 7.
54 Astor, above n 47, 26.
55 Ibid.
56 Ibid.

While courts and tribunals provide the most obvious form of external dispute resolution,[57] there are other avenues available to students which are relatively quick, free and leave intact the further option of going to court if all else fails. One important free dispute resolution service to be found outside the university is the public sector ombudsman. This institution is discussed in Chapter 11 by Kamvounias, as it provides the best example of this form of external oversight of university grievance handling.[58] Whichever internal grievance handling process is instituted in a public university, if a student is not satisfied with the outcome, a complaint can be lodged with the relevant parliamentary ombudsman.

Reviews of university decision-making by external bodies, such as ombudsmen, courts, tribunals and human rights commissions may include examining the actual decision as well as the process or application of proper procedure in making the decisions. Thus in investigating the resolution of a student complaint, the procedural fairness of the original university decision-maker may be reviewed. Procedural fairness or 'natural justice' is a fundamental principle of dispute resolution.[59] The goal of procedural fairness is to support rational decision-making and often requires prior notice that a decision will be made, disclosure of the substance of the information upon which the decision will be based and an opportunity for the student to respond.[60]

The challenge for universities in observing procedural fairness when resolving student grievances is one of striking a balance between 'fairness to the individual, as against practical administrative considerations, such as the importance of finality, efficiency and lack of formality in administrative decision-making'.[61] The application of the principle is important as a university which fails to comply with the requirements of procedural fairness risks having decisions declared invalid by a court or tribunal. This will be on the grounds, not because the decision itself was wrong, but because the decision-making process was wrong in some way.[62] The requirements of procedural fairness have been described as 'ambulatory. They will vary from one legal context to another and from one fact situation to another'.[63] However there are two basic principles of procedural fairness – the 'bias rule' and the 'hearing rule' requiring a decision-maker to inform a person of the case against them or their interests and give

---

57 Kamvounias and Varnham, above n 2. Astor notes that only a small fraction of disputes in universities are heard by a judge, magistrate or tribunal: see Hilary Astor, 'Australian Universities in Court: The Causes, Costs and Consequences of Increasing Litigation' (2008) *Legal Studies Research Paper*, No 08/133, 5.

58 Depending on the nature of the complaint there may be other external agencies, such as the Australian Human Rights and Equal Opportunity Commission or the Independent Commission against Corruption, to which a student may appeal rather than commencing litigation.

59 John McMillan and Robin Creyke, *Control of Government Action* (3rd ed, LexisNexis, 2009); William Lane and Simon Young, *Administrative Law in Australia* (Thomson Reuters, 2007).

60 Ibid.

61 John McMillan, 'Natural Justice: Too Much, Too Little or Just Right?' Paper delivered to the Australian Institute of Administrative Law, National Administrative Law Forum (Canberra, 2007), 1.

62 *O'Rourke v Miller* (1985) CLR 342, 353 (Gibbs J).

63 Justice French, 'Administrative Law in Australia: Themes and Values Revisited' in M Groves (ed), *Modern Administrative Law in Australia: Concepts and Context* (Cambridge University Press, 2014), 47.

them an opportunity to be heard.[64] It is accepted that a hearing is unlikely to be fair when a decision-maker receives material or representations in the absence of one party, or does not disclose relevant material obtained from another source – if disclosure is inadequate, a fair hearing will not be possible[65] (see also Chapter 9 by Lindsay).

VI Current Issues

A *Complexity of Student Issues*

The diversity of models established by universities demonstrates how the sector may provide internal redress for student grievances. It must be recognised that student complaints are often complex, serious and may have many conflicting stakeholders,[66] requiring a resourced, considered and transparent framework for the investigation and determination of student concerns.

The creation by universities of specialist internal bodies to deal with complainants is therefore likely to be one of the more effective mechanisms to ensure procedural fairness and compliance with external oversight in dealing with student grievances. To be effective, practitioners in the area of student complaints must be trained in the university processes and be skilled in conflict resolution and negotiation. To avoid problems resulting from a lack of training, universities should address the issue of training as part of their strategy to improve processes for dealing with student complaints.[67]

Discussions in the university sector have also concerned a perceivable increase in students displaying signs of mental health concerns.[68] Two approaches to improving the outcomes for all students, including those experiencing high levels of distress, are to establish a 'first resort' office where students with both formal and informal complaints are 'triaged' to the appropriate person or unit within the university and secondly, to provide mental health training to all staff who engage with aggrieved students. The challenge will be to ensure ongoing refinement, resourcing and support for these bodies given ever changing internal and external requirements.

B *One Model*

The current main models for the handling of student complaints discussed in this chapter are generally uniform in nature across the Australian university sector. For this reason, and others such as consistency of decisions, common application of procedural fairness and removal of 'forum shopping', the UK model of an independent adjudicator for higher education has been debated in Australia.[69] It may be that there are

64 *Kioa v West* (1985) 159 CLR 550, 583.

65 Mark Aronson and Matthew Groves, *Judicial Review of Administrative Action* (5th ed, Thomson Reuters, 2013), 526-527, [8.180].

66 Astor, above n 47, 28.

67 Jackson et al, above n 7, 80.

68 Varnham and Evers, above n 19, 234.

69 See Bronwyn Olliffe and Anita Stuhmcke, 'A National University Grievance Handler? Transporting the UK Office of the Independent Adjudicator for Higher Education (OIA) to Australia' (2007) 29(2) *Journal of Higher Education and Policy Management* 203. Jackson et al, above n 7, 85 also recommended further research and discussion of the need and effectiveness

Constitutional challenges caused by Australia's federal legal system with this model, but the establishment of the Overseas Student Ombudsman as a Commonwealth scheme working across States and Territories demonstrates that a Commonwealth model is possible.

VII Conclusion

This chapter has outlined that Australian universities are subject to extensive legislative, regulatory and common law requirements with respect to the resolution of student grievances. The regulation of, and reporting by, student ombudsman and equivalent grievance handling offices are part of the structure by which universities are held accountable. Compliance with these requirements is critical. Lack of compliance may have serious risk consequences for the university, including deregistration, expense and reputation loss and for the students, including non-completion of study, financial consequences and health and safety issues.

A commonality shared by universities is that internal grievance handling procedures are an integral part of the university structure and that university decision-makers may be subject to external review by courts, ombudsman, tribunals and other administrative bodies. Importantly, the focus of universities and external bodies in resolving student grievances is a shared one, that being to ensure that the university decision-making with respect to the student experience of higher education is both fair and transparent. Therefore, while this chapter evidences that the approach to dispute resolution by Australian universities is idiosyncratic, this shared focus (together with extensive external oversight) facilitates universities having similar procedures and policies which aim to effectively resolve student disputes within the university.

---

of a national student ombudsman in Australia managing complaints from across the higher education sector.

Chapter 11

Public Sector Ombudsmen and Higher Education

Patty Kamvounias

I Introduction

Complaints about the conduct of universities can find their way into courts and tribunals.[1] Alternatively, complainants may have the option of bringing their concerns to the attention of the relevant Commonwealth, State or Territory Ombudsman. Although extensively regulated by the Commonwealth, public universities also fall within the jurisdiction of one of the nine parliamentary ombudsmen in Australia. An independent ombudsman is also available to overseas students with complaints about private higher education providers.

This chapter deals with the jurisdiction of parliamentary ombudsmen and their role in relation to higher education and includes an analysis of how ombudsmen deal with complaints about the sector. The chapter also includes a discussion of comparable developments in other jurisdictions and whether there is a need for a national university ombudsman in Australia.

II Background and Jurisdictional Issues

A *Jurisdiction of Parliamentary Ombudsmen in Relation to Universities*

With its origins in Sweden in 1809[2] and first introduced into Australia in the 1970s, the role of the parliamentary ombudsman's office has expanded and evolved and now includes ensuring 'that powers of whatever agencies specified to be within jurisdiction are exercised in a way that produces responsible, fair and reasonable outcomes'.[3]

1 See Hilary Astor, 'Australian Universities in Court: Causes, Costs and Consequences of Increasing Litigation' (2008) 19 *Australasian Dispute Resolution Journal* 156; Patty Kamvounias and Sally Varnham, 'Legal Challenges to University Decisions Affecting Students' (2010) 34(1) *Melbourne University Law Review* 140.

2 See Swedish Parliamentary Ombudsmen website <http://www.jo.se/en/About-JO/History/>.

3 Bruce Barbour, 'The Ombudsman and the Rule of Law' (2005) 44 *Australian Institute of Administrative Law Forum* 17, 18-22. See also Anita Stuhmcke, 'The Evolution of the Classical Ombudsman: A View from the Antipodes' (2012) 2(1) *International Journal of Public Law and Policy* 83.

Legislation exists at Commonwealth level and in each State and Territory appointing an ombudsman as an independent officer of parliament to receive and investigate complaints about the actions of public bodies.[4]

Any person has a right to complain to the ombudsman about 'the conduct of a public authority'.[5] According to Goldring, 'the ombudsmen's relation to Australian universities flows from the public nature of universities'.[6] As almost all universities in Australia are public institutions established under State or Territory legislation they are subject to the scrutiny of the ombudsman of the relevant State or Territory. The Australian National University, the only university established under Commonwealth legislation, is the only university within the jurisdiction of the Commonwealth Ombudsman.[7]

Although the language used in the legislation varies slightly across the jurisdictions, the fundamental role of parliamentary ombudsmen is to keep public agencies accountable through the handling of complaints about 'administrative actions'. In relation to universities, these actions would include the appointment and promotion of staff and decisions about admission and exclusion of students.[8] The ombudsman will not get involved in the assessment of students and is not concerned with determining academic merit but will focus on ensuring that the procedures for determining issues such as merit are fair and transparent.[9] Allegations of unfair policies, procedures and decisions and allegations of unreasonable conduct (for example, delay in decision making and decisions without reasons) would also fall within the ombudsman's remit.

B Complaint Handling in Universities: Views of Parliamentary Ombudsmen

As noted in Chapter 10 by Stuhmcke, Olliffe and Evers, all universities have their own policies and procedures to deal with complaints and grievances. Regardless of the

4 *Ombudsman Act 1976* (Cth); *Ombudsman Act 1974* (NSW); *Ombudsman Act 2001* (Qld); *Ombudsman Act 1972* (SA); *Ombudsman Act 1978* (Tas); *Ombudsman Act 1973* (Vic); *Parliamentary Commissioner Act 1971* (WA); *Ombudsman Act 1989* (ACT); *Ombudsman (Northern Territory) Act 1978* (NT).

5 *Ombudsman Act 1974* (NSW) s 12. 'Conduct' is defined to mean 'any action or inaction relating to a matter of administration, and any alleged action or inaction relating to a matter of administration: *Ombudsman Act 1974* (NSW) s 5. See also *Ombudsman Act 1976* (Cth) s 5(1) 'a matter of administration ... by a prescribed authority'; *Ombudsman Act 2001* (Qld) s 14(1) 'administrative actions of agencies'; *Ombudsman Act 1972* (SA) s 13(1) 'any administrative act' defined in s 3 to mean 'a matter of administration on the part of an agency to which this Act applies'; *Ombudsman Act 1978* (Tas) s 12(1) 'any administrative action of a public authority'; *Ombudsman Act 1973* (Vic) s 13(1) 'any administrative action taken by or in an authority'; *Parliamentary Commissioner Act 1971* (WA) s 14(1) 'a matter of administration by any department or authority to which this Act applies'; *Ombudsman Act 1989* (ACT) s 5(1) 'a matter of administration ... by an agency'; *Ombudsman (Northern Territory) Act 1978* (NT) s 10(1) 'administrative actions of public authorities'.

6 Jack Goldring, 'Ombudsmen and Australian Universities' (1987) 1 *Australian Universities' Review* 31, 36. The 'public' nature of universities also brings them with the jurisdiction of the courts applying administrative law remedies. See also Chapter 9 by Lindsay.

7 The conduct of private universities and private higher education providers is outside the authority of parliamentary ombudsmen.

8 Goldring, above n 6.

9 Bruce Barbour, 'Handling Student Grievances: What Lessons are There for Institutions in the Cases Brought Before the Ombudsman in Australia' in Organisation for Economic Co-operation and Development, *Responding to Student Expectations* (OECD Paris, 2002), 145.

type of complaint handling processes maintained by a university, if a person is not satisfied with the outcome of that process, a complaint can be lodged with the relevant parliamentary ombudsman.

Complaints about universities have been described as 'amongst the most difficult and resource intensive complaints, in part because they are not initially handled well by the university and by the time they reach [the parliamentary ombudsman] … may be protracted and entrenched'.[10] The ombudsmen in Victoria and in New South Wales have both investigated complaint handling by universities[11] and were signatories to a letter to *The Australian* expressing concerns about the quality of complaint handling and the rising number of complaints about universities from students and staff. In that letter the ombudsmen warned that:

> failure by universities to address this issue could be damaging to their reputations and capacity to attract quality staff and students, both locally and internationally.[12]

Best practice guidelines for complaint handling by universities were subsequently published[13] and formed the basis of a collaborative project between ombudsmen in Australia and New Zealand to set minimum standards for universities.[14] *Complaint Handling at Universities – Australasian Best Practice Guidelines*[15] was launched in 2014 'to assist universities to make their complaint handling systems more robust and effective … [by] identify[ing] best practice minimum standards that will protect the rights of students, staff and the university itself'.[16] These guidelines cover a range of matters such as complaint management systems; taking, assessing and investigating complaints; following-up on complaints and issues; providing protections and support; and working with overseas students.

C Scope of Powers of Parliamentary Ombudsmen

Even when the university is within jurisdiction and the action or decision complained about relates to a matter of administration, the ombudsman is not obliged to investigate. The ombudsman may decline to investigate if the complainant has not tried to resolve the problem directly with the university or if the university is still investigating the complaint. The ombudsman may also exercise discretion not to investigate if the complaint is frivolous, vexatious or not in good faith; the subject-matter is trivial; the complainant does not have sufficient personal interest in the matter; or the matter

10 Ombudsman Victoria, *Review of Complaint Handling in Victorian Universities* (May 2005), 2.

11 Ibid. See also New South Wales Ombudsman, *Discussion Paper: Complaint Handling in NSW Universities* (2004).

12 Bruce Barbour, David Bevan, GE Brouwer, Vic Feldman, John McMillan, Jan O'Grady and Deidre O'Donnell, 'Complaints Give Rise to Concern' (27 April 2005) *The Australian* 34.

13 New South Wales Ombudsman, *Complaint Handling at Universities: Best Practice Guidelines* (December 2006). The New South Wales Ombudsman and the Victorian Ombudsman also now hold annual forums specifically targeted at university complaint handlers.

14 Victorian Ombudsman, *Annual Report 2014*, 36.

15 Victorian Ombudsman, *Complaint Handling at Universities: Australasian Best Practice Guidelines,* 2014; available at <https://www.ombudsman.vic.gov.au/Publications/Guidelines/Complaint-handling-at-universities-Australasian-be>.

16 Ibid 5.

occurred at too remote a time to justify investigation.[17] Unlike litigation, where the complainant has control of the legal proceedings that will be heard in public, the investigation of a complaint to an ombudsman is totally at the discretion and within the control of the ombudsman and must be conducted in private.[18]

Parliamentary ombudsmen have a wide jurisdiction but their powers are limited to making recommendations.[19] They cannot change decisions of public authorities. Nonetheless, if an ombudsman is not satisfied that sufficient steps have been taken in due time after an investigation, the ombudsman can report the public authority's default.[20]

D Role of Parliamentary Ombudsmen in Relation to Overseas Students

Public sector ombudsmen have a special role under the *Education Services for Overseas Students Act 2000* (Cth) (*ESOS Act*). The *National Code of Practice for Registration Authorities and Providers of Education and Training to Overseas Students* (*National Code*) was introduced under the *ESOS Act* as part of the Commonwealth's regulatory framework for international education services. Education providers have had to comply with a number of standards in the *National Code* since 1 July 2007 (see also Chapter 5 by Ramia). Standard 8 requires education providers to ensure that overseas students are advised of their external appeal rights if students have been unsuccessful in an internal appeal against exclusion. Most universities have nominated the public sector ombudsman in their State or Territory to perform this external appeals function. Ombudsmen in some States have recognised the importance of their role in relation to the *National Code* and have developed specific resources to assist overseas students.[21]

III Investigating Complaints About Public Universities

Public sector ombudsmen are required to submit annual reports of their activities to parliament.[22] There is no prescribed format so the form and content of the annual reports

17 *Ombudsman Act 1974* (NSW) s 13. See also *Ombudsman Act 1976* (Cth) s 6; *Ombudsman Act 2001* (Qld) s 23; *Ombudsman Act 1972* (SA) s 17; *Ombudsman Act 1978* (Tas) s 21; *Ombudsman Act 1973* (Vic) s 15A; *Parliamentary Commissioner Act 1971* (WA) s 18; *Ombudsman Act 1989* (ACT) s 6(1); *Ombudsman (Northern Territory) Act 1978* (NT) s 33.

18 *Ombudsman Act 1974* (NSW) s 17. See also *Ombudsman Act 1976* (Cth) s 8(2); *Ombudsman Act 2001* (Qld) s 25; *Ombudsman Act 1972* (SA) s 18; *Ombudsman Act 1978* (Tas) s 23A; *Ombudsman Act 1973* (Vic) s 13A; *Parliamentary Commissioner Act 1971* (WA) s 19(2); *Ombudsman Act 1989* (ACT) s 9(3); *Ombudsman (Northern Territory) Act 1978* (NT) s 49(1).

19 Goldring, above n 6, 32.

20 *Ombudsman Act 1974* (NSW) s 27. See also *Ombudsman Act 1976* (Cth) s 15; *Ombudsman Act 2001* (Qld) s 51; *Ombudsman Act 1972* (SA) s 25; *Ombudsman Act 1978* (Tas) s 23; *Ombudsman Act 1973* (Vic) s 25; *Parliamentary Commissioner Act 1971* (WA) s 25; *Ombudsman Act 1989* (ACT) s 19; *Ombudsman (Northern Territory) Act 1978* (NT) s 63.

21 See, for example, Victorian Ombudsman, *Fact Sheet 12 – Overseas Students and the Role of the Ombudsman*; and Ombudsman Western Australia, *Information Sheet for Overseas Students–Complaints by Overseas Students* and *Complaint Form for Overseas Students.*

22 *Ombudsman Act 1974* (NSW) s 30. See also *Ombudsman Act 1976* (Cth) s 19; *Ombudsman Act 2001* (Qld) s 52; *Ombudsman Act 1972* (SA) s 29; *Ombudsman Act 1978* (Tas) s 30; *Ombudsman*

vary across jurisdictions and may also change within a jurisdiction from time to time. Generally, annual reports will identify all universities within the jurisdiction and the number of complaints received against each one. The notable exception is Victoria where the annual reports provide only aggregated data for complaints about that State's public education sector. This is an unfortunate limitation as there are eight public universities in Victoria including some of the largest universities in Australia in terms of student enrolments. Nonetheless, annual reports remain a rich source of information about complaints involving universities, as reflected in the discussion that follows.

A *Number of Complaints*

Table 1 (*pages 130-131*) shows the number of complaints about universities received by the Commonwealth, State and Territory Ombudsmen for each financial year from 2004 through to 2014.

All nine parliamentary ombudsmen deal with complaints about public universities but the extent of their involvement and experience of the university sector is dependent on the number of public universities within their respective jurisdictions. As shown in Table 1, the number of universities within each jurisdiction varies considerably.

The number of complaints received about public universities is small compared to the number of students enrolled in public universities in Australia[23] and also small compared to the overall number of complaints received about public authorities.[24] Although the raw numbers are relatively low, the data reinforce the earlier findings[25] that the number of complaints about universities has been increasing and the upward trend is likely to continue.

Reasons for the increase in the number of complaints and for the disparity between jurisdictions may include matters such as:

1. *The level of awareness of the parliamentary ombudsman's role in relation to public universities.* Students and staff in some jurisdictions may simply be more aware of the availability of the ombudsman in relation to university complaints and so may be relying on the service provided by the ombudsman's office more frequently than in other jurisdictions.

Act 1973 (Vic) s 25; *Parliamentary Commissioner Act 1971* (WA) s 27; *Ombudsman Act 1989* (ACT) s 21; *Ombudsman (Northern Territory) Act 1978* (NT) s 152.

23 In 2013 there were a total of 1,313,776 domestic and international students enrolled at higher education institutions: Australian Government, Department of Education, Higher Education Statistics, Student Data <https://www.education.gov.au/selected-higher-education-statistics-2013-student-data>.

24 For example, in the 2007-2008 Annual Report (p 16), the Queensland Ombudsman recorded the following numbers in relation to complaints: State Government (4238); Local Government (1843); Universities (130) and other State Agencies (931).

25 See Bronwyn Olliffe and Anita Stuhmcke, 'A National University Grievance Handler? Transporting the UK Office of the Independent Adjudicator for Higher Education (OIA) to Australia' (2007) 29(2) *Journal of Higher Education Policy and Management* 203, 205 where the authors attribute the gradual increase in the number of complaints over the period 1997-2005 to the fast pace of change in the higher education sector, increased student numbers, the growth of fee paying students and the lack of attention paid to developing and implementing acceptable complaints policies and procedures.

Table 1: Number of Complaints About Universities Received by the State, Territory and Commonwealth Ombudsman Offices

Jurisdiction	University	2003-4	2004-5	2005-6	2006-7	2007-8	2008-9	2009-10	2010-11	2011-12	2012-13	2013-14
Australian Capital Territory	University of Canberra											
	ACT TOTAL:	**2**	**2**	**3**	**8**	**10**	**6**	**3**	**6**	**14**	**14**	**14**
Commonwealth	*Australian National University*											
	CTH TOTAL:	**11**	**4**	**9**	**12**	**12**	**18**	**11**	**17**	**27**	**24**	**20**
New South Wales	*Charles Sturt University*	5	3	7	6	3	5	2	6	7	15	7
	Macquarie University	5	3	6	5	15	14	13	17	12	7	9
	Southern Cross University	7	7	3	6	3	5	2	6	8	12	4
	University of New England	6	4	5	3	2	9	6	6	2	1	11
	University of New South Wales	13	7	4	10	12	11	10	15	14	15	14
	University of Newcastle	10	5	4	11	10	11	13	8	12	7	9
	University of Sydney	15	13	10	4	9	20	8	8	24	27	32
	University of Technology, Sydney	5	0	3	1	11	2	3	7	6	7	17
	University of Western Sydney	20	10	15	5	10	9	15	24	21	18	20
	University of Wollongong	1	3	3	1	4	8	9	7	6	4	12
	NSW TOTAL:	**87**	**55**	**60**	**52**	**79**	**94**	**81**	**104**	**112**	**113**	**135**
Northern Territory	*Charles Darwin University*											
	NT TOTAL:	**13**	**22**	**3**	**3**	**3**	**3**	*	**3**	**2**	**15**	**20**
Queensland	*Central Queensland University*	*	*	6	12	8	16	26	49	*	*	*
	Griffith University	*	*	11	23	46	89	75	88	*	*	*
	James Cook University	*	*	13	9	11	18	33	15	*	*	*
	Queensland University of Technology	*	*	11	15	18	11	42	26	*	*	*
	University of Queensland	*	*	29	30	30	30	69	66	*	*	*
	University of Southern Queensland	*	*	1	14	13	7	2	13	*	*	*
	University of the Sunshine Coast	*	*	1	9	1	5	12	7	*	*	*
	Other	*	*	2	1	3	6	3	6	*	*	*
	QLD TOTAL:	**71**	**74**	**74**	**113**	**130**	**182**	**262**	**270**	**333**	**367**	**338**

Jurisdiction	University	2003-4	2004-5	2005-6	2006-7	2007-8	2008-9	2009-10	2010-11	2011-12	2012-13	2013-14
South Australia	*Flinders University*	*	7	6	3	2	2	7	12	21	15	9
	University of Adelaide	*	10	10	6	11	7	11	13	20	15	6
	University of South Australia	*	10	11	18	15	15	19	15	34	27	37
	SA TOTAL:	*	**27**	**27**	**27**	**28**	**24**	**37**	**40**	**75**	**57**	**52**
Tasmania	*University of Tasmania*											
	TAS TOTAL:	**5**	**3**	**5**	**2**	**5**	**13**	**11**	**6**	**5**	**8**	**6**
Victoria	*Deakin University*	*	*	*	*	*	*	*	*	*	*	*
	La Trobe University	*	*	*	*	*	*	*	*	*	*	*
	Monash University	*	*	*	*	*	*	*	*	*	*	*
	Royal Melbourne Institute of Technology	*	*	*	*	*	*	*	*	*	*	*
	Swinburne University of Technology	*	*	*	*	*	*	*	*	*	*	*
	University of Ballarat	*	*	*	*	*	*	*	*	*	*	*
	University of Melbourne	*	*	*	*	*	*	*	*	*	*	*
	Victoria University	*	*	*	*	*	*	*	*	*	*	*
	VIC TOTAL:	*	*	*	*	*	*	*	*	*	*	*
Western Australia	*Curtin University*	7	19	5	11	7	25	29	38	30	32	33
	Edith Cowan University	1	1	8	3	13	17	14	10	19	33	35
	Murdoch University	10	7	7	4	9	8	9	8	9	18	20
	University of Western Australia	5	3	10	4	1	3	4	6	6	8	9
	University of Notre Dame Australia	*	*	*	*	*	*	*	*	3	2	*
	WA TOTAL:	**23**	**30**	**30**	**22**	**30**	**53**	**56**	**62**	**67**	**93**	**97**
	TOTAL FOR ALL JURISDICTIONS (excluding Victoria): * indicates data not available	**212**	**217**	**211**	**239**	**297**	**393**	**461**	**508**	**635**	**691**	**682**

Source: Annual Reports from 2003-2004 to 2013-2014

2. *The existence of a university or campus ombudsman.* Some universities have their own dedicated offices 'of last resort' on campus to deal with grievances before they escalate into more serious disputes (see also Chapter 10 by Stuhmcke, Olliffe and Evers). Would more ombudsmen on campus mean fewer complaints to external ombudsmen? Although this seems compelling, evidence also exists that students distrust campus ombudsmen,[26] so no firm conclusions can be drawn.

3. *The number of international students at a particular university.* As discussed above, public sector ombudsmen have an important role in the ESOS framework. Ombudsmen in four jurisdictions (New South Wales, Queensland, Victoria and Western Australia) have referred specifically to the *National Code* in their annual reports since 2007-2008 and attribute the increase in the number of complaints against universities to this new area of responsibility. Given the implications a university decision to terminate enrolment may have for a student's visa status, it is not surprising that 'international students are highly motivated to pursue all avenues of review and appeal'.[27]

Table 1 shows that in the 10-year period from 2004 to 2014, the total number of complaints to ombudsmen increased from 212 to 682. This upward trend is likely to continue given the requirements of the *National Code* in relation to external review of decisions to exclude overseas students. But these national figures do not give an accurate picture of what is happening in a particular State or at a particular university and without the inclusion of data from Victoria these figures understate the extent of recourse to the public sector ombudsmen.[28]

B Types of Complaints

Some of the complaints about the 'administrative actions' of universities are highlighted and presented in the annual reports as 'case studies'. These case studies are useful indicators of the areas of concern about the sector. Case studies involving staff include complaints about selection and recruitment processes; unfair disciplinary action; complaint handling processes; and freedom of information requests. Those involving students include complaints about admission, exclusion, assessment, special consideration, fees and penalties and 'maladministration'. 'Maladministration' generally includes matters such as unreasonable delays in decision making; inadequate investigation of complaints; unfair practices; and bias and has specifically been found when, for example, an appeals process did not comply with the *National Code* or was inconsistent with university policies and where insufficient notice of probationary status was given to a student prior to exclusion.

26 Jim Jackson, Helen Fleming, Patty Kamvounias and Sally Varnham, *Student Grievances and Discipline Matters Project: Final Report to the Australian Learning and Teaching Council* (Australian Learning and Teaching Council, May 2009), 33.

27 Queensland Ombudsman, *Annual Report 2008-2009*, 47.

28 In the 2013-2014 Annual Report (p 36) the Victorian Ombudsman noted that complaints about universities had grown substantially since 2007 and that 631 complaints, mainly from students, were closed in 2013-2014.

C Outcomes of Investigations of Complaints

When a complaint is sustained after an investigation, the ombudsman must provide a report giving reasons for the findings and making recommendations (for example, that the conduct be considered or reconsidered by the university; that action be taken to rectify mitigate or change the conduct or its consequences; that reasons be given for the conduct; that any practice relating to the conduct be changed; that compensation be paid to any person; or that any other step be taken).[29]

Examples of assistance received by individual complainants include: providing a staff member a detailed statement of reasons for the decision of a grievance committee; rehearing a student's appeal against academic assessment by a newly constituted committee to ensure principles of procedural fairness were applied; removal of a finding of breach of the student discipline rules against a student; accepting an out of time appeal from a student.

The ombudsman can also make recommendations to a university for systemic change (including amendments to policies, processes and systems). With the power to recommend improvements in administrative practices to prevent recurrence of the conduct that is the subject of the complaint, an ombudsman can correct the cause of the problem before it affects others.[30] It is this aspect of an ombudsman's investigation of a complaint that can have the greatest impact on the administrative processes of public agencies including public universities. Examples of systemic changes recommended by ombudsmen to universities include: review of a university's conflict of interest policy to address situations that give rise to apprehension of bias; review of selection and promotion procedures to clarify requirements; and reviews of student appeals procedures to ensure students are aware of their entitlement to have a support person in any appeals hearing, to be given detailed reasons for decisions and to allow further submissions to appeals committees where special circumstances apply.

D Other Investigations of Public Universities

In addition to investigating complaints made by the public, parliamentary ombudsmen may also instigate investigations on their own motion. For example, the Victorian Ombudsman conducted an investigation into how universities deal with international students.[31] The report highlighted problems with English language proficiency, academic standards and regulatory arrangements and made a number of recommendations about good practice in these areas.[32] Although the universities were critical of the investigation

29 *Ombudsman Act 1974* (NSW) s 26. See also *Ombudsman Act 1976* (Cth) s 15; *Ombudsman Act 2001* (Qld) s 50; *Ombudsman Act 1972* (SA) s 25; *Ombudsman Act 1978* (Tas) s 28; *Ombudsman Act 1973* (Vic) s 23; *Parliamentary Commissioner Act 1971* (WA) s 25; *Ombudsman Act 1989* (ACT) s 18; *Ombudsman (Northern Territory) Act 1978* (NT) s 59.

30 See Bruce Barbour, 'The Impact of External Administrative Law Review: Courts, Tribunals and Ombudsmen' (2008) 57 *Australian Institute of Administrative Law Forum* 507.

31 Victorian Ombudsman, *Investigation into How Universities Deal with International Students* (October 2011). Four universities were selected for the investigation (Deakin, RMIT, Swinburne and the University of Ballarat) partly based on complaints to the ombudsman's office and partly to ensure the sample covered urban, regional, large and small universities [13].

32 Ibid.

and in many cases disputed the ombudsman's conclusions,[33] the investigation and report served to highlight the important role of the ombudsman in relation to public universities in that State.[34]

Public sector ombudsmen also have a wide range of other responsibilities and functions many of which do not impact at all on public universities[35] but responsibilities in relation to, for example, public interest disclosures can and sometimes have led to investigations of university conduct[36] (see also Chapter 6 by Fleming).

IV Developments in Other Jurisdictions

One of the recommendations of the Dearing Report on higher education in the United Kingdom was that 'institutions ... review and, if necessary, amend their arrangements for handling complaints from students, to ensure that they reflect the principles of natural justice; they are transparent and timely; they include procedures for reconciliation and arbitration; [and] they included an independent, external element'.[37] The UK government responded by providing this 'external element' in the form of the Office of the Independent Adjudicator for Higher Education (the OIA). The OIA is a 'purpose-built independent, student complaints scheme ... [as] an alternative to expensive and time-consuming litigation'.[38] The structure of the OIA is similar to that of ombudsmen in industries such as telecommunications and banking[39] with powers determined by the terms of reference and operational costs shared by each higher educational institution in England and Wales.[40] But, like, public sector ombudsmen, the OIA is an ombudsman of 'last resort' (students must exhaust the internal complaints procedures of their universities before lodging their complaints with the OIA) and the service is free to students.

33 See, for example, Andrew Trounson, 'Unis Brush Off Quality Concerns' (28 October 2011) *The Australian*.

34 It has also been argued that the report 'provides evidence that Australian higher education providers may be failing to meet their legal obligations to international students': Stephen Corones, 'Consumer Guarantees and the Supply of Educational Services by Higher Education Providers' (2012) 35 *University of New South Wales Law Journal* 1.

35 For example, the New South Wales Ombudsman also has functions that relate to deaths of children and people with disabilities in care, the administration of the witness protection program and police powers. See Chris Wheeler, 'Review of Administrative Conduct and Decisions in NSW Since 1974 – an Ad Hoc and Incremental Approach to Radical Change' (Paper presented at the *National Administrative Law Conference*, 19 July 2012, Adelaide, South Australia).

36 See Ombudsman Victoria, *An Investigation into a Complaint about Preferential Treatment of a Student by The University of Melbourne – Report of the Ombudsman*, June 2002; Ombudsman Victoria, *Whistleblowers Protection Act 2001 – Investigation into an Allegation of Improper Conduct within RMIT's School of Engineering (TAFE) Aerospace* (July 2010).

37 National Committee of Inquiry into Higher Education, 'Dearing Report' (Final Report, 1997), para 15.59.

38 Mike Reddy, 'The Office of the Independent Adjudicator for Higher Education: Preparing for the Statutory Scheme' (2004) *Education Law Journal* 1, 2.

39 See Anita Stuhmcke, 'Privatising Administrative Law: The Telecommunications Industry Ombudsman Scheme' (1998) 5 *Australian Journal of Administrative Law* 15.

40 Office of the Independent Adjudicator for Higher Education, *Annual Report* (2008), 61.

In New Zealand and Scotland, it is also the public sector ombudsmen that have jurisdiction to hear complaints about further and higher education institutions.[41] However, in both these jurisdictions there is only one public sector ombudsman's office involved in receiving, assessing, investigating and following up on complaints about public universities, whereas in Australia there are nine independent public sector ombudsmen involved to a greater or lesser extent in dealing with complaints about universities.

V One Ombudsman to Unite them All?

There have been a number of recommendations that the Commonwealth establish an independent ombudsman for the higher education sector in Australia.[42] Although these recommendations received widespread support,[43] they were not implemented. The *Baird Review* also recommended the establishment of a statutorily independent body to handle complaints against education providers.[44] This recommendation was accepted and the ESOS legislation and the *Ombudsman Act 1976* (Cth) were amended accordingly.[45] The new Overseas Student Ombudsman (OSO), established within the office of the Commonwealth Ombudsman, began operation on 9 April 2011.

The OSO investigates complaints overseas students make about private education providers and considers, free of charge, external appeals under Standard 8 of the *National Code*. The 2013-2014 annual report indicates that OSO received 518 complaints about private education providers that were mainly about refunds and fee disputes, providers' decisions to refuse a student transfer to another provider, and providers' decisions to report students to the Department of Immigration and Border protection for failing to meet attendance and progress requirements.[46] OSO also provides information about best practice complaints handling to help private

41 The *Ombudsmen Act 1975* (NZ) gives jurisdiction to investigate complaints about the administrative acts and decisions of government agencies including tertiary education institutions. The *Further and Higher Education (Scotland) Act 2005* extended the remit of the Scottish Public Sector Ombudsman to include further and higher education institutions from 3 October 2005.

42 See Department of Employment, Education, Training and Youth Affairs, *Learning for Life: Review of Higher Education Financing and Policy* (the West Report) (Final Report, 17 April 1998), 110, Recommendation 10; Senate Employment, Workplace Relations, Small Business and Education Committee, *Universities in Crisis* (Final Report, 27 September 2001); Senate Education, Employment and Workplace Relations References Committee, *Welfare of International Students* (Final Report, November 2009), 64.

43 J Wells, 'Why an Ombudsman is Essential for Higher Education' (22 October 2001) *Sydney Morning Herald*.

44 Department of Education, Employment and Workplace Relations, *Stronger, Simpler, Smarter ESOS: Supporting International Students: Review of the Education Services for Overseas Students (ESOS) Act 2000* (the Baird Review) (Final Report, 26 February 2010), 28-29.

45 See Department of Education, Employment and Workplace Relations Legislation Committee, *Education Services for Overseas Students Legislation Amendment Bill 2010* (Final Report, 22 November 2010).

46 Commonwealth Ombudsman, *Annual Report 2013-2014*, 59.

providers manage internal complaints effectively[47] and reports on trends and broader issues arising from investigations.[48]

VI Conclusion

Having an independent external review body is a key component of any robust complaint handling system. There are 10 independent ombudsmen services across Australia involved to some extent in higher education. Nonetheless, local students, staff members and the general public are without recourse to an external independent ombudsman if they have a complaint about a private university or private higher education provider. To avoid the inefficiencies of multiple ombudsmen investigating similar types of complaints and to avoid the unfairness of gaps in the external review system that now exists in Australia, perhaps it is time to reconsider the idea of a 'one-stop' national higher education ombudsman. Having a specialist ombudsman would also allow the development of expertise in dealing with the types of complaints that are made about higher education providers and universities. Furthermore, a singular approach to data collection would make it easier to identify trends and systemic problems and so make it easier for policy-makers and law-makers to better respond to concerns about higher education.

The idea of a national higher education ombudsman has had widespread support and academic commentators have evaluated how the proposal could be implemented using the OIA as a model.[49] The Commonwealth would require a consensus between the States and Territories to introduce appropriate legislation or could tie a national university ombudsman to the funding and quality control arrangements it currently has with the higher education sector.[50] Although the Abbott government has announced proposals for major regulatory reforms of the sector, independent external review of complaint handling does not appear to be a policy priority.

---

47 See, for example, the OSO's Better Practice Complaint Handling for Education Providers (February 2011) available at <http://www.oso.gov.au/docs/better_practice_complaint_handling_for_education_providers.pdf>.

48 For example, in August 2014 the OSO released an issues paper on overseas student health cover available at <http://www.oso.gov.au/docs/Overseas_Students_Ombudsman_Issues_Paper_Overseas_Student_Health_Cover.pdf>.

49 See Hilary Astor, 'Improving Dispute Resolution in Australian Universities: Options for the Future' (2005) 27(1) *Journal of Higher Education Policy and Management* 49; Olliffe and Stuhmcke, above n 25.

50 See Greg Craven, 'Commonwealth Power Over Higher Education' (2006) 1(1) *Public Law* 1; Jim Jackson, 'Commonwealth Controls Over Australian Schools, TAFEs and Universities Via Tied Funding: Time for Constitutional Reform?' (2008) 13(2) *Australia and New Zealand Journal of Law and Education* 101.

Chapter 12

Diversity, Affirmative Action and Higher Education

Joy Cumming and Ralph Mawdsley

I Introduction

Increasing participation in higher education by under-represented groups from remote areas, Indigenous background and low socio-economic backgrounds has been a focus of Australian higher education policy at federal and State level for more than 20 years, based on the premise that failure to realise the full potential of all capable people is 'a significant economic issue for the nation'.[1] Australian State and Territory anti-discrimination legislation that set parameters for non-discriminatory behaviour also allows for affirmative action, referred to as special measures,[2] to address factors perceived to disadvantage participation. This chapter examines diversity and special measures for entry to Australian higher education, and case law that has challenged such measures in general. The conclusion is that while Australian courts would most likely endorse special entry measures as meeting special measure conditions, or concerning internal university policy, Australian universities may be establishing potential liability for ensuring the success of students enrolled under these. The issue addressed in this chapter is the application of law to solve a perceived education inequality. In order to examine Australian law and higher education on this issue, US case law in the area is first briefly discussed. Educators and lawyers gave their attention to a recent seminal case on affirmative action and university admission which prompted examination of the Australian legal context for such actions.

II The US Context

A seminal US education law case, *Fisher v University of Texas at Austin* (UTA) (*Fisher*),[3] attracted considerable attention from both education law and education research communities in the United States. Fisher, a white student, challenged special entry or affirmative action quotas adopted by the university to address underrepresentation of

1 Australian Government Department of Education, Employment and Workplace Relations (AGDEEWR), *Review of Australian Higher Education* (*Bradley Review*) 10 hdl.voced.edu.au/10707/44384.

2 'Special measure' is the term used in international conventions such as the UN *International Convention on the Elimination of All Forms of Racial Discrimination.*

3 Cert granted 2012; remanded to 5th Circuit in June 2013.

students from disadvantaged backgrounds, especially black and Hispanic applicants. Educators argued for the respondents that such actions were necessary to address inequity; lawyers argued for the plaintiff that to be Constitutional, such measures, following precedents from earlier cases from over a quarter of a century, needed to meet the highest level of scrutiny (strict scrutiny), a compelling public interest, be narrowly tailored and the least restrictive means to achieve the interest, and cease when the goal has been achieved.

Miss Fisher challenged affirmative action processes that resulted in denial of her place in the university she preferred. In brief, the UTA admission procedures involved automatic admission of the top 10 per cent of high school graduates to a Texas university (but not necessarily UTA) and for 80 per cent (later changed to 75 per cent) of UTA admissions. Remaining UTA places were allocated on the basis of academic records (Academic Index) and a Personal Achievement Index (PAI). The latter included two essays, non-academic achievements, and information on socio-economic status and family responsibilities. These were considered holistically to 'provide the fullest possible understanding of the student as a person and to place his or her achievements in context'.[4]

Miss Fisher was offered a place at a non-Austin University of Texas campus. Her challenge was based on the Equal Protection Clause of the US Constitution and discrimination.[5] Challenges in US law that discrimination has occurred on the basis of race are held to strict scrutiny, with the government interest identified as compelling.[6] *Fisher* had several landmark precedents on which to draw, including *Bakke*,[7] where an admission process that reserved a quota of places for disadvantaged students was found to be to imprecise, and *Gratz*,[8] where a process that allocated 20 out of 100 points for persons with underrepresented race or ethnicity was found to not meet the strict scrutiny standard despite a compelling interest. In *Gruetter*,[9] however, an affirmative action admission policy for minority groups that evaluated each student individually on a range of factors was held Constitutional, with judicial aspiration that in 25 years, such policies would no longer be necessary.

The challenge by Fisher was heard by the 5th Circuit, which found that UTA met the compelling interest and narrowly tailored approach, then on appeal by Fisher in the Supreme Court which vacated the case and remanded it once more to the Fifth Circuit Court of Appeals,[10] identifying five points for more careful consideration than in the initial judgment.

The final 2-1 decision by the Fifth Circuit again upheld UTA's admission policy as a tailored approach to meet equity goals and address educational disadvantage. The policy was seen to consider race as a factor in 'the unique context of each applicant's entire experience' whereby a student who would otherwise miss out excelled, with no numerical value assigned to racial membership.[11] The dissenting judge found lack

4 Ibid 22.
5 The Fourteenth Amendment to the US Constitution (Equal Protection Clause).
6 See, for example, *Brown v Board of Education* 347 US 483 (1954) (ending segregation in schools).
7 *Regents of University of California v Bakke* 438 US 265 (1978) (*Bakke*).
8 *Gratz v Bollinger* 539 US 244 (2003) (*Gratz*).
9 *Gruetter v Bollinger* 539 US 306 (2003) (*Gruetter*).
10 *Fisher v University of Texas at Austin* No 11-345 (2013) (remanded to 5th Cir).
11 *Fisher v University of Texas at Austin* No 09-50822 (5th Cir, 15 July 2014), 4.

of clarity of goals and objectives with respect to race-conscious policy. Given the educational and legal significance of this case for equity in higher education in the United States, Australian legal contexts for affirmative action, or 'special measures' are considered.

III Australian Special Measures

The Australian Constitution does not grant individual rights such as those in the US Constitution, and no Australian student could claim a right to entry to a higher education institution. Australian discrimination laws do prevent discrimination in higher education enrolment on the grounds of race or other identified attributes.[12] In Australia, discrimination is identified as direct, 'if a person treats, or proposes to treat, a person with an attribute less favourably than another person without the attribute is or would be treated in circumstances that are the same or not materially different', or indirect, through imposition or proposing to impose 'a term (a) with which a person with an attribute does not or is not able to comply; and (b) with which a higher proportion of people without the attribute comply or are able to comply'.[13] Discrimination, if established, is unlawful.

Exemptions for practices that are discriminatory are allowed under special circumstances and applications may be made for exemption.[14] Applications for exemption are different, however, from 'special measures' – actions endorsed in Australian legislation similar to affirmative actions in the United States.[15]

Australian anti-discrimination legislation allow for 'special measures', 'positive discrimination' and 'equal opportunity measures' to 'secure advancement' for special groups or to ensure equal enjoyments or exercise of human rights.[16] For example, the

12 See, for example, for race, *Racial Discrimination Act 1975* (Cth) s 9; *Discrimination Act 1991* (ACT) s 7(1); *Anti-Discrimination Act 1977* (NSW) s 7; *Anti-Discrimination Act* (NT) s 3; *Anti-Discrimination Act 1991* (Qld) s 7; *Equal Opportunity Act 1984* (SA) s 51; *Anti-Discrimination Act 1988* (Tas) s 16; *Equal Opportunity Act 2010* (Vic) s 6; *Equal Opportunity Act 1984* (WA) s 36.

13 See, for example, *Discrimination Act 1991* (ACT) s 8(1)(a) (direct), s 8(1)(b) (indirect); *Anti-Discrimination Act 1991* (Qld) s 10 (direct), s 11(indirect).

14 While under Australian anti-discrimination law, an application is made for an exemption to undertake an action that is on the face discriminatory, determination of a special measure occurs if an action is challenged as discriminatory.

15 For example, in *Downer EDI Mining* [2013] QCAT 99, a company applied for an exemption to advertise for Indigenous workers, denied as the company was already exceeding its own Indigenous employee targets. However, if the goal was a special measure under s 105 of the *ADA* to promote equal opportunity, then an exemption would not be needed. In *King's International College* [2011] QCAT 231, a college sought exemption under s 113 of the *ADA* to run a 'nanny' course for males only, due to lack of male students and workers in area. The exemption was denied, as the content of the course was not adapted to be more suitable for male students. Insufficient evidence was provided to warrant a special measure.

16 *Racial Discrimination Act 1975* (Cth) s 8 (special measures); *Discrimination Act 1991* (ACT) s 27 (measures to achieve equality); *Anti-Discrimination Act 1977* (NSW) s 21 (special needs programs and activities); *Anti-Discrimination Act* (NT) s 57 (special measures); *Anti-Discrimination Act 1991* (Qld) s 105 (equal opportunity measures); *Equal Opportunity Act 1984* (SA) s 65 (projects for benefit or persons of a particular race); *Anti-Discrimination Act 1998* (Tas) s 25 (special needs), s 26 (equal opportunity); *Equal Opportunity Act 2010* (Vic) s 12

Racial Discrimination Act 1975 (Cth), which imports the *International Convention on the Elimination of All Forms of Racial Discrimination* (*ICEAFRD*) to which Australia is signatory,[17] notes that discrimination 'does not apply to, or in relation to the application of, special measures to which of paragraph 4 of Article 1 of the Convention applies'.[18]

Article 1(4) of the *ICEAFRD* states that:

> *Special measures* taken for the *sole purpose* of securing adequate advancement of certain racial or ethnic groups or individuals requiring such protection as may be necessary in order to ensure such groups or individuals equal enjoyment or exercise of human rights and fundamental freedoms shall not be deemed racial discrimination, *provided*, however, that such measures do *not*, as a consequence, lead to the *maintenance of separate rights for different racial groups* and that they shall *not* be *continued after the objectives for which they were taken have been achieved.* (emphasis added)

Similar expectations are expressed, for example, in the Victorian *Equal Opportunity Act 2010* (*EOA*). A 'special measure' for the purpose of promoting or realising substantive equality for members of a group with a particular attribute must:

(a) be undertaken in good faith for achieving the purpose
(b) be reasonably likely to achieve the purpose
(c) be a proportionate means of achieving the purpose
(d) be justified because the members of the group have a particular need for advancement or assistance.[19]

The special measure must be undertaken solely for that purpose or in conjunction with other purposes.[20] When the purpose has been achieved, the measure 'ceases to be a special measure'.[21] 'Reasonable' restrictions may be placed on eligibility for the special measure. The EOA is incorporated in general terms in the *Charter of Human Rights and Responsibilities Act 2006* (Vic) (*Charter of Human Rights*) in s 8(4). Section 7(2)(e) of the *Charter of Human Rights* on restrictions of human rights has been interpreted to replicate the principle noted in US case law as to whether 'any less restrictive means [were] reasonably available to achieve the purpose that the limitation seeks to achieve'.[22]

Without reference to US case law, but reflecting the *ICEAFRD*, and US precedents on university affirmative action, Australian anti-discrimination law identifies principles underpinning special measures as:

- 'in good faith', 'justified' and 'to achieve a (legitimate) purpose';
- 'proportionate', 'likely to achieve the purpose' and 'reasonable' reflecting 'narrowly tailored', with '[generally] no less restrictive option available';[23]
- to cease on achievement of the goal.

(special measures); *Equal Opportunity Act 1984* (WA) s 51 (measures to achieve equality, equal opportunities, access to meet special needs).

17 Opened for signature on 21 December 1965 and entered into force on 2 January 1969.

18 *Racial Discrimination Act 1975* (Cth) s 8(1).

19 *Equal Opportunity Act 2010* (Vic) s 12(3).

20 *Equal Opportunity Act 2010* (Vic) s 12(4).

21 *Equal Opportunity Act 2010* (Vic) s 12(7).

22 *Lifestyle Communities Ltd (No 3) (Anti-Discrimination)* [2009] VCAT 1869, [79].

23 Ibid [79].

These principles from legislation on 'special measures', therefore, create potential tests for whether Australian special admission schemes to higher education would be categorised as discriminatory actions or as special measures under anti-discrimination law.

There is a dearth of judicial considerations of 'special measures' to confirm these tests.[24] In *Gerhardy v Brown*,[25] Brennan J indicated four characteristics of a special measure for racial equality:

> a special measure
> (1) confers a benefit on some or all members of a class
> (2) the membership of which is based on race, colour, descent or national or ethnic origin
> (3) for the sole purpose of securing adequate advancement of the beneficiaries in order that they may enjoy and exercise equally with other human rights and fundamental freedoms
> (4) in circumstances where the protection given to the beneficiaries by the special measure is necessary in order that they may enjoy and exercise equally with other human rights and fundamental freedoms.[26]

Again, Brennan J noted that special measures should be discontinued when their objectives have been achieved.

In a more recent case regarding the introduction of 'inflexible quotas' by unions for 50 per cent of representatives to executive positions to be women,[27] Crennan J noted that a special measure under s 7D of the *SDA* must be considered broadly as a subject test in terms of its 'context, object and purpose'.[28] Council for the Human Rights Commissioner, as *amicus curae*, had submitted that to determine whether a special measure was appropriate:

> the Court needs to objectively test first whether the entity propounding a special measure acted reasonably in assessing the need for the special measure, and secondly the capacity of the special measure to achieve the purpose of substantive equality. It was also submitted that appropriate factors to be considered included the field of activity in which the special measure was taken, the correct comparator in relation to substantive inequality, the causes of inequality, the proportionality of the special measure and whether the special measure was still required.[29]

'Intention and purpose' of a special measure govern its characterisation.[30] Similar principles of special measures were stated in an unsuccessful application for exemption:

> Equality does not imply absolute equality without any distinctions. Purely formal equality can produce and entrench substantive inequality. Some differentiation

24 *Walker v Cormack* [2011] FCA 861.
25 (1985) 159 CLR 70.
26 Ibid [32].
27 *Jacomb v Australian Municipal Administrative Clerical and Services Union* [2004] FCA 1250 (*Jacomb*). The challenge claimed discrimination on the grounds of sex under the *Sex Discrimination Act 1984* (Cth) (*SDA*) as the quotas did not reflect 'attainable levels of representation' proportionate to membership of women and men.
28 See *Jacomb*.
29 Ibid.
30 Julie O'Brien, 'Affirmative Action, Special Measures and the Sex Discrimination Act' (2004) 27(3) *UNSW Law Journal* 840.

> between people may be justified and is not prohibited discrimination. Measures taken to redress inequalities arising from past treatment or historical circumstances are not violations of the equality and nondiscrimination principles ... differentiation which is reasonable, objective and aims to achieve a purpose which is legitimate ..., and is proportionate to that purpose.[31]

In cases considered in Australia, numerical quotas as an approach have not been rejected as in the United States, however, these cases have involved special measures to promote equal opportunity on the basis of gender, where the population ratio can be estimated. After consideration of international law with respect to quotas, Crennan J concluded that the purpose of the quotas in *Jacomb* was to achieve 'substantive equality between men and women members' that had not been achieved to date. The quota was to be discontinued if no longer needed.

Australia is not noted for its volume of legal challenges in education law, although increasingly these are occurring in higher education. In order to consider likely outcomes of such challenges in Australian courts, the following discussion examines a further number of legal challenges against special measures, the nature of the judicial reasoning that establishes the legality of special measures in Australian law and outcomes.

IV Australian Legal Challenges to Special Measures[32]

Challenges by individuals against special measures or by organisations applying to introduce special measures have occurred in a number of areas outside higher education in Australia, for example, individuals seeking access to restricted housing 'designed to meet the special needs of disadvantaged persons',[33] and to restricted medical services provided to patients who were from Aboriginal or Torres Strait Islander or non-English speaking background or were under 25 years of age,[34] identified as 'having the greatest difficulty in accessing mainstream health services' as well as 'often having complex and chronic health problems'.[35] In both these cases, the special measures were found to be appropriate. It was noted that to meet identified and targeted needs, they did not require 'strict construction'[36] and that the medical services 'may be expected to have a termination date'.[37]

Of some relevance to higher education, in *Bruch v Commonwealth*,[38] a non-Aboriginal student challenged the provision of rental assistance to Indigenous students under ABSTUDY. The question for determination was whether the rental assistance under ABSTUDY was a special measure. The applicant received a different form of

---

31 *Lifestyle Communities Ltd (No 3) (Anti-Discrimination)* [2009] VCAT 1869, [4], [5].

32 Legal decisions with respect to special measures for Indigenous people of Australia and land rights (see, for example, *Gerhardy v Brown* (1985) 159 CLR 70) or introduction of controls in areas such as alcohol consumption and gambling are not considered in this chapter.

33 *Richardson v ACT Health & Community Care Service* [2000] FCA 654 (*Richardson*).

34 *Central Northern Adelaide Health Service v Atkinson* [2008] SASC 371 (*Atkinson*).

35 Ibid [31].

36 See *Richardson.*

37 *Atkinson*, [112].

38 [2002] FMCA 29.

allowance that did not include rental assistance. ABSTUDY was argued to be a special measure under s 8 of the *Racial Discrimination Act 1975* (Cth) to advance education of Indigenous disadvantaged students. Rental assistance was taken to meet the requirements for special measures indicated in *Gerhardy v Brown* and further that the need for such special measures had been established with the 'sole purpose [of] securing the adequate advancement of indigenous Australians and that at present and indeed in the foreseeable future that group requires protection to ensure equality of opportunity in tertiary education which in turn I regard as equal enjoyment of the exercise of human rights'.[39]

Overall, cases regarding special measures arise when a complainant mounts a challenge that an action is discriminatory. The legal burden is then on the respondent to provide the evidence that establishes the action as a special measure, including, context and purpose of the action; considerations that have occurred that have led to the action; that the approach is proportionate and is reasonable to achieve the stated goal of equality of opportunity; and that measures are in place to cease the activity when the goal is obtained. In principle courts and tribunals heed these elements. Most notably, however, the interpretations of elements have been broad, not strict, with apparent leeway given to measures identified as addressing identified disadvantage and equality. Strict scrutiny has not applied to whether alternative less restrictive measures were available. Focus has turned to whether an identifiable group or groups are the recipients of the special measure and how their needs are to be met. The cases considered, with the exception of *Jacomb* discussed earlier, have related to service provision – that is, the special measures are about the provision of an activity or service that will better the opportunities offered to groups identified as in need and which will address those needs.

V Potential Legal Challenges to Australian Universities' Special Measures

Australian universities admit students through a range of policies and approaches. A number have in place what seem, on the face, to be special measures – admission policies designed to address disadvantage or underrepresentation, and to promote equality of opportunity for students. No legal challenges to special measures for admission, as have occurred in the United States, have been identified in Australian law. Given increasing pressure on entry in some disciplines such as medicine, however, it is possible that Australian students who are not admitted on the basis of their grades may wish to challenge the admission of students with lower grades on the basis of special measures, especially if they are unsuccessful in obtaining a higher education place in a preferred and prestigious, high entry demand course such as medicine or law.

Table 2 (see *over page*) provides an overview of types of special entry admission schemes promoted by Australian universities on their 2013-2014 websites and the

39 Ibid [53].

Table 2: Summary of Special Measures and Admissions Schemes – Australian Universities 2014

		No of Universities
Types of Special Entry Offered	Financial	25
	Rural	29
	Difficult Circumstances	26
	Mature Age	18
	Women /Men in under-represented disciplines	6
	Under-represented schools	17
	Indigenous Special Entry	38
Nature of Schemes	Per cent of positions dedicated to Special Entries	2 (20%; 10%)
	Bonus points - EAS / SEAS	19
	Bonus points - relevant subjects	13
	Bonus points - other	17
	Direct Entry (other than Indigenous)	6
Support Offered	Bridging Programs	30
	Unit subject programs	2
	Course advice	7
	Counselling	7
	Indigenous Higher Education Unit/Support	39
	Study Assistance	11
	Institution Equity Scholarships	19

numbers of institutions identified as offering these schemes.[40] Overall, the types of schemes available enable students to make application for admission on the basis of: financial disadvantage; rural disadvantage; other difficult personal circumstances; mature age; graduation from underrepresented schools; Indigenous or Torres Strait Islander background. Admission schemes in a small number of universities are also gender-related for areas where either women or men are underrepresented.

It should be noted first that Australian courts are reluctant to engage with matters of policy of universities and other educational institutions. However, a complaint of discrimination would need to be addressed, and for many of these schemes, the defence of special measure would need to be raised. A complaint of discrimination under legislation, of course, can only occur on the basis of protected attributes such as race, sex, marital status, age, political belief, disability, and in some legislation, family responsibilities. Financial or personal circumstances or geographic location identified in some special admission schemes are not protected attributes; complaints against admission policies addressing these on grounds of discrimination could not arise. Thus, while a number of admission schemes have the nature of special measures to address equality of opportunity, they are not special measures within the legal sense, but reflect identified Australian federal higher education policy initiatives.

To be a special measure, the university admission schemes would need to demonstrate not only the need to address equality of opportunity but also that the approach taken addresses the need and is proportionate. Different universities have taken different approaches in making special admission offers. A common approach is to lower the entry requirements for a course below those specified for students who do not quality for special entry. For example, The University of Melbourne indicated that special entry through Access Melbourne required only an Australian Tertiary Admission Ranking (ATAR) of 88 for commerce, with the minimum for other students expected to be 93.[41] If challenged, in terms of legal consideration of special measures, it would appear from previous case law that the university would need to demonstrate considerations that led to this difference in entry levels and how it was identified that this would be appropriate in reaching the goal, and at what point such measures would not be needed. The University of Melbourne also indicates that it has a desired quota of 20 per cent of supported places to be allocated to students for graduate programs admitted through Access Melbourne.[42] Australian case law to date on quotas in special measures has occurred in equal opportunity for men and women, where notional populations can be identified. It would be of interest to see how courts would reason when faced with a quota of 20 per cent if no clear rationale for such a ratio could be provided other than government policy.

40 Every endeavour has been made to ensure accuracy of information in Table 2 at the time of writing. Some omissions may have occurred because of terminology differences across websites and the manner in which information on admission processes or support is interwoven across websites.

41 University of Melbourne, Access Melbourne (2014) <http://futurestudents.unimelb.edu.au/admissions/access_melbourne_and_equity_programs/access-melbourne/guaranteed-entry-for-access-melbourne-applicants>.

42 Ibid. See also <http://futurestudents.unimelb.edu.au/admissions/access_melbourne_and_equity_programs/graduate-access-melbourne/benefits_of_graduate_access_melbourne>.

Another common approach is to provide bonus points to boost entry rankings for students on the basis of characteristics. Again, a legal challenge to the scheme would need the institution to provide evidence that some forethought had gone into the allocations of points, that they are proportionate to the goal, and that there is an end in sight when the goals are reached. The non-specificity of backgrounds of students who will gain special entry may or may not create a problem for Australian courts.

The final types of special entry schemes offered by Australian universities are not to address perceived inequality of opportunity, that is legally or not legally defined special measures, but are more commercial in nature to gain the most academically-able students. These are schemes that offer bonus points for students who have studied specific subjects, such as languages, offer places to students in schools linked to universities, or offer direct entry to students who may have undertaken some university studies as a part of their secondary schooling. These are clearly not challengeable on grounds of discrimination or defendable as special measures.

Overall, following the guidelines that have been set in Australian case law on special measures, it is unlikely that a challenge against university schemes on the basis of discrimination, based on a protected attribute, would be successful in Australia, if the various elements of defence can be argued by the universities.

This analysis does give rise to concern, however, that the special admission schemes that universities have put in place do not clearly demonstrate that the approach is reasonable to achieve the goal. Adding points, reducing entry requirements, setting quotas may increase the diversity of students entering universities, originally identified as the goal of schemes in the United States, and address lack of educational opportunity that some students experience. The admission schemes do not, however, relate to services to address need, as in the cases previously discussed.

In and of themselves, the schemes may not be reasonable in achieving a goal of increasing the diversity of students who *graduate* from universities, the concern further raised in US cases such as *Fisher*. To achieve this, additional support mechanisms throughout studies must be in place and integrated with the admission scheme. Table 2 includes information gained from university websites on the nature of supports available to students who have been admitted through special admission schemes, including special measures to create equal opportunity. While nearly all universities indicate support for Indigenous students, and some indicate general advice about financial assistance and counselling, there is not consistency of evidence of what universities will do for students who have gained admission with identified lower academic achievement standards than other students. While nearly all universities offer bridging programs that enable students to make a transition from early studies or work experience to university-level studies, these are not indicated as compulsory for students gaining special admissions.

This analysis therefore raises the concern that while students who are not admitted may not be successful in challenging special admission schemes on the basis of discrimination for a protected attribute, students who are successfully admitted under a special measure may challenge universities for misrepresentation and false and deceptive conduct that they would be capable of undertaking their studies, under s 18 of the

Australian Consumer Law (sch 2 to the *Competition and Consumer Act 2010* (Cth); previously s 52 of the *Trade Practices Act 1974*).

Concerns were raised in various forums in 2014 about possible abuse of admission schemes by universities and in particular bonus point schemes to fill student numbers,[43] general lack of transparency as to whether students have adequate academic resources to undertake their proposed programs of study,[44] and the appropriate level of quotas or targets for disadvantaged student entry.[45] Students who accept special entry or bonus scheme admission will have foregone earnings, will have made commitments, but may find, without adequate support to address any gaps in their academic preparation, which they are unable to succeed or to succeed at the level necessary for future employment. To achieve 'substantive' equality,[46] it can be argued, special measures that affect admission but not ongoing support and study should fail the test of proportionality and reasonableness to address the identified needs of intended recipients. This is more significant in Australian higher education than in US institutions, given direct entry for most students into vocationally-oriented degrees with academically-focused expectations.

VI Conclusion

This chapter has examined Australian statute law, policy and case decisions in the area of special measures, actions undertaken to address disadvantage and need, specifically enabled both through international conventions and federal, State and Territory anti-discrimination legislation. The focus was instigated in response to a seminal law case in the United States, building on previous legal decisions from over 25 years, challenging a university's affirmative action policy to increase the diversity of students from disadvantaged backgrounds.

Examination of Australian law and case law identified that similar elements are in place in Australia to establish that an action that is, apparently, direct discrimination can be characterised as a special measure. Australian case law has, and most likely will continue to have, broader tests of these elements than US case law, with more recognition of the policy-making responsibilities of Australian universities. Each of the identified elements has been considered.

The conclusion drawn from a legal perspective is that if Australian universities can provide evidence of the rationale and considerations behind special measures for admission, legal challenges on grounds of discrimination will not succeed. The analysis raises the more potentially serious question, however, as to whether special measures

43 Julie Hare, 'Uni Admissions Racket Thrives on Fake Cut-Offs' (13-14 September 2014) *The Weekend Australian* (Sydney) 21: 'Accepting up to 25 bonus points is not unheard of' (with reports that in South Australia in future students will gain a maximum of five bonus points for disadvantage and four for subject choice).

44 Andrew Trounson, 'Spell Out Courses Maths Demands' (17 September 2014) *The Australian (Higher Education)* (Sydney), 31.

45 Andrew Trounson, 'Fallout From Dropping Targets "Will Be Short-lived"' (23 April 2014) *The Australian (Higher Education)* (Sydney), 26: '"Arbitrary" targets risked encouraging universities to enrol underprepared students who were at higher risk of dropping out, simply to meet the target'.

46 *Jacomb*, Submission of Council for the Human Rights Commissioner as *amicus curiae*.

that address only admission may be misleading for students who, following entry, are not supported to succeed. Increased equitable participation 'for all capable people'[47] is federal policy. Support funding programs to address these goals are available to higher education institutions and students. Where special measures have occurred to enable students to enrol in courses for which they did not meet preliminary academic requirements, institutions must be on notice to demonstrate that appropriate funding expenditure and support are in place.

Potential challenges may not arise in Australian law. If they do, the evidence of the higher education institutions about prior considerations, rationales and justifications will be extremely informing as to the considerations that tribunals and courts must make in determining whether the admission schemes can be characterised as special measures. The point of law on which such considerations may turn is whether the special measures will achieve 'substantive equality'. 'Special measures' as an area of discrimination law is underrepresented in Australian writing but an area with considerable import for individuals and groups, under the auspices of international conventions on human rights, and worthy of further exploration. To attain overall equality, of course, the goal is that such special measures will cease to be required.

47 *Bradley Review*, above n 1, 6.

Chapter 13

Disability Standards for Education

Elizabeth Dickson

I Introduction

The *Disability Discrimination Act 1992* (Cth) (*DDA*) prohibits discrimination by education institutions against students with disability[1] and obliges Australian education providers, including universities, to make reasonable adjustments to policies and procedures so as to avoid discrimination.[2] The *Disability Standards for Education 2005* (Cth) (*Disability Standards*), subordinate legislation passed under the authority of the *DDA*, set out a scheme to support the making of reasonable adjustments. The *Disability Standards* were expected to increase the effectiveness of the *DDA* by clarifying the scope of the action which must be taken by education providers to avoid discrimination against students with disabilities.[3]

The *Disability Standards* acknowledge that students with disability have a right to an education 'on the same basis' as students without disability.[4] They set out the obligations which must be met by education providers as they deliver upon that right, and they set out measures of compliance to assist them to determine whether those obligations have been met. As such, the *Disability Standards* shift, from the university student to the university, the burden of ensuring the removal of barriers to equal opportunity in higher education. A university can no longer wait for a complaint of discrimination to be made before remedying practices and policies which have the effect of limiting the educational opportunities of their students with disabilities.

Although the *Disability Standards* have been in force for almost a decade,[5] evidence suggests that there is still confusion in the Australian university sector about their scope and effect. A recent review of the *Disability Standards* reported 'disparity between institutions in the levels of assistance provided to students with the same disability',[6] highlighted lack of university staff awareness of the *Disability Standards* 'as a major

1 *DDA* s 22.

2 *DDA* ss 5 and 6. Note that of the State and Territory Acts, only the *Equal Opportunity Act 2010* (Vic) mandates reasonable adjustment for people with disability: s 40.

3 Sev Ozdowski, *Advancing Equality in Education and Beyond* (Paper presented at Eastern Metropolitan Region Student Disability Conference, 1 September 2005, Melbourne). Dr Ozdovski was acting Disability Discrimination Commissioner at the time the *Disability Standards* came into force.

4 *Disability Standards* ss 4.2, 5.2, 6.2, 7.2.

5 The *Disability Standards* came into force on 18 August 2005.

6 Department of Education, Employment and Workplace Relations, Australian Government, *Report on the Report on the Review of Disability Standards for Education 2005* (June 2012), 29.

factor affecting provider compliance'[7] and suggested that compulsory staff training[8] and even external monitoring[9] may be required to improve compliance within individual universities and across the sector.

This chapter aims to improve compliance by universities and educational opportunity for university students. It will explain the scheme of the *Disability Standards*, their intersection with general discrimination law, and ramifications for university education.[10]

II The Standards and Discrimination Law

A *Cases Interpreting the Disability Standards*

It is interesting to note that, to date, there has not been a tertiary education discrimination case where the *Disability Standards* have been litigated.[11] Indeed, to date, there have been only four Federal Court cases where the *Disability Standards* have been considered in any detail:[12] *Walker v Victoria* (*Walker*),[13] *Sievwright v Victoria* (*Sievwright*),[14] *Abela v Victoria* (*Abela*)[15] and *Kiefel v Victoria* (*Kiefel*).[16] While each of these cases concerns the compulsory education sector, the way the law is interpreted in each applies also to the tertiary sector. Unfortunately, however, none of the cases completely explains the scope of the *Disability Standards*. It is possible to make informed comment on that scope too, and particularly upon the scope of the primary obligation under the *Disability Standards*, the obligation to make 'reasonable adjustment', by drawing upon other education discrimination decisions which consider concepts relevant to the *Disability Standards* such as reasonableness and unjustifiable hardship.[17] Most of those cases will 'turn on their own facts' and not set

---

Note that a second review of the Disability Standards commenced in May 2015. It is anticipated that the report on that review will be published later in 2015.

7 Ibid 35.

8 Ibid 8.

9 Ibid 64.

10 For more detailed analysis of the efficacy of the *Disability Standards* as a tool towards the elimination of discrimination see Elizabeth Dickson, 'Disability Standards for Education 2005 (Cth): Sword or Shield for Australian Students with Disability' (2014) 19(1) *International Journal of Law and Education* 5.

11 What this suggests about the effectiveness of the *Disability Standards* as a tool towards the elimination of discrimination is discussed below.

12 There have been several cases involving allegations of a breach or breaches of the *Standards* which have been settled, and where the Federal Court has ratified the settlement pursuant to an applicant under the *Federal Court Rules 2011* (Cth) r 9.71. See, for example, *A on behalf of B v New South Wales (Department of Education and Training) (No 2)* [2013] FCA 551. In each of the cases which did proceed to trial, the complainant was unsuccessful in proving either a breach of the *Disability Standards* or of the *DDA*.

13 [2011] FCA 258 (*Walker*). The decision was upheld in *Walker v Victoria* [2012] FCAFC 38.

14 [2012] FCA 118.

15 [2013] FCA 832.

16 [2013] FCA 1398.

17 Australian anti-discrimination legislation has always addressed reasonableness in the context of indirect discrimination, where it will render lawful an otherwise discriminatory condition imposed upon a person with disability. See, for example, *DDA* s 6. Moreover, express exemptions to discrimination, and, in particular, the unjustifiable hardship exemption which applies only

any precedent in respect of the application of the *Disability Standards*, but they will illustrate the potential for certain adjustments to be sought and the considerations relevant to their reasonableness.

B Intersection of the Disability Standards and the DDA

The relevant wording of the *DDA* suggests that the *Disability Standards* may work to protect education providers from liability under the *DDA*. The *DDA* provides that compliance with the *Disability Standards* amounts to compliance with the *DDA*.[18] The decided cases demonstrate, however, that actions are now being brought against education providers which allege both a failure to make reasonable adjustment amounting to non-compliance with the *Disability Standards*, and direct or indirect discrimination as prohibited by the *DDA*. Direct discrimination is less favourable treatment of a person. Determination of less favourable treatment requires analysis of the treatment of the complainant and a comparator in circumstances that are not materially different.[19] Indirect discrimination arises when an unreasonable condition is imposed on the complainant, he or she cannot comply with the condition and it disadvantages him or her.[20]

Breach of the *Disability Standards* was argued in conjunction with direct and indirect discrimination claims in all four Federal Court cases which address the *Disability Standards*: *Walker*, *Sievwright*, *Abela* and *Kiefel*. Tracey J, in the *Walker* case upon appeal, explains that breach of the *Disability Standards* is a cause of action separate from direct or indirect discrimination:

> [T]he purpose of the *Standards* is to prescribe processes, such as consultation, which must be observed when determining how best to assist a disabled student. A failure to comply with one of the requirements does not give rise to discrimination within the meaning of the *DDA*. It gives rise to a contravention of s 32.[21]

C Intersection of the Disability Standards and the DDA with Other Discrimination Laws

Australia has a two-tiered system of prohibition of discrimination on the basis of disability or impairment. Each State and Territory has generic anti-discrimination or equal opportunity legislation which prohibits discrimination against students with disability or impairment.[22] A student may choose to bring a complaint of discrimination

in respect of discrimination against people with disability, have required courts and tribunals to consider matters which are relevant to the reasonableness of less favourable treatment. See, for example, *DDA* s 11.

18 *DDA* s 34.

19 *DDA* s 5.

20 *DDA* s 6. Until 2009, the formula for indirect discrimination was as follows: a condition is imposed with which the complainant cannot comply; a higher proportion of people without the complainant's disability could comply; the condition is not reasonable.

21 *Walker*, [273].

22 *Anti-Discrimination Act 1977* (NSW) s 49L; *Equal Opportunity Act 1984* (SA) s 74; *Equal Opportunity Act 1984* (WA) s 66I; *Anti-Discrimination Act 1991* (Qld) ss 7, 37-39; *Discrimination Act 1991* (ACT) ss 6(1)(j), 18; *Anti-Discrimination Act 1998* (Tas) ss 16(k), 22; *Anti-Discrimination Act* (NT) ss 19(1)(j), 29; *Equal Opportunity Act 2010* (Vic) ss 6(e), 38.

under State legislation rather than under the *DDA* and *Disability Standards*.[23] Because of the operation of *DDA* s 13(3A), which has the effect that State law which is inconsistent with the operation of the *Disability Standards* is displaced, however, compliance with the *Disability Standards* will be a relevant consideration for State courts and tribunals adjudicating upon complaints of discrimination brought under State law.[24] While the New South Wales Administrative Decisions Tribunal (NSWADT) (Appeal Panel) case, *Phu v New South Wales Department of Education and Training*[25] has acknowledged the relevance of the *Disability Standards* to State law 'as providing a norm or reasonable expectation of the *Disability Standards* an educational institution should seek to achieve', it is interesting that they are not routinely pleaded in the context of matters brought under State legislation.[26]

III The Scope of the Disability Standards

A *Institutional and Staff Obligations*

The *Disability Standards* are binding on all universities, schools and school systems across the government and independent sectors. The legislation binds 'education providers'. 'Education provider' is further defined to cover 'education authorities' and 'education institutions'.[27] Moreover, the *Disability Standards* apply in respect of a complete range of modes of education delivery, 'including in-class tuition, distance education, flexible delivery, computer-assisted learning, on-line delivery, part-time study for post-compulsory students and the various combinations of these modes, and on-the-job training'.[28]

The clear trend in discrimination litigation is for a complainant to sue the education authority which administers the institution where the unlawful treatment is alleged to have occurred, or the institution itself. There have been discrimination actions, however, in which staff have been joined as respondents.[29] An educational

23 Indeed, students, who are often self-represented, may prefer to bring claims in costs-neutral State jurisdictions where available, in order to avoid Federal Court costs ramifications should they fail to prove a breach of the *Disability Standards* or unlawful discrimination. See *Walker v Victoria* [2012] FCAFC 38, [114] (Flick J) for an example of the Federal Court approach to costs in this jurisdiction: 'As a result of the orders for costs made at first instance and in this appeal, if the respondent should see fit to enforce those orders, the effect on the appellant's family will no doubt be ruinous. The interests of the appellant have certainly not been advanced in the conduct of litigation of this kind in the manner in which it has been conducted'.

24 In Victoria, the *Equal Opportunity Act 2010* (Vic) s 40(3)(i) expressly acknowledges the relevance of the *Disability Standards*.

25 [2010] NSWADTAP 76, [20].

26 An exception is the school case, *AB v Ballarat Christian College* [2013] VCAT 1790 which concerned a claim brought under the *Equal Opportunity Act 2010* (Vic). As noted, *Equal Opportunity Act 2010*, above n 2, imposes an obligation to make reasonable adjustment for students with disability. Further, it acknowledges the relevance of the *Disability Standards* to the reasonableness enquiry for the purpose of that Act: s 40(4).

27 See *DDA* s 4 (definitions of education provider, educational authority and educational institution); *Disability Standards* s 2.1.

28 *Disability Standards* s 1.5 Note 3.

29 See, for a recent example, *Kancheff v Charles Darwin University* [2013] FCCA 1564. The complainant student, alleging direct and indirect discrimination, commenced action under

authority or institution will likely be deemed liable for the wrongs of a staff member committed on its behalf and 'within the scope of his or her actual or apparent authority' unless the authority or institution 'took reasonable precautions and exercised due diligence to avoid the conduct'.[30] An educational authority or institution which 'causes, instructs, induces, aids or permits' discriminatory acts may be directly liable.[31] The weight of case law suggests that it will be rare for an educational authority or institution to escape liability for the discriminatory acts of one of its staff. As such, it is important for universities to ensure staff awareness of obligations upon them pursuant to discrimination law.

B *Disability and Disclosure*

Australian universities receive Commonwealth funding under the Additional Support for Students with Disability (ASSD) component of the Higher Education Disability Support Program to provide support and services to their domestic students with disability. Education providers 'may claim for expenditure incurred for domestic students who are enrolled with the higher education provider, who have been assessed by the higher education provider as having a disability, and who have received educational support related to that disability'.[32]

It is interesting to note that the relevant Commonwealth funding legislation[33] does not define disability, and simply stipulates that higher education providers must 'must obtain evidence of the student's disability and support needs and must undertake a needs assessment process, in accordance with the higher education provider's usual procedures'.[34] To support this assessment process, providers 'must publish their eligibility assessment procedures in a format that is readily available and accessible to people with a disability'.[35]

In the absence of any guidance as to the scope of disability for funding purposes, and in order to avoid allegations of a discriminatory failure to provide support, higher education providers would be wise to align their disability assessment categories with the definition in the *DDA* and *Disability Standards*.[36] In that legislation, disability is very broadly defined to encompass physical, intellectual, behavioural, psychiatric and sensory impairments. It is particularly important for education providers that the definition specifically includes 'a disorder or malfunction that results in the person learning differently from a person without the disorder or malfunction'.[37]

The 2012 report of the review of the *Disability Standards* noted that 'there continues to be some reluctance for students with disability and mental illness to identify disability

the *DDA* against the university, the Dean of the Faculty of Education, Health and Science and the supervisor of the course work component of a unit in which the student was enrolled.

30 *DDA* s 123.
31 Ibid s 122.
32 *Higher Education Support Act 2003 – Other Grants Guidelines (Education) 2012* (Cth) s 1.100.5.15.
33 Ibid.
34 Ibid s 1.100.10.1.
35 Ibid s 1.100.10.10.
36 *Disability Standards* s 1.4; *DDA* s 4 (definition of 'disability').
37 *DDA* s 4(1) (definition of 'disability') para (f).

when commencing at university'.[38] While university enrolment forms may now routinely allow an opportunity for students to disclose disability, there is no legal requirement for students to do so. Even if a student does not disclose on the enrolment form, there will be opportunities for him or her to put the university on notice after enrolment. In *Bishop v Sports Massage Training School*, for example, the tribunal found, that although a formal disclosure process had not been utilised, the education institution knew about the disability once the student had told teaching staff about his dyslexia.[39]

Disability, and any imperative to disclose, may also manifest after enrolment. Many university teaching staff may not appreciate that the student who seeks an extension on account of a broken arm[40] or bout of the flu[41] will have a 'disability' for the purpose of the *DDA* and *Disability Standards* and that any extension may amount to a reasonable adjustment for that disability and not a concession. Not all, or, arguably, even most disabilities are managed by disability support staff.

It should also be noted that since *Purvis v New South Wales* (*Purvis*),[42] which confirmed a 'true basis' rather than a 'but for' test for causation,[43] it is unlikely that a university will be held liable for direct discrimination in respect of action taken – or not taken – in respect of an unknown disability. If there has been no disclosure of disability, it will be difficult to prove that any less favourable treatment flowing from a failure to make reasonable adjustment was 'because of'[44] the disability of the student concerned.

C Education 'On the Same Basis' and 'Reasonable Adjustment'

As noted above, the *Disability Standards* acknowledge that students with disabilities have a right to an education 'on the same basis' as students without disability. Education 'on the same basis' does not mean that all students are to be treated the same way. Rather, the *Disability Standards* contemplate that students with disabilities may need to be treated differently in order to access education rights 'on the same basis' as students without disability. The overarching obligation under the *Disability Standards* is to make 'reasonable adjustment' to policies and practices, facilities and curriculum, so as to facilitate access and inclusion.[45] The *Disability Standards* address four aspects

38 Department of Education, Employment and Workplace Relations, above n 6, 43.

39 [2000] HREOC No H99/55.

40 *DDA* s 4(1) (definition of 'disability') para (a) (total or partial loss of the person's bodily or mental functions); or para (e) (the malfunction, malformation or disfigurement of a part of the person's body).

41 *DDA* s 4(1) (definition of 'disability') para (c) (the presence in the body of organisms causing disease or illness).

42 (2003) 217 CLR 92.

43 Disability must be the 'true basis' of the discriminatory treatment (Gleeson CJ), 102; the 'real reason' (McHugh and Kirby JJ); 'the central question will always be – *why* was the aggrieved person treated as he or she was' (Gummow, Hayne and Hayden JJ), 163.

44 *DDA* s 5.

45 *Disability Standards* s 3.4(1). Since relevant amendments came into effect in August 2009, pursuant to the *Disability Discrimination and Other Human Rights Legislation Amendment Act 2009* (Cth), the *DDA* has acknowledged that discrimination may flow from a failure to make reasonable adjustment. See ss 5(2), 6(2).

of the education experience where reasonable adjustment is relevant: enrolment;[46] participation;[47] curriculum development, accreditation and delivery;[48] and student support services.[49] They also create obligations to take 'reasonable steps' to prevent the harassment and vilification of students with disabilities.[50]

Whether an adjustment is reasonable will be established by 'balancing the interests of all concerned'.[51] 'All relevant circumstances' should be considered including the following specified matters:

- the relevant disability;
- the views of the student about the adjustment;
- the effect on the student of the adjustment;
- the effect on others of the adjustment; and
- the costs and benefits of the adjustment.[52]

D Consultation

As part of the process of determining which adjustments may be appropriate and their reasonableness, universities must consult with affected students and, where appropriate and with the consent of the relevant student, their associates. Associates may include a student's parents or guardians, and medical and therapy professionals involved in the management of his or her disability. Consultation must occur upon enrolment[53] and, in anticipation of the fact that what is reasonable may change over time,[54] throughout the duration of the enrolment.[55] The *Disability Standards*, therefore, ensure that a student has some influence upon decisions which are made about how his or her education is delivered.

Student views, however, are not determinative of a regime of adjustments to be made. In both *Walker*[56] and *Sievwright*[57] it was accepted that, while a student must be consulted, it is the staff members of the education institution who are best placed to decide whether a particular adjustment, or group of adjustments, will be implemented. They are 'qualified education providers' who are 'in the best position to understand the breadth of … [a student's] educational needs'.[58] It goes without saying, perhaps, that a student unhappy with the university's decision may seek to challenge it by claiming a breach of the *Disability Standards* or other discrimination legislation.[59]

---

46 *Disability Standards* Part 4.
47 Ibid pt 5.
48 Ibid pt 6.
49 Ibid pt 7.
50 Ibid pt 8.
51 *Disability Standards* s 3.4(1).
52 Ibid s 3.4(2).
53 Ibid s 4.2(3).
54 Ibid s 3.4(1) Note.
55 Ibid ss 5.2(3), 6.2(3), 7.2(7).
56 *Walker,* [284].
57 *Sievwright,* [162].
58 Ibid.
59 Sixty-eight complaints of discrimination in education were made under the *DDA* in 2012-2013. See Australian Human Rights Commission, *Annual Report 2012-2013* (8 October 2013), 139.

While consultation, per se, is mandated, the form and timing of that consultation is not.[60] Nevertheless, it is advisable for universities to implement systems which provide for regular tracking of student progress and regular, personal contact between students and their disability advisors and, where appropriate, their teachers. Regular consultation maximises the likelihood of ongoing reasonable adjustment, maximises the likelihood of educational success and minimises the likelihood of litigation.[61] Tertiary institution submissions to the review of the *Disability Standards* suggested that the consultation could be supported by 'a formal signed agreement that sets out student's rights, the provider's responsibilities and the agreed adjustments and mechanisms for review and support'.[62]

E *Implementing the Disability Standards*

1 Standards for Enrolment

Part 4 of the *Disability Standards*, Standards for Enrolment, does not guarantee enrolment in a university for students with disability. As Tracey J explains in *Abela:*

> The provider is not obliged to enrol the student in a school of the student's choosing. Nor does the Standard confer on a student a right to admission to a particular school.[63]

The Standards for Enrolment focus on adjustment to enrolment policies and procedures so that students with disability are able to access information about an education institution and what it has to offer on the same basis as students without disability. This may simply mean that a university should make staff available to explain and assist students with disabilities when they make enquiries and during any ensuing enrolment. Universities should also consider exploiting available technology to maximise the accessibility of any promotional and enrolment materials available on their websites.

It is clear from the express terms of the *Disability Standards*, however, that an education provider should not refuse an enrolment simply because it considers that a place would be available for that student at another institution. To refuse an enrolment on this basis would mean that the education provider 'does not treat a prospective student on the same basis as a prospective student without a disability' unless a student without disability would also be refused a place.[64] As such, a university is exposed to allegations of a breach of the *Disability Standards* and of direct discrimination (less favourable treatment) if it rejects the enrolment of an otherwise qualified student with a disability, before it has considered whether it is able to make reasonable adjustments to support that student's enrolment.[65]

Separate statistics for university discrimination in education claims are not publically available.

60 *Walker,* [284].

61 See the discussion of the *Sluggett* case, below n 67, for an illustration of how easy-to-solve problems may result in litigation when regular updating of disability-related information by students does not occur.

62 Department of Education, Employment and Workplace Relations, above n 6, 28.

63 *Abela,* [214].

64 See *Disability Standards* s 2.2(2).

65 See *Abela,* [172]-[199] and [215]-[218] for an example of extensive consultation pre-enrolment.

2 Participation, Curriculum and Student Support Services Standards

There is significant overlap across these three areas in terms of what is anticipated by the *Disability Standards*. Collectively, the relevant *Disability Standards* will oblige universities to consider both curricular and co-curricular aspects of the education opportunities that they provide. Moreover, the *Disability Standards* provide that an 'education provider must take reasonable steps to ensure that any adjustment required to be made is made within a reasonable time'.[66] What is a 'reasonable time', however, will be affected by whether a student has 'in a timely way' informed the university 'about how the disability affects ... [him or her] in relation to education or training'.[67]

(a) Physical Access

Education providers should ensure that grounds and facilities are accessible to students.[68] Attention should also be given to the accessibility of places attended by students during the course of their studies – excursion destinations,[69] work placements,[70] and graduation venues,[71] for example. It makes sense, wherever possible, to choose places and placements for co-curricular activities based on whether they will be accessible to all.

(b) Learning and Teaching

As noted above, the *Disability Standards* regulate a variety of modes of delivery of education, 'including ... distance education, flexible delivery, computer-assisted learning, on-line delivery'.[72] 'Blended learning', learning which combines online and traditional learning and teaching forums and strategies, has been called 'the defining transformative innovation for higher education in the 21st century',[73] and has become, perhaps, the dominant model for university education in Australia.

What is the scope of reasonable adjustment in a blended learning environment? It may be that universities are obliged to provide reasonable alternative learning and teaching contexts for students who cannot navigate the online learning elements of a course. In some instances, computer technologies may be utilised to translate materials

66 *Disability Standards* s 3.7.

67 Ibid s 3.7(2)(a). See, for example, *Sluggett v Flinders University of South Australia* [2003] FCAFC 27 (*Sluggett*) for an example of allegations of discrimination failing because of a student's delay in informing the university of the ramifications for access of her disability.

68 See *Sluggett*, ibid. See also *A School v Human Rights and Equal Opportunity Commission* (1998) 55 ALD 93: room allocations for student with mobility impairment.

69 See *Kancheff v Charles Darwin University* [2013] FCA 1252 (*Kancheff*), excursion travel arrangements for student with back and vision impairment. The merits of the complainant student's case were considered in the context of a successful application by the respondent university for an order for security for costs. An appeal for leave to appeal against the order was dismissed by the Federal Court of Australia.

70 See *Sluggett*, work placement for student with mobility impairment.

71 See *Kinsela v Queensland University of Technology* [1997] HREOC No H97/4, accessibility of graduation ceremony.

72 *Disability Standards* s 1.5 Note 3.

73 Randy Garrison and Heather Kanuka, 'Blended Learning: Uncovering its Transformative Potential in Higher Education' (2004) 7 *The Internet and Higher Education* 95, 95-96.

into an accessible format in much the same way as they are used to translate course readings and lectures delivered in an on-campus context. In other cases, it may be necessary to provide alternative learning experiences altogether. This is one area where it is important for academics to be aware of the risk of unintended discrimination in the management of their online delivery of course materials. It is important for academics to be aware of the consequences for learning of the disabilities of their students so that appropriate decisions can be made about the selection and structure of learning activities. It may be easier, and more efficient, to adopt, as far as possible, the principles of universal design and to prefer activities and resources which will not exclude students with disabilities enrolled in a subject.

Reasonable adjustment to curriculum may also require changes to assessment conditions and procedures and adjustment of assessment items to remove barriers to a student's ability to display his or her knowledge and skills.[74] The variety of subject areas studied at university, individual disabilities and assessment circumstances make it difficult to state that any one variety of adjustment will always be reasonable. Australian case law, however, indicates that the following kinds of adjustments may be considered:

- extra time to finish an exam or assignment;[75]
- completing a course over a longer than usual time;[76]
- supervised rest, food and medication breaks in examinations;[77]
- adjustment to the format of an exam paper – font, paper colour and size, paper 'masks';[78]
- separate venues to minimise distraction or to accommodate assistance animals;
- alternatives to writing – *viva voce*, examination, scribe, assistive technology;[79]
- alternatives to reading – brailled and/or taped materials, assistive technology;[80]
- alternatives to hearing – written stimulus materials, translators, assistive technology;[81]
- alternatives to speaking – written rather than spoken responses allowed;
- adjusted scheduling of assessment;[82]
- adjusted level of achievement thresholds where performance has been affected by disability;[83] and

74 *Disability Standards* s 6.3(f). For further detail on this topic see Elizabeth Dickson, 'The Assessment of Students with Disabilities: The Australian Law as to Reasonable Adjustment and Academic Integrity' (2012) 17(2) *International Journal of Law and Education* 49. Parts of the commentary on assessment in this section of the chapter are adapted from that article.

75 See, for example, *Bishop* [2000] HREOC No H99/55; *BI v Board of Studies* [2000] NSWSC 921 (*BI*) (*BI* is a judicial review case, not a discrimination case); *Brackenreg v Queensland University of Technology* [1999] QADT 11; *W v Flinders University of South Australia* [1998] HREOCA 19 (*W*).

76 See, for example, *Beanland v Queensland and Queensland Studies Authority* [2008] QADT 5 (*Beanland*); *BKY v University of Newcastle* [2014] NSWCATAD 39 (*BKY*).

77 See, for example, *BI* [2000] NSWSC 921.

78 See, for example, *Hinchliffe v University of Sydney* [2004] FMCA 85.

79 See, for example, *Beanland*.

80 See, for example, *Beanland*; *Hinchliffe*.

81 See, for example, *Hurst v Queensland* [2006] FCAFC 100.

82 See, for example, *Brackenreg* [1999] QADT 11; *W v Flinders University of South Australia* [1998] HREOCA 19.

83 See, for example, *Brackenreg*.

- adjusted weighting of assessment for students who have missed an assessment item because of disability.[84]

It is clear that reasonable adjustment does not require any compromise of academic integrity:

> In assessing whether an adjustment to the course of the course or program in which the student is enrolled, or proposes to be enrolled, is reasonable, the provider is entitled to maintain the academic requirements of the course or program, and other requirements or components that are inherent in or essential to its nature.[85]

Universities are not required, therefore, to erode the level of difficulty of an assessment item, or of a course of study, so that a person with disability will pass. In order to minimise the potential for error, and litigation, however, universities should work towards articulating the 'academic' and other 'inherent' requirements of the subjects and courses that they offer. Such an approach should be embedded in the curriculum development process. It would clarify for students what must be achieved to complete those subjects and courses. Moreover, it would clarify for academics and disability support staff the limits beyond which adjustment must not be made. When universities claim that particular requirements are inherent, however, they should be prepared to defend the claim.[86] This is an area, perhaps, where the unquestioned acceptance of 'the way things have always been done' may inform assertions about what students must be able to do, to complete a particular subject or course.

3 Support Services

Students with disabilities must have access to support services which are offered by the university to students without disability – careers and general counselling, for example. But reasonable adjustment may also require education providers to make available specialist equipment and specialist support services to facilitate inclusion. This may encompass such services as Auslan translation,[87] transcription, note taking, brailling, taping[88] and accessibility 'buddies'. If a university does not provide onsite specialist support it may need to facilitate the provision of external support to its students, 'including through collaborative arrangements with specialised service providers'.[89]

In that funding for university disability support is calculated on a different basis from funding for support in the compulsory sector, it may also be the case that some services which are commonly provided at school, may not be required at university. Personal care support is a good example. While school staff may assist with toileting and medication, such services are not typically part of the university support regime. While the rationale for the provision of such support in the compulsory sector may be inferred to be that it allows attendance at school as a prerequisite to access to education, funding

84 See, for example, *W*.

85 *Disability Standards* s 3.4(3).

86 See, for example, *BKY v University of Newcastle* [2014] NSWCATAD 39.

87 See *Hurst v Queensland* [2006] FCAFC 100 and *Ferguson v Department of Further Education* [2005] FMCA 954: Auslan interpretation for students with hearing impairment.

88 See *Hinchliffe v University of Sydney* [2004] FMCA 85: font enlargement and taping of learning materials for a student with vision impairment.

89 *Disability Standards* s 7.3(b).

regulations in the tertiary sector explicitly prohibit claims for 'the ongoing operation of general disability support services or for the provision of personal care for students with a disability'.[90] The inference here is that by the time students are old enough to attend university, they will need to manage their own personal support regimes. In the higher education sector, funding is expressly linked to 'educational support'.[91] In the absence of funding for personal support, it may be possible to mount arguments that providing such support is not 'reasonable adjustment'.

4 Harassment and Victimisation

The *Disability Standards* oblige universities to take steps to prevent the harassment[92] or victimisation[93] of students with disability and to deal with complaints of harassment and victimisation 'promptly and with due regard to the severity of the matter'.[94] It is not enough for a university to rely on a generic anti-bullying policies or codes of conduct to demonstrate compliance with the *Disability Standards* in this respect. Specific staff and student policies prohibiting harassment and victimisation must be developed along with 'fair, transparent and accountable' procedures for managing complaints.[95] Both staff and students must be educated in these policies and procedures.[96] Moreover staff should be 'trained to detect, and deal with, harassment in education and training settings'.[97]

F *Limits on Reasonable Adjustment*

Tracey J in *Walker* makes it plain that '[t]here may … be cases in which an adjustment is necessary but no reasonable adjustment is able to be identified which will ensure that the objectives contained in the relevant Disability *Standards* are achieved'.[98] By implication, an adjustment will not be required if it is not reasonable. Even a reasonable adjustment, moreover, will not be required if one of the exceptions provided for in the *Disability Standards* is engaged. The exceptions align with equivalent exceptions in the *DDA*.

An adjustment will not be required if it is inconsistent with an act authorised by regulation or a court order.[99] This exemption may support, for example, the decision of a university to exclude from campus-based activities a student who is the subject

90 *Higher Education Support Act 2003 – Other Grants Guidelines (Education) 2012* (Cth) s 1.100.5.15.
91 Ibid.
92 See *Disability Standards* s 8.1(a) where harassment is defined as follows: 'in relation to a person with a disability, includes an action taken in relation to the person's disability that is reasonably likely, in all the circumstances, to humiliate, offend, intimidate or distress the person.
93 See *DDA* s 42 for the meaning of victimisation. In summary, victimisation is to subject a person to a detriment because he or she has made a complaint of discriminatory treatment or has indicated that he or she intends to make a complaint.
94 *Disability Standards* s 8.5(f).
95 Ibid s 8.5(c).
96 Ibid s 8.3(2), s 8.5(d).
97 Ibid s 8.5(e).
98 *Walker,* [284].
99 *Disability Standards* s 10.3; *DDA* s 47.

of an apprehended violence order as the result of aggressive or harassing on-campus behaviour.[100]

If it is 'reasonably necessary' to protect the health and welfare of the university community, a university may 'isolate' a student with disability, or 'otherwise discriminate' against him or her, 'if the disability is an infectious disease or other condition'.[101] This exemption would allow a university to exclude a student from campus access while they were in the infectious stages of diseases such as tuberculosis or measles.

While the above exemptions may allow exclusion from campus, either temporarily or on an ongoing basis, reasonable adjustment may require off-campus support for affected students during the period of exclusion. Moreover, where the exclusion is related to illness and incapacity, reasonable adjustment may require adjustments to assessment schedules. It is clear, therefore, that while the authorised by law and health and safety exemptions may legitimise the refusal of one kind of adjustment – access to campus facilities – they should not be taken as legitimising the refusal of all adjustments to affected students.[102] Indeed, they may necessitate the making of reasonable adjustments to replace the on campus experience.

A university may 'provide special measures (including specialised units or institutions) intended specifically for the benefit of students with disabilities'.[103] This exemption authorises, therefore, 'positive discrimination' to support students with disability and means that special programs implemented to benefit students with a particular disability will not amount to less favourable treatment of other students.

Perhaps the most significant, and the most controversial, exemption to reasonable adjustment is the unjustifiable hardship exemption.[104] There is an overlap in terms of the considerations relevant to reasonableness and unjustifiable hardship. Both enquiries will consider the nature of the disability, its effects, and the costs and benefits for all concerned in making an adjustment.[105] In respect of hardship, however, the financial circumstances of the education provider are also relevant.[106]

Early education discrimination case law suggests that unjustifiable hardship may be proved where a student's disruptive or dangerous behaviour threatens the learning environment or health and safety of others in the university environment.[107] Since

---

100 See, for example, *Firestone v Australian National University* [2009] ACTDT 1 (*Firestone*). While this is a case brought under the *Discrimination Act 1991* (ACT), and while it was decided on the basis that a causal link could not be established between the complainant's disability and his treatment, the facts around the exclusion from campus of the student illustrate a set of circumstances where the authorised by law exemption under the *Disability Standards* s 10.3 may be available.

101 *Disability Standards* s 10.4; *DDA* s 48.

102 In *Firestone*, it could be argued that it was relevant to the finding that there had been no discrimination in refusing access to the campus that Firestone had been provided with off campus learning support.

103 *Disability Standards* s 10.5; *DDA* s 45.

104 *Disability Standards* s 10.2; *DDA* s 29A. Note that the unjustifiable hardship exception cannot be relied upon by an education provider to excuse it from its obligations under the harassment and victimisation: *Disability Standards* s 10.2(1).

105 Compare *Disability Standards* s 3.4(2) and *DDA* s 11.

106 See *DDA* s 11(1)(c) and (d).

107 See, for example, *L v Minister for Education for Queensland (No 2)* [1995] 1 QADR 207; *P v Director-General, Department of Education* [1995] 1 QADR 755.

Purvis, however, it is now difficult to prove discrimination in such a fact situation, even when the behaviour is a manifestation of a disability, obviating the need to raise the hardship exemption.

A variety of unjustifiable hardship which may prove to be of increasing relevance, however, is unjustifiable hardship flowing from the cost of accommodating a student with disability. Some disabilities may indicate a need for extensive and expensive adjustments. There will inevitably be situations where the cost of providing student support stresses the budget and compromises the ability to provide other services.

Most universities in Australia are publicly funded. Until quite recently, case law suggested that it would be difficult for a public institution to argue that it could not afford to provide for a student with disability.[108] Increasingly complex claims for support, including claims for full time one-on-one support, coupled, perhaps, with a more practical view of government budgetary restraints, have, however, resulted in a willingness on the part of some courts to consider claims of unjustifiable hardship arising from cost.[109]

IV Conclusion

While the *Disability Standards* regulate the actions of education authorities and institutions, in practice, they will have ramifications for a wide variety of university staff. The issues canvassed in this chapter suggest that the activities of facilities management, enrolment, examinations, academic, administrative and disability support staff are all within the scope of the *Disability Standards*. The cases canvassed suggest that there remains some ignorance on the part of both staff and students as to the kind of adjustments that may be sought and made and the considerations relevant to reasonableness. It is curious that among the most recent actions commenced against universities, the *Disability Standards* appear not to have been pleaded. This is despite their relevance to State discrimination laws as well as to compliance with the *DDA*. Does this suggest ignorance, even on the part of lawyers practising in this area, of the guidance as to reasonable adjustment provided in the *Disability Standards* and of the potential for proof of compliance with the *Disability Standards* to defeat discrimination claims? To date, then, perhaps it could be said that the potential of the *Disability Standards* to improve compliance with disability discrimination law has not been fully realised. Perhaps it could also be said that the *Disability Standards* will only deliver better outcomes for students and protection from litigation for universities when their scope and impact are better understood by both students and staff, and their legal advisors.

108 Ibid.
109 See *Victoria v Turner* [2009] VSC 66, [102]; *Sievwright*, [207]-[210].

Chapter 14

Employment Law

Jacquie Seemann and Katie Kossian

I Introduction

In Australia, employment relationships operate 'within a framework defined by statute and by common law principles, informing the construction and content of the contract of employment'.[1] The various sources of law overlap and create a complex and dynamic system of regulation of employment. This is complicated in the higher education sector because some aspects of the context in which the sector operates are unique. The engagement of university academic staff in particular is not solely driven by commercial considerations, but must also take into account the fundamental purpose of the university. The purpose of this chapter is to provide an overview of how employment relationships in universities are regulated in Australia, and what particular legal issues may arise in the engagement of academic staff.

II University as Employer

From a legal perspective, universities are corporations and their employees are like other employees; however, their relationships differ significantly from other employment relationships as a result of the overlapping effect of four significant aspects of the university structure.

First, each university is regulated by separate and specific legislation (State-based, except the Australian National University, which is governed by Commonwealth legislation. See Chapter 1 by Squelch). Though the wording of each Act differs, in broad terms, the legislation sets out the framework within which the university will operate, including 'the entire control and management of the affairs and concerns of the university'.[2]

Secondly, universities are distinct from other corporations because they are not established simply to generate a financial profit. So much is clear, for instance, from s 6(1) of the *University of Sydney Act 1989* (NSW):

> The object of the University is the promotion, within the limits of the University's resources, of scholarship, research, free inquiry, the interaction of research and teaching, and academic excellence.

Thirdly, the employment of academics by a university has a 'distinctive feature':

1 *Commonwealth Bank of Australia v Barker* (2014) 312 ALR 356, [1].
2 *University of Western Australia v Gray* (2009) 259 ALR 224, quoting trial judge at [96].

> [A]cademic staff are part of the membership that constitutes the corporation and as such are bound by the statutes, regulations, etc of the university. Their membership is integral to their status and place in the university. To define the relationship of an academic staff member with a university simply in terms of a contract of employment is to ignore a distinct dimension of that relationship.[3]

Although the relevant legislation does not deal directly with the rights and obligations of members, it appears conceivable that, at least from a corporate law perspective, members would enjoy the same rights as company shareholders and thereby have input into the control of a university.[4] Cases, at least to date, do not translate this into substantively different rights in employment, but might in future.

Fourthly, unlike other corporations and most other employers, universities must grapple with the notion of academic freedom, a matter that is considered in Chapter 17 by Stobbs. In this context, questions arise around the extent to which, if any, a university is required to provide academics with freedom to publish their views, and to tolerate an academic's dissenting opinions about its operation and functions.[5]

Provision for the exercise of academic freedom is sometimes made in university policies and enterprise agreements. In the absence of explicit references, there is at least an argument that there is an implied right within the employment relationship for an academic to publish research and information, provided that it is truthful and published for the purpose of increasing knowledge.[6]

In addition to these inherent characteristics of universities, they are often involved in complicated arrangements which make it not necessarily straightforward to identify the employer of a particular individual. In many cases, although it might appear that the university that is the employer, this assumption might be quite wrong. The actual employer might be a residential college, a services company, a teaching hospital, a commercialisation or clinical research entity – there are many different combinations. Yet in all these situations, university policies may apply, and the university may have other quasi-employer rights or obligations.

It is apparent from case law that the courts are willing to recognise the unique features of employment relationships within universities. Accordingly, in determining university employment disputes, courts apply basic contract law principles, overlaid with both the special principles of employment contracts and specific consideration of the university environment, including the factors discussed above.[7]

III Employees and Independent Contractors

Before dealing with sources of employment regulation it is important to note the difference between 'contracts of service' (contracts of employment) and 'contracts for service' (independent contractor agreements). Determining whether an individual is

3 Ibid [185].

4 Jim Jackson and Sally Varnham, *Law for Educators School and University Law in Australia* (LexisNexis Butterworths Australia, 2007), 28-29.

5 See, for example, *University of Wollongong v National Tertiary Education Industry Union* [2002] FCAFC 85.

6 Jackson and Varnham, above n 4, 328-329.

7 See, for example, *Victoria University of Technology v Wilson* [2004] VSC 33.

an employee or contractor is not always easy, and Australian courts have long grappled with the task. Courts will consider and balance a number of indicia to determine the nature of the relationship, with a focus on the economic reality of that relationship.[8]

This chapter is concerned only with employment contracts. However, the distinction between an employee and an independent contractor is one to which any employing entity (including a university) should give careful attention. This is because a true independent contractor will not be entitled to many of the benefits of employees, including leave and superannuation. However, if a person properly characterised as an employee is treated as a contractor, substantial backpay and penalties can apply, under the legislation creating entitlements, under 'sham contracting' legislation and under taxation law.

IV Statutory Sources of Employment Regulation

As noted earlier, employment relationships are regulated through a number of different sources, each of which will be discussed in further detail below.

A Federal and State Laws

The *Fair Work Act 2009* (Cth) (*FW Act*) is the central legislative framework for industrial relations and employment entitlements in Australia. The *FW Act* covers all 'national system employees': those employed by a Constitutional corporation and also, in cases where the States have conferred law-making power on the Commonwealth, employees of partnerships and individuals. The *FW Act* does not cover non-constitutional corporation employers in Western Australia, which has retained its State system.

All national system employers must comply with the 10 minimum National Employment Standards (NES) contained in the *FW Act*.[9] The NES provide for maximum weekly hours of work, flexible working arrangements, parental leave, annual leave, personal/carer's leave, compassionate leave, community service leave, long service leave (calculated in accordance with State legislation), public holidays, notice of termination and redundancy pay, and the requirement to issue a Fair Work Information Statement (summarising *FW Act* entitlements) to new employees.[10]

The *FW Act* also affords employees various rights and protections, including protection from unfair dismissal and adverse action. These will be dealt with later in this chapter.

B Modern Awards and Enterprise Agreements

The *FW Act* makes provision for awards[11] and enterprise agreements,[12] which – when they apply to particular employees' employment – provide for an additional safety net, building on NES entitlements and regulating other terms and conditions of employment.

8 See, for example, *Stevens v Brodribb Sawmilling Co Pty Ltd* (1986) 160 CLR 16; *Hollis v Vabu Pty Ltd* (2001) 207 CLR 21; *On Call Interpreters and Translators Agency Pty Ltd v Commissioner of Taxation (No 3)* [2011] FCA 366; *Baker v Markellos* [2012] SASCFC 114; and *Tattsbet Limited v Morrow* [2015] FCAFC 62.

9 *FW Act* ch 2 pt 2-2.

10 *FW Act* ch 2 pt 2-2.

11 *FW Act* ch 2 pt 2-3.

12 *FW Act* ch 2 pt 2-4.

Awards are industry- and occupation-based industrial instruments made by the Fair Work Commission, which typically provide for minimum wages for specified classifications, types of employment, arrangements for working hours (rosters etc), overtime and penalty rates, allowances, leave, superannuation, consultation, representation and dispute resolution. In 2010, after an extensive 'modernisation' process, historical awards were replaced by new 'modern' awards.

While historically university employment was regulated by industrial awards, in the last 15-20 years, a significant change in the industrial relations landscape, propelled by governments from both sides of the political fence, has seen a move towards bargaining at enterprise level. Under the *FW Act*, enterprise agreements may be created between an employer and its employees.[13] An enterprise agreement may operate to exclude an otherwise applicable modern award, but will only be approved if employees are 'better off overall'[14] under the agreement than if the agreement did not operate. Neither a modern award nor enterprise agreement can exclude or in any way undermine the entitlements created by the NES.

The employment of the majority of university employees is now covered by an enterprise agreement, which will typically set out employment classifications, salaries, allowances, leave entitlements, provisions for termination of employment and redundancy, requirements related to change management, consultation and dispute resolution.

The university sector is highly unionised. According to statistics published by the National Tertiary Education Union (NTEU) in the Recruitment Brochure 2014 on its website, the union now represents 28,000 members across Australia (16,000 of whom are academic staff members).[15] This high level of union participation has a considerable impact on negotiations for enterprise agreements. Bargaining involves large numbers of parties and can be very slow. This may impact on morale and the dynamics of the environment, and consequently sometimes on the delivery of educational services. Also, enterprise bargaining is the arena in which the unions seek to influence and sometimes to reverse changes in the university context.

Unlike enterprise agreements in many other sectors, a marked feature of university enterprise agreements is that they contain very detailed provisions relating to discipline and performance management and sometimes reference particular policies and procedures which are then incorporated by reference into the enterprise agreement. This can sometimes be problematic for universities, as perceived breaches of procedures within enterprise agreements have given rise to litigation.[16]

The 'special' nature of university life sometimes emerges in the context of enterprise bargaining and agreements. University enterprise agreements often provide for unique sector-specific rights and obligations, such as the right to demote an employee.[17] Conversely, sometimes (despite their traditional attitudes) universities learn that they must make enterprise agreements in line with general community norms. Thus, in

13 *FW Act* pt 2-4 div 2.

14 *FW Act* s 193.

15 See <https://www.nteu.org.au/library/view/id/4886>.

16 See, for example, *University of Western Sydney v Fletcher* [2009] AIRCFB 368 and *NTEIU v University of Wollongong* [2001] FCA 1069.

17 *Lollback v University of Southern Queensland* [2014] FWC 2011.

Australian Catholic University,[18] the NTEU and Community and Public Sector Union (CPSU) contended that a proposed enterprise agreement included an unlawfully discriminatory term. The term would have allowed the university to pay lesser severance payments to staff members whose employment had proceeded beyond their 'normal retirement date', after which they would have access to their superannuation. Fair Work Australia (as the Fair Work Commission was then called) held that the term was discriminatory, and therefore could not stand. Perhaps implicit in the judgment, though not discussed, was that the university assumed it was acceptable to treat differently those staff who had passed the usual tenure period. The decision confirms what might have been obvious – that universities are subject to the same anti-discrimination principles as other employers, and should not assume that special retirement rules based on tenure will be permitted to apply.

V Employment Contracts

There is no legal requirement in Australia to have a written employment contract. However, whether or not it is written down, there is always an employment contract that exists when one person is employed by another, which imposes obligations beyond those set out in statute and industrial instruments. Much of the controversy in employment disputes relates to what terms form part of that employment contract.

A Implied Terms

Apart from the express (written or oral) terms of an employment contract, an employment contract also includes terms implied in fact or in law. As with contracts generally, terms will only be implied if they are not inconsistent with the express terms of the contract.

For a term to be implied in fact, it must be shown that it was intended by the parties that it apply, although it was not expressly included into the contract. It must be necessary for the 'reasonable and effective operation of the contract'.[19]

For a term to be implied in law, it must be able to be said that, without the term, 'the enjoyment of the rights conferred by the contract would or could be rendered nugatory, worthless, or, perhaps, be seriously undermined or the contract would be deprived of its substance, seriously undermined or drastically devalued'. For this reason, 'implications which might be thought reasonable are not, on that account only, necessary'.[20]

The common law has recognised that employees and employers have the implied contractual duties set out in 'VI Employee Obligations at Common Law' and 'VII Employer Obligations at Common Law' below. While the existence of these implied duties in employment contracts is fairly well settled generally, the courts have identified an added layer of complexity in the scope of employment of university academic staff. For example, it is recognised that academics enjoy a level of self-determination in their work that is not typically afforded to other professions:

18 [2011] FWA 3693.
19 *Byrne v Australian Airlines* (1995) 185 CLR 410.
20 *Commonwealth Bank of Australia v Barker* (2014) 312 ALR 356, quoting *Gray* [29].

> the seeming freedom to choose the subject or line of research and the manner of its pursuit and the freedom to decide when and how to publish the products of one's research to the extent that these subsist, sits uneasily with notions such as an implied duty of an employee to obey all lawful and reasonable instructions of the employer within the scope of the employee's employment ...[21]

This chapter considers some features of the appearance of these duties in university contracts.

As the cases illustrate many times over, implied terms and conflicting express terms cause problems for both parties to the relationship. A well-written contract helps to avoid costly and damaging disputes.

Where there is an apparent conflict in contractual terms, 'what matters is what each party by words and conduct would have led a reasonable person in the position of the other party to believe. References to the common intention of the parties to a contract are to be understood as referring to what a reasonable person would understand by the language in which the parties expressed their agreement'.[22] Hence in *Campbell v University of Adelaide*[23] it was held that, despite conflicting views being expressed on what had been agreed regarding continuity of service, the conduct of the parties demonstrated their respective intentions.

B Incorporation of Awards, Enterprise Agreements and Policies?

It is important to note parenthetically that an award or enterprise agreement need not be incorporated into the employment contract to be enforceable. As noted in *Byrne*, neither 'from the point of view of the employer nor the employee is there any need to convert those statutory rights and obligations to contractual rights and obligations'.[24] Similarly, 'there is no need for express incorporation in the contract of employment for the terms of the EBA [Enterprise Bargaining Agreement] to be both identifiable and enforceable'.[25]

Nor do policies need to be incorporated in order to be enforceable. In some circumstances, legislation requires employers to have policies on specific subject-matters (for instance, privacy) but on the whole, policies are adopted voluntarily by employers to regulate work and inform employees. Whether a policy will form part of the contract of employment will depend upon the way in which the policy, the contract and in some instances the enterprise agreement (which may refer to policies of the university) are drafted. If policies are expressly incorporated into the employment contract, a breach of policy may constitute a breach of contract. The language used in both policy and contract is critical to whether the policy is a contractual term.[26] However, if it is not, then it may be enforceable as an employer direction – as to which, see below.

21 Ibid [186].
22 *Toll (FGCT) Pty Ltd v Alphapharm Pty Ltd* (2004) 219 CLR 165, [40].
23 [2006] SASC 92.
24 (1995) 185 CLR 410, 421.
25 *Gramotnev v Queensland University of Technology* [2013] QSC 158, [40].
26 See, for example, *McCormick v Riverwood International (Australia) Pty Ltd* (1999) 167 ALR 689; *Goldman Sachs JB Were Services Pty Ltd v Nikolich* (2007) 163 FCR 62; *Gramotnev v Queensland University of Technology* [2013] QSC 158, [98].

Even if a policy is deemed to be contractual, that finding alone will not automatically result in a successful claim for damages. In *Gramotnev v Queensland University of Technology*,[27] a physics professor argued that the university had breached several of its own policies and, in doing so, had breached his employment contract. In considering his claims, the court noted that it 'is not simply whether a policy can possibly be contractual in nature that is in issue but whether the policy gives rise to the precise contractual obligation on which Dr Gramotnev relies to advance his claim for damages'.[28]

VI Employee Obligations at Common Law

A *Duty to Obey Directions*

The common law says that there is an implied duty that employees must act in accordance with the reasonable and lawful directions of the employer. By extension, this may require an employee to comply with the employer's policies and procedures, which – depending on their scope and nature – can often be characterised as directions of the employer.

However, an employee is not required to comply with an unlawful direction – for instance, a direction to engage in fraud – and that the direction must be reasonable. What will be considered reasonable will depend on the circumstances of the case, and the nature and scope of the employment relationship. In *Miller v University of New South Wales*,[29] the court determined that the university's direction to Professor Miller to undertake more teaching hours was a reasonable direction after regard was had to his employment contract and the duties that related to his position.[30]

B *Duty of Skill and Care*

An employee must perform work with the skill and care that would be expected of someone with his/her qualifications, experience and training. This is particularly the case where an employee holds him/herself out to have a specific skill-set and then fails to undertake work in accordance with that skill-set.[31] Moreover, employees have a duty to take reasonable care to ensure their own safety and the safety of others (see Chapter 16 by Squelch).

C *Duty of Good Faith and Fidelity*

The relationship between an employee and employer is a fiduciary one. Accordingly, the employee is obliged, in the course of their employment, to act in the best interests of the employer. The scope of this duty (also called the duty of loyalty) was explored in *Victoria University of Technology v Wilson* (*Wilson*),[32] where a professor working

27 [2013] QSC 158. Contrast with *Victoria University of Technology v Wilson* [2004] VSC 33.
28 Ibid [83].
29 (2001) 110 IR 1.
30 A similar finding was made in *Sheikholeslami v University of New South Wales (No 3)* [2008] FMCA 35.
31 *Harmer v Cornelius* (1858) 141 ER 94.
32 [2004] VSC 33.

with a senior lecturer and former student, initially as representatives of the university and later on their own behalf, developed a profitable software program and purported to sell it for their own benefit. In determining that both employees had breached the implied duty of good faith and fidelity, the court noted that 'the law is clear that a fiduciary is not allowed to put himself in a position where his interest and duty conflict and a fiduciary who profits outside the scope of his undertaking can be accountable if the information about the opportunity to make the profit came to him through his fiduciary position'.[33]

D Intellectual Property

Generally speaking, intellectual property created in the course of employment will belong to the employer (see Chapter 18 by Fraser and Chapter 19 by Wyburn). Notwithstanding this, it is possible for an employee to retain ownership of intellectual property rights – for example, in some cases, if it can be shown that the work from which the rights arose did not involve the resources of the employer. Similarly, if an employment contract does not contemplate the creation of intellectual property of a kind that is ultimately created, it will also not be considered to be the property of the employer. In *Gray*, the university tried to claim ownership of a method of treatment for liver cancer, but the claim was refused. The court found, notwithstanding Dr Gray's duty to research, that:

> Dr Gray's employment duties did not even require him to perform the tasks from which inventions might result. The subject matter and manner of discharge of his duty to research were in his discretion. He was not employed to invent.[34]

In addition, the court emphasised that the mere fact that an employment relationship existed between Dr Gray and the university did not automatically give the university ownership of inventions made by the employee during the term of the employment.[35]

This case can be contrasted with *Wilson*, where the court found that two senior employees were retained to perform the work which they undertook, which subsequently led to a profitable invention. In that case, because Professor Wilson had the ability to determine what he and another employee should work on, it followed that 'both men were for relevant purposes retained for the time being to invent the system'.[36]

E Confidentiality

The requirement to keep an employer's confidential information confidential is an equitable duty, which recognises that employers would be vulnerable to the misappropriation of their confidential information by employees who have access to such materials. The obligation of confidentiality extends beyond the termination of employment.[37]

33 Ibid [142].
34 *University of Western Australia v Gray* (2009) 259 ALR 224, [195] (*Gray*). Note, however, that the court did find at [194] that Dr Gray was employed to conduct research.
35 Ibid [150].
36 *Wilson*, [122].
37 Andrew Stewart, *Stewart's Guide to Employment Law* (5th ed, Federation Press, 2015).

VII Employer Obligations at Common Law

A Duty of Care

An employer owes its employees a duty of care. This duty is codified in work health and safety legislation,[38] but the implied term still continues to exist. Accordingly, a failure to provide a safe working environment may create liability for breach of both statute and contract. In *Wolters v University of the Sunshine Coast*,[39] it was held that the university breached its duty of care to an on-campus security guard when it failed to properly investigate and discipline another employee whose aggressive behaviour towards the security guard caused her to develop a debilitating psychiatric illness.

B Duty of Indemnity

An employer is taken to indemnify its employees with respect to any liability they incur during the course of their employment, if such a liability was performed in the course of their normal duties. Again, this is sometimes codified in legislation.[40]

C No Duty of Mutual Trust and Confidence

Until very recently, there was considerable debate in Australia as to whether the common law implied a term of 'mutual trust and confidence' in employment contracts. That proposed term was formulated in the United Kingdom as a duty on both parties not, without reasonable and proper cause, to conduct themselves in a manner calculated or likely to destroy or seriously damage the relationship of confidence and trust between them.[41]

However, the Australian position on this matter has now been resolved definitively by the High Court, which in *Commonwealth Bank of Australia v Barker*[42] determined unanimously that no such common law duty exists in Australia. The High Court determined that the term would, if accepted, impose wider obligations than necessary to make the employment contract work.[43] This decision will no doubt be a controversial one, with many employment law academics in particular being proponents of the duty.[44]

VIII Possible Claims and Disputes

As with any employment relationship, disputes may arise between an employee and a university about the employment relationship. The spectrum of disputes ranges from grievances about the application of particular policies through to challenges to

38 See Chapter 16 by Squelch.
39 [2013] QCA 228.
40 See, for example, *Employees Liability Act 1991* (NSW).
41 *Malik v Bank of Credit and Commerce International SA (in liq)* [1998] AC 20, [49].
42 (2014) 312 ALR 356.
43 Ibid [37]-[38].
44 See, for example, Joellen Riley, 'Before the High Court "Mutual Trust and Confidence" on Trial: At Last' (2014) 36 *Sydney Law Review* 15.

summary termination of employment following findings of serious misconduct. This section summarises the most common claims brought within the sector.

A Unfair Dismissal Claims

Part 3-2 of the *FW Act* protects tertiary education employees from unfair dismissal if they:

(a) have completed a minimum period of employment of six months;
(b) are covered by a modern award;
(c) are subject to an enterprise agreement applies; or
(d) have an annual rate of earnings less than the 'high income threshold' (as at 1 July 2014, $133,000).[45]

A person is deemed to be unfairly dismissed if the Fair Work Commission is satisfied that:

(a) the person has been dismissed;
(b) the dismissal was harsh, unjust or unreasonable; and
(c) the dismissal was not a genuine redundancy.[46]

'Dismissal' means that the employment was terminated at the employer's initiative or, conversely, that the employee was effectively forced to resign because the employer's conduct made continued employment untenable ('constructive dismissal').

The question of whether an employee has actually been dismissed (constructively or otherwise) is perhaps a little more complicated that one might expect. For instance, in *Lollback v University of Southern Queensland*,[47] Mr Lollback was demoted following an investigation into allegations of serious misconduct made against him. The demotion involved a significant reduction in Mr Lollback's salary and duties. Under general common law principles, a unilateral demotion of this nature would be a repudiation of the employment contract, and Mr Lollback argued that the demotion resulted in the termination of his employment. In dismissing his application for relief from unfair dismissal, Deputy President Gooley determined that the Vice Chancellor was authorised by the university's enterprise agreement to demote Mr Lollback, and noted that 'where the Agreement has been complied with, a demotion authorised by an enterprise agreement is not a termination of employment'.[48]

The Fair Work Commission must take into account various factors when considering whether a dismissal was harsh, unjust or unreasonable.[49] Those considerations include whether:

- there was a valid reason for dismissal and the person was notified of that reason;
- the person was offered an opportunity to respond to the reason;

45 *FW Act* s 382.
46 *FW Act* s 385.
47 [2014] FWC 2011.
48 Ibid [58].
49 *FW Act* s 387.

- if dismissal relates to unsatisfactory performance, the person was on notice about their performance; and
- a support person was present when the matter was discussed.

This list is not exhaustive; the Fair Work Commission may also take into account any other matters it considers relevant. What is clear is that the Act is concerned with both substance (merit) and process. As noted in *Byrne v Australian Airlines*:

> It may be that the termination is harsh but not unjust or unreasonable, unjust but not harsh or unreasonable, or unreasonable but not harsh or unjust. In many cases the concepts will overlap. Thus, the one termination of employment may be unjust because the employee was not guilty of the misconduct on which the employer acted, may be unreasonable because it was decided upon inferences which could not reasonably have been drawn from the material before the employer, and may be harsh in its consequences for the personal and economic situation of the employee or because it is disproportionate to the gravity of the misconduct in respect of which the employer acted.[50]

The primary remedy if a dismissal is found to be unfair is reinstatement – unless the Fair Work Commission considers this inappropriate, in which case it can award compensation equivalent to up to six months' remuneration.[51]

Recent decisions on unfair dismissal in the university context include:

- *D v Charles Sturt University*[52] – senior lecturer dismissed following allegations from an international student that the lecturer made inappropriate sexual advances towards her. The lecturer denied the allegations and claimed the investigation process was defective. The Fair Work Commission disagreed, and the dismissal was upheld.
- *Dr Li v Edith Cowan University*[53] – associate professor dismissed following allegations of plagiarism. It was held at first instance that the dismissal was unfair because, even though there was a valid reason, the university investigated whilst the professor was overseas, thereby not giving him an opportunity to respond to the allegations. An order was made for compensation as reinstatement was deemed inappropriate. On appeal, the first instance decision was upheld.
- *Sheikholeslami v University of NSW (No 3)*[54] – university professor dismissed following her refusal to undertake teaching of undergraduate students. At hearing, the professor contended that her suspension (without pay) and the subsequent termination of her employment were in breach of her employment contract. The court held that the professor had serious misapprehensions about her employment and that the direction to teach undergraduate students was a reasonable direction.
- *Jin v University of Newcastle*[55] – professor dismissed from employment following claims of misappropriation of grant funds and inappropriate expense

50 (1995) 185 CLR 410, [128].
51 *FW Act* ss 390-393.
52 [2013] FWC 5446.
53 [2014] FWCFB 2857.
54 [2008] FMCA 35.
55 [2013] FWC 418.

claims. The Commission held that his conduct was serious but not 'serious misconduct'. Given the particular nature of the allegations, reinstatement was inappropriate, but the Commission awarded compensation.

B Adverse Action

The *FW Act*[56] protects employees and prospective employees from 'adverse action'[57] based on a prohibited reason, including:

- that the employee has or has not exercised, or proposes to exercise, a 'workplace right' and workplace right. A 'workplace right' includes an entitlement or benefit of, or role or responsibility under, a workplace law, workplace instrument or order made by an industrial body (including under an enterprise agreement or award). The types of relevant entitlements include the entitlement to make a complaint;[58]
- industrial activity;[59] and
- sex, race, disability, age and other discriminatory grounds.

Adverse action includes dismissal; injuring the employee in his/her employment; altering the employee's position prejudicially; and discriminating against the employee. In the case of a prospective employee, adverse action includes refusing to employ. Adverse action claims have a 'reverse onus of proof'. This means that it is the employer who must show that any adverse action was not taken for a prohibited reason.[60]

Adverse action claims may be brought against both the university and an employee of a university, if that individual is personally involved in the alleged contravention.

Claims can result in reinstatement or uncapped compensation, and also penalties of up to $51,000 being awarded against respondents.[61]

In *NTEU v Royal Melbourne University of Technology*[62] the NTEU contended on behalf of a professor that her termination (said to have been on the basis of redundancy) was in fact due to the professor's tense relationship with the Head of School, and her complaints about his behaviour. The Federal Court found that 'even if the reasons advanced as actual reasons for the decision are accepted as such, the absence of evidence

56 *FW Act* ch 3 pt 3-1.
57 *FW Act* s 342.
58 *FW Act* s 342.
59 *FW Act* ss 346-347. See, for example, *Board of Bendigo Regional Institute of Technical and Further Education v Barclay* (2012) 248 CLR 500. In this case, Mr Barclay was suspended after he, in his capacity as a union delegate, sent an email to members of the Australian Education Union in which he raised allegations of inappropriate behaviour on the part of the TAFE in its course re-accreditation preparation. He was suspended on the basis that it considered that he had breached his employment contract by sending the email without first bringing these serious allegations to management. Mr Barclay alleged that this action amounted to adverse action on the basis of his union membership. The matter reached the High Court, which determined that the action was taken independent of Mr Barclay's union membership, but because his actions were contrary to the terms of his employment. Accordingly, TAFE had not taken unlawful adverse action against him.
60 See *FW Act* s 361.
61 *FW Act* ss 545 and 546.
62 [2013] FCA 451.

that there were no additional reasons, or that the actual reasons did not include the alleged proscribed reasons, will usually result in a failure to rebut the presumption.'[63] In that case, the professor was reinstated and the university was fined $37,000.

1 Discrimination and Harassment

There is anti-discrimination legislation at both federal and State level which prohibits discrimination on the basis of particular 'attributes' (or unlawful 'reasons' or 'grounds').[64] The attributes vary between jurisdictions, but generally include:

- sex, pregnancy and breastfeeding;
- marital/relationship status;
- family/carer's responsibilities;
- race, colour, descent, nationality, national origin, ethnicity, ethno-religious origin;
- sexual orientation, gender identity and intersex status;
- disability;
- age;
- political or trade union activity; and
- voluntary defence force service.[65]

Sometimes, discrimination is not unlawful even if it is based on one of the protected attributes. For example, it is not unlawful to refuse to employ a person whose disability makes it impossible for the person to carry out the 'inherent requirements' of the particular job. Unlawful discrimination can be direct or indirect. Direct discrimination means treating one person less favourably than another for an unlawful reason. For example, it is usually unlawful direct race discrimination to refuse to employ an individual because he or she is of a particular nationality. Indirect discrimination means imposing an unreasonable condition or requirement which has the effect of disadvantaging someone for an unlawful reason.[66] For example, directing all staff to work certain hours will disadvantage a person who has carer's responsibilities. Unlawful harassment is a subset of unlawful discrimination.

2 Work Health and Safety

The common law duty to provide a safe working environment has been largely (but not totally) eclipsed by legislation in every jurisdiction, which in the second decade of the 21st century has been the subject of much-needed 'harmonisation' resulting in greater similarity than before between the provisions of the different laws.[67] Like all

63 Ibid [20].

64 Federally, see *Age Discrimination Act 2004* (Cth), *Sex Discrimination Act 1984* (Cth); *Racial Discrimination Act 1975* (Cth) and *Disability Discrimination Act 1992* (Cth). For State-based legislation, see *Anti-Discrimination Act 1977* (NSW); *Anti-Discrimination Act 1991* (Qld); *Equal Opportunity Act 2010* (Vic); *Equal Opportunity Act 1984* (WA); *Equal Opportunity Act 1984* (SA) and *Anti-Discrimination Act 1998* (Tas).

65 See also *Defence Reserve Service (Protection) Act 2001* (Cth).

66 See, for example, *Kapoor v Monash University* [2001] VSCA 247.

67 For federal legislation, see *Work Health and Safety Act 2011* (Cth). For State and Territory-based legislation, see *Work Health and Safety Act 2011* (NSW); *Work Health and Safety Act 2011* (Qld);

employers and 'persons conducting a business or undertaking', have significant and detailed obligations to do what is reasonable to protect the health, safety and welfare of those attending their workplaces. This includes demanding risk management strategies and systematic consultation with staff (see Chapter 16 by Squelch).

A failure to comply with safety obligations can result in a criminal prosecution. Often, a prosecution is sparked by a workers compensation claim (see below) which alerts the relevant safety authority to the existence of a safety issue within an employer's operations.

3 Bullying

Traditionally, workplace bullying has been considered to be a work health and safety issue, and accordingly a university whose staff are bullied can be prosecuted for breaches of safety law. From 1 January 2014, workers have also been able to apply to the Fair Work Commission to make a 'stop bullying order'.[68]

'Worker' here has the same meaning as under Work Health and Safety legislation, and includes an individual who performs work in any capacity, including as an employee, a contractor, a subcontractor, an outworker, an apprentice, a trainee, a student on work experience or a volunteer.

A worker is bullied if, while at work, an individual or a group repeatedly behaves unreasonably towards the worker, or a group of workers of which the worker is a member, and that behaviour creates a risk to health and safety. Reasonable performance management is not bullying. This is consistent with the common law approach to bullying generally.

The purpose of these provisions is to resolve tensions in the workplace and have workers return to their workplace without further bullying conduct. Accordingly, an application for an order to stop bullying will not be dealt with if the employee is no longer working for the employer. Equally, the purpose of the provisions is not to provide financial compensation. The Commission will only issue fines if it is satisfied that an employer has failed to comply with an order.

4 Workers Compensation

As with anti-discrimination and safety legislation, each State and Territory has its own workers compensation legislation.[69] The legislation outlines the basis on which workplace injuries can be compensated, together with the rights and obligations of

---

Work Health and Safety Act 2011 (ACT); *Work Health and Safety (National Uniform Legislation) Act 2011* (NT); *Work Health and Safety Act 2012* (SA); *Work Health and Safety Act 2012* (Tas); *Occupational Health and Safety Act 2004* (Vic) and *Occupational Safety and Health Act 1984* (WA).

68 *FW Act* s 789FC.

69 In New South Wales: *Workers Compensation Act 1987* and *Workplace Injury Management and Workers Compensation Act 1998*; in Queensland: *Workers Compensation and Rehabilitation Act 2003*; in Victoria: *Accident Compensation Act 1985*; in South Australia: *Workers Rehabilitation and Compensation Act 1986*; in Western Australia: *Workers Compensation and Injury Management Act 1981*; in Tasmania: *Workers Rehabilitation and Compensation Act 1988*; in ACT: *Workers Compensation Act 1951*; and in the Northern Territory: *Workers Rehabilitation and Compensation Act 1986*.

employees and their employers with respect to workplace injuries. To claim workers compensation, a worker must be able to demonstrate a connection between the injury and the employment.

Increasingly, workers compensation claims have been made with respect to psychological injuries where an employee has felt stressed, bullied or harassed – particularly in circumstances involving performance management or disciplinary proceedings. Employers have no control over the receipt of such claims, but well-documented processes and adherence to policies on discipline and performance management will help to defend those claims. In particular, the legislation bars claims where psychological injury has arisen out of reasonable performance management.[70]

5 Enterprise Bargaining – Industrial Action

Perhaps because of their high level of unionisation, university employees are more prepared than those in some other sectors to use the provisions of the FW Act which provide for 'protected industrial action' – action taken during enterprise bargaining – the only form of strikes that are lawful. For example, in 2013 (when many universities were re-negotiating enterprise agreements), there were several cases of protected industrial action, including results bans and academics walking out of work in protest of what they perceived to be unsatisfactory pay and work conditions.[71]

IX Conclusion

A university is a unique employer for a number of reasons. Owing to its unique character, it faces challenges that are not shared by other corporate entities when dealing with employment arrangements.

Given recent changes in work arrangements of academic staff, it seems apparent that both universities and the academics they employ are becoming acutely sensitive to managing workplace rights and obligations. Future challenges will invariably continue to be tied to the role and function of academics and other staff within a university, and universities' assessment of their fundamental purpose.

---

70 See, for example, s 11A(1) of the *Workers Compensation Act 1987* (NSW). No compensation is payable under this Act in respect of an injury that is a psychological injury if the injury was wholly or predominantly caused by reasonable action taken or proposed to be taken by or on behalf of the employer with respect to transfer, demotion, promotion, performance appraisal, discipline, retrenchment or dismissal of workers or provision of employment benefits to workers.

71 Recent examples of such activity include: in March 2014, Monash University employees walked off the job after failing to negotiate a new enterprise agreement; and employees at the University of Queensland commenced protected industrial action which included a ban on emails, attendance at university events and performing overtime. See 'Monash University Workers Go Out, as Tertiary Sector Bargaining Intensifies' (3 March 2014) *Workplace Express* <http://www.workplaceexpress.com.au/nl06_news_selected.php?selkey=52106>.

Chapter 15

The Tort of Negligence and Higher Education

Robert Horton, Kerry Smith and Abigail Tisbury

I Introduction

Universities may be liable for negligence under common law and statute for wrongful acts and omissions which cause damage to persons or property. Most tort-based court actions arise from personal injuries allegedly caused by a defendant's negligence.[1] There are few decided cases involving universities probably, in part, because insurers tend to resolve personal injury claims and actions before judgment. This chapter will focus on the tort of negligence, particularly as it relates to personal injury,[2] including some particular risks for higher education institutions.

II Negligence

The tort of negligence 'imposes liability on a defendant' who 'unjustifiably fails to take reasonable care' to avoid or prevent harm from occurring to another person.[3] For liability to arise, the necessary elements of negligence must be present, namely, the existence of a duty of care, a breach of that duty, and compensable damage which is caused by the breach.[4] In the seminal case of *Donoghue v Stevenson*, Lord Aitken stated that in 'an action for damages for negligence the complainant has to show that he has been injured by the breach of a duty owed to him in the circumstances by the defendant to take reasonable care to avoid such injury'.[5] Most Australian jurisdictions introduced legislation in 2002-2003 to modify the common law to restrict some causes of action and reduce damages pay-outs (the *Civil Liability Act* regimes, CLAs).[6]

1 The law of torts covers a number of intentional and unintentional actions including trespass, assault and battery and defamation. A discussion of torts in general is beyond the scope of this chapter; however, for a comprehensive discussion on the law of torts in Australia, see RP Balkin and JLR Davis, *Law of Torts* (Butterworths, 2013).

2 For discussion of the intentional torts, nuisance or the economic torts amongst others, see, for example, Carolyn Sappideen and Prue Vines (eds), *Fleming's The Law of Torts* (Thomson Reuters, 2011).

3 Julia Davis, *Connecting with Tort Law* (Oxford University Press, 2012), 314.

4 Ibid 337.

5 *Donoghue v Stevenson* [1932] AC 562.

6 *Civil Liability Act 2002* (NSW); *Civil Law (Wrongs) Act 2002* (ACT); *Personal Injuries (Liabilities and Damages) Act 2003* (NT) and *Personal Injuries (Civil Claims) Act 2003* (NT); *Civil Liability Act 2003* (Qld); *Civil Liability Act 1936* (SA); *Civil Liability Act 2002* (Tas); *Wrongs Act 1958* (Vic); and *Civil Liability Act 2002* (WA).

A Duty of Care

Negligence is not actionable without a duty of care which a defendant must owe to a plaintiff. The law recognises certain categories of relationships in which a duty of care is owed. Established categories include teachers who owe a duty of care to students and employers who owe a duty of care to employees.[7]

The general duty, following the CLAs,[8] is to take reasonable care to avoid a foreseeable and not insignificant risk of injury. The duty is owed to a person that ought reasonably be in contemplation as being affected by the act or omission.[9]

Some duties are non-delegable, which imports an additional obligation to ensure that reasonable care is taken by any person delegated to carry out the functions of the defendant. The duty cannot be discharged merely by engaging a competent person to carry out the task. The employment relationship is one giving rise to such a duty,[10] and a university will therefore owe its employees a non-delegable duty of care to exercise reasonable care and skill or to take reasonable steps to avoid risk of harm.[11]

There is little specific Australian authority on the nature of a university's duty of care to its students, who are members of their universities.[12] It is unlikely that a distinct duty of care is owed to a student solely because of that membership. However, a university will owe the general duty to a student on its premises, as it would to any other entrant, and will owe a student a duty of care in other circumstances where there is a sufficiently proximate relationship.

This view was qualified, however, in *Waters v Winter and University of New England*[13] in which the plaintiff student failed in his claim for damages against his university after being assaulted at a residential college social function for which he was an organiser. He alleged the university should have provided greater security for the event, despite the university not having arranged it. The Court of Appeal upheld the District Court judgment in favour of the university. Although there was a general duty of care towards students to protect them from risk of injury of which the university was or ought to have been aware, the particular circumstances of this case did not fall within that duty. This was because 'it was not reasonably foreseeable that a failure to provide paid professional security guards would be likely to lead to harm to the plaintiff or any other student in his position. The decision illustrates that each case will be decided on its particular facts'.[14]

7 Davis, above n 3, 359-360.

8 For the Northern Territory and classes of actions excluded from the CLAs (for example, employment injuries in New South Wales s 3B(1)(f)), see *Wyong Shire Council v Shirt* (1989) 146 CLR 40.

9 *Donoghue v Stevenson* [1932] AC 562, in which the 'neighbour principle' was enunciated.

10 *Kondis v State Transport Authority* (1984) 154 CLR 672.

11 See, for example, *Czatyko v Edith Cowan University* (2005) 79 ALJR 839, [12].

12 While the relationship has not been definitively established by case law in Australia, there is precedent from comparable jurisdictions, for example, New Zealand, which states that the relationship is partly statutory by which students are members of the university, and partly contractual: *Staines, Woolley, Grant & Staines*, reported as *Grant v Victoria University of Wellington* [2003] NZAR 185.

13 [1998] NSWSC 248.

14 See Stanley Yeo, 'The Responsibility of the Universities for their Student's Personal Safety' (2002) 6 *Southern Cross University Law Review* 77 for a discussion of United States cases, decided either way.

Where a duty of care is owed by a university to a student, it is unlikely to be as a consequence of the kind of special relationship giving rise to a non-delegable duty. This may differ in a situation where a university has the direct control of an activity involving school age children, such as summer vacation courses.[15]

B Breach of Duty of Care

For the duty of care to be breached, the risk of harm flowing from the breach must be reasonably foreseeable. The common law test is that the risk is foreseeable unless it is 'far-fetched or fanciful'.[16] That has been modified by the CLAs in all jurisdictions except the Northern Territory. Section 5B of the *Civil Liability Act 2002* (NSW) is representative of the statutory provisions[17] and says that a person is not negligent in failing to take precautions against a risk of harm unless the risk was foreseeable, not insignificant, and in the circumstances, a reasonable person would have taken those precautions. A reasonable person will weigh, amongst other things, the probability and seriousness of the harm with the burden of taking precautions and the social utility of the subject activity.

C Causation

A plaintiff must prove that the damage suffered was caused by the defendant's negligent act or omission. Under the common law there may be more than one cause or cumulative causes of the plaintiff's loss. Causation will be found where the defendant's act is a material cause though not the sole cause of the loss. It is sufficient to be a material cause that it is not 'negligible'.[18]

The CLAs have modified the common law for determining causation in all jurisdictions except the Northern Territory.[19] Under the CLAs, there are two arms of causation – that the negligence was a necessary condition of the harm (*factual causation*), and that it is appropriate for the scope of liability to extend to the harm (*legal causation*).[20]

Factual causation under the CLAs is a 'but for' test,[21] which asks whether the plaintiff would have suffered damage but for the breach of duty by the defendant. If damage would have been suffered anyway, the plaintiff will fail on causation. If not, the court has to consider the scope of liability.

15 See *Commonwealth v Introvigne* (1982) 150 CLR 258 regarding a school authority's non-delegable duty to school students.

16 *Wyong Shire Council* v *Shirt* (1989) 146 CLR 40.

17 Wording varies slightly between States. See (Vic) s 48; (Qld) s 9; (Tas) s 11; (SA) s 32; (WA) s 5B; (ACT) s 43.

18 *Western Australia v Watson* [1990] WAR 248.

19 (NSW) s 5D; (Vic) s 51; (Qld) s 11; (Tas) s 13; (SA) s 34; (WA) s 5C; (ACT) s 45; no NT equivalent section.

20 For a discussion of causation, see Pam Stewart and Anita Stuhmcke, *Australian Principles of Tort Law* (Federation Press, 2012), 407.

21 See *Adeels Palace Pty Ltd v Moubarak* (2009) 239 CLR 420.

If a defendant's breach of duty is accepted by the court, causation will be established if a plaintiff's injury would not, on the probabilities, have occurred had the defendant complied with its duty of care.[22]

If the causal link is severed, the defendant's actions will be found not to be the cause of the loss and the defendant will not be liable for the damage.[23] However, a defendant cannot escape liability for deliberate or voluntary acts of a third party when the event that occurred was the risk which it was the defendant's duty to avoid.[24]

D Remoteness of Damage

A defendant is only liable for damage which is reasonably foreseeable. The plaintiff need only show that the kind of damage was foreseeable and not that the precise type or the full extent of damage was foreseeable.[25] The 'eggshell skull' rule[26] means that a defendant may be liable for extreme consequences of an otherwise minor incident.[27] A defendant may also be liable for a subsequent injury which is brought about by an initial injury for which it is liable and which caused the plaintiff to be susceptible.[28]

Mental harm may also be compensable at common law and under the CLAs, though liability for a solely psychiatric injury is more restricted than for physical or mixed physical and psychiatric injury.[29] At common law, issues relevant to determining whether a person is entitled to damages for pure mental harm consequent to the death or injury of another person include whether the plaintiff directly saw the death or injury, the relationship between the plaintiff and the person in peril, the nature of the shock and whether there is a pre-existing relationship with the person killed or injured.[30]

To be compensable, the harm must be 'a recognised psychiatric injury'.[31] The CLAs restrict liability to injury foreseeably suffered by a person of normal fortitude, and in New South Wales, Tasmania and Victoria, recovery is restricted to limited classes

22 See *Strong v Woolworths Limited* (2012) 246 CLR 182, the plaintiff will not fail simply because there is no evidence positively establishing the causal link.

23 The 'but for' test was criticised by the High Court in *March v E & MH Stramare Pty Ltd* (1991) 171 CLR 506 and is not the common law test.

24 *Chomentowski v Red Garter Restaurant* (1970) 92 WN (NSW) 1070 for criminal assault, and *Mahony v J Kruschich (Demolitions) P/L* (1985) 156 CLR 522 for the consequences of subsequently received negligent medical attention.

25 *Hughes v Lord Advocate* [1963] AC 837.

26 Where a person suffers more severe damage than would others because of particular susceptibility, otherwise described as the wrongdoer 'takes the plaintiff as he finds him'. See *Shorey v PT Ltd* (2003) 197 ALR 410, [44]-[45] (Kirby J).

27 See *Commonwealth v McLean* (1996) 441 NSWLR 389 where the court stated that the 'eggshell skull' principle makes a defendant liable for damage of an unforeseeable extent, but not for unforeseeable damage of a different kind. The defendant was not liable for the plaintiff's throat cancer caused by excessive tobacco and alcohol use stemming from a psychological injury caused by the defendant's negligence.

28 *Pyne v Wilkenfeld* (1981) 26 SASR 441.

29 Psychiatric or psychological illness not caused by or related to a physical injury is also referred to as 'nervous shock'.

30 *Annetts v Australian Stations P/L; Tame v New South Wales* (2002) 211 CLR 317.

31 (NSW) s 31; (SA) s 53(2); (Tas) s 33; (Vic) s 72(1); (WA) s 55(1); (ACT) ss 34(1), s 35; and NT as per common law.

of persons.[32] Damages are proportionately reduced commensurate with the victim's contributory negligence.[33]

E Vicarious Liability

Pursuant to a principle known as vicarious liability, an employer or a principal will be liable for the torts of their employees or agents in most circumstances. This liability requires proof that the tortfeasor was an employee or agent of the defendant and that they were acting within the scope of that employment or agency.[34] A university is not vicariously liable for the torts of its students.

III Defences to Negligence

Under a principle known as contributory negligence, a defendant can reduce his or her liability to a plaintiff by demonstrating that the plaintiff's own failure to take reasonable care for their safety contributed to the damage suffered.[35]

At common law, it is a complete defence to an action for damages that the plaintiff acted with full knowledge of the risk of being injured, and voluntarily assumed that risk.[36] This defence of voluntary assumption of risk, in modified form, is incorporated in various of the CLAs restricting liability with respect to obvious risks and inherent risks[37] and dangerous recreational activities,[38] and in some States[39] a university may deflect liability through risk warnings. Nonetheless, the defence of voluntary assumption of risk remains available at common law although it is extremely difficult to prove, as the court must be satisfied that the plaintiff assumed the risk with full knowledge of the circumstances.

IV Some Areas of Particular Risk for Universities

There are various activities and situations in the university context that may give rise to claims for negligence if foreseeable risks are not identified and acted upon in a reasonable manner. Some of these key areas are highlighted below.

---

32 For example, *Civil Liability Act 2002* (NSW) pt 3 s 30. Direct witnesses to the primary victim being killed or injured, and particular categories of relatives of such a person.

33 *Civil Liability Act 2002* (NSW) pt 3 s 30.

34 See *Hollis v Vabu Pty Ltd* (2001) 207 CLR 21 regarding the fact of employment, and *New South Wales v Lepore* (2003) 212 CLR 511 as to the scope of employment.

35 Originally, a complete defence at common law (*Butterfield v Forrester* (1809) 103 ER 296) which was ameliorated by legislation in all Australian jurisdictions (for example, *Law Reform (Miscellaneous Provisions) Act 1965* (NSW) s 59(1)) and modified again by CLAs in NSW, Qld, Vic and ACT to allow for a reduction of up to 100 per cent of damages.

36 *Smith v Baker* [1891] AC 325 (HL).

37 In New South Wales, Victoria, Queensland, Tasmania, South Australia and Western Australia.

38 In New South Wales, Queensland, Tasmania and Western Australia. For a recent judicial application, see *Campbell v Hay* [2014] NSWCA 129 where the activity was recreational flying.

39 In New South Wales, Tasmania and Western Australia.

A University as Occupier

When a university is an occupier of premises it will have a duty of care to an entrant to avoid a foreseeable risk of injury,[40] but the use and nature of the occupation is relevant to determination of liability.[41]

A university is usually not the occupier of premises leased to third parties and in those circumstances the university, lacking the element of control, is unlikely to be liable for damage suffered by entrants onto the premises. Occupation of premises may be shared and a university may remain an occupier of premises licensed to a third person. A university is unlikely to have the requisite control to be an occupier of residential colleges.

Liability may flow from circumstances such as injury as a consequence of hidden dangers, failure to maintain grounds or buildings, presence of dangerous works, but not where a danger is minor, obvious and unexceptional.[42]

B Bullying and Cyberbullying

Workplace health and safety requirements mean universities are required to have anti-bullying and harassment policies applicable to staff and students.[43] Universities would be advised to have in place a reporting system and a welfare/pastoral care system for students. It is likely that a non-delegable duty of care will be owed to employees[44] and it is arguable that anti-bullying initiatives taken by the university could give rise to a duty of care to students based on an assumption of responsibility and control. If so, failure by a university to adhere to its own policies in this regard could amount to a breach of the duty of care.[45]

C Workshops, Machines, Laboratories and Dangerous Substances

Often during the course of their studies students will be required to work in such situations where there will be a clear and foreseeable risk of injury to both students and employees. A court will expect reasonable precautions to be taken to avoid harm including, for instance, insistence on the wearing and use of appropriate safety equipment, provision of adequate safety instructions and compliance with handling and storage protocols for hazardous materials.[46]

---

40 *Australian Safeways Stores P/L v Zaluzna* (1987) 162 CLR 479 for statutory modifications of duty in Victoria, South Australia, Western Australia and Australian Capital Territory.

41 *Thompson v Woolworths (Qld) P/L* (2005) 221 CLR 234.

42 *Neindorf v Junkovic* (2005) 222 ALR 631.

43 Joan Squelch and Robert Guthrie, 'Workplace Health and Safety: Managing the Risk of Workplace Bullying' (2012) *Legal Issues in Business* 14, 9-18.

44 *Nationwide News P/L* v *Naidu* [2007] NSWCA 377, and see *Wolters v University of the Sunshine Coast* [2012] QSC 248.

45 For an example of a school decision awarding damages to a student, see *Oyston v St Patrick's College* [2013] NSWCA 135.

46 *Johnson v Rea Limited* [1961] 3 All ER 816; for an example of breach of duty through inadequate safety instructions, see *Roberts v Northern Melbourne Institute of TAFE* [2008] VCC 181 (eye damage from 'welder's flash').

D Animals

Universities will primarily have exposure in relation to injury caused by or as a consequence of animals being kept for research purposes, as livestock breeds maintained for vocational training or for dangerous activities such as horse riding. The complex common law rules creating different classes of animals for liability purposes have been largely subsumed into the modern law of negligence[47] and in any event abolished by statute in New South Wales, South Australia and the Australian Capital Territory, and modified in Western Australia. The obligations of universities to provide for animals' physical health and behaviour needs as per *The Australian Code for the Care and Use of Animals Used for Scientific Purposes* (2013)[48] are to be noted.

E Work Placements, Field Trips and Excursions

Where field trips and excursions are organised by the university with students under the control and direction of the institution's staff, a duty of care will be owed, the content of which will vary depending on the nature of the activity. Where a work placement or internship is arranged by the student directly to comply with course requirements, it is unlikely a duty of care will be owed. However, in the case of the institution arranging the work placement, a duty of care may be owed, but possibly limited to circumstances where the university had notice of circumstances placing the student at risk. A host employer will generally bear liability for the student.[49]

F Travel

Liability for injuries to employees may arise where arrangements are made for domestic or international travel, without due precautions being taken in respect of known risks. Reasonable measures should be taken to protect employees from harm including ensuring the availability of emergency and medical care. Department of Foreign Affairs and Trade travel advice updates should be monitored for overseas travel and appropriate directions issued to employees, such as restrictions on unnecessary travel in dangerous regions. A duty of care to students could arise where travel arrangements have been made by a university or where there has been an assumption of responsibility or introduction of control in some way by the university such as providing the means of conveyance or accommodation or perhaps by providing accompanying university staff.

G Provision of Security, Sexual Assaults and Major Security Incidents

An occupier does not owe a duty to protect persons on its land from the unpredictable criminal behaviour of strangers even if the risk of harm is foreseeable.[50] The exception

47 See Sappideen and Vines, above n 2, 407.
48 National Health and Medical Research Council Guideline, 8th edition, 2013 <https://www.nhmrc.gov.au/guidelines-publications/ea28>.
49 *Southern Area Health Service v Brown* [2003] NSWCA 369; *Simundic v University of Newcastle* [2005] NSWSC 586.
50 *Lesandu Blacktown P/L v Gonzalez* [2013] NSWCA 8.

to this rule is where a special relationship exists such as that of employer and employee, or school and pupil that gives rise to a duty to take reasonable care to protect the other from the criminal behaviour of third parties, random and unpredictable as such behaviour may be.[51] No such special relationship has yet been found by Australian courts to date between universities and its students. However, a university was found to have owed an employee of a contractor a duty of care to secure her personal safety against the foreseeable risk of physical attack in circumstances where the university was on notice of an attacker in the vicinity, had care and control of the location and was responsible for the system of her entry and exit to her place of work.[52]

H Liability for On-campus Groups/Associations

Generally, there is no legal duty on one person to control the actions of another to prevent them from causing injury to other people.[53] Although there are exceptions to this rule (such as a school's duty to control young children), a university does not have such a close level of control over other groups and associations, and is unlikely to owe such a duty. This will be subject to the extent to which the university becomes involved in the activity.

I Student Activities

As outlined above, a university will owe the general duty to students and their invitees with respect to its premises. However, in the absence of control or an assumption of responsibility the student activity may not fall within the duty of care. In circumstances where it was not foreseeable that not providing professional security guards for a closed student function would be likely to lead to harm, there was no duty to do so.[54]

Many student activities will involve the imbibing of alcohol which may impact on a student's ability to assess risk. Nonetheless, there is likely to be no duty to warn against danger the existence of which would have been obvious had the plaintiff been sober.[55] Furthermore, some CLAs have modified the effect of intoxication on the duty of care owed. A presumption of contributory negligence applies in some States when a person is intoxicated at the time of injury.[56] The fact of intoxication does not of itself increase the standard of care owed and there will be no recovery of damages unless the court is satisfied that the injury would likely have occurred even if the person had not been intoxicated.

51 *Modbury Triangle Shopping Centre P/L v Anzil* (2000) 75 ALJR 164.

52 *Karatjas v Deakin University* [2012] VSCA 53.

53 *Smith v Leurs* (1945) 70 CLR 256, [162] (Dixon J).

54 *Waters v Winter and University of New England* [1998] NSWSC 248.

55 *Council of the Shire of Muswellbrook v Lettice* [2000] NSWCA 359; however, see *Coghlan v Beta Theta Pi Fraternity* 987 P 2d 300 (Idaho 1999) where the University of Idaho was liable for injury sustained at a fraternity drinking party <http://www.ecases.us/case/idaho/1401395/coghlan-v-beta-theta-pi-fraternity>.

56 *Civil Liability Act 2002* (NSW) pt 6; *Civil Liability Act 1936* (SA) pt 7.

J Sport and Other Recreational Activities

The CLA defences may apply in the case of sports and recreational injuries, depending on the nature of the risk leading to harm. The 'dangerous recreational activities' defence[57] where available may prevent a duty of care arising in circumstances such as those pertaining in an American case where a university cheerleader suffered brain damage and serious bodily injury in falling from a human pyramid. The court found that the voluntary provision of safety information by the university led to an obligation to do so in a non-negligent manner.[58]

V Is there a Tort of Educational Negligence in Australia?

Whether an educational institution or its teaching staff can be liable in negligence ('educational malpractice') for a loss sustained by a student as a consequence of the institution's or the teacher's failure to educate the student at an appropriate standard is presently unresolved in Australia.

Anecdotally, the higher costs of obtaining a university education and competition amongst providers have contributed to students viewing themselves as consumers of tertiary education services, with greater expectations of their universities than in the past and a perceived greater willingness to take legal action for disappointed expectations. Such factors suggest Australian courts will be required to consider the existence of the tort before long.

The tort of educational negligence has succeeded in the United Kingdom in relation to school students with disabilities, but has been generally rejected in the United States on public policy grounds.[59] Whether it may be successfully argued in the university context was left open by the High Court of New Zealand.[60]

In the United Kingdom, the House of Lords in 1995 recognised there was an arguable cause of action in negligence for the failure of a school education authority to properly diagnose the learning disability of a school student.[61] In 2000, the House of Lords in *Phelps*[62] upheld a judgment for damages awarded against another education authority for the negligent provision of professional or specialist services. This case involved a former school student who sued for the failure of an educational psychologist employed by the local educational authority to diagnose her dyslexia. The court rejected

57 (NSW) s 5L; (Qld) s 19; (Tas) s 20; and (WA) s 5H.

58 *Davidson v University of North Carolina at Chapel Hill* 353 NC 724, 550 SE 2d 771 (2001).

59 See, for example, Ralph Mawdsley and Joy Cumming, 'Educational Malpractice and Setting Damages for Ineffective Teaching: A Comparison of Legal Principles in the USA, England and Australia' (2008) 20(1) *Education and the Law* 25.

60 Ibid. *Grant v Victoria University of Wellington* [2003] NZAR 185.

61 *X (Minors) v Bedfordshire County Council* [1995] UKHL 9 – five appeals of which three were from strike out applications of claims that school education authorities failed to diagnose a learning disability. The court accepted there was an arguable claim for vicarious liability for the negligent provision of professional services.

62 *Phelps v London Borough of Hillingdon* [2000] 4 All ER 504, which was heard with another three related cases against school authorities.

policy arguments against the duty of care existing and by way of dicta, suggested the action could apply to a teacher and that logically, the duty would be owed to all students, not only those with special needs. However, the court did warn that 'the existence of a duty of care owed by teachers to their pupils should not be regarded as a basis for mounting of generalised educational malpractice claims'.[63]

Phelps has not resulted in a rush of claims, and success appears limited to students with special needs.[64] But the tort, nonetheless, now has its bridgehead in England and this may well be persuasive to an Australian court.

The tort has not been recognised in Australia. However, if recognised, the risk to universities may be of claims arising from circumstances, among others, such as failing to teach set course content, teaching at a poor standard, failing to conduct assessments or examinations appropriately, failing to make adequate arrangements during the absence of a lecturer or tutor, failure of technology or other resources necessary for the course, or inadequately supporting students with disabilities, or students from non-English speaking backgrounds who have nonetheless, been encouraged to enrol (see Chapter 8 by Kamvounias).

A plaintiff would first need to establish the nature of the harm suffered and whether it was an injury, or a claim for pure economic loss. The type of claim would impact on the existence, scope and content of the duty of care. A tertiary student whose entry into the workforce is delayed is likely to have suffered a pure economic loss but no injury and the law on recovery for pure economic loss would apply. However, development of a diagnosable psychiatric condition as a result of the university's breach of duty would result in an injury with consequential economic loss.

If a relevant duty of care and breach are established, the plaintiff would next need to establish causation to be entitled to damages. This is likely to be the major practical barrier to a claim succeeding, as the student's educational outcome is what is in issue, and whether the student would have been in a better position but for the claimed breach of duty. Should factual causation be established, the court under the second limb of causation would consider whether it is appropriate for the defendant's liability to extend to the harm or damage claimed. In considering causation and remoteness, the court will take policy issues into consideration and could decide at this point that the tort has no place in Australian law.

The general law, and in some States the CLAs, restrict liability of 'professionals'. Academics and teachers are likely to fall within the definition of 'professional' in some States but not others.[65] In those States a 'professional' does not incur liability in negligence if they acted in a manner widely accepted in Australia by peer professional opinion as competent professional practice[66] unless the court determines that the

63 Ibid. Lord Jauncey of Tullichettle agreeing with Lord Nicholls.

64 See *Abramova v Oxford Institute of Legal Practice* [2011] EWHC 613 (QB) where the plaintiff law student failed in alleging negligence against her teachers/examination markers.

65 Queensland, New South Wales, Victoria, Tasmania and South Australia, but not Australian Capital Territory or Northern Territory. In Western Australia, the protection is restricted to 'health professionals' which could cover diagnostic failures such as occurred in *Phelps*.

66 The wording varies among States, see (Qld) s 22; (NSW) s 5O; (Vic) s 59; (Tas) s 22; (SA) s 41; (WA) s 5PB.

opinion is unreasonable[67] or irrational[68] or contrary to a written law.[69] The defence[70] may not be available if the conduct complained of does not fall within an actual 'practice'.[71] The common law applies in the other States and would apply to claims which do not relate to conduct of 'professionals'.[72]

VI Conclusion

It can be expected that the boundaries of duty of care will be tested in the future by students and others presenting a greater range and variety of claims. However, the lack of decided cases against universities to date would suggest that in absolute terms, claim numbers are low and they are likely to remain so with most university-based litigation occurring with respect to other areas of law. Universities will best preserve their position by proactive risk management and maintenance of appropriate insurance arrangements.

67 (Vic) s 59(2) and (WA) s 5PB(4).
68 (NSW) s 5O(2); (Tas) s 22(2); (SA) s 41(2).
69 (Qld) s 22(2).
70 See above n 66, provisions referred to operate as a defence; *Dobler v Halvorsen* [2007] NSWCA 335.
71 *McKenna v HNELHD* [2013] NSWCA 476. Judgment overturned on appeal to High Court, *Hunter and New England Local Health District v McKenna; Hunter and New England Local Health District v Simon* (2014) 89 ALJR 39 but s 5O point not considered.
72 Examples would be allegations of negligent resourcing by institution management, which is an administrative rather than a professional issue.

Chapter 16

Workplace Health and Safety

Joan Squelch

I Introduction

The establishment and management of a safe and healthy working environment is a key joint responsibility of employers and workers. Higher education institutions are generally large and complex organisations and workplaces that are subject to a myriad of Commonwealth and State or Territory laws and regulations that govern workplace health and safety. They, of necessity, have specialist divisions that oversee health and safety matters and risk management. This chapter provides an overview of some of the key provisions of the recently enacted model *Work Health and Safety Act* as it pertains to universities. It is beyond the scope of this chapter to cover all related health and safety legislation, but it is necessary for those responsible for the management of health and safety in a higher education institution to be familiar with such legislation as it forms the corpus of health and safety law.

II Legislative Framework

The Commonwealth, States and Territories are responsible for the regulation of occupational health and safety in their jurisdiction and so each has its own laws on workplace health and safety.[1] Although the laws deal with similar matters and processes, it is recognised that there are 'differences between jurisdictions in the details and application of these laws'.[2]

There have been several attempts to harmonise health and safety laws across multiple jurisdictions, which was achieved to a large extent by 2012.[3] In 2008, the Council of Australian Governments (COAG) signed the *Intergovernmental Agreement for Regulatory and Operational Reform in Occupational Health and Safety* (*IGA*) that provided an undertaking by the Commonwealth, State and Territory governments to cooperate to develop and implement a national work health and safety legislative

1 *Occupational Health and Safety Act 1989* (ACT); *Occupational Health and Safety Act 1991* (Cth); *Occupational Health and Safety Act 2000* (NSW); *Workplace Health and Safety Act 2007* (NT); *Workplace Health and Safety Act 1995* (Qld); *Occupational Health, Safety and Welfare Act 1986* (SA); *Workplace Health and Safety Act 1995* (Tas); *Occupational Health and Safety Act 2004* (Vic); *Occupational Safety and Health Act 1984* (WA). See below n 8.

2 COAG, *Inter-governmental Agreement for Regulatory and Operational Reform in Occupational Health and Safety*.

3 Belinda Reeve and Ron McCallum, 'The Scope of Employers' Responsibilities Under Australian Occupational Health and Safety Legislation' (2011) 24 *Australian Journal of Labour Law* 189.

scheme.[4] The *IGA* describes harmonisation as the 'national uniformity of the OHS legislative framework (comprised of a model OHS Act, supported by model OHS regulations and model codes of practice) complemented by a nationally consistent approach to compliance policy and enforcement policy'.[5] A primary purpose of harmonising the work health and safety laws is to 'enable the development of uniform, equitable and effective safety standards and protections for all Australian workers'.[6]

The model work health and safety scheme was developed through an extensive process of consultation[7] and the final model *Work Health and Safety Act* was completed in 2011 and available to be enacted in all jurisdictions. It is not mandatory for a jurisdiction to adopt the model law and to date, the States of Victoria and Western Australia have not adopted the legislation.[8] Therefore, in Victoria and Western Australia,[9] the current State legislation applies.

III Model Work Health and Safety Law

The model *Work Health and Safety Act 2011* (Cth) (*WHS Act*) came into operation in January 2012. The primary object of the *WHS Act* is to provide for 'a balanced and nationally consistent framework to secure the health and safety of workers and workplaces by protecting workers and other persons against harm to their health, safety and welfare through the elimination or minimisation of risks arising from work'.[10] Most jurisdictions have enacted the model law and implemented corresponding legislation which continues to be administered and regulated within each jurisdiction.[11] Although some variations may be found in the corresponding legislation, the core components covered in this chapter are reflected in the State and Territory legislation.

4 COAG <https://www.coag.gov.au/node/276>.

5 COAG, above n 2, cl 1.2.

6 COAG, above n 2, cl 1.4.

7 For an overview of the consultation process see Safe Work Australia, *Harmonisation Background* <http://www.safeworkaustralia.gov.au/sites/swa/model-whs-laws/background/pages/background>.

8 Safe Work Australia, the new model work health and safety laws, commenced in New South Wales, Queensland, the Australian Capital Territory, the Commonwealth and the Northern Territory on 1 January 2012. South Australia and Tasmania commenced on 1 January 2013. *Work Health and Safety Act 2011* (NSW); *Work Health and Safety Act 2011* (Qld); *Work Health and Safety Act 2011* (ACT); *Work Health and Safety (National Uniform Legislation) Act* (2011) (NT); *Work Health and Safety Act 2012* (SA); *Work Health and Safety Act 2012* (Tas). Western Australia and Victoria have elected not to adopt the model legislation in its current form; the current State legislation remains in force. See above n 1.

9 On 23 October 2014, the Western Australia Work Health and Safety Bill was tabled in parliament by the Minister for Commerce. The Bill is based on the model *Work Health and Safety Act 2011* with changes to suits the WA workplace context <http://www.commerce.wa.gov.au/sites/default/files/atoms/files/list_of_change_to_the_model_whs_bill_0.pdf>.

10 *WHS Act* s 3.

11 The *WHS Act* sets out a range of jurisdictional matters that provides for some jurisdictional differences. Each jurisdiction identifies and determines the courts, regulators and local authorities for its corresponding legislation.

A Who is Covered by the Act?

The *WHS Act* has wide coverage and applies to those who carry out work for a person conducting a business or undertaking.[12] Therefore, employees, contractors, subcontractors, apprentices, trainees, outworkers[13] and volunteers[14] are included. Workplace health and safety legislation applies to private and public universities. In the university context, students, students gaining work experience, sessional teaching staff, and casual administrative and teaching staff all fall within the scope of the *WHS Act*. Other people such as visitors and customers are also covered, for example, visiting academics and scholars.

The *WHS Act* also broadly defines the workplace to cover workers in 'a place where work is carried out for a business or undertaking and includes any place where a worker goes, or is likely to be, while at work'.[15] 'Place' includes a vehicle, vessel, aircraft or other mobile structure; and any waters and any installation on land, on the bed of any waters or floating on any waters.[16] Therefore, university workers such as researchers working in these kinds of locations fall within the ambit of the legislation.

B Health and Safety Duties

A fundamental component of the *WHS Act* is the health and safety duties that are imposed on entities employing people, workers and other persons. The first key object of the legislation is to secure the health and safety of workers and workplaces by protecting workers and other persons against harm to their health, safety and welfare through the elimination or minimisation of risks arising from work.[17] To this end, it is a shared duty of entities, workers and others to create a safe workplace and not to engage in conduct that poses a risk to the health and safety to oneself and others.

1 Primary Duty of Care

There is a primary duty on persons conducting a business or undertaking (PCBU)[18] to ensure, so far as reasonably practicable, the health and safety of workers and others who may be affected by the carrying out of work.[19] The *WHS Act* does not use the term 'employer' but the concept is broad and covers a wide range of people.[20] The PCBU

12 *WHS Act* s 5.

13 Labour hire staff, for example, casual or part-time university administrative staff employed through an agency.

14 The *WHS Act* does not cover volunteer associations who do not have employees.

15 *WHS Act* s 8. For an analysis of the phrase 'while at work' see *Bowker, Coombe, Zwarts v DP World Melbourne; Maritime Union of Australia, Victorian Branch* [2014] FWCFB 9227.

16 But note exclusion in *WHS Act* s 12A.

17 *WHS Act* s 3(1)(a).

18 The PCBU is the employer, which is broadly defined, see *WHS Act* s 5.

19 *WHS Act* div 2 s 19.

20 A person is a worker if the person carries out work in any capacity for a person conducting a business or undertaking, including work as an employee; or a contractor or subcontractor; or an employee of a contractor or subcontractor; or an employee of a labour hire company who has been assigned to work in the person's business or undertaking; or an outworker; or an apprentice or trainee; or a student gaining work experience; or a volunteer; or a person of a prescribed class: *WHS Act* s 7.

concept intends to be broad to include employers and various forms of contractors and managers of workplaces and therefore expands the group of persons who might be liable for breaches of workplace safety. The duty imposed is similar to the common law duty of care owed by employers to employees, but Creighton and Stewart note that a breach of the s 19 duty cannot be used as a 'basis for the award of damages to persons who are injured as a consequence of that breach'.[21]

Universities, both private and public, fall within the definition of a PCBU and therefore have a primary duty to protect the health and safety of workers. Universities as body corporates and separate legal entities may undertake a 'business' or an 'undertaking', which do not have to be a for-profit enterprise. In the context of the *WHS Act*, a business is 'an enterprise usually conducted with a view to making a profit and have a degree of organisation, system and continuity' while an 'undertaking' has the 'elements of organisation, systems and possibly continuity, but are usually not profit-making or commercial in nature'.[22] A university may have elements of both.

2 Duties of Officers

The *WHS Act* places a positive duty on officers[23] of a PCBU to comply with duties under the Act and to exercise due diligence to ensure that the person conducting the business or undertaking complies with the duty[24] to establish a healthy and safe environment. The term officer has the meaning found in s 9 of the *Corporations Act 2001* (Cth). In universities, an 'officer' will apply to executive and senior members of academic and administrative staff, including executive staff, a board of trustees, deans, heads of schools and departments, and directors of research institutes.

Volunteers, namely persons acting on a voluntary basis regardless of whether the person receives out-of-pocket expenses,[25] also have duties under the *WHS Act*. In universities, there may be various 'officers' who are acting in a voluntary capacity, such as the chair of an academic board, external people and students sitting on university councils, and academic union officials. Volunteer officers in universities are required to exercise due diligence, but they are exempt from prosecution for failing to comply with this compliance standard. However, they may be prosecuted as a worker under the Act.[26]

An officer of a PCBU (for example, of a university) may be convicted or found guilty of an offence under s 27 of the *WHS Act* irrespective of whether or not the PCBU has been convicted or found guilty of an offence under the *WHS Act* relating to the duty or obligation.[27]

---

21 Breen Creighton and Andrew Stewart, *Labour Law* (Federation Press, 2010), 456.

22 Safe Work Australia, *Interpretive Guideline – Model Work Health and Safety Act. The Meaning of Person Conducting a Business or Undertaking* 1 <http://www.safeworkaustralia.gov.au/sites/swa/about/publications/pages/interpretive%20-guideline-pcbu>.

23 Officers are defined as per s 9 of the *Corporations Act 2001* (Cth). It includes officers of corporations and unincorporated associations.

24 *WHS Act* s 7(1).

25 *WHS Act* s 4.

26 *WHS Act* s 34(1).

27 *WHS Act* s 27(4).

3 Due Diligence

An officer of a PCBU is required to exercise due diligence to ensure that the PCBU meets its health and safety obligations under the *WHS Act*. Due diligence means to take 'reasonable steps' to eliminate or minimise risks to health and safety; to ensure appropriate processes are in place for receiving and considering information regarding incidents, hazards and risks; and responding in a timely way to information and processes for complying with any duty or obligation under the *WHS Act*.[28]

For officers of a university, for instance, this will mean taking reasonable steps to:

- ensure appropriate policies and process are in place to meet health and safety obligations;
- ensure officers and workers receive appropriate training in health and safety matters;
- make necessary resources available to implement health and safety policies;
- monitor and review policies and processes;
- report notifiable incidents;[29]
- consult with workers;[30]
- comply with notices issued to the university under the Act;[31] and
- ensure that health and safety representatives receive their entitlements to training.[32]

4 Duties of Workers and Other Persons

The *WHS Act* refers to workers, not employees, which recognises the different kinds of people and relationships in the workplace. Pursuant to the Act, workers and other persons[33] are required to take reasonable care for their own health and safety, and take reasonable care that their acts or omissions do not adversely affect the health and safety of other persons. This is illustrated in *Hillman v Lawless*[34] in which a worker (the defendant) was fined $4400 for failing to take reasonable care to ensure the safety of other workers. Workers must also comply, to the extent that the worker or other person is reasonably able, with any reasonable instruction that is given by the PCBU to allow the person to comply with this Act.[35] Additionally, workers are required to cooperate with any reasonable policy or procedure of the PCBU relating to health or safety at the workplace that has been notified.[36]

---

28 *WHS Act* s 27(5).

29 *WHS Act* s 38. A notifiable incident means the death of a person; or a serious injury or illness of a person; or a dangerous incident: s 35.

30 *WHS Act* s 47.

31 *WHS Act* ss 90-102, 191-194.

32 *WHS Act* s 19(1)(f).

33 'Other persons' in the university context include visitors to the university and clients.

34 *Hillman v Lawless* [2010] SAIRC 27. In this case, the worker caused serious injury to a fellow worker when the defendant lit a cigarette in an area where smoking was prohibited owing to the presence of inflammable substances.

35 *WHS Act* ss 28, 29.

36 *WHS Act* ss 28, 29.

5 Reasonably Practicable Standard

Workers and other persons are afforded a high standard of health and safety protection, so far as is 'reasonably practicable'.[37] The *WHS Act* prescribes that a duty imposed on a person to ensure health and safety requires '(a) the person to eliminate risks to health and safety, so far as is reasonably practicable; and (b) if it is not reasonably practicable to eliminate risks to health and safety, to minimise those risks so far as is reasonably practicable'.[38]

The compliance standard 'reasonably practicable' qualifies the duty of a PCBU and in essence means 'what could reasonably be done at a particular time to ensure health and safety measures are in place'.[39] Factors that are considered when determining whether an action is 'reasonably practicable' include:

- the likelihood of a hazard or risk occurring;
- the degree of harm that might result if the hazard or risk occurred;
- what the person concerned knows, or ought to reasonably know, about the hazard or risk and ways of eliminating or minimising it;
- ways to eliminate or minimise the hazard or risk; and
- the cost of eliminating or minimising the hazard or risk.[40]

The standard is an objective test which means that a 'duty holder must meet the standard of behaviour expected of a reasonable person in the duty holder's position and who is required to comply with the same duty'. The two elements of 'reasonably practicable' are that: 'A duty holder must first "consider what can be done – that is, what is possible in the circumstances for ensuring health and safety", and then determine "whether it is reasonable in the circumstances to do all that is possible"'.[41]

The duty is illustrated in *Symons v Cedar College Incorporated*[42] in which the defendant educational institution was prosecuted for failing to ensure 'so far as was reasonably practicable' that persons under their management and control were not exposed to risk and injury. In this case, two parents and a student, were injured at the workplace when part of a tree fell on them at a sports day event. It was held that the risk of injury was reasonably foreseeable, and was exacerbated by the fact that activities were conducted near and under the tree during very windy conditions. It was held that the removal of the tree was a reasonable practical measure based on an arborist report that had been received some time before the event.

C Consultation and Representation

The *WHS Act* requires that a person conducting a business or undertaking must, so far as is reasonably practicable, consult with workers who carry out work for the business

37 Safe Work Australia, *Guide to the Model Work Health and Safety Act* (October 2012), 5 <http://www.safeworkaustralia.gov.au/sites/swa/about/publications/pages/guide-to-the-work-health-and-safety>.

38 *WHS Act* s 17.

39 *WHS Act* s 18.

40 *WHS Act* s 18.

41 Work Safe Australia, *How To Determine What is Reasonably Practicable to Meet a Health and Safety Duty* (May 2013), 7 <http://www.safeworkaustralia.gov.au/sites/SWA/about/Publications/Documents/774/Guide-Reasonably-Practicable.pdf>.

42 *Symons v Cedar College Incorporated* [2012] SAIRC 1.

or undertaking who are, or are likely to be, directly affected by a matter relating to work health or safety. The importance of consultation is reflected in the penalty that may be imposed for failing to comply is currently $20,000 in the case of an individual and $100,000 in the case of a body corporate.[43]

Consultation is described as a collaborative process between the PCBU and its workers and it 'does not require agreement to be reached'.[44] To this end, the *WHS Act* prescribes minimum requirements for the process of consultation, which requires ensuring that relevant information about the matter is shared with workers and that workers are given a reasonable opportunity to express their views and to raise work health or safety issues in relation to the matter. Workers must also have a reasonable opportunity to contribute to the decision-making process relating to the health and safety matter and that their views are taken into account by the PCBU. Workers are also entitled to be advised of the outcome of the consultation in a timely manner.[45]

The manner in which the information or advice is conveyed to workers is not prescribed in the *WHS Act*. If the PCBU has an agreed consultation procedure then this must be followed.[46] For instance, universities generally have a consultation process set out in the enterprise bargaining agreement or specifically in the internal health and safety policy and procedures.[47] The *WHS Act* does however make provision of 'work groups' to be formed before consultation.

The code of practice which applies to consultation lists the following factors that may be taken into consideration when determining when consultation is 'reasonably practicable':

- size and structure of the business;
- nature of the work that is carried out;
- nature and severity of the particular hazard or risk;
- nature of the decision or action, including the urgency to make a decision or take action;
- availability of the relevant workers and any health and safety representatives;
- work arrangements, such as shift work and remote work; and
- characteristics of the workers, including languages spoken and literacy levels.[48]

Consultation may take place through health and safety representatives, health and safety committees and various informal arrangements. The *WHS Act* only requires the establishment of these consultation mechanisms if a worker requests a health and

---

43 *WHS Act* s 47(1).

44 Safe Work Australia, *Guide to the Model Work Health and Safety Act* (October 2012), 15 <http://www.safeworkaustralia.gov.au/sites/swa/about/publications/pages/guide-to-the-work-health-and-safety>.

45 *WHS Act* s 48(1).

46 Safe Work Australia, above n 44, 15.

47 See, for example, University of Melbourne, *OHS Consultative Arrangements Procedure* <http://policy.unimelb.edu.au/MPF1184>; University of New South Wales, *HS337 Health and Safety Consultation Procedure* <https://www.gs.unsw.edu.au/policy/documents/HS337.pdf>.

48 Safe Work Australia, *Code of Practice: Work Health and Safety Consultation, Co-operation and Co-ordination* <http://www.workcover.nsw.gov.au/formspublications/publications/Documents/whs-consultation-cooperation-coordination-code-of-practice-3568.pdf>.

safety representative,[49] or a safety representative for a work group of workers carrying out work at that workplace or a group of five or more workers request a committee.[50]

Health and safety matters on which workers should be consulted include making decisions about ways to eliminate or minimise risks,[51] proposing changes that may affect the health or safety of workers[52] and making decisions about procedures that includes providing information and training for workers.[53]

1 Health and Safety Representatives

The *WHS Act* makes provision for the appointment of health and safety representatives committees. Any worker may request the PCBU to organise the appointment of health and safety representatives (HSRs). The functions of HSRs are primarily to represent the group of workers in consultations and negotiations with the PCBU regarding health and safety matters, to investigate complaints, and to monitor the implementation of health and safety measures.[54] If requested, a PCBU must provide training for HSRs.[55] The PCBU is required to publish the list of health and safety representatives. Generally, universities have comprehensive information on health and safety matters on their websites that include lists of current health and safety representatives.[56]

A 'work group' is a group of workers who share similar areas of work,[57] for example, all workers employed in the research office of a university or in the property and maintenance section of the university. A work group is set up for the purpose of being represented by one or more HSRs. A work group may be determined for workers at one or more workplace.[58] If a university work group requests the election of an HSR, the university must commence negotiations with workers within 14 days to determine the number and composition of the work group(s), the number of HSRs and deputy HSRs, and the workplace(s) to which the work group(s) apply.[59]

The general powers and functions of HSRs are to:[60]

- represent the workers in the work group in matters relating to work health and safety;
- monitor the measures taken by the person conducting the relevant business or undertaking or that person's representative in compliance with this Act in relation to workers in the work group;

49 *WHS Act* s 50.
50 *WHS Act* s 75.
51 *WHS Act* s 49(b).
52 *WHS Act* s 49(c).
53 *WHS Act* s 49(e)(v).
54 *WHS Act* s 50.
55 *WHS Act* s 72.
56 See, for example, Flinders University <http://www.flinders.edu.au/whs/ohsflinders/oh&s-representatives.cfm>; University of Tasmania <http://www.utas.edu.au/work-health-safety/whs-essentials/health-safety-representatives>.
57 *WHS Act* s 51.
58 *WHS Act* s 51(3).
59 *WHS Act* s 52(2).
60 *WHS Act* s 68(1).

- investigate complaints from members of the work group relating to work health and safety; and
- inquire into anything that appears to be a risk to the health or safety of workers in the work group, arising from the conduct of the business or undertaking.

2 Health and Safety Committees

Health and safety committees play an important role in overseeing the coordination and implementation of health and safety obligations and internal policies. They are also one of the key structures through which consultation takes place. The primary functions of health and safety committees are to:

- facilitate cooperation between the person conducting a business or undertaking and workers in instigating, developing and carrying out measures designed to ensure the workers' health and safety at work;
- assist in developing standards, rules and procedures relating to health and safety that are to be followed or complied with at the workplace; and
- undertake any other functions prescribed by the regulations or agreed between the person conducting the business or undertaking and the committee.[61]

D The Regulator and Safety Inspectors

The *WHS Act* provides for the establishment of a regulator and the appointment of safety inspectors who have an important role to play in promoting health and safety in the workplace. They also have wide statutory powers and functions to ensure and enforce compliance with the law where necessary.

1 The Regulator

Each jurisdiction has its own regulator (agency)[62] that oversees the administration and implementation of the health and safety legislation. The regulator has the following general functions:

- advise and make recommendations to the Minister and report on the operation and effectiveness of the Act;
- monitor and enforce compliance with the Act;
- provide advice and information on work health and safety to duty holders under the Act and to the community;
- collect, analyse and publish statistics relating to work health and safety;
- foster a cooperative, consultative relationship between duty holders and the persons to whom they owe duties and their representatives in relation to work health and safety matters;

61 *WHS Act* s 77.

62 For example, WorkCover, New South Wales; Work Place Health and Safety Queensland (WHSQ); and SafeWork, South Australia. See also, Safe Work, Australia <http://www.safeworkaustralia.gov.au/sites/swa/about/who-we-work-with/regulators/commonwealth-national/pages/commonwealth-national-regulators>.

- promote and support education and training on matters relating to work health and safety;
- engage in, promote and coordinate the sharing of information to achieve the object of the Act, including the sharing of information with a corresponding regulator;
- conduct and defend proceedings under the Act before a court or tribunal; and
- carry out other functions conferred on the regulator by this Act.[63]

In 2011, the National Compliance and Enforcement Policy was adopted, which provides the framework for a consistent approach to compliance and enforcement. The policy sets out the 'principles endorsed by the Workplace Relations Ministers' Council that underpin the approach work health and safety regulators ("the regulators") will take to monitoring and enforcing compliance with the Work Health and Safety Act and Regulations'.[64]

2 Safety Inspectors

The regulator responsible for monitoring and enforcing compliance of the *WHS Act*[65] may appoint inspectors who provide information and advice about compliance with the Act and who assist with resolving work health and safety issues at workplaces.[66]

The *WHS Act* extends extensive powers to inspectors. Safety inspectors have the power to enter a workplace at any time with or without the consent of the PCBU and conduct and investigate health and safety matters. Inspectors must, however, within a reasonable time advise the PCBU that they have entered the workplace and their purpose for doing so. They may seek information and documents pertinent to the matters being investigated.[67] Importantly, employers and workers are obliged to answer questions put to them by inspectors unless they have a 'reasonable excuse' to refuse to answer.[68] The burden is on the individual to show that the excuse is reasonable. This means that employers and workers will not be able to exercise the right to silence even if the information provided may incriminate them. However, information provided in these circumstances may not be used in civil or criminal proceedings, except in cases concerning misleading and deceptive conduct.[69] Significant penalties apply if a person refuses to cooperate with the inspectors or hinders their investigations.[70]

63 *WHS Act* s 152.

64 Safe Work Australia, *National Compliance and Enforcement Policy* <http://www.safeworkaustralia.gov.au/sites/swa/about/publications/pages/national-compliance-enforcement-policy> 1.

65 Model *Work Health and Safety Act*, Jurisdictional Note 156: A jurisdiction will need to include local provisions to ensure that appropriate arrangements are made for the appointment as an inspector of a person who is an inspector under a corresponding WHS law.

66 *WHS Act* s 160.

67 *WHS Act* s 171.

68 *WHS Act* s 165(2). A breach of this section attracts a penalty of $10,000 for individuals and $50,000 for corporate entities.

69 *WHS Act* s 172.

70 *WHS Act* s 188.

E Offences, Penalties and Enforcement

The primary aim of workplace health and safety legislation is to create safe working environments and to reduce the incidents of injury. To this end, the *WHS Act* imposes important health and safety duties on entities, employers and workers. A breach of duties and failure to comply with the law may result in significant penalties. The *WHS Act* provides for a range of enforcement measures and substantial penalties for criminal offences, as outlined in this section.

1 Health and Safety Offences

The *WHS Act* classifies health and safety offences into three criminal offence categories with each carrying maximum penalties for PCBUs and individuals:

- Category 1 concerns the reckless conduct of a person. An offence arises when a duty holder engages in conduct that *recklessly* exposes an individual to whom that duty is owed to a risk of death or serious injury or illness.[71]
- Category 2 offences arise when a duty holder fails to comply with a health and safety duty and the failure exposes an individual to a risk of death or serious injury or illness.[72]
- Category 3 deals with more minor contraventions and arises when the duty holder fails to comply with the health and safety duty.[73] In such cases, there is no risk of death or serious injury or illness.

2 Key Enforcement Measures

The *WHS Act* contains various measures for enforcing compliance. Administrative measures include issuing improvement notices in writing[74] aimed at remedying a contravention or likely contravention,[75] prohibition notices that aim to prohibit actions that involve an actual or potential risk to health and safety,[76] and non-disturbance notices that aim to preserve a site at which a notifiable incident has occurred for a specified period or to prevent the disturbance of a particular site.[77] To ensure compliance with such notice, the regulator may apply to a court for an injunction requiring a person to comply with a notice or restraining a person from contravening a notice.[78]

Enforceable undertakings are another measure used to compel compliance with the *WHS Act* and deter contraventions. They are essentially legal binding agreements that are enforceable by a court that are made by a PCBU or person to the regulator

---

71 *WHS Act* s 31(1). Current penalty: corporations ($3 million); individual as PCBU or officer ($600,000, five years in jail or both); individual as worker or other person ($300,000, five years in jail or both).

72 *WHS Act* s 32. Currently penalty: corporation body ($1.5 million); individual as PCBU or officer ($300,000); individual as worker or other person ($150,000).

73 *WHS Act* s 33. Current penalty: corporations ($500,000); individual as PCBU or officer ($100,000); individual as worker or other person ($50,000).

74 *WHS Act* s 203.

75 *WHS Act* s 191.

76 *WHS Act* s 195.

77 *WHS Act* s 198.

78 *WHS Act* s 215.

to take or cease certain actions.[79] They are an alternative to civil or administrative actions. Enforceable undertaking may be accepted by the regulator in relation to a matter; however, they cannot be accepted for a contravention or alleged contravention that is a Category 1 offence.[80] An enforceable undertaking is one way in which the party can undertake to address health and safety matters, and to remedy contraventions, but which does not constitute an admission of guilt by the person giving the undertaking in relation to the contravention or alleged contravention.[81] It is important for a PCBU and workers to be aware of undertakings and for officers to ensure undertakings are complied with because a contravention of an enforceable undertaking attracts a significant civil penalty of $50,000 in the case of an individual and $250,000 in the case of a body corporate, for example, the university.

F Legal Proceedings

A breach of the *WHS Act* is generally a criminal offence. Legal proceedings for offences under the *WHS Act* may be brought by the Director of Public Prosecutions, the regulator; or an inspector with the written authorisation of the regulator.[82] Individuals cannot bring an action in their own name. If a person reasonably considers an action against the *WHS Act* falls within a Category 1 offence or a Category 2 offence, and no prosecution has been brought after six months and no later than 12 months after that occurrence, then that person may make a written request to the regulator that a prosecution be brought.[83] Upon receiving such a request, the regulator must advise the person on whether or not the matter has been investigated and completed, and whether the matter will be prosecuted.[84]

The regulator must also notify the alleged offender of these matters. Further, if the regulator advises the person that an 'investigation has been conducted and that a prosecution for a Category 1 or Category 2 offence will not be brought, the regulator must advise the person that the person may ask the regulator to refer the matter to the Director of Public Prosecutions for consideration; and if the person makes a written request to the regulator to do so, refer the matter to the Director of Public Prosecutions within 1 month of the request'.[85] The Director of Public Prosecutions must consider the matter and advise the regulator in writing 'as soon as is practicable as to whether the Director considers that a prosecution should be brought'.[86]

1 Civil Penalty Provisions

In the *WHS Act* certain provisions attract a civil penalty which is a monetary fine imposed for contravening a civil penalty provision. The contravention does not amount to an offence.[87]

---

79 Marina Nehme, 'Enforceable Undertakings: A New Form of Settlement to Resolve Alleged Breaches of the Law' (2007) 11(1) *University of Western Sydney Law Review* 104.
80 *WHS Act* s 216(2).
81 *WHS Act* s 216.
82 *WHS Act* s 230.
83 *WHS Act* s 231(1).
84 *WHS Act* s 231(2).
85 *WHS Act* s 231(3).
86 *WHS Act* s 231(4).
87 *WHS Act* s 257.

2 Orders

In addition to or as an alternative to penalties, the following orders may be made by the court.

1. Adverse publicity orders that require information pertaining to the offence, its consequences, the penalty imposed and any other related matter to be publicised and/or a specified person to be notified of information pertaining to the offence, its consequences, the penalty imposed and any other related matter.[88]
2. Restoration orders that direct an offender to take action that is within the offender's power and within a specified period to remedy any matter caused by the offence.[89]
3. Work health and safety project orders that require the offender to undertake a specified project for the general improvement of work health and safety within the period specified in the order.[90]
4. Court-ordered work health and safety undertakings which arise when the court adjourns proceedings for an offence for up to two years, with or without a conviction, and the court releases an offender on specified condition that they give a work health and safety undertaking.[91]
5. Training orders that require a person to undertake or arrange for one or more workers to undertake a specified course of training.[92]

IV Conclusion

This chapter has outlined the application of the model *Work Health and Safety Act* to universities. Other than the States of Victoria and Western Australia, the Commonwealth and all other States and Territories have adopted corresponding legislation to enact the model legislation. Although there may be some differences among State and Territory legislation, the model legislation that has been enacted aims to provide greater coherence, consistency and uniformity across the various jurisdictions. In this chapter, some of the key themes and provisions of the model *Work Health and Safety Act* have been highlighted, in particular the health and safety duties as they apply to persons conducting a business or undertaking (such as a university), officers, workers and other persons. A significant aspect of the legislation is the recognition that health and safety in the workplace is the responsibility of everyone and that the legislation provides for wide coverage of persons who fall within the ambit of the legislation. The legislation also enjoins universities and its officers to ensure there are the necessary structures, strategies and measures in place to fully and effectively implement, manage, monitor and review compliance with the legislation and regulations, and to report on health and safety matters. In this regard, provisions relating to health and safety representatives and committees and the duty to consult are important. It is also incumbent on

88 *WHS Act* s 236.
89 *WHS Act* s 237.
90 *WHS Act* s 238.
91 *WHS Act* s 239.
92 *WHS Act* s 241.

universities and officers to ensure that all officers, workers and relevant persons are fully informed about their health and safety duties and obligations and the consequences for non-compliance, especially since the legislation provides for substantial penalties that apply to both individuals and the organisation for breach of health and safety duties.

Chapter 17

Academic Freedom and University Autonomy

Nigel Stobbs

I Introduction

This chapter examines the law in relation to the doctrines of university autonomy and academic freedom, in the Australian context. It first considers some traditional misconceptions and surrounding these doctrines, which seem to have obscured the real nature of the relationship between universities and the state.

It then examines some laws and legal instruments at an international, federal and State level which define and regulate these freedoms. It considers some contemporary controversies, to illustrate both the strengths and weaknesses surrounding how alleged infringements of academic freedom and independence have been managed. It concludes with a look at an important emerging challenge which has implications for how we might avoid and manage such controversies in the future.

A Autonomy as a Prerequisite for Innovation and Prosperity

Apart from the marketing value of any claim to 'innovation', there is a sound rationale for linking innovation to freedom of inquiry. A university is both a monument to, and a crucible of, rational inquiry. Rational inquiry can only be conducted on the understanding that no position, belief or value can be arbitrarily quarantined from rigorous and critical scrutiny, since the goal and the product of rational inquiry is objective knowledge. Any external pressure to limit the rational academic process by giving privileged status to subjective factors (be they political, economic, religious or cultural), confounds this process. Such factors can of course be legitimate determinants of policy, but they need to be factored in expressly, and after the process of rational inquiry has concluded.

Knowledge is the most valuable product of a university. Scientific knowledge, in particular, has immense intrinsic and instrumental value, in that it is the raw material for technological innovation – and innovation is endlessly commodifiable. When seen as a commodity or resource, innovation needs to be nurtured and treated strategically in order to deliver its potential.

Wicked social and technological problems threaten to devour resources which are not strategically nurtured. Anthropogenic global warming and climate change, food security, developing sustainable energy sources and reconciling health care costs with increased longevity are problems which will only be solved through innovation. Solving these problems is arguably the greatest challenge to maintaining human prosperity and promoting the equitable distribution of resources. Without freedom to follow where rational inquiry leads, prosperity would be hamstrung.

The functions of an Australian public university are stated in general terms in its enabling statute.[1] The functions of a private university are mostly a matter for the company which owns and operates it.[2] Freedoms to pursue these institutional functions independent of external influence are provided for in a range of sources as discussed in the next section. Institutions are, fundamentally, a collection of individuals pursuing similar goals, so this freedom extends to the academic employees who exercise the functions of a university. These freedoms are not unfettered. The community expects to see some practical returns on their investment. The current political agenda, focused on the reconceptualising and repositioning of our institutions of higher learning within the wider polity, needs to be grounded in a consensus as to both the nature and limits of institutional autonomy and academic freedom, if either of these phenomena are to survive.

B Autonomy and Freedom – the Romance and the Reality

Martin observes that 'whatever the status of academic freedom "in reality," belief in its importance can be a powerful force'.[3] Disputes about perceived or actual breaches of academic freedom and independence tend to arouse passions, and cause damage, disproportionate to the incident(s) which triggered the dispute. This underscores the fact that there are deep values, but also a powerful mythology surrounding principles of academic freedom, and its origin. It is as much from that mythology, as from the formal instruments which provide for it, that these academic rights seem to derive their normative force.

Academic freedom, like many of our cultural conventions, is largely a legacy of 19th century English liberal thought. Menzies declared it 'utterly undesirable' that any government should tell a university what and how to teach.[4] He said that 'the greater the university's dependence upon government finance, the more becomes the importance of this principle'. The reality is that government is intimately involved in what universities do and how they do it, because they control the rules of the higher education market and the six billion dollar Commonwealth Grants Scheme which underwrites it. Universities have significant autonomy in relation to what courses to offer, who to employ, whether to be research or teaching intensive, whether to open

1 The statutory functions of the University of Queensland (for example) pursuant to s 5 of the *University of Queensland Act 1998* (Qld) are to disseminate knowledge and promote scholarship; to provide education at university standard (to meet the needs of the community); to provide facilities for, and encourage research; and to exploit commercially, for the university's benefit study, research or knowledge, or the practical application of study, research or knowledge, belonging to the university, whether alone or with someone else.

2 See, for example, *Bond University Act 1987* (Qld) s 3.

3 Brian Martin, 'Dilemmas of Defending Dissent: The Dismissal of Ted Steele from the University of Wollongong' (2002) 45(2) *Australian Universities' Review* 7.

4 RG Menzies, *The Modern Problems of Higher Education* (The University of Texas, 1969).

overseas campuses et cetera, but almost every choice involves a meta choice related to how they will position themselves in the market.

The idea of a university as a centre for the delivery of a broad liberal education, patronised by students who come to learn the skills of critical scholarship has arguably only ever been rhetoric in Australia, preserved as a polite mask for the intensely commercial relationship between universities, government and students.

Although academic freedoms are still routinely referred to as 'traditional rights', their origin and function needs to be understood in a pragmatic historical context. An 18th century society characterised by a *laissez-faire* capitalism was relatively tolerant of universities isolated from market values, on the grounds that they were the custodians of more fundamental principles. Political and economic evolution has inevitably impacted on the role of the university.[5] Our current neoliberal environment seeks to homogenise professions and allow market forces, rather than intellectual curiosity and scholarly consensus alone, to determine what universities research and teach.

Large student cohorts looking for marketable skills have little interest in the classical liberal ideal of a pluralist civil society composed of self-regulating professions and institutions as a hedge against excessive state or corporate interference in their lives – except perhaps as an object of historical analysis. Australian universities have always been predominantly focused on vocation readiness rather than on knowledge for its own sake; producing professionals for Australian industry and enterprise, and the choices of students in a relatively deregulated market. Tempering this pragmatic economic context is the deep commitment which both the courts and academics themselves have always shown (and continue to show) to these doctrines.

'Academic freedom' is the freedom which academics enjoy to pursue whatever avenues of research their intellectual curiosity and disciplinary expertise draw them to. It extends to disseminating and proclaiming the results of that research and the individual's personal conclusions, regardless of the implications for those external to the research team, without fear of recrimination. It refers, to a lesser extent, to decisions about what to teach and how to teach it. This sort of freedom can be conceived of as both a right and an obligation. Punishing an academic for endeavouring to comply with this powerful obligation would be unconscionable. Jensen observes that:

> One of the jobs of intellectuals is to identify the issues to which we should be paying attention, even when, especially when, people would prefer to ignore problems. Intellectuals today should be apocalyptic, focusing attention on the hard-to-face realities of an unjust and unsustainable world.[6]

'University autonomy' is the independence which universities have to pursue their broad statutory functions (to disseminate knowledge and promote scholarship and

5 Glyn Davis (Vice Chancellor at the University of Melbourne) observes that '[t]he incentive to remain close to the original idea has proven compelling, defeating even legislated initiatives to create diversity. As a result, Australian higher education is dominated by autonomous, professional, comprehensive, secular, public and commuter universities sharing very similar mission ... this model has a powerful hold on the public imagination ... yet ... may be approaching the end of its influence': Glyn Davis, *The Australian Idea of a University* (The Conversation, 23 August 2013) <http://theconversation.com/the-australian-idea-of-a-university-17433>.

6 Robert Jensen, *We Are All Apocalyptic Now: On the Responsibilities of Teaching, Preaching, Reporting, Writing, and Speaking Out* (MonkeyWrench Books Collective, 2012).

to provide education) in ways which are 'morally and intellectually independent of all political authority and economic power'.[7]

II Sources of University Autonomy and Academic Freedom

A *International Instruments*

The *Magna Charta Universitatum* (to which Australia is a signatory) is a useful foundation for interpreting traditional principles on which universities were founded. Its main function is to facilitate cooperation between European universities, but universities from outside Europe, including Australia, are signatories.[8]

Freedom of intellectual discourse, and of the dissemination of knowledge, are recognised, and to some degree,[9] protected under international law.[10] Article 15 of the *International Covenant on Economic, Social and Cultural Rights* (*Covenant*) (to which Australia is a signatory) prescribes, for example, that everyone has a right to participate in the cultural life of the community and to enjoy the benefits which emerge from the practical outcomes of science and to have their own material and moral interests protected where they are the author of literary, artistic or scientific endeavour. The *Covenant* provides that signatory States have obligations to fully realise this right by the conservation, development and 'diffusion' of science and culture. They must do this in the context of respecting 'the freedom indispensable for scientific research and creative activity'. That includes (the *Covenant* expressly provides) the encouragement and development of international contact and cooperation in these fields. The fact that the *Covenant* provides that there are such explicit, positive obligations attached to academic freedom expands the doctrine well beyond a simple protection from outside interference in research and teaching.[11]

B *Domestic Legislation*

The *Higher Education Support Act 2003* (Cth) (*HESA*) requires publicly-funded universities to enter into a mission-based compact with the Commonwealth as a condition of receiving their annual funding grant. *HESA* imposes statutory obligations on the universities to produce a range of policies, such as strategies for teaching and learning,

7 *Magna Charta Universitatum* (Balogna, 18 September 1988), Fundamental Principle 1.

8 It originated at the University of Bologna and was drafted in Barcelona in 1987. The current Australian signatories are: Deakin University, Flinders University, La Trobe University, The University of Melbourne, The University of Tasmania, University of Sydney, University of Western Australia, Adelaide University. Full text of the Charter is available online at <http://www.aic.lv/ace/ace_disk/Bologna/maindoc/magna_carta_univ_.pdf>.

9 The actual protections afforded by these sorts of treaties is often a function of the commitment of particular signatory states.

10 *International Covenant on Civil and Political Rights* opened for signature 16 December 1966, General Assembly Resolution 2200 A (XXI) (entered into force 23 March 1976) art 19.2 (ICCPR).

11 Discourse and dissemination are an essential prerequisite for converting raw knowledge into innovation.

for undertaking research, research training and innovation.[12] It also requires that each institution have 'a policy that upholds free intellectual inquiry in relation to learning, teaching and research'.[13] The *Higher Education Standards Framework (Threshold Standards) 2011* provides at 4.2 that: 'The higher education provider promotes and protects free intellectual inquiry and expression in its higher education learning, teaching, and research activities'. The *Higher Education Standards Framework (Threshold Standards) 2011* are under review and the equivalent in the proposed replacement Higher Education Standards Framework is less robust providing that: 'The governing body takes steps to create an organisational culture where freedom of intellectual enquiry is upheld and protected ...' (cl 6.1.3).

The enabling statutes for public universities prescribe some broad functions or objectives which fundamentally impact on the nature of the relationship between academics and universities.

In the United States, academic freedom is ultimately enforceable under the First Amendment right to free speech. The US Supreme Court has defined academic freedom as deriving from a 'special concern of the First Amendment which does not tolerate laws that cast a pall of orthodoxy over the classroom', in *Keyishian v Board of Regents*.[14]

The situation here is fundamentally different. In *University of Western Australia v Gray (No 20)* (*UWA v Gray (No 20)*)[15] the full Federal Court grounds the freedoms in the nature of the relationship between the university and the academic. The court held that an academic staff member is more than simply an employee. They are a member of the 'special purpose statutory corporation' created by a university's enabling legislation and therefore bound by its statutes, rules and regulations. French J said that Gray was, 'by virtue of the definition of the "university" in the UWA Act[16] a member of it and linked historically by that definition to the idea of the university as a community of teachers and scholars ... traced back at least to the 16th century statute by which Oxford University was incorporated'.[17]

C Contractual Agreements and Institutional Policies

Universities have academic freedom clauses within their Enterprise Bargaining Agreements. These clauses are drafted in generic language which reflects that used in the international treaties and statutory instruments. A typical clause contains a statement such as this:

---

12 *HESA* s 19.110.

13 *HESA* s 19.115. Division 19 of the Act requires provides that supported providers of higher education must comply with certain quality standards, although these are quite generally articulated and currently subject to review. See also *Higher Education Standards Framework (Threshold Standards) 2011* (Cth).

14 385 US 589 (1967).

15 [2008] FCA 498. The dispute related to ownership of potentially valuable patent rights for the production and use of microspheres for targeted treatment of tumours, in the context of an employed academic who was not contractually bound to 'invent' as part of their work duty.

16 See *University of Western Australia Act 1911* (WA) s 4(1).

17 [2008] FCA 498, [1361].

> Academic staff members have the right to express unpopular or controversial views, but this does not mean that they have a right to harass, vilify, defame or intimidate.[18]

In a comprehensive survey of references to academic freedom in these agreements, Jackson found express statements about 'critical and open inquiry', 'public debates and expressing opinion', 'collegiality', 'rights to state opinions about the university' academic freedom in teaching, 'academic freedom linked to research', 'freedom from institutional censorship' and others. Some universities choose to manifest these principles in an institutional policy, thereby affording the protections more stable recognition – and these may even expressly provide that they operate regardless of the contractual conditions under which the employee is appointed.[19]

Such express statements are preferable (and necessary) because courts are unlikely to imply them into employment contracts. Equally, a university may not be able to contractually exclude rights and interests relating to academic freedom.[20] A contract of employment for an academic is not simply a subset of contracts between employers and employees, it differs in kind. The court in *UWA v Gray (No 20)* held that any obligation imposed upon academics was different in kind from that imposed upon an employee of a private, commercial entity. UWA wrongly assumed that there was an implied term in an academic's contract of employment which imposed a duty on the employee not to disclose the results of research, even where dissemination could destroy the patentability of some commercially valuable invention. There can be no such implication, because academics are not engaged to simply advance the institution's commercial interests, but also to research (often contingent upon successfully seeking external research funding).[21]

III Disputes, Controversies and the Impact of the Common Law

Disputes most often occur between university management and academics, often originating in low key disagreements about the interpretation and application of institutional policies as they apply to promotions and dismissals, but quickly escalating when

---

18 Queensland University of Technology, *Queensland University of Technology Enterprise Agreement (Academic Staff) 2010-2012* (31 December 2010) Cl 38 Intellectual and Academic Freedom <http://www.nteu.org.au/library/view/id/490>. The university's Code of Conduct (at 8.1.5 'Commitment to the system of government') is more specific in providing for the 'traditional right of academics to engage in free enquiry and active criticism on matters of public concern, or to pursue research within their field of expertise on matters which may be controversial or unpopular, even where this involves challenge or criticism to ideas, methods or practices of government or governmental agencies.'

19 See Jackson, below n 25. See, for example, the *Academic Freedom Policy* enacted by the Melbourne Institute of Technology (see especially 'Scope') <http://www.mit.edu.au/about-mit/institute-publications/policies-procedures-and-guidelines/academic-freedom-policy>.

20 See below 'III Disputes, Controversies and the Impact of the Common Law' in the discussion of *UWA v Gray (No 20)*. See Chapter 19 by Wyburn.

21 The High Court subsequently refused the University of Western Australia's application for special leave to appeal this decision of the full Federal Court, Gummow observing that 'on a practical level the lesson of this case may be [that] there is a need for express arrangements'; *University of Western Australia v Gray* [2010] HCATrans 11.

rights to academic freedom are invoked. Growing cynicism about the rapidly evolving nature of higher education among academics, stoked by increasing corporatisation and managerialism and its questionable compatibility with collegiality, transparency and intellectual rigour, is one of the greatest challenges facing the sector. Management preoccupation with reputation, image and branding in a ruthlessly competitive market is unsurprising. But when combined with a growing trend of employing managers at the level of Faculty Dean (and above) from outside of academia, there is a possibility that those tasked with transforming the sector at the institutional level have inadequate understanding of, and inclination to take seriously, the traditional rights of academics they manage to engage in 'free inquiry' and 'active criticism'. Add to this the uncertainty which exists in relation to whether and how terms of academic freedom are incorporated in an academic's contract of employment, and disputes are inevitable. Recent common law suggests that unless rights to academic freedom are expressly and unambiguously written into these contracts, they will not be implied.

In *Gramotnev v Queensland University of Technology*,[22] McMeekin J was asked to consider whether various university documents and policies created implied terms within the contract of employment of academics.[23] One clause of the relevant university policy manual said that QUT had an organisational value of providing 'a consultative communication framework which will respect academic freedom and will facilitate informed decision making, effective planning and full accountability'. The academic's letter of appointment constituted his actual employment contract – a common practice in universities. That letter included a statement that '[the] *terms and conditions of your appointment* are *prescribed* [emphasis added] by the relevant enterprise bargaining agreements … a Manual of Policies and Procedures (MOPP) and … Statutes and Policies.' Gramotnev submitted that the letter of appointment expressly and unambiguously incorporated those terms into his contract and therefore contractually bound the university. He was mistaken. McMeekin J held that 'No objective reader could assume that the statements (in the policy documents) are anything more than aspirational. There is nothing at all that suggests a contractual promise to employees to achieve the stated aims, no matter how much the University administrators desire their achievement'.[24] Although this matter is under appeal and was litigated in an attempt to obtain contractual damages, it underscores the reality that an academic seeking to rely on 'guarantees' of academic freedom in institutional policies, cannot rely on them as contractual obligations. The practical implication being that contractual remedies will not be available where either party is in breach.

Where the university has made promises of academic freedom in policy documents, enterprise agreements and the like, and has intended that academics act in reliance on these, the university may be estopped from denying any of these rights. Equitable damages may be available where the academic has relied on these promises to

22 [2013] QSC 158.

23 McMeekin noted that '[t]he letter of appointment constitutes the academics' employment contract at QUT, and actually includes a statement that: "[t]he terms and conditions of your appointment are prescribed by the relevant enterprise bargaining agreements a Manual of Policies and Procedures (MOPP) and Statutes and Policies"'.

24 *Gramotnev v Queensland University of Technology* [2013] QSC 158, [128].

their detriment, regardless of McMeekin J's characterisation of some of these statements as 'aspirational'.

What seems to be a set of reasonably common complaints among university academics contributes to a working environment which creates fertile grounds for 'whistleblowing' and sometimes for litigation. These complaints tend to cluster around perceptions by academics that their independence is under threat as standards are falling; that assessment lacks the necessary rigour and validity; and that they are under pressure not to fail too many students or to go easy on fee paying students.[25] Accusations of unwarranted interference by university management with the exercise of academic freedom are common, both anecdotally and as a matter of record. On the other hand, universities are keen to be seen to defend the academic freedom of their staff, on the grounds that to discipline them for promoting controversial views would damage the institution's scholarly reputation more than simply issuing statements distancing the university from the views held.[26]

The rhetoric of academic freedom, once invoked, inflames passions which can devastate careers, professional relationships and faculties. Individual academics can become ostracised from their colleagues and suffer disproportionate trauma and stress, managers can become bogged down in endless procedural remediation and litigation;[27] faculties and universities may suffer blows to their reputation and the public can become cynical. The doctrine of academic freedom does not seem to become any more precisely articulated or nuanced as a result.

In *NTEIU v University of Wollongong*,[28] public criticism of his department for alleged 'soft marking' in relation to the honours work of full fee paying foreign students resulted in summary dismissal of molecular immunologist Ted Steele from his tenured position at the University of Wollongong. The dispute morphed into something of a national ideological outrage concerning management attacks on academic freedom

---

25 Surveys and discussions of a wide range of these cases can be found in: James Jackson, 'Express Rights to Academic Freedom in Australian Public University Employment' (2005) 9 *Southern Cross University Law Review* 107; Martin, above n 3; Michael Herriman, 'Academic Freedom in Australia' [1984] *Interchange* 82.

26 See, for example, the statement of support issued by the University of Sydney in response to criticism of academics within its Centre for Peace and Conflict Studies who apparently expressed support for the Assad regime in Syria or promoted a boycott of academics from Israeli universities University of Sydney press release: Professor Stephen Garton, Acting Vice-Chancellor, 'University Defends Academic Freedom' (Press release, first published in the Australian, 10 January 2014) <http://sydney.edu.au/news/84.html?newsstoryid=12883>. The Federal Minister for Education, although acknowledging that the matter was solely the concern of the University, urged the university 'to maintain the reputation and the quality of their institution'. Christian Kerr, 'Uni Faces Heat Over Lecturer's Syrian Talks' (7 January 2014) *The Australian* <http://www.theaustralian.com.au/national-affairs/policy/uni-faces-heat-over-lecturers-syrian-talks/story-fn59nm2j-1226796129326#>.

27 The Gray litigation, for example, involved 20 interlocutory hearings, numerous counterclaims by Gray and the two other defendant parties against UWA, a cross-claim against Gray for breach of director's duties and contravention of the *Fair Trading Act 1987* (WA) by one of the other defendants – and a final trial which went for 50 days and required 4568 pages of transcript, with over a thousand documents tendered, after which Chief Justice French delivered a written judgment of 1619 paragraphs in the *UWA v Gray (No 20)*. See Chapter 19 by Wyburn.

28 [2001] FCA 1069.

and industrial litigation which reached the full bench of the Federal Court.[29] The court eventually held that the university had not complied with the requirements of the relevant employment agreement in reaching the decision to summarily dismiss (without making any comment in relation to the substance of Steele's criticism or to the nature and ambit of any rights to academic freedom) and ordered Steele's reinstatement. Other academics in the department had strongly disagreed with the substance of Steele's view on the validity of the marking process and made their displeasure at the situation public in the national press.[30] Ultimately, Steele did not return to the department and there was a confidential settlement between the parties. Both the vigour with which the aggrieved academic pursued the perceived attack on his academic freedom and the precipitous (and as it turned out unlawful) decision to summarily dismiss him does not seem to have led to any significantly positive outcome. Commenting on a range of similar disputes, Herriman concludes that the greatest threats to Australian academics, in terms of their academic freedom, seem to come from their colleagues.[31] A fear of expressing unpopular or unorthodox opinions does not sit well with a supposed culture of encouraging doctrinal critique as a catalyst for innovation.

Questions occasionally arise as to whether academics in religious institutions in exercising their freedom to question or critique any assumed knowledge or position, should be permitted to challenge religious doctrines if that becomes relevant to their research. An article in the August 2013 issue of *The Journal of Religious Education*[32] (a journal published by the Australian Catholic University[33]) in which the author included a quote from a publication by another scholar to the effect that the gospel narratives of the birth of Jesus ought to be taken as 'sacred stories' or as 'Christian drama' rather than as literal records of historical events. The latter author then discussed whether this was the best approach to take in the religious education of children. In a later issue of the journal, a 'Note to Readers' by the university's Dean of Education and Arts[34] stated, *inter alia*, that 'Robert Crotty thinks that Jesus was conceived in the normal way by two Jewish parents named Joseph and Mary'. The Note observed that 'this assertion … does not reflect the opinion of the ACU nor the Faculty of Education' and warned teachers to

29 Steele had previously expressed concern at the effect which his published work on Jean Lamarck, which challenged some orthodox views on the heritability of traits only acquired during a parent's lifetime, had on his academic freedom; Edward Steele, Robyn A Lindley, and Robert V Blanden, *Lamarck's Signature: How Retrogenes are Changing Darwin's Natural Selection Paradigm* (Basic Books, 1999).

30 Patrick Lawnham, 'Staff Refuse to Work with Steele' (10 April 2002) *The Australian* 32; and more locally in Lisa Sewell, 'Staff Reject Steele Claims' (6 April 2002) *Illawarra Mercury* 5. Martin, above n 3, 16; (another academic at the university) recounts that '[e]very single academic member of the department signed a letter which, among other things, said: "As the staff who are as yet undefended victims of his [Steele's] accusations we request that all parties work quickly towards an agreement on a process that gives us the opportunity to have the facts heard, our reputations repaired, and our past, present and future students cleared"'.

31 Herriman, above n 25, 85.

32 Maurice Ryan, 'Where was Jesus Born? Challenges for Religious Educators Teaching the Infancy Narratives' (2013) 61(2) *Journal of Religious Education* 30.

33 Which, by virtue of its recognition as a university in Queensland pursuant to s 4 of the *Australian Catholic University (Queensland) Act 2007* (Qld), qualifies for some public funding.

34 Professor Wyatt-Smith.

use 'due caution and prudence'. The mini furore that ensued saw little if any published support from academic or senior ACU management for the Dean's alleged attempt at censorship, with a number of people expressing concerns[35] that it reflected badly on the standing of the university in the eyes of the taxpayer.

Nobody seems to have benefitted from this dispute, and nothing has been added to our understanding of the relevant doctrines. Managers and administrators, however, need to take seriously perceptions by staff that their academic integrity is under threat. Policies and processes for airing and resolving complaints related to academic freedom (rather than generic grievance procedures) may avoid disproportionate damage. In the current 'maturation' phase of higher education we may be well advised to reframe the intellectual and rhetorical debate over the parameters of academic freedom, away from the realm of law and policy to a focus on the dignity and wellbeing of all the people who constitute a university.[36]

IV Emerging Issue – Limits on Dissemination

Whether rights to communicate and disseminate information can be limited by statute, and if so to what extent, is a question of growing concern.[37]

The issue has arisen in relation to legislation which imposes export controls over so-called 'dual-use' technologies which may have military as well as industrial applications. The existing mechanisms for regulating such technology relate to physical export of specified, tangible goods but are silent as to intangible transfers of relevant technology. This may be through indirect dissemination between researchers at academic conferences or symposia – which could potentially be via online webinars, email discussion groups or face-to-face meetings.

The *Defence Trade Controls Act 2012* (Cth) gives effect to the *Australia-United States Defence Trade Cooperation Treaty* by tightening the regulation of defence export controls over dual-use goods and technologies which appear on the Defence and Strategic Goods List (DSGL). There are 10 categories of controlled 'DSGL technology' provided for in the current DGSL.[38] The Act makes it an offence, attracting potentially

35 Maurice Ryan, 'Contrary to Church Teachings, or Contrary to the Spirit of Academia?' (2 April 2014) *The Australian* <http://www.theaustralian.com.au/higher-education/opinion/contrary-to-catholic-teachings-or-contrary-to-the-spirit-of-academia/story-e6frgcko-1226871255844#>; Julie Hare, 'VC "Played No Role" in Virgin Birth Dispute' (2 April 2014) *The Australian* <http://www.theaustralian.com.au/higher-education/vc-played-no-role-in-virgin-birth-dispute/story-e6frgcjx-1226871303931#>.

36 Yamada notes that, in the context of American industrial disputes involving alleged breaches of academic freedom that 'the courts and legal process offer marginal solace for mistreated employees'. He advocates for a more 'dignitarian framework' for resolving disputes in which 'there is [still] plenty of room for market-based competition, entrepreneurship, individual responsibility, and sound management prerogative'; David Yamada, 'Human Dignity and American Employment Law' (2009) 43 *University of Richmond Law Review* 523, 526.

37 This would be much more difficult in the United States given the grounding of academic freedom within the ambit of the First Amendment. No such Constitutional right exists in Australia.

38 Including Nuclear Materials; Materials, Chemicals, Micro-organisms and Toxins; Materials Processing; Electronics; Computers; Telecommunications and Information Security; Sensors and Lasers; Navigation and Avionics; Marine; Aerospace and Propulsion; *Defence and Strategic Goods List Amendment 2011 (No.1)* (Cth) made under s 112(2A)(aa) of the *Customs Act 1901*

severe penalties,[39] to publish or disseminate DSGL technology without Ministerial approval. This potentially catches academics in their research and commercialisation activities, where they supply or transfer (or 'broker the supply' of) DSGL technology to international research partners, other institutions or 'the public' outside of Australia. This could include indirect dissemination at conferences, or even via the increasingly common teaching of graduate courses overseas.[40] Making the sharing and dissemination of academic research a criminal offence, contingent upon the discretion of an agency of the executive branch of government would be a very significant breach of rights to academic freedom and anathema to innovation. US academics are protected by significant statutory exclusions.[41]

The relevant offence creating provisions comes into effect on 16 May 2015. If Australian university advocacy groups and peak bodies are unable to lobby successfully for exemptions equivalent to those enjoyed by educational institutions in the United States, then university administrators will need to develop policies to manage compliance and to educate individual academics in how to mitigate their risk.[42]

Consultation with Universities Australia – involving a pilot program based at two major research institutions[43] – continues to gauge the extent of any issues to do with implementation, compliance and monitoring that may arise. Universities Australia has expressed concern about time pressures involved in putting in place the necessary procedures before the end of the transition period.[44] This is especially the case,

---

(Cth). Items listed in the index to the List include 'recovery parachutes', 'goat pox virus' and 'safety cabinets for biological agents'.

39 Imprisonment for 10 years or 2500 penalty units (ie currently $425,000) or both; *Defence Trade Controls Act 2012* (Cth).

40 Section 14A of the *Defence Trade Controls Act 2012* (Cth) provides that a person commits an offence if they publish (otherwise disseminate) to the public, or a section of the public, by electronic or other means, DSGL technology, without an approval from the Minister. Approval will only be given (to a person) where the Minister is satisfied that it is in in the public interest to do so. The maximum penalty for breaching this provision is currently imprisonment for 10 years or a $425,000 fine or both. The effect of s 15.2 of the *Criminal Code* (Cth) regarding extended geographical jurisdiction would mean that this offence then applies to something done by an Australian citizen (or a university in its capacity as a body corporate incorporated in a State or Territory) wholly outside Australia, or even by a person who is merely a resident of Australia at the time of the alleged offence. But note now the Defence Trade Controls Amendment Bill 2015, see Universities Australia Media Release <https://www.universitiesaustralia.edu.au/news/media-releases/Defence-Trade-Controls-Amendment-Bill-is-a-positive-outcome-for-universities#.VWArhLCJjIU>.

41 Statutory exclusions provide that external approvals are not required in order for academics to disclose technical information if that information is either in the public domain or disseminated through 'fundamental research in science and engineering (at accredited institutions) where the information is ordinarily published and shared broadly in the scientific community' – § 734.8 *Export Administration Regulation* and 120.11(8) of the *International Traffic in Arms Regulation*.

42 The Department of Defence has a dedicated internet site for disseminating information regarding compliance issues related to the *Australia-United States Defence Trade Cooperation Treaty* which claims to be current as at 29 May 2014 <http://www.defence.gov.au/ustradetreaty/default.asp>. Relevant information is also contained on the Defence Export Control Office site at <http://www.defence.gov.au/deco/>.

43 The University of Queensland and Curtin University.

44 There is understandable concern to optimise communications with the Sanctions area of the Department of Foreign Affairs and Trade.

given that other statutes impose compliance and monitoring burdens on universities in relation to autonomous sanctions – particularly in the areas of material science, manufacturing and physics. Autonomous sanctions are non-military, punitive measures which the government chooses to apply to further its foreign policy objectives in relation to situations 'of international concern (such as significant human rights abuses by a foreign government or organisation,[45] the proliferation of weapons of mass destruction or the prosecution of armed conflicts).

V Conclusion

Yamada observes that '[t]hose who are privileged with the protections of tenure and academic freedom should embrace a social responsibility to be researching, understanding, and speaking out on matters of importance.' Academics and universities cannot live to do this without substantive, enforceable guarantees of those protections.

Australian universities retain a diversity which covers a broad disciplinary agenda. But that diversity is increasingly likely to be a function of positioning within the market, rather than a reflection of the intellectual interests of its academics and students. Future disputes over academic freedom may have a stronger industrial flavour and be triggered in response to perceived limits on commercial activities which may be only tangentially aligned with university business, or to perceptions of restrictive trade practices. The ideological and intellectual passions which seem to intensify these disputes are unlikely to dissipate and will probably create an environment in which governments and universities need to be more aware of, and responsive to the associated risks.

That is the reality that our universities need to prepare for – not for the sort of faux ideological battles which pit intellectual freedom against market forces. There will always be room for debate about the 'true' nature and purposes of scholarly institutions, but polarising the debate between these two forces is counterproductive in that it dooms one of them to the status of loser.

45 *Autonomous Sanctions Act 2011* (Cth). The Act imposes sanctions against: Burma, Fiji, the former Federal Republic of Yugoslavia Iran, North Korea, Syria, Ukraine and Zimbabwe.

Chapter 18

Copyright Law and Higher Education

Michael Fraser

I Introduction

Until recently, academics in Australia operated in a 'copyright-free zone' in dealings with their employing universities.[1] As increased funding pressures force universities to seek alternative sources of income, greater attention is now being given to the copyright materials created within universities. Previously, copyright creations, particularly in the humanities, were considered an inconsequential source of revenue for universities.[2] Now, universities in Australia (and overseas) commonly harness technology to create 'marketable teaching products',[3] such as those offered within Massive Open Online Courses (MOOCs).[4] These developments re-focus attention on the copyright ownership of academic-created materials.[5]

This chapter outlines the position on copyright ownership under Commonwealth legislation,[6] and considers the treatment of academic-created copyright materials in university employment contracts and policies. Under Australian legislation, and commonly under university contractual terms, there may remain uncertainty about the copyright ownership of academic-created materials. Uncertainty about ownership damages transactional efficiency. Equally, as lecture notes and recordings become potentially marketable materials,[7] it remains unclear whether lecturers will have rights

1 Ann Monotti and Sam Ricketson, *Universities and Intellectual Property: Ownership and Exploitation* (Oxford University Press, 2003), 10.

2 In comparison, the patentable inventions of those in science faculties have been of interest to universities for some time. Ibid 10; Rochelle Cooper Dreyfuss, 'Collaborative Research: Conflicts on Authorship, Ownership, and Accountability' (2000) 53 *Vanderbilt Law Review* 1161, 1185; Robert A Gorman, 'Copyright Conflicts on the University Campus: The First Annual Christopher A Meyer Memorial Lecture' (2000) 47 *Journal of the Copyright Society of the USA* 291, 297.

3 Monotti and Ricketson, above n 1, 500.

4 Tim Dodd, 'New Wave of MOOCs About to Go Live' (24 February 2014) *Australian Financial Review* <http://www.afr.com/p/national/education/new_wave_of_australian_moocs_about_MTUMD1L17U6vgpP0brs2WP>. This is consistent with a worldwide trend: Educause, 'Copyright Challenges in a MOOC Environment' (2013), 1.

5 Although initially not much attention was paid to who might own intellectual property in MOOCs, for example (Monotti and Ricketson, above n 1, 3), the question of intellectual property ownership of academic ideas and copyright works 'remains very much alive, and in need of attention': Justine Pila, 'Who Owns the Intellectual Property Rights in Academic Works?' (2010) 32 *European Intellectual Property Review* 609.

6 The *Copyright Act 1968* (Cth) (*Copyright Act*).

7 'For commercial MOOC providers, and increasingly for campuses, course content is potentially profitable': Educause, above n 4, 2.

to receive a return from the exploitation of them. This is problematic from a policy perspective.

Accordingly, a new general rule is proposed. Employed academics should own copyright in any materials created by them, subject to a pre-licensing regime in favour of their employer. This would permit the operation of a new, mutually beneficial network of databases for the management of academic content, described as a 'Content Services Network'.

II Introduction to Copyright

A *What is Copyright?*

Copyright is a 'bundle of rights'[8] that subsists in certain materials. Since, to a large extent, copyright protection is internationally standardised,[9] fruitful comparisons may be drawn between Australian copyright law and that of other jurisdictions.

In Australia, copyright is regulated by the *Copyright Act 1968* (Cth) (*Copyright Act*). In order for copyright to subsist in a 'work', or in other subject-matter, the work or subject-matter must fall within prescribed categories under the *Copyright Act*. Relevantly, one category of 'work' is that of 'literary works'.[10] Common 'literary works' include books, articles, and academics' lecture notes.[11] For copyright to subsist in a 'literary work', it must be 'original'.[12] In addition to 'literary works', brief mention is made here of two types of 'subject-matter' in which copyright can subsist, namely, sound recordings and films,[13] for which there is no requirement of 'originality'.[14] Importantly, copyright protects only the expression (or 'material form') of ideas, and not ideas themselves.[15] Where copyright subsists in material, the copyright owner is granted certain exclusive rights in relation to that material.[16] For example, the owner of copyright in a literary work has the exclusive right to reproduce that work.[17]

---

8 Alma Swan, 'Overview of Scholarly Communication' in Neil Jacobs (ed), *Open Access: Key Strategic, Technical and Economic Aspects* (Chandos Publishing, 2006), 7.

9 The *Berne Convention for the Protection of Literary and Artistic Works* opened for signature 9 September 1886, 1161 UNTS 30 (entered into force 5 December 1887) sets 'general standards for copyright protection in member countries', which now comprise many of the world's nations: William van Caenegem, *Intellectual and Industrial Property in Australia* (LexisNexis Butterworths, 2009), 33.

10 *Copyright Act* s 32(1).

11 '[L]ecture notes' are defined (in s 40(1B) of the *Copyright Act*) as 'any literary work produced for the purpose of the course of study or research by a person lecturing or teaching in or in connection with the course of study or research'.

12 Section 32(1) and (2) of the *Copyright Act* make clear that copyright may subsist in a literary, dramatic, musical or artistic work only if it is 'original'.

13 Section 89 of the *Copyright Act* provides that copyright may subsist in a sound recording. Section 90 of the *Copyright Act* provides that copyright may subsist in a 'cinematograph film'.

14 Contrast ss 89 and 90 of the *Copyright Act* (dealing with sound recordings and films, respectively) with s 32(1) of the *Copyright Act* (dealing with original works).

15 Van Caenegem, above n 9, 33, 37.

16 See s 31(1) of the *Copyright Act* (in relation to works), s 85 (in relation to sound recordings) and s 86 (in relation to cinematograph films).

17 *Copyright Act* s 31(1)(a)(i).

The owner of copyright in a sound recording or film is usually the 'maker' of the sound recording or film,[18] being the person who owned the first record of the recording at the time of production (in the case of sound recordings) and the person who made the arrangements necessary for filming (in the case of films).[19]

The owner of copyright in a work is usually the work's individual 'author',[20] being the person who gives 'material form' to the ideas expressed in the work.[21]

The university context gives cause to consider the statutory exception to this rule.

B An Exception: Circumstances of Employment

The *Copyright Act* provides that, in circumstances of employment, the usual rule on copyright ownership in original works is displaced.[22] Where an original work is created by an author 'in pursuance of the terms of his or her employment' under a 'contract of service or apprenticeship', the author's employer will – subject to contrary agreement[23] – own copyright in that work.[24] The *Copyright Act* contains a similar provision on films, under which employee directors cede copyright to their employers.[25]

Where an employer asserts copyright in a work created by a putative employee, this prompts investigations into:

- whether the author of the copyright work is, in fact, an employee;
- if so, what is scope of the employment arrangement;[26] and
- whether the work was created within that scope.

The first of these enquiries may often be resolved by reference to an employment contract. Yet, as discussed below, the scope of employment may remain unclear.[27]

In particular, the academic's changing role can create uncertainty about the scope of an academic's employment duties, in turn creating uncertainty about the copyright position as between an academic and their university employer.

---

18 *Copyright Act* s 97 (in relation to sound recordings) and s 98 (in relation to cinematograph films).

19 *Copyright Act* s 22(3) (in relation to sound recordings) and s 22(4) (in relation to cinematograph films).

20 *Copyright Act* s 35(2).

21 *Copyright Act* s 22(1): the time at which a work is 'made' is the time at which it is reduced to writing or some other material form. By implication of s 32(1) of the *Copyright Act*, it is the author who 'makes' a work.

22 *Copyright Act* s 35(6).

23 *Copyright Act* s 35(3).

24 *Copyright Act* s 35(6).

25 *Copyright Act* s 98(5). The *Copyright Act* does not contain an analogous provision on sound recordings, yet copyright in sound recordings created by employees is likely to be owned by the employer in any case, due to the definition of 'maker' for sound recordings.

26 In other words, '[w]hat is it that [the employee] is employed to do?': see *University of Western Australia v Gray* (2009) 259 ALR 224 (*UWA v Gray*), [258]. See Chapter 19 by Wyburn.

27 Despite the fact that there exists developed case law on the kinds of works (for example, those created outside working hours, at home with use of an employee's own resources) that will clearly fall outside the scope of employment: Van Caenegem, above n 9, 62-63.

C Private Agreement

The *Copyright Act* allows contracting parties to allocate rights as between each other by agreements,[28] which may either exclude or modify the ownership provisions of that Act.

III Universities and Copyright

Universities, and those working and studying within them, are both users and potential creators of copyright material.[29]

A Academic Staff and Universities as Copyright Creators

Until recently, little thought was given to the role of universities as copyright *creators*. Now, due in part to decreasing funding,[30] 'most Australian universities ... operate as global businesses',[31] with revenue-producing products and services.[32]

In this context, universities depend upon market sources of income.[33] Fee paying students constitute one such source.[34] Another is the commercialisation of knowledge.[35]

With their ability to generate income through assignment or licensing, copyright materials have therefore become increasingly important to universities. Advances in technology have allowed copyright materials to be marketed in new forms, to broader audiences.[36] MOOCs are an example of the packaging and distribution to market of copyright materials created by faculty members.[37]

B University Treatment of Academic-created Copyright Materials

A mark of universities' invigorated interest in copyright materials is their zeal in 'staking out copyright claims' against staff and students.[38] A frequent practice

28 *Copyright Act* s 35(3).
29 Gorman, above n 2, 310.
30 Monotti and Ricketson, above n 1, 39. Decreasing government funding is a feature of the university experience in the United Kingdom (see William R Cornish, 'Rights in University Innovations: The Herchel Smith Lecture for 1991' (1992) 14 *European Intellectual Property Review* 13; Pila, above n 5, 609) and the United States (see, for example, Gorman, above n 2, 298) also.
31 Simon Marginson and Mark Considine, *The Enterprise University: Power, Governance and Reinvention in Australia* (Cambridge University Press, 2000), 48. See also Monotti and Ricketson, above n 1, 38.
32 On appeal, the full Federal Court in *UWA v Gray* agreed and noted that '[b]y at least the 1990s the governmental incentive for universities in some degree to "commercialise" – a word of many colours – was a matter of notoriety': *UWA v Gray*, [251].
33 Marginson and Considine, above n 31, 50.
34 Monotti and Ricketson, above n 1, 39.
35 Ibid. Cornish, above n 30, 13.
36 Cooper Dreyfuss, above n 2, 1185; Gorman, above n 2, 298.
37 The internet allows teaching materials to be packaged and distributed as 'distance learning'. Cooper Dreyfuss, above n 2, 1185.
38 Gorman, above n 2, 298. Pila notes that increased funding pressures will likely cause universities to expressly claim copyright rights, if they have not yet done so: Pila, above n 5, 610.

of universities is to assert, in contracts and policies, ownership of all intellectual property (including copyright) created by academics during the course of their employment.[39] While such terms reflect the statutory position under the *Copyright Act* in respect of 'works',[40] some universities assert copyright ownership in creations falling outside the 'course' of employment,[41] or contractually deem certain categories of intellectual property to have been created 'in or during the course of employment'.[42]

Two categories of material – 'scholarly works' and 'teaching materials' – are often dealt with explicitly by university employment documents. Commonly, the academic retains copyright in 'scholarly works' (typically defined to include academic articles and books), unless these have been created further to an express direction by the institution.[43] However, the university will typically take a perpetual, royalty-free licence to use scholarly works created by academics, sometimes for limited purposes (such as the university's teaching, educational and research purposes).[44]

Conversely, universities frequently assert copyright in 'teaching materials' – being those materials created by an employed academic for use 'in teaching' at the employer university, such as course outlines and slides.[45] Mirroring the treatment of scholarly works, academics typically take a perpetual, royalty-free licence to use teaching materials created by them (although, again, for limited purposes).[46]

---

39 See, for example, *University of Technology Sydney Intellectual Property Policy* s 5.1.1; *University of Sydney (Intellectual Property) Rule 2002* r 3.1; *University of Melbourne, Statute 14.1 – Intellectual Property*, s 14.1.2.1; *University of Queensland Policy 4.10.13 Intellectual Property for Staff, Students and Visitors*, cl 5.1(a). This practice is in line with a trend in US universities towards increased university control over works: Cooper Dreyfuss, above n 2, 1184. Likewise, in the United Kingdom it has been suggested that '[s]ome personnel and legal officers take a bullish view of copyright ownership': Derek Law, Ralph Weedon and Margaret R Sheen, 'Universities and Article Copyright' (2000) 13 *Learned Publishing* 141, 146.

40 This is the case in the United Kingdom also: Pila, above n 5, 610.

41 See, for example, *University of Sydney (Intellectual Property) Rule 2002*, r 3.2.

42 See, for example, *University of Queensland Policy 4.10.13 Intellectual Property for Staff, Students and Visitors*, cll 5.1(c)-(g).

43 See, for example, *University of Technology Sydney Intellectual Property Policy*, s 5.1.3; *University of Sydney (Intellectual Property) Rule 2002*, r 4.1; *University of Melbourne, Statute 14.1 – Intellectual Property*, s 14.1.2.1; *University of Queensland Policy 4.10.13 Intellectual Property for Staff, Students and Visitors*, cl 5.7.

44 See, for example, *University of Technology Sydney Intellectual Property Policy*, s 5.1.3; *University of Sydney (Intellectual Property) Rule 2002*, r 4.1.1; *University of Melbourne, Statute 14.1 – Intellectual Property*, s 14.1.4.1; *University of Queensland Policy 4.10.13 Intellectual Property for Staff, Students and Visitors*, cl 5.7.

45 Note that, in contrast to the other universities considered here, the University of Technology Sydney expressly does not assert ownership of the intellectual property in 'course and educational materials', except where created or developed for specific purposes (of which some non-exhaustive examples are given): *University of Technology Sydney Intellectual Property Policy*, s 5.1.3.

46 See, for example, *University of Sydney (Intellectual Property) Rule 2002*, r 4.2; *University of Queensland Policy 4.10.13 Intellectual Property for Staff, Students and Visitors*, cl 5.8.

C Remaining Uncertainty

Notwithstanding the explicit treatment of scholarly works and teaching materials in many Australian universities' contracts and policies,[47] there can be ambiguity as to whether materials were created 'during the course of' an academic's employment.

The changing nature of the university and its activities[48] has implications for the role of the academic. Whereas academics were traditionally employed only to deliver lectures,[49] the transition of the university from academy to commercial enterprise[50] means academics may have a broader range of academic duties. The consequence is that a broader range of academic-authored works may fall to university ownership.[51] Unless specifically enumerated in employment documents or made clear by practice, however, it may be uncertain which works have been created in pursuance of work duties.

This uncertainty affects universities, academics, and third parties. Universities with an uncertain understanding of their rights in copyright materials cannot efficiently market them.[52] Academics cannot confidently deal with publishers, new employers, external colleagues, or other third parties. And third parties are necessarily unsure about whom to approach for rights clearances.

D Particular Forms of Copyright Material

Some forms of copyright material, commonly used within MOOCs, bring this uncertainty into focus.[53]

1 Lecture Notes

As noted above, copyright protects only the particular expression of a work or subject-matter. This can be significant in the university context, as an unrecorded lecture given to students has no 'material form', whereas written notes of a lecture may have 'material form' as a 'literary work'.[54]

Arguably, academics are employed to orally deliver lectures, but not to write them down.[55] Therefore, the delivery of an unrecorded lecture would likely be 'in the course of employment' as an academic, whereas the reduction of the lecture to material form (in the way of notes) would arguably not be.[56] Unless expressly addressed in an employment contract, this would have the effect, under the *Copyright Act*, that copyright in the

47 Note that not all universities deal explicitly with both scholarly works and teaching materials, meaning the question of ownership has be resolved with reference to other, general, contractual terms.

48 Cornish notes that an increased emphasis on commercialisation of knowledge is 're-defining the very concept of a university': Cornish, above n 30, 13.

49 Monotti and Ricketson, above n 1, 270.

50 Or in the terminology of Cornish, from the 'Academe' to the 'Technopolis': Cornish, above n 30, 14.

51 Monotti and Ricketson, above n 1, 270.

52 Ibid 434.

53 Educause, above n 4, 1, 2.

54 Gorman, above n 2, 301, draws an analogous conclusion when applying the similar legislative provisions of the United States.

55 Monotti and Ricketson, above n 1, 270. See also Cornish, above n 30, 15.

56 For a contrasting opinion in the United States, see Gorman, above n 2, 302: 'books, articles and courseware fall within the scope of employment; they are created in furtherance of the faculty

lecture notes would remain with the academic author.[57] The application of university contracts and policies dealing expressly with teaching materials, meanwhile, might result in a different outcome.

If notes of a lecture were taken by a student (and then, perhaps, made freely accessible or sold for a profit, as can occur online with ease[58]), ownership would be determined by principles of authorship. This would require consideration of whether the student had injected sufficient originality into the notes such as to author a new, original, copyright work.[59] As this seems unlikely,[60] it is unclear who would be the copyright owner under the *Copyright Act* (although the issue can, perhaps, be addressed contractually, by imposing conditions on students).[61]

2 Recorded Lectures

Sound and video recordings of lectures raise further issues.

Under the *Copyright Act*, the owner of copyright in a sound recording or film is usually the 'maker' of the sound recording or film.[62] Accordingly, a university can be expected to be the *prima facie* owner of a recording made by it or under its direction.[63] Similarly, if a student made a sound or video recording of lecture – for example, using their personal smart phone while attending the lecture – the student would be the expected owner of copyright in that recording under the *Copyright Act*. This outcome could, again, perhaps be avoided contractually.

If, instead, a 'star' academic produced their own recordings of tuition in a subject (perhaps in their own time, at home, yet with some reliance on research done during the course of their employment), on general principles they would likely be the copyright owner.

E Policy Considerations

Having explored the legal context for ownership of copyright in academic-created materials, it is worth considering whether current approaches are appropriate from a policy perspective.

---

member's responsibilities and the university's mission' and therefore fall within the US 'works for hire' doctrine, meaning ownership lies with the university.

57 In analogous circumstances, this was the result in the English case of *Stevenson Jordan & Harrison v MacDonald & Evans* [1952] 1 TLR 101.

58 Gorman, above n 2, 299.

59 Ibid 305. The English precedent of *Walter v Lane* [1900] AC 539, in which it was decided that the faithful transcription of a speech constituted a new copyright work authored by the transcriber, seems unlikely to be followed after recent Australian case law setting a much higher bar for originality: see the decisions of the High Court and full Federal Court in *IceTV Pty Ltd v Nine Network Australia Pty Ltd* (2009) 239 CLR 458 and *Telstra Corporation Ltd v Phone Directories Co Pty Ltd* [2010] FCAFC 149 respectively.

60 Gorman, above n 2, 306.

61 Ibid 301.

62 *Copyright Act* ss 97 and 98.

63 It is considered, below, whether it is good policy that a university should own, and have the ability to exploit, all rights in recordings made of academic lectures. Separate from the issue of copyright ownership, it remains unclear whether the permission of a lecturer, as a performer, must be sought before their lecture may be recorded.

At the outset, it should be noted that the attitudes of faculty members towards copyright ownership have tended to be relaxed.[64] In contrast to other authors of copyright works, academics do not rely on financial returns from the exploitation of their copyright content. Typically, they receive salaries from their employing institution, and funding for specific research projects.

Moreover, the academic's imperative is to publish, and the common practice of academics is to openly share their research through journal articles, as well as the 'usual avenues of conference presentations ... books, staff transfers and teaching'.[65]

Nonetheless, as educational copyright materials become increasingly marketable, it would be natural for academics to become more protective of their copyright interests as against their employers and consumers.[66] Evidence suggests that this process has already begun in the United States.[67]

1 Academic Freedom

Academic freedom ensures that academic staff may disseminate their views and research results without fear or favour, and enables the free flow of ideas within and between institutions, and to the public. This freedom is essential to the public functions of the university, and to democracy itself.

Not only do employed academics have purposes additional to the commercial objectives of their employers, they have traditionally had latitude in the discharge of their duties. Academics determine their own research agendas (including how to conduct research and whether and how to publish research results);[68] they are also free – although perhaps to a lesser degree[69] – to choose what and how to teach.[70] These liberties are aspects of academic freedom.[71] To the extent that they constrain academics' freedom of agency and control over their creative output, laws and policies which vest ownership of academic materials in universities are arguably inconsistent with academic freedom.[72]

---

64 Law, Weedon and Sheen, above n 39, 143.

65 Ann Monotti, 'Is it Time to Codify Principles for Ownership of Academic Employee Inventions? The Disconnect Between Policy and the Law' (2012) 38 *Monash University Law Review* 102, 103.

66 Despite the fact that little thought was given to the question of intellectual property rights in the early days of MOOCs, for example: Monotti and Ricketson, above n 1, 3.

67 Letter from University of California Santa Cruz Faculty Association to Renee Mayne, Senior Manager, Employee & Labor Relations, University of California Santa Cruz, 5 March 2013 <https://www.documentcloud.org/documents/624323-scfa-online-ed-rfi-3-5-13.html>.

68 Cornish, above n 30, 14.

69 Ibid 15.

70 Ibid 14.

71 This notion receives support in the federal *Higher Education Support Act 2003* (Cth) (s 19.115 of which requires institutions to have a policy ensuring 'free intellectual inquiry'), and institutional policies which recognise the existence of the freedom.

72 Cornish argues that the rights comprised in copyright can 'not reasonably be taken from the individual academic whose research generates the information at stake', as this flies in the face of basic ideas about the university: Cornish, above n 30, 16. He further argues that academic copyright ownership is a 'necessary requirement' if control of copyright materials is to remain with academics: at 16. This does not prevent the granting of licences to others in order that revenue may be shared.

The exclusivity of copyright means that a university copyright owner has the ability to exclude the academic creator from accessing or using the copyright material. This compromises the academic's freedom to determine whether and how to publish or share research results with colleagues and the public. Even where academics are granted a licence to use copyright materials created by them – for example, for teaching purposes – the university, as copyright owner, retains the power to reproduce and publish such materials for other purposes (including commercial purposes), or 'prevent publication altogether'.[73] The choice to publish, and/or commercially exploit, the materials is taken out of the hands of the academic.

Accordingly, the *Copyright Act*'s provisions on copyright ownership in circumstances of employment, which function well to reward investment in organisations with purely commercial functions,[74] are arguably ill-suited to the university environment. As sound and video recordings are increasingly used in the education context, the suitability and applicability of existing provisions regarding these should also be questioned. In addition, private university contracts and policies, which reflect and sometimes expand upon the statutory provisions to vest ownership of academic-created materials in universities, are arguably inappropriate from a policy perspective.

While universities increasingly engage in commercial activities, the Australian university's primary functions remain teaching and research for eventual public purposes.[75] University employees are not required solely to advance its commercial purposes.[76] For these reasons (amongst others), it can be 'hard to see in the academic relationship any of the hallmarks of employment or agency'[77] (or at least those which justify the application of the *Copyright Act*'s employment provisions to all academics' original works and subject-matter).

2 Provision of Incentive

There is a further reason why employer ownership of copyright is inappropriate in the university setting. Copyright ownership, and the consequent ability to receive financial rents in return for providing access and usage rights, operates as a strong incentive to produce copyright materials.[78]

As discussed above, in contrast to 'typical' employees in commercial organisations, academics are rarely given specific directions to create particular copyright materials.[79] Rather, they have liberty to pursue their own lines of inquiry, whether or not these are

73 Ibid 15.

74 Monotti and Ricketson, above n 1, 42. Cornish notes that this was likely the purpose of the equivalent UK statutory provision vesting ownership in employers: Cornish, above n 30, 15.

75 Monotti and Ricketson, above n 1, 39, 43. The older enabling Acts of Australian universities recognise these twin aims as the primary object of each institution: see, for example, the preamble to the *University of Western Australia Act 1911* (WA); s 4A of the *University of Adelaide Act 1971* (SA). This is consistent with the aims of universities elsewhere: see, for example, Cornish, above n 30, 13-14.

76 *UWA v Gray*, [264]-[265].

77 Cooper Dreyfuss, above n 2, 1202.

78 'At the most basic level, intellectual property rights ... are said to provide an incentive for the production of intellectual goods that are of cultural or practical value to society': van Caenegem, above n 9, 10.

79 Cornish, above n 30, 15.

likely to result in marketable copyright materials. It has been suggested that academics are more akin to independent authors than standard employees.[80]

Consequently, and as the materials created by academics generally have social utility, it is important to provide academics with a strong incentive to create copyright materials. Granting academics copyright ownership in their materials would likely provide such an incentive.[81]

It is true that the university contracts and policies examined here already typically disclaim ownership in scholarly works, whilst claiming ownership in teaching materials. Equally, concerns about academic freedom and incentive are stronger in respect of scholarly works, as distinct from teaching materials. Academic claims of ownership may be harder to justify in respect of the latter category.[82] Yet, there are benefits to a consistent approach to ownership as between scholarly works and teaching materials. The two categories of material tend to cross-fertilise,[83] and some are of the opinion that 'any attempted distinction [between the two] is untenable'.[84]

F A Proposal: A Content Services Network

One solution to a number of the issues raised above is a Content Services Network (CSN), which would allow a more sophisticated means of managing the rights comprised in academic-created materials. The CSN model suggested here would have a number of other benefits, including better management of the relationship between academic creators, content publishers, and the public (including researchers and students).[85] The model has benefits for copyright owners to better manage their rights and also benefits users, who would have increased flexibility in accessing and using content. An important prerequisite for the proposed CSN would be copyright ownership by academics of all materials they create. This would need to be supported by uniform private agreements overriding the statutory provisions, where they might otherwise apply.[86]

The Intellectual Property Ordinance of Cambridge University, in the United Kingdom, provides a precedent for expansive copyright ownership of materials by academic creators.[87]

---

80 Law, Weedon and Sheen, above n 39, 147.

81 Monotti and Ricketson, above n 1, 503.

82 Ibid 500.

83 Ibid.

84 Gorman, above n 2, 303. Cornish and Pila also advocate a consistent position on copyright ownership of scholarly works and teaching materials: see, generally, Cornish, above n 30; Pila, above n 5.

85 While it is sometimes suggested that universities are better positioned to negotiate on terms with third parties, such as content publishers, this does not itself justify university copyright ownership: Pila, above n 5, 610-611. Academic copyright ownership at least ensures that academics play a part in the conversation with third parties desiring rights to copyright materials.

86 Changes at institutional level are perhaps preferable to wholesale legislative changes, given that 'no one strategy on copyright is likely to suit all institutions': Law, Weedon and Sheen, above n 39, 143. See also Cornish, above n 30, 14.

87 *University of Cambridge Statutes and Ordinances*, Ordinances Chapter XIII, Intellectual Property Rights, reg 7.

There are some limited exceptions to academic copyright ownership under this provision.[88] Further, the university is granted a licence to use teaching materials created by academics in its employ.[89] It is proposed that a pre-licensing regime, such as exists at Cambridge, would also be a prerequisite to the proposed CSN.[90] This would retain the important right enjoyed by universities to use teaching materials.

Academics would agree, under uniform employment terms, to grant a non-exclusive licence of their copyright materials to universities for certain purposes, and to share with universities the revenue received from exploitation of the materials. Whilst uniform revenue minimums might be set (using collective bargaining processes, if necessary), exact shares could be negotiated between the parties in each case.

The CSN would consist of a network of databases, hosted perhaps at institutional level, where academics would register their content. The content, no matter where it is held, would be linked to the CSN. Academics would register rights management information for their content, to enable automated content and rights transactions through the CSN, without the need for usage rights and terms to be negotiated in each case. Content could be in 'traditional' forms, such as journal articles and conference papers, or newer forms such as videos and sound recordings.

Users would have the ability to access the network directly, selecting only those particular items (or parts of items) of content that they wish to use. Where required, users would pay for access to content, and those particular rights they wish to use. The system would allow the generation of specific data relating to actual access and re-use of content, indicating content usage and quality through actual demand levels.

A consistent and clear copyright ownership position would allow automated full rights clearance in each case. Users could then be confident about their ability to use content, with certainty that the full clearance had been granted by the actual copyright owners. Academic colleagues at different institutions could likewise use the CSN to share and collaborate on content, with confidence in their rights to do so.

Importantly (and subject to the pre-licensing regime discussed above), the CSN model would return control of copyright materials to the hands of academic creators. Content creators would determine first, whether to submit content to the network, and secondly, whether materials should be subject to price barriers or made open access. This decision could be further refined – for example, a creator might choose to make content available for free to certain categories of users only (such as colleagues within their own or at other institutions).

---

88 *University of Cambridge Statutes and Ordinances*, Ordinances Chapter XIII, Intellectual Property Rights, regs 28, 29.

89 *University of Cambridge Statutes and Ordinances*, Ordinances Chapter XIII, Intellectual Property Rights, reg 30.

90 Uniform pre-licensing is preferred by Robert P Merges as a means of retaining the benefits of pre-assignment whilst avoiding a 'loss of creator autonomy': Robert P Merges, 'Individual Creators in the Creative Commons' (2010) 95 *Cornell Law Review* 793, 797, 798. Retention of copyright ownership by academics, together with a licence to universities for specific purposes, is also in practice elsewhere: see Law, Weedon and Sheen, above n 39, 145. In Germany, a similar regime exists for patentable inventions, under which academics are entitled to ownership but share revenues with their employing institutions: Cornish, above n 30, 16.

Academic content creators would set content prices and adjust these on the basis of market demand. Access and use payments by users would, importantly, provide a financial incentive to academics to continue producing educational copyright materials, with ultimate benefit to the public.

As discussed above, the CSN would also preserve the rights of universities to receive revenue from exploitation of some copyright works, through licensing and minimum revenue shares. The CSN solution would allow the calibration, through the tested practice of licensing, of the intellectual property rights provided under copyright legislation.[91]

IV Conclusion

The landscape of the higher education sector in Australia has changed, and with it the role and expected output of employed academics. Previously, relatively little thought was given to ownership of copyright in materials created by academics. Instead, reliance was placed on unspoken practices,[92] some of which are now reflected in employment documents and policies at institutional level.

Applying statutory provisions, and the terms of private agreements, still sometimes results in uncertainty as to whom, as between a university and its employee academic, will be the owner of copyright in particular materials. This is inefficient, as it requires investigation into the changing scope of the academic's employment, and the circumstances of creation, only to produce a potentially uncertain response. In particular, when increasingly important (and potentially profitable) educational copyright materials are considered, it is clear that the position on ownership will not be certain or consistent.

A consistent approach to ownership of copyright in academic-created materials would allow the operation of a CSN. The proposed CSN, based on a uniform position of academic copyright ownership, would allow the efficient sharing and use of new, diverse and granular copyright materials.

Importantly, the CSN (and its prerequisite, academic copyright ownership) would return control of academic-created content to faculty members. Academic control of scholarly works is essential to the preservation of academic freedom; by extension, teaching materials which build upon, or draw from, scholarly works should also fall within academic control.

Likewise, the CSN would allow a financial return to academics, based on the useful metric of content usage levels. While the choice to allow open access would be in the hands of the academic copyright owner, the option would exist to charge access and usage fees.

At the same time, crucial university rights of use would be preserved, by means of a pre-licensing scheme at institutional level. This would ensure the ability of universities

91 Whilst academic copyright ownership should be the 'starting point', universities should be permitted to 'benefit directly or indirectly from the exploitation of academic work': Pila, above n 5, 613.

92 Such as the long-standing practice of letting academics deal freely with their scholarly works (including research in progress): Monotti and Ricketson, above n 1, 277. See also Gorman, above n 2, 297; Law, Weedon and Sheen, above n 39, 146.

to use materials for teaching purposes. Similarly, universities would have the right to revenues from the exploitation of academic-owned copyright materials. However, this would be done without compromising academic freedom, or academics' rights to a direct financial return for their contribution to marketable works and teaching products.

Chapter 19

Intellectual Property Rights and Commercialisation of Research in Higher Education

Mary Wyburn

I Introduction

This chapter is about the ownership of intellectual property when research in Higher Education Institutions (HEIs) is commercialised. It looks at the nature of the key intellectual property rights relevant for commercialised HEI research and the legal principles applied in determining the ownership of the intellectual property generated. The chapter then briefly examines a legal dispute over commercially valuable research outputs in order to illustrate the types of problems that can arise in this context.

II Intellectual Property in HEI Research

There are a number of different categories of intellectual property rights. The chapter will concentrate on those categories most relevant for the commercialisation of HEI research in Australia, ie patent, confidential information and copyright.[1] Other relevant categories include designs, circuit layouts and plant breeder's rights and these are discussed briefly.[2] Both the nature of these intellectual property rights and the rules about their ownership, have a significant impact on the conduct of research within HEIs.

A *Nature of Intellectual Property in HEI Research*

1 Patent

Patent protects the way a technology works or how it is made. Under patent law exclusive rights are granted to the owner of a patent registered with the Patent Office. The criteria

1 Protection for intellectual property is afforded at the national level. Often intellectual property protection is also sought in overseas jurisdictions and there are several international treaties and administrative arrangements that facilitate this, for example for patents, the Patent Cooperation Treaty.

2 For further information see A Stewart, P Griffith, J Bannister and A Liberman, *Intellectual Property in Australia* (5th ed, LexisNexis Butterworths, 2014), chs 9, 10 and 15. Also included in the categories of intellectual property are various types of trade marks and trade names, for example registered trade marks and business reputation (which covers the tort of passing off and misleading or deceptive conduct or false representations prohibited under the Australian Consumer Law), domain name registration and geographical indications.

for registration[3] include novelty (a new invention) and inventive step[4] (not developed by merely following an obvious line of inquiry). Once obtained, the rights granted are extensive.[5] The patent system reflects a bargain under which broad exclusive rights are granted for a 20-year term[6] in return for the patent owner publicly revealing the technology in the patent documents filed with the Patent Office and in this respect there is a minimum level of disclosure required for there to be a patent validly registered.

In order for novelty to be established for the patent application, the invention must not have been revealed either by way of publication or use, in or outside Australia, prior to the application being lodged.[7] There are some exceptions to this rule.[8] The requirement for novelty means that disclosure of details about the claimed invention by HEI researchers, for example in journal articles, conference proceedings, research theses, in the press or on social media, must wait until after the patent application has been lodged.

2 Confidential Information

The closest intellectual property law gets to the protection of a bare idea is in the area of confidential information. Confidential information obligations may arise at general law or under an express contract with a third party or by way of express or implied employee obligation.[9]

For the general law obligation to apply there must be information that is confidential (not public), disclosure of the information in circumstances importing an obligation of confidence and unauthorised use to the detriment of the disclosing party.[10] There is often valuable knowhow associated with an invention not disclosed in the patent application that will be potentially protectable as confidential information under general law. To attract and maintain protection of technology as confidential information steps will need to be taken to prevent the information becoming public knowledge. Unlike the information that becomes public knowledge when published as part of the patent process, the confidentiality of associated knowhow will need to be maintained even after the patent documents have been published.

The scope of a contractual obligation of confidence will depend on the contract's express terms or on the relationship giving rise to an implied term. In an employment situation, where express terms of confidentiality are not agreed, there may be an implied obligation of confidence the scope of which will depend on the particular circum-

3 *Patents Act 1990* (Cth) s 18.

4 For an innovation patent, an innovative step is required: *Patents Act 1990* (Cth) s 7.

5 *Patents Act 1990* (Cth) s 13. There are some exceptions to the wide scope of the exclusive rights of the owner of a registered patent. These include uses of the registered patent for certain experimental purposes: *Patents Act 1990* (Cth) s 119C.

6 For a standard patent: *Patents Act 1990* (Cth) s 67. The term for an innovation patent is eight years: *Patents Act 1990* (Cth) s 68.

7 *Patents Act 1990* (Cth) s 7(1).

8 *Patents Act 1990* (Cth) s 24. The exceptions include a grace period in respect of a disclosure made during the 12 months before the filing of the complete patent application (*Patents Regulations 1991* (Cth) reg 2.2C) but such a disclosure will put at risk the registration of the patent in overseas jurisdictions that do not recognise a grace period.

9 *Faccenda Chicken Ltd v Fowler* [1987] Ch 117.

10 *Coco v AN Clark (Engineers) Ltd* [1969] RPC 41.

stances.[11] Express terms that seek to unduly restrict the freedom of a party to carry on trade or to seek other employment will be subject to the restraint of trade doctrine.[12]

In some areas of research there is considerable value in confidential research data. Data created as part of the testing of a process or product in order to obtain the authorisation of health or other government authorities for the marketing of a new product, is potentially valuable confidential information.[13] However, the HEI research community's practices make it difficult to preserve confidentiality in respect of the data underlying published research. There is an expectation that some data will be available in order for academic papers based on it to be tested by the referees vetting the research paper prior to its publication in an academic journal or in the published proceedings of an academic conference. After publication, other researchers will expect sufficient data to be available as the results revealed in a published paper must be found to be replicable in order to be accepted by the wider research community.

The secrecy required for patent and confidential information rights to be obtained and in the case of confidential information, to be maintained, contrasts with the increasing pressure on HEIs to make their research outputs available on an open access basis ('open science' or 'open innovation'[14]), for example through open access journals.

3 Copyright

Copyright law is another important potential area of protection for research outputs generated at HEIs, for example a journal article or a computer program. Copyright rights arise in relation to works (literary, dramatic, musical and artistic) and subject-matter other than works (sound recordings, cinematograph film, broadcasts and published editions), when the material is created provided certain criteria are met (for example, originality for works). The term of copyright differs for the various types of copyright material, but in general, copyright in published works operates until the end of the 70th year after the end of the year in which the author died (life plus 70: *Copyright Act 1968* (Cth) (*Copyright Act*) s 33). A discussion of copyright law appears in Chapter 18 by Fraser.

There are two areas of copyright law that are of particular interest in the context of research data developed or used in HEI commercialised research. They relate to current and emerging issues in the protection of compilations of data.

Whereas in the past a database of research information would generally be recognised under copyright law as a literary work,[15] recent case law has found that a

11 In *Faccenda Chicken Ltd v Fowler* [1987] Ch 117 the court distinguished between three categories of information in the employment context: information that is accessible to the public and not protectable as confidential either during or after employment has ceased, information the employee must treat as confidential during their employment but which becomes part of their skill and knowledge and can be used after employment ceases and the true trade secret which must be kept confidential both during employment and after the employment ceases.

12 Stewart, Griffith, Bannister and Liberman, above n 2, 89.

13 For example, the value of test data in the pharmaceutical area is recognised in the *Therapeutic Goods Act 1989* (Cth) s 25A.

14 Productivity Commission, *Public Support for Science and Innovation* (Research Report, 2007), 197.

15 *Copyright Act* s 32.

compilation of data created without "independent intellectual effort" contributed by its author, will not satisfy the requirement of originality.[16] This is especially true when the data is collected and arranged by a computer process.[17] There are alternative means for protecting this data. Like valuable knowhow, it may be protected as confidential information provided its confidentiality is maintained. Another way to protect it is to impose contractual obligations limiting its use by any third parties given access to it.

A second area of interest is the developing research technique of data mining. Text or data mining uses software for automated searching, extracting and indexing of data, such as online research articles, in order to find patterns that can be used in scientific research.[18] This is an area of conflict. On the one hand, there are journal publishers who own copyright in the published material and provide it on a subscription basis to HEIs. On the other hand, there are researchers who are seeking access to the data for uses going beyond the terms of use provided for in the current subscription frameworks and which would generally involve acts of infringement of copyright.

The nature of the intellectual property rights as discussed above, combined with the increasing commercialisation of HEI research, results in a situation where, simultaneously, there will be parts of a single HEI attempting to obtain for the technology they are generating intellectual property rights with the broadest possible scope and other parts seeking access to third party knowledge and technology on the widest possible open access terms.

B Ownership of Intellectual Property in HEI Research

The ownership of intellectual property generated by HEI research plays an important role in this context. Contracts between HEIs and their business partners will invariably include express terms determining the ownership of intellectual property in project outputs. Outside of these express contract terms, the ownership of intellectual property generated by HEI research is determined by legal rules (statute and case law) and these are supplemented by codes of conduct and principles developed to encourage best practice in publicly funded research. A further complicating factor is that there are developed practices in HEIs about how a participant's contribution to research will be recognised and these practices do not always conform to the definitions of inventorship and authorship recognised in intellectual property law.

1 Patent

Under s 15 of the *Patents Act 1990* (Cth), a patent for an invention may be granted to a limited range of persons including the inventor or inventors.[19] The legislation does

16 *IceTV Pty Ltd v Nine Network Australia Pty Ltd* (2009) 239 CLR 458.

17 *Telstra Corporation Ltd v Phone Directories Co Pty Ltd* [2010] 194 FCR 142.

18 JISC, *The Value and Benefit of Text Mining to UK Further and Higher Education* (2012). See also A Guadamuz and D Cabell, 'Data Mining in UK Higher Education Institutions: Law and Policy' (2014) 4(1) *Queen Mary Journal of intellectual Property* 3; Australian Law Reform Commission, *Copyright and the Digital Economy Final Report* (Report 122, 2013), 260-266; European Commission, *Standardisation in the Area of Innovation and Technological Development, Notably in the Field of Text and Data Mining Report from the Expert Group* (2014).

19 *Patents Act 1990* (Cth) s 15(1)(a).

not define who is to be regarded as the inventor. Case law indicates that inventorship is a question of fact to be determined in the particular circumstances. To be regarded as an inventor, the person must have contributed to the 'inventive concept' of the patent (*University of Western Australia v Gray*,[20] *Polwood Pty Ltd v Foxworth Pty Ltd*[21]). The one invention may combine a number of elements and there may be more than one inventive concept (*Polwood Pty Ltd v Foxworth Pty Ltd*). Determining inventorship in technology produced by a research team, the favoured form for modern scientific research, may be a difficult exercise.

Correctly identifying inventorship is important not only for the grant of a registered patent but also for avoiding its revocation. Lack of entitlement to the grant of a patent (for example, because a nominated person is not the inventor) is a ground for opposition to the grant of a patent[22] as well as a ground for revocation (wholly or in part) of the registered patent,[23] in the latter case, only where the court is satisfied that 'in all the circumstances, it is just and equitable to do so'.[24]

Another party who may be granted a patent for an invention pursuant to s 15 is a person who would on the grant of the patent 'be entitled to have the patent assigned' to them.[25] An example of someone who may be so entitled is the employer of the inventor. Although s 15 contemplates ownership of patent rights being assigned from an employee to their employer, the legislation leaves the details of how this arises to express agreement and to case law. For instance, an employer's entitlement to an assignment of patent rights may arise through an express clause in a contract of employment or a term implied under general law.

In an employment situation, where there is no express contract term determining the ownership of a patent, there is an implied term to the effect that an invention created by an employee will be owned by the employer where it has been created in the course of the inventor's employment, that is, as part of the performance of duties the employee was hired to undertake.[26] The work an employee is retained to perform may change over the period of employment, so the scope of employment is to be determined by reference to the work performed at the relevant time.[27] Where the creation of the invention was not part of the employee's duties, the employer will not own the invention even though it was created during working hours and using the employer's resources. In *University of Western Australia v Gray* (discussed below) the full Federal Court found the HEI employee was hired to teach and research but not hired to invent, even though patentable inventions may have been produced by him.

---

20 (2009) 259 ALR 224.
21 (2008) 75 IPR 1.
22 *Patents Act 1990* (Cth) s 59(a).
23 *Patents Act 1990* (Cth) s 138(3)(a).
24 *Patents Act 1990* (Cth) s 138(4). See also ss 34 and 36. A patent is not invalid merely because the patent, or a share in it, 'was granted to a person who was not entitled to it' or 'was not granted to a person who was entitled to it': s 22A.
25 *Patents Act 1990* (Cth) s 15(1)(b).
26 *Sterling Engineering Co Ltd v Patchett* [1955] AC 534; *Spencer Industries Pty Ltd v Collins* (2003) 58 IPR 425.
27 *Victoria University of Technology v Wilson* (2004) 60 IPR 392; *University of Western Australia v Gray* (2009) 259 ALR 224.

2 Confidential Information

The next key area of intellectual property, confidential information, is not governed by legislation and unlike the other forms of intellectual property, it is not regarded as a proprietary right.[28] The general law obligation is owed to the disclosing party.[29] The scope of contractual obligations of confidentiality will depend on the terms of the agreement.

3 Copyright

According to s 35(2) of the *Copyright Act*, the first owner of copyright in a work is the author, that is, the person who first reduced the work to a material form and not the mere supplier of ideas.[30] There may be more than one author (joint authorship) in relation to a single copyright work.[31]

Under s 35(6), where a copyright work is made by its author 'in pursuance of the terms' of their employment, the employer will own copyright, although this rule can be modified by agreement.[32] Determining whether a copyright work was made in pursuance of the terms of employment will depend on the nature of the individual's employment. The nature of academic employment has changed considerably over the years and it continues to change. Consequently, there is some disagreement about the current operation of s 35(6) in relation to the wide range of copyright material produced in HEIs such as lecture material, compilations of course readings, online learning materials, scholarly journal articles and conference presentations.[33] The copyright ownership picture is further complicated by past practices over a considerable period under which HEIs impliedly waived their rights in scholarly copyright material (for example, journal articles, monographs and textbooks) and allowed HEI staff to contract as copyright owners with publishers.

An author who is an independent contractor, rather than an employee, will be the first owner of copyright in a work by virtue of s 35(2). Where an author is commissioned to make a work, unless there is an express agreement about copyright ownership,[34] except for some types of artistic work,[35] the author will be the first owner of copyright pursuant to s 35(2) and the commissioning client will have a licence to use the material in the manner contemplated by the parties.

For subject-matter other than works, such as sound recordings and cinematograph film, it is the maker (as defined in s 22) who first owns copyright but where the material is commissioned, the commissioning client will own copyright.[36] For television and radio broadcasts the broadcaster will own copyright and for a published edition the owner will be the publisher.[37]

---

28 *Moorgate Tobacco Co Ltd v Philip Morris Ltd (No 2)* (1984) 156 CLR 414.
29 *Fraser v Evans* [1969] 1 QB 349.
30 *Donoghue v Allied Newspapers Ltd* [1938] Ch 106.
31 *Copyright Act* s 10 defines 'work of joint authorship'.
32 *Copyright Act* s 35(3), (6).
33 A Monotti and S Ricketson, *Universities and Intellectual Property: Ownership and Exploitation* (Oxford University Press, 2003), 269-283.
34 *Copyright Act* s 35(3).
35 *Copyright Act* s 35(5).
36 *Copyright Act* ss 97, 98.
37 *Copyright Act* ss 99, 100.

4 Designs, Circuit Layouts and Plant Breeder's Rights

Other types of intellectual property may be relevant to the commercialisation of technology in HEIs. A brief discussion of the ownership provisions of three of these other categories is useful before turning to intellectual property ownership issues of a more general nature.

Registration under the *Designs Act 2003* (Cth) provides the owner with a range of exclusive rights in relation to the visual appeal of a product (as opposed to how the product works or is made, matters potentially protectable by patent) for up to 10 years[38] if certain criteria are met (ie the design is 'new and distinctive'[39]).[40] The visual features protected include 'the shape, configuration, pattern and ornamentation' of the product.[41] The ownership rules for registered designs provide in the first instance that the person who created the design (the designer, ie the person who 'conceives' the design and 'reduces it to visible form'[42]) will be entitled to ownership (there may be more than one designer).[43] Registered designs created 'in the course of employment' or 'under a contract with another person' will be owned by the employer or the other person, unless the parties agree to the contrary.[44]

Circuit layouts (semiconductor chips) and their designs are protected under the *Circuit Layouts Act 1989* (Cth) provided certain criteria are met (for example, originality as defined in s 11), for a term up to 20 years (depending on when the layout is first commercially exploited).[45] The maker, or joint makers, of an eligible layout[46] is, or are, the first owner or owners of the rights.[47] Where the eligible layout is made 'under the terms of' the maker's employment, the employer is regarded as its maker.[48]

Plant variety rights are protected under the *Plant Breeder's Rights Act 1994* (Cth) for 25 years in the case of trees and vines and 20 years for other varieties.[49] The rights may be applied for by a breeder of a plant variety.[50] The term breeder is defined to include two or more persons involved in the joint breeding of a variety or a body (incorporated or unincorporated) where the development of the variety was by a person 'performing duties or functions as a member or employee' of the body.[51]

5 HEI By-laws

The rules of ownership provided for in the various intellectual property statutes and under general law can be altered by express contract. HEIs often achieve this result

38 *Designs Act 2003* (Cth) s 46.
39 *Designs Act 2003* (Cth) s 15.
40 The overlap between protection for artistic works under copyright and for designs under designs law is addressed in the *Copyright Act* pt III div 8.
41 *Designs Act 2003* (Cth) s 7.
42 *Chris Ford Enterprises Pty Ltd v BH & JR Badenhop Pty Ltd* (1985) 4 IPR 485.
43 *Designs Act 2003* (Cth) s 13(1)(a).
44 *Designs Act 2003* (Cth) s 13(1)(b).
45 *Circuit Layouts Act 1989* (Cth) ss 5, 17.
46 *Circuit Layouts Act 1989* (Cth) s 5.
47 *Circuit Layouts Act 1989* (Cth) s 16(1).
48 *Circuit Layouts Act 1989* (Cth) s 16(2).
49 *Plant Breeder's Rights Act 1994* (Cth) s 22.
50 *Plant Breeder's Rights Act 1994* (Cth) s 24.
51 *Plant Breeder's Rights Act 1994* (Cth) s 3.

by way of their by-laws, incorporated by reference in their contracts of employment. For instance, the *University of Sydney (Intellectual Property) Rule 2002* sets out ownership rules for intellectual property generated by its staff (Division 2). The rule also refers to intellectual property owned by students who are not university employees (Division 3).[52]

6 Codes of Conduct, Principles and Policies

In addition to the legal rules about ownership of intellectual property rights and HEI by-laws, there are a number of codes of conduct, principles and policies recommending particular practices in relation to the management of intellectual property that are relevant for HEIs. One of these codes is the *National Principles for Intellectual Property Management for Publicly Funded Research* (2013),[53] a set of broad principles developed by the federal government to encourage best practice in intellectual property management. Another is the National Health and Medical Research Council and Australian Research Council's *Australian Code for the Responsible Conduct of Research* (2007).[54] These documents are general in their scope. They recommend research institutions have policies in respect of the ownership and licensing of intellectual property rights, that ownership of intellectual property be clearly agreed when research is undertaken in collaboration with business or other research organisations and that intellectual property management systems be established. At the same time, they seek to promote the wide dissemination of research findings for the benefit of the research community and the public.[55]

The main HEI employer organisation, Universities Australia (formerly the Australian Vice Chancellor's Committee), has published a practice guide: *Ownership of Intellectual Property in Universities Policy and Good Practice Guide* (2002).[56] Individual HEIs also have their own policies and guidelines for the ethical conduct of research that will include provision for matters such as appropriate attribution of the authorship of research.[57]

Where an employed academic, and not the HEI, owns the intellectual property generated by a research project and the technology is commercialised by a business entity in which the academic has equity, there are obligations owed by the academic to the HEI that will be relevant but are not discussed in this chapter.[58] For instance, for an

52 It recognises the intellectual property rights will be owned by the student in the first instance and that in order for the university to obtain ownership, the student must agree to assign their rights (r 6). The student cannot be forced to assign their intellectual property in order to enrol in a course but where they are engaged in projects involving a third party, assignment of their rights may be made a condition of their participation (r 7.2). In a project involving a third party, where the student must assign rights, they may be entitled to share in the 'commercial benefits' the project brings to the university (rr 8 and 14). For further discussion of the operation of HEI by-laws, see Monotti and Ricketson, above n 33.

53 See <http://www.arc.gov.au>.

54 See <http://www.nhmrc.gov.au>.

55 See Australian Research Council, *Open Access Policy* (version 2013.1).

56 See <http://www.universitiesaustralia.edu.au>.

57 For example, University of Sydney, *Research Code of Conduct 2013.*

58 See, for example, National Health and Medical Research Council and Australian Research Council, *Australian Code for the Responsible Conduct of Research*, pt A, s 7, Conflicts of Interest.

academic in these circumstances there is potential for a conflict of interest (including a 'conflict of commitment'[59]) to arise which in most instances will be governed by HEI rules and codes of conduct.

7 Academic Practices

There is a further complicating factor that must be taken into account when considering the application of the legal rules and codes relevant to the determination of ownership of intellectual property rights. This is the operation of developed practices in HEI academic communities about how a participant's contribution to research will be recognised in published academic research, in particular when the published research is an output from a team research project. These academic practices do not always correlate with accepted definitions of inventorship or authorship in intellectual property law.

Appropriate recognition of another's contribution is required under ethical rules about plagiarism that are well recognised in the HEI community (for example, when using the ideas or words of another, the source must be indicated). However, inventorship and authorship are questions of law determined on the particular facts. An HEI academic may consider their contribution to a research output sufficient to attract some form of attribution, but it is not always the case that the contribution will amount to inventorship or authorship as those terms are defined in intellectual property law. Problems may arise, for instance, where a person whose contribution does not amount to inventorship is nominated as one of the inventors in a patent application (see above) or where part authorship of copyright material is gifted by way of a joint authorship credit to a person whose contribution does not amount to authorship and without there being some form of assignment or agreement to assign any part of the copyright rights from the true author.

III Disputing Ownership of Intellectual Property in HEI Research: UWA v Gray

A brief case study illustrates the practical application of the legal principles in this area. In the case study, the court found the HEI employee owned the patented invention and not his employer.

When Bruce Gray took up his appointment as University of Western Australia (UWA) Chair of Surgery at Royal Perth Hospital (jointly funded by UWA and RPH) in January 1985, he had already been researching the use of microspheres to deliver targeted anti-cancer therapies to the liver for some years. From an early stage and for a considerable time, Gray cooperated with the various university entities that had the job of fostering UWA research, including its commercialisation but these attempts were unsuccessful. Throughout the relevant period Gray was careful to ensure appropriate intellectual property protection was obtained for research outputs from the various parts of his research team's work. He lodged the first of several patent applications in 1988.

59 R Jensen and M Thursby, 'Proofs and Prototypes for Sale: The Licensing of University Inventions' (2001) 91(1) *American Economic Review* 240, 255.

In 1995, Gray commenced planning for a public fundraising to support the commercialisation of the microspheres technology and for this purpose a public company was incorporated (Sirtex Medical Ltd (Sirtex)). At that time Gray revealed his intentions to UWA. From March 1997 Gray moved from full time to a fractional appointment, wholly funded by RPH. In May 1997, various purchase agreements were entered into under which the intellectual property rights in the microspheres technology, including various patent rights, then in the ownership of Gray and the research institute associated with the funding of Gray's research, were transferred to Sirtex in return for the issue of Sirtex shares. The agreements included warranties and indemnities from Gray and the research institute about the ownership of the intellectual property and any proceedings, current or threatened, in respect of it. Gray did not disclose the potential for claims by UWA in relation to the intellectual property. During 1999, UWA began to assert a claim in respect of the microspheres intellectual property created by Gray as its employee, a claim Gray continued to deny. Gray left UWA in November 1999.

The public float for the venture was launched in July 2000. Although aware of the claims being made by UWA in respect of the microspheres technology, Gray did not mention the matter during the due diligence process and no indication of UWA's claims appeared in the prospectus for the capital raising. In 2003, when publicity about a takeover bid for Sirtex highlighted the considerable potential value of the microspheres technology, UWA sought outside legal advice about the matter and in December 2004 it commenced proceedings in the Federal Court against Gray and Sirtex.

The court at first instance found the relevant university intellectual property regulations relied on the general law rule about ownership of patent rights generated by employees. Newer regulations, not formally adopted until very late in the period, purporting to vest rights in staff-generated intellectual property in UWA, were found to be invalid.[60] The court was of the view that the statute establishing UWA allowed it to make regulations about the management and control of its own property but it did not permit the university to make regulations acquiring property from others or interfering with those rights by way of the operation of the regulations themselves.[61] In order to acquire such rights, UWA would have to provide for assignment of the rights in its employment contracts.

The court found the implied term as to ownership of employee inventions did not give ownership of the microspheres patents to UWA in the circumstances. Gray was hired to teach and research. Patentable inventions may have been produced by Gray but he was not hired to invent.[62] The court found a duty to research did not carry with it a duty to invent. Gray's obligation to research could be met in a variety of ways and the manner of meeting this obligation was at his discretion. The implied term as to ownership of employee inventions was also not applicable in light of other factors. These included the fact that the public purposes of the university encouraged disclosure of research findings, even though this might affect the patentability of inventions and a researcher in Gray's position was expected to obtain most of their funding from external

60 *University of Western Australia v Gray* (2008) 246 ALR 603, 618.
61 Ibid 635.
62 Ibid 929.

sources and to engage in collaborative research with third parties.[63] Even if the implied term did apply to Gray, the court was of the view that the scope of Gray's employment had significantly changed over the period and the work done for Sirtex fell outside the scope of his employment with UWA.[64]

UWA's subsequent appeal to the full Federal Court was unsuccessful. The appeal was essentially limited to the matter of the general law implied term as to ownership of employee inventions. Like the court at first instance, the appeal court found several factors weighing against a finding in favour of UWA ownership of the invention under the implied term: the lack of confidentiality limits on publication of the research findings; the extent of Gray's dependence on funding from external sources and the extent of collaboration, including the exchange of information, between different institutions involved in the research.[65]

The appeal court felt constrained in its consideration of the issue of employee inventions in the HEI context because important areas had not been included in the arguments presented by the parties. These areas included the employee's implied duty of good faith and fidelity, obligations of confidentiality and the fiduciary duty not to misappropriate an opportunity of the employer. Therefore, the appeal judgment cannot be said to establish the full scope of the law in the area of HEI employee inventions. The appeal court also noted that its judgment had not fully examined other types of intellectual property, such as copyright, that were relevant in the HEI employee context.[66]

IV Current Issues

There are a number of emerging issues in this area. One of these is 'big data'. As discussed above, data mining will continue to develop as an important research tool and will require negotiation between HEI researchers and the owners of published data such as journal publishers. Another research process gaining popularity is crowd science. Crowd science or citizen science engages communities of enthusiasts who, after some basic training, assist in labour intensive scientific projects that require human intelligence, rather than computer analysis, to interpret large amounts of data (for example, classification of images of galaxies).[67] Crowd science will require consideration of the expectations of the numerous participants as to appropriate attribution of their contribution. There is also the further issue of maintaining confidentiality when it is necessary to give many participants access to parts of the project materials in order for them to make their contribution.[68] The online nature of these contributing communities of enthusiasts will attract the added problem of determining intellectual property rights operating across national boundaries. These new developments will ensure continuing interest in the area of intellectual property ownership of commercialised HEI research.

63 Ibid 930.
64 Ibid 934-935.
65 *University of Western Australia v Gray* (2009) 259 ALR 224, 267-269.
66 Ibid 264.
67 C Franzoni and H Sauermann, 'Crowd Science: The Organization of Scientific Research in Open Collaborative Projects' (2014) *Research Policy* 1.
68 Ibid 7.

Chapter 20

Alternate Dispute Resolution in Higher Education

*Myles Stilwell**

I Introduction

This chapter considers how matters of difference arising in higher education might best be dealt with through informal or consensual processes. Within this context, it will discuss the balance between the rights and responsibilities of the institution and its staff and students, and their interests.

When a dispute occurs, the preferred outcome will be achieved via consensual resolution by the parties[1] based on common interests, rather than an imposed resolution based on the legal rights of the parties. Case law, at times, demonstrates how rights-based processes may achieve 'justice' while still failing to satisfy the parties' interests. If agreement is not achieved, then guidance is provided on how best to follow principles of natural justice[2] to ensure a fair process.

II The Higher Education Environment

The nature of the relationships between an educational institution and its students, or the institution and its staff, provides fertile ground for the development of disputes.

The institution/student relationship has its distinctions from conventional notions of exchange typical of most commercial contracts, in that it involves not just the provision of learning experiences by the institution, but a requirement for some degree of active engagement by a student in order to gain a qualification. This relationship will occur over an extended period of time, with particular importance on the development, or failure to develop, a positive relationship between the parties based on mutual respect.

The rights and responsibilities of students and the institution are balanced by the provision of disciplinary procedures for student misconduct and grievance procedures for student complaints. Such processes should be easily accessible, easily understood by

---

* I wish to acknowledge the assistance of my colleague at Massey University, Virginia Goldblatt, in the preparation of this chapter.

1 For the purposes of this chapter, disputes are being considered as matters between two parties, although matters may involve more than two parties, or groups.

2 Also described as 'procedural fairness'.

both staff and students, and applied with a degree of consistency that avoids confusion while allowing for flexibility according to the varying circumstances of the case.[3]

III Principles of Dispute Resolution

Dispute resolution includes all processes relating to disputes and their management on a continuum, between avoidance at one end, and legal resolution by judicial decision in the courts at the other. Options between these two extremes may be divided into consensual and non-consensual processes. For both, the object is that resolution is best achieved as soon as possible, following the raising of the matter, and that the process used be perceived as fair by the parties. The Satisfaction Triangle[4] identifies three types of need that should be addressed if an enduring agreement is to be reached. The three sides of the triangle consist of the Psychological needs (the emotions of a party in relation to the matter in question), the Procedural needs (the sense that the process is fair), and the Substantive needs (the subject-matter of the dispute or negotiation).[5]

A *Consensual Processes*

Typically, these will be negotiation between the parties, or the involvement of a third party, a mediator, in a non-decision-making role between the parties.

Negotiation between the parties is the usual way matters in dispute are resolved. The reality is that negotiation may be a positional[6] process-based on the respective power (or rights) of the parties. However, a more 'interest-based' process, where the need for an ongoing positive relationship between the parties is important, as in the tertiary education context, may be more successful.[7]

It is possible that an audience with a person of authority in itself may satisfy a disgruntled complainant, highlighting a critical characteristic of successful interest-based negotiation – that is, the ability to listen to the other party, while demonstrating the seriousness with which the institution is treating the issue.

The courts recognise and support early negotiation or mediation of matters in dispute by granting them (except in limited circumstances) confidentiality

3 See Jim Jackson, Helen Fleming, Patty Kamvounias and Sally Varnham, Australian Learning and Teaching Council, Final Report, Student Grievances and Discipline Matters Project May 2009 (ALTC Report), for extensive coverage of this area. See also Chapter 7 by Rochford, Chapter 9 by Lindsay and Chapter 10 by Stuhmcke, Olliffe and Evers.

4 A conflict diagnosis tool developed by Christopher Moore, in his book *The Mediation Process* (Jossey-Bass, San Francisco, 2003).

5 ALTC Report, above n 3. This found the quality of the process and treatment of the student through the process was more important (to the student) than the university being right or wrong in the decision-making process, 81 [11.5].

6 For a very readable consideration of positional vs interest-based approaches to negotiation, see Roger Fisher, William Ury and Bruce Patton, *Getting to Yes: Negotiating an Agreement without Giving In* (Random House UK, 2012).

7 The notion of 'success' in negotiation could be widely explored, but here is used in the sense of the ability to achieve an agreement, and one that is likely to endure.

and without prejudice privilege,[8] in the reasonable expectation that agreement between the parties will reduce the number of cases that need to be resolved by a judicial process. Such confidentiality increases the likelihood that parties may be creative and possibly generous in their offerings of satisfaction to the other side, when no further legal consequences result from admissions or concessions in negotiation or mediation.

Mediation employs a non-decision-making neutral third party to assist the parties in their negotiations.[9] This may be an in-house mediator[10] or one may be contracted in. While a mediator does not have the power to make a decision on the substance of the matter for the parties, it is nonetheless critical that the mediator is perceived as neutral[11] and impartial. Because the successful conclusion to a consensual process is an agreed decision between the parties and is essentially a contract rather than an imposed result, there is not a specific requirement for natural justice to apply, in contrast with a non-consensual process.

B Non-consensual Processes

It is common for the default position in dispute resolution procedures to be formalised and non-consensual,[12] looking backwards to past events to determine fault, emphasising the rights of the parties, and often giving brief attention to the possibility of negotiated agreements or the importance of future relationships, if any. Investigation and subsequent decision on an issue will result in consequences imposed on the parties. Any such imposed decision is subject to the requirement that a fair process has been followed, complying with the principles of natural justice.[13] The failure to comply with this obligation is probably the main source of problems with investigative processes.

---

8 Meaning, for example, that concessions made by one side to induce the agreement of the other, may not be used in subsequent formal processes as admissions of liability. Long recognised, with some exceptions, in common law, and in statute in the *Evidence Act 1995* (Cth) s 131.

9 National Alternative Dispute Resolution Advisory Council definition of mediation: 'Mediation is a process in which the parties to a dispute, with the assistance of a neutral third party (the mediator), identify the disputed issues, develop options, consider alternatives and endeavour to reach an agreement. The mediator has no advisory or determinative role in regard to the content of the dispute or the outcome of its resolution, but may advise on or determine the process of mediation whereby resolution is attempted. Mediation may be undertaken voluntarily, under a court order, or subject to an existing contractual agreement.' *ADR Terminology: A Discussion Paper* (June 2002).

10 See University of Melbourne, Student Complaints and Grievances Procedure, for an example using in-house options <https://policy.unimelb.edu.au/MPF1067>.

11 An in-house mediator, funded by the Institution, may give rise to concerns as to that person's neutrality. The ALTC Report, above n 3, 83 states in its recommendations that 'Mediators and facilitators should be appropriately qualified and trained, and importantly, independent (and seen to be independent).'

12 ALTC Report, above n 3, 19 notes few institutions promote ADR or mediation in their procedures/policies.

13 Broadly defined as a duty to act fairly, which includes a requirement that the decision-maker not be biased, and the right to a fair hearing.

IV Conflict Assessment Considerations

Established procedures in the form of regulations or policies of the institution, will need to be followed. However, practical considerations may include the parties agreeing to revert to negotiation or mediation processes. Successful resolution via such a reversion may provide valuable learning for avoiding similar issues turning into formal disputes in the future.

The critical question is what process will best resolve a particular matter, leading to an outcome where both parties feel the process has been fair, avoiding unnecessary costs, delay, damage to relationships and providing ample opportunity to present their side of the issue.

First steps involve some kind of conflict diagnosis of the situation, and if it is clear that the institution is at fault in some way, an appropriate response is to express regret, take responsibility for any damage caused, and undertake to make good the situation with the aggrieved party.

The matter in dispute may have a level of seriousness that requires a formal investigative process to be undertaken. In the tertiary context, examples of this may be issues of plagiarism that are considered to be beyond remedy by simple educative approaches or grading penalty and are therefore serious disciplinary matters, and allegations of serious misconduct (whether by staff or student) that may involve the safety of property, others or the reputation of the institution. Public interest considerations may also guide decisions to seek a public or judicial decision on a matter rather than pursue a mediated outcome.[14]

It must be remembered that both parties influence the choice of process, and an individual complainant may choose to use formal processes that may thwart an institution's attempts to resolve a matter informally. Whichever approach is taken, in the context of a dispute, the institution concerned has the principal responsibility as the ostensibly more powerful party, to handle it in a manner that accords with natural justice principles where necessary and complies with the stated procedures of the institution.[15]

In a complaint by a student against a staff member, there is a risk of separate matters becoming intermingled. In such a case the student complaint should be considered and resolved (whether informally or by formal processes), separately from the matter of whether the activity complained of warrants an investigation of a staff member. It is also best practice to separate any investigator of fact and fault from the final decision-maker as to consequences.

With any dispute, there is a risk that ultimately it may finish up in a judicial setting.

Courts and tribunals will generally expect institutional staff will be familiar with their disciplinary and complaints procedures, and have access to institutional resources.

---

14 The decision as to the appropriateness of mediation in a broad sense is given consideration in Laurence Boulle, Virginia Goldblatt and Phillip Green, *Mediation: Principles Process Practice* (2nd NZ ed, LexisNexis Butterworths, 2008), 177-190.

15 See Patty Kamvounias and Sally Varnham, 'Doctoral Dreams Destroyed: Does Griffith University v Tang Spell the End of Judicial Review of Australian University Decisions?' (2005) 10(1) *Australia & New Zealand Journal of Law and Education* 5, 9, 10 for consideration of Kirby J's statements and reference to earlier Australian and UK case law.

In contrast, students (or individual staff) may feel isolated and powerless against an institution, and it is important that procedures available to them are readily accessible.[16] Any party to a dispute will have their own needs or concerns and these are considered below.

V Parties

A *Students*

A student may be either a complainant or the subject of disciplinary action by the institution. While there may be avenues for contesting assessment, the decision on these matters of substance remains with the institution and the courts have been unwilling to interfere, unless there have been allegations of incorrect process.[17] This may occur where it is alleged that the decision was unreasonable in all the circumstances, or departed from the established procedures of the institution or showed some form of bias against the individual.

It is quite possible that a student may avoid raising a complaint because of a fear of intimidation or retribution, stress or costs. Avoidance is undesirable,[18] in that the lingering sense that they have not been treated well may result either in the issue arising again in an inflamed form, or ongoing damage to the reputation (possibly of both the institution and the individual) by continued airing of discontent. Social media sites easily spread such dissatisfaction to a wide audience.

Most student grievance procedures give some attention to informal processes as first options, and these may be by direct negotiation between student and staff member, or an assisted negotiation process like mediation, or they may default to an investigative process.[19] In a formal investigation, the student's desires for a particular outcome may be given less attention,[20] compared with a consensual process such as mediation.

B *Staff*

The institution as a workplace is subject to applicable employment legislation and the provisions of employment contracts. Staff have rights and responsibilities within the

16 As noted in the ALTC Report, above n 3, there is considerable variation in the ease of access to and clarity of options for dispute resolution on university websites and recommendation 3 at 11.6.3 specifically focuses on these issues.

17 See the dissenting judgment of Kirby J in *Griffith University v Tang* (2005) 221 CLR 99, considering the special position of universities in the section 'Of Academic Independence and Other Concerns'.

18 The ALTC Report, above n 3, 25 discusses reasons for students not pursuing complaints.

19 The separation of the two processes may require some clarification to the student in the process of dealing with the grievance. Reference to the University of Melbourne's Complaints and Grievances Procedure online links to Related Documents, which includes the Responsible Conduct of Staff Policy, leading to the Misconduct Procedure which sets out the rights and responsibilities of the staff member. See <https://policy.unimelb.edu.au/MPF1067>.

20 For example, *Lenart v Massey University* WEC 15/97, and *Conaglen v Vice Chancellor of University of Auckland* [2011] NZERA Auckland 377. For a discussion of *Conaglen*, see Virginia Goldblatt, 'Why it is Not Enough Not to be Wrong' (Paper presented at the Australia and New Zealand Education Law Association (ANZELA) Conference, Hobart, 2013).

institution, and mutual trust and confidence between employer and employee in the workplace is critical to the effective functioning of the institution.

Just as there are indications that student complaints may be on the rise against institutions,[21] an increasing sense of entitlement[22] expressed by students may heighten the stresses in the teaching and assessment function. Staff stress may result in less helpful responses to complaints when raised, email use may rapidly sharpen points of difference, and exasperation may see a reversion to formal processes. This may have the virtue of consistency, but limits flexibility. The remedies available under regulation are generally more restricted than those that may be agreed between the parties themselves, such as apology, for example.

C Institution

The concern of institutions to maintain academic standards underpins their assessment of students' work and will likely lead some of those students to fail. Courts have been reluctant to interfere with matters of academic judgment as to quality, although judicial review may follow allegations of abuse of process, bias or departure from the institution's procedures.

Progress in dealing with any dispute will depend on the abilities of those involved to see through the difficulties being experienced and to optimistically consider the possibility of agreement between the parties. It is useful if regulations are seen as a backstop rather than an inevitable pathway through a dispute. Prominence given to informal resolution is useful to avoid reflexive reference to formality. In the struggle over who is right and who is wrong in a formal process, parties may forget that a negotiated agreement remains possible.

There are personalities on both sides of any dispute, and issues of ego, respect and recognition are often important to one side or both. An institution is not, at the earliest or lowest level of a dispute, an impassive monolith, but an entity composed of human beings with all their various personalities and perceptions.

Allegations by the institution against the student are likely to fall into two main categories. On the one hand are matters of academic integrity, most frequently plagiarism, and on the other, matters of misconduct where damage or misuse of institutional property or teaching environments is alleged.

Allegations by an institution against staff are generally covered by the provisions of the employment contract and the applicable employment legislation. Staff have rights that sit alongside the rights of students, and as noted earlier, matters dealing with these distinct areas need to be kept separate.

Employment relationship issues are similar to student issues in their level of importance in the life of an individual. A concern with consistency of treatment can

21 Hilary Astor, 'Australian Universities in Court: Causes, Costs and Consequences of Increasing Litigation' (2008) 19 *Australian Dispute Resolution Journal* 156, and further considered in ALTC report, above n 3, 11-13.

22 ALTC Report, above n 3, 76, notes that 'consumer' does not fit comfortably in this context. For a consideration of the implications and case law relating to this issue, see Patty Kamvounias and Sally Varnham, 'Getting What They've Paid For: Consumer Rights of Students in Higher Education' (2006) 15(2) *Griffith Law Review* 306.

see management of the institution turning early to formal processes. Representatives of the parties can be a moderating influence, but also may influence whether consensual or non-consensual approaches are pursued. Exchanges between the parties in informal processes will be expected to be confidential, and compliance with confidentiality will be assisted by fair and constructive approaches by both sides.

VI Choice of Process

There may be concerns by institutional staff about early informal processes impacting on formal processes later if the matter remains unresolved. The critical point (in reference to the matter of privilege raised earlier) is that information disclosed in a negotiation or mediation process cannot later be used in a non-consensual process, except with consent of the parties or by independent proof. Given that most disputes are resolved by negotiation (whether sooner or later), it is valuable to assist staff with training in dispute resolution to focus on early and mutually satisfactory consensual dispute resolution, wherever possible.

Representatives (union or legal) may feel a pressure to take a strong position in order to show the client their willingness to 'fight' for them. The client may also have a desire for a 'day in court' to be heard in public. Such approaches may lead to a sense of justice having been done, at some cost, but may also lead to an unhelpful result due to legal issues.[23]

The nature of informal processes with their focus on direct communication between the parties may expose strong emotions or personal vulnerabilities. However, they also offer an unrestricted range of possible outcomes to be agreed between the parties, whereas remedies available via imposed processes are generally more limited, a situation that continues into the options available to the courts.

Learning and reflections are always valuable in guiding future dealing with similar issues. Among these are that reversion to negotiation will be possible in most situations at any time – we needn't stay committed to a formal process simply because the matter was initiated in that way, and both parties can influence a different approach. In this regard it is useful to bear in mind the widely acknowledged tendency to reciprocity[24] that characterises parties' dealings with each other in negotiation or disputes. By this it is meant that the form of the initial complaint may tend to generate a response in a like manner – so that a formal written notification of an issue may result in a formal written response, and a continuance of formality. It may require a 'risky' move by either side to informality in order to explore mutual interests in a less guarded way. A factor that may work against this is the perception by either side that the initiator of an informal response may be seen as weak, or not having a strong case to pursue.

While relatively few disputes actually conclude with court action, such an outcome may reflect a failure at some point in the process to fully consider the alternatives

23 *Griffith University v Tang* (2005) 221 CLR 99, [17], where the majority held that the issue of fairness did not arise because of an absence of jurisdiction for judicial review, and *Bell v Victoria University of Wellington* [2010] NZHC 2200, where the result of judicial review did not lead to a decision for one side or the other, but a need to re-visit the process undertaken on the matter in question.

24 Ray Fells, *Effective Negotiation* (2nd ed, Cambridge University Press, 2012), 20.

available to the parties for resolution between themselves, or the real consequences of putting the resolution of their matter into the hands of a third party judicial decision-maker. The courts themselves sometimes suggest that the parties make stronger efforts to reach agreement.[25]

Parties need to remain aware that at any time they may choose to depart from a rights-based process and pursue an outcome of mutual satisfaction. While this may fall short of a 'win' for either side, it may also avoid the 'loss' that one party (at the very least) inevitably suffers in a rights-based process, as well as the possible publicity that may be given to court action.

VII Conclusion

Relationships and their maintenance will continue to be critically important in higher education. Consensual approaches should be central to disputes or complaints procedures, except in rarer cases where it is necessary to follow formal processes to resolution. Staff training in established procedures should include emphasis on the skills of negotiation to agreement. Similarly, dispute systems design should see emphasis on informal approaches, usefully supporting in-house mediation services, aiming at familiarising all (including student advocates and union personnel), with the benefits of successful consensual dispute resolution.

Regardless of the process, the principal consideration should be that the parties feel some degree of satisfaction, or at least fairness, as a result of the process, and this should be achieved as early and at as low a level, as possible.

It helps if there is an agreed framework of procedures with which both parties are familiar. These may be part of a student contract with the institution, and need not be extremely complex or detailed. Often if they are stated at an appropriate level of principle rather than specific attempts to cover all situations, they may be more useful than detailed regulations. Of themselves, regulations are not enough. The resort to formalised procedures is seldom going to substitute for the desire that the parties will have for respect and recognition from the other.

The fundamental purpose of any higher education institution is to educate, and this opportunity should be especially encouraged, whether for staff or for students, when disagreements arise. A willingness to negotiate to a consensual outcome is not a sign of weakness, but a practical response to conflict, and a positive experience of this will provide a model for future dealings in dispute resolution.[26] As Kenneth Cloke states: 'Even minor, insignificant conflicts can be transformed into exercises that improve

25 *Bell v Victoria University of Wellington* [2010] NZHC 2200, [201]. Further discussed in Myles Stilwell, 'Can't We Talk About This? Dispute Resolution in the Education Context' (Paper presented at the ANZELA Conference Rotorua, New Zealand, 2012).

26 Referring to student issues, 'very educational things may happen as a referral gets channelled through the process, but it is a formalised conduct process nonetheless. As such, it is structurally predetermined that someone other than the student will be empowered to make a decision about how to manage the incident, and the case may result in sanctions more punitive in nature than educational or restorative.' Jennifer Meyer Schrage and Nancy Geist Giacomini, *Reframing Campus Conflict: Student Conduct Practice Through a Social Justice Lens* (Stylus Publishing, Sterling, Virginia, 2009), 192.

everyone's skills in listening, collaborative negotiations, and creative problem solving. Each one can deepen our capacity for integrity, patience, compassion, and forgiveness, and increase our ability to learn from our conflicts and transform them into sources of wisdom, insight, and personal and social improvement'.[27]

27 Kenneth Cloke, *The Crossroads of Conflict: A Journey into the Heart of Dispute Resolution* (Janis Publications, 2006), 5.

Index